THE UMBRELLA ACADEMY™

GERARD WAY & GABRIEL BÁ

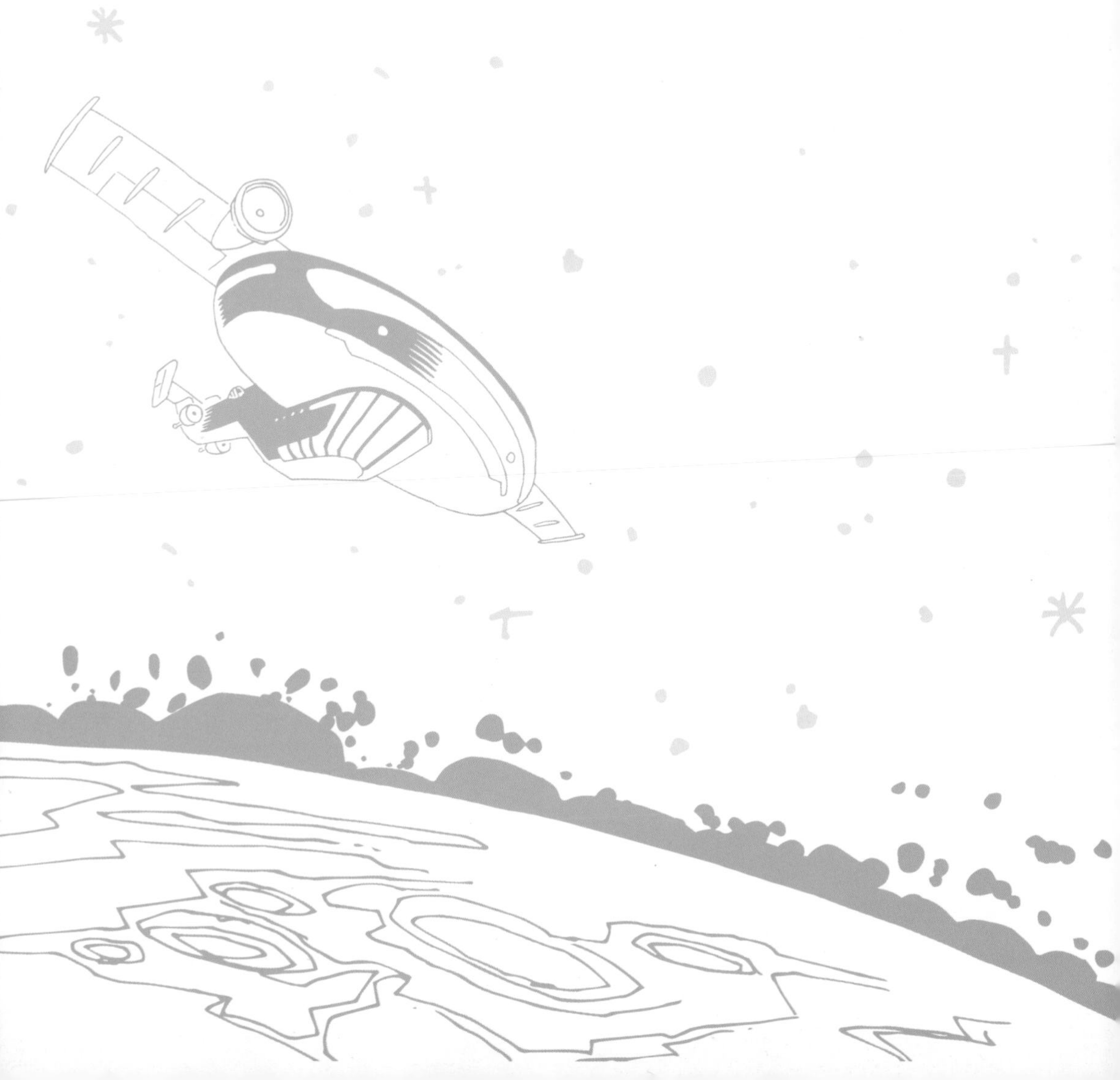

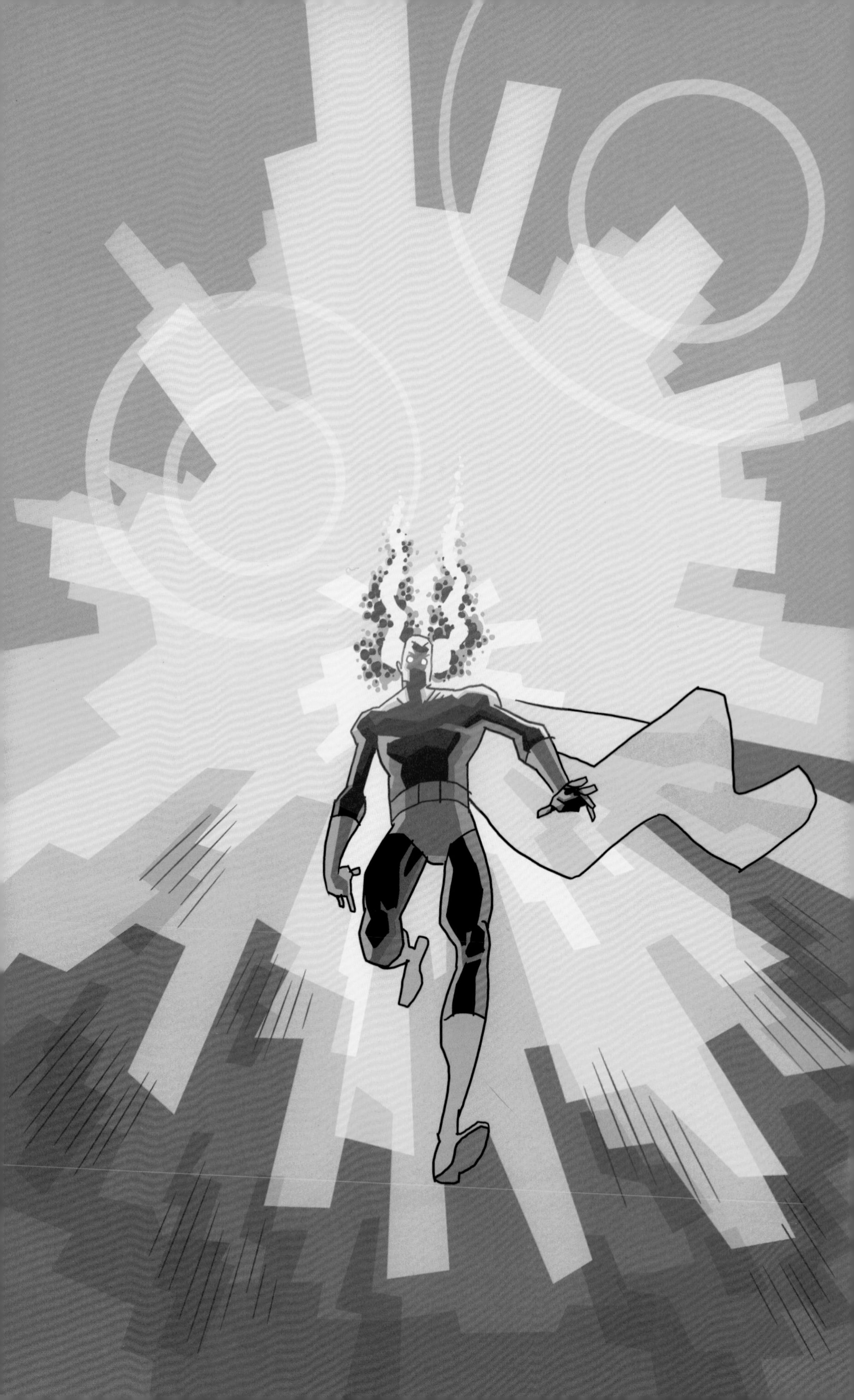

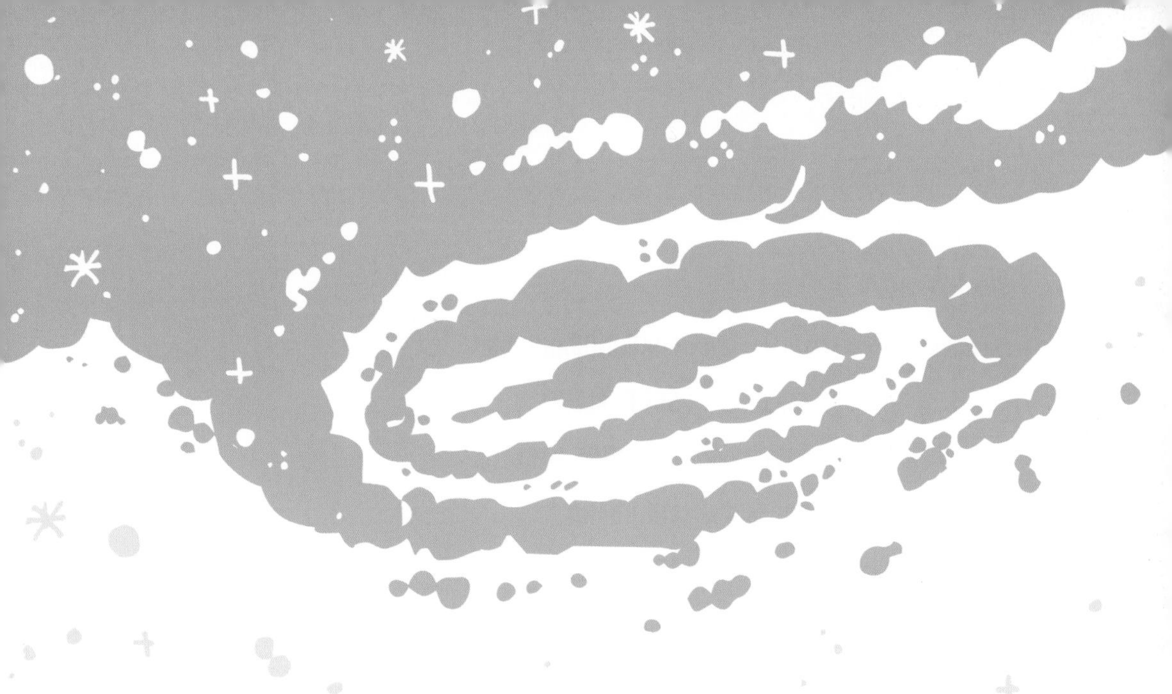

THE UMBRELLA ACADEMY™

VOLUME 3: HOTEL OBLIVION

STORY GERARD WAY

ART GABRIEL BÁ

COLORS NICK FILARDI

LETTERS NATE PIEKOS OF BLAMBOT®

DARK HORSE BOOKS®

PRESIDENT & PUBLISHER **MIKE RICHARDSON**

EDITOR **SCOTT ALLIE**

ASSISTANT EDITOR **SUNSHINE BARBITO**

COLLECTION DESIGNER **LIN HUANG**

DIGITAL ART TECHNICIAN **ALLY HALLER**

NEIL HANKERSON Executive Vice President • TOM WEDDLE Chief Financial Officer • RANDY STRADLEY Vice President of Publishing • NICK McWHORTER Chief Business Development Officer • DALE LaFOUNTAIN Chief Information Officer • MATT PARKINSON Vice President of Marketing • CARA NIECE Vice President of Production and Scheduling • MARK BERNARDI Vice President of Book Trade and Digital Sales • KEN LIZZI General Counsel • DAVE MARSHALL Editor in Chief • DAVEY ESTRADA Editorial Director • CHRIS WARNER Senior Books Editor • CARY GRAZZINI Director of Specialty Projects • LIA RIBACCHI Art Director • VANESSA TODD-HOLMES Director of Print Purchasing • MATT DRYER Director of Digital Art and Prepress • MICHAEL GOMBOS Senior Director of Licensed Publications • KARI YADRO Director of Custom Programs • KARI TORSON Director of International Licensing • SEAN BRICE Director of Trade Sales

THE UMBRELLA ACADEMY™
VOLUME THREE: HOTEL OBLIVION

This volume reprints the comic-book series *The Umbrella Academy Volume 3: Hotel Oblivion*, issues #1-7 published by Dark Horse Comics.

Published by Dark Horse Books
A division of Dark Horse Comics LLC
10956 SE Main Street
Milwaukie, OR 97222

DarkHorse.com
Advertising Sales: (503) 905-2315
To find a comics shop in your area, visit comicshoplocator.com

First Edition: August 2019
ISBN 978-1-50671-142-3
Digital ISBN 978-1-50671-143-0

10 9 8 7 6 5 4 3 2 1
Printed in China

INTRODUCTION

The Umbrella Academy was following me around, and it took me a while to figure out why.

Last year, the co-creators of *Umbrella Academy*, Gerard Way and Gabriel Bá, were in my home town of Toronto, Canada, where filming of the *Umbrella Academy* television adaptation was about to get underway. Gabriel's brother, the wonderful Fábio Moon, was also there to lend his support. Fábio and I hooked up for lunch one day. He came down to my studio and we talked about comics and had a great time. That was my first contact with all things *The Umbrella Academy.*

The second brush with fate came about a week later. I was at my studio and went for my usual coffee break. And as I walked by the bookstore that is near my coffee shop, there was Ellen. There was a full film crew there too. You see, they were filming scenes from *The Umbrella Academy.* Second contact. And about a month or two later, I was in the airport and guess who was lined up in security right in front of me? Ellen Page again. Contact three.

Okay, here was the big one. I was at a convention in North Carolina this past fall and Gerard Way was also a guest at the con, and we found ourselves on a panel together one morning. I had never met Gerard, but as soon as we began to talk backstage, and on the panel, I could immediately tell he was a creative kindred spirit. So, finally, after a year of *The Umbrella Academy* following me around…I decided to actually read it.

"*What?!*" you say, "you'd never read *The Umbrella Academy*?!" I know, I know! What can I say, other than the fact that there are *a lot* of comics out there to read, and I make a few myself, so I'm busy, and what can I say, you can't read everything. I just never got around to reading *The Umbrella Academy.* I love Bá's art and always have, so there was really no excuse. So, after meeting Gerard, I finally corrected my egregious oversight, sat down, and dove head first into this extraordinary world that he and Gabriel created.

So where do I begin? First of all, I love superheroes. But this isn't a superhero book. Not *really.* It's about a family. And if there is one thing I love more than comics about superheroes, it's comics about families. And this family is incredible. I tore through the first two *Umbrella Academy* volumes and absolutely fell in love with Spaceboy, Rumor, Kraken, Séance, and Number 5 … especially Number 5.

And then came *Hotel Oblivion,* the very volume you now hold in your hands. A few weeks after reading it, I received an email from my editor at Dark Horse, asking if I would like to write the intro for this book! See, it *is* following me! And now I get it. Now I know *why*—it was leading to *this,* so that I could finally read these wonderful comics and spread the word to you!

And what a word it is.

Comic books are the single greatest invention of humankind. I think we can agree on that much, right? And *The Umbrella Academy* is as good a comic book as I've ever read. Some intros tend to recap or spoil plots. There is no point in doing that here. Instead I will just say, if, like me, you haven't yet read *The Umbrella Academy,* but maybe heard about it, or saw the Netflix show, then do yourself a favor and take the plunge. These are really, *really* good comics. And *Hotel Oblivion* isn't just the third volume in the ongoing *Umbrella* saga—it may also be the best. It feels like the lives and stories of Hargreeves's children have all been building to this. And of course, they have. Gabriel Bá's art has never looked more vital, kinetic, and so full of life. And Gerard Way's characters all succumb to the wonderfully insane and mind-bending circumstances he surrounds them with. No matter what he throws at them—and in *Hotel Oblivion* he throws a lot—they still come through as deeply human, deeply flawed, and deeply compelling.

So that's it. Read this book and enjoy it was much as I did. Trust me, you don't want to make the same mistake I did. Don't wait for *The Umbrella Academy* to come after you, because it will.

Trust me. These stories are alive. And they were meant for you.

JEFF LEMIRE
Toronto, Canada
April 2019

Dedicated to the USA Hostels, San Diego.

—GABRIEL BÁ

To the Benson Hotel in Portland, Oregon. Thank you for providing me with years of refuge and inspiration.

—GERARD WAY

CHAPTER ONE

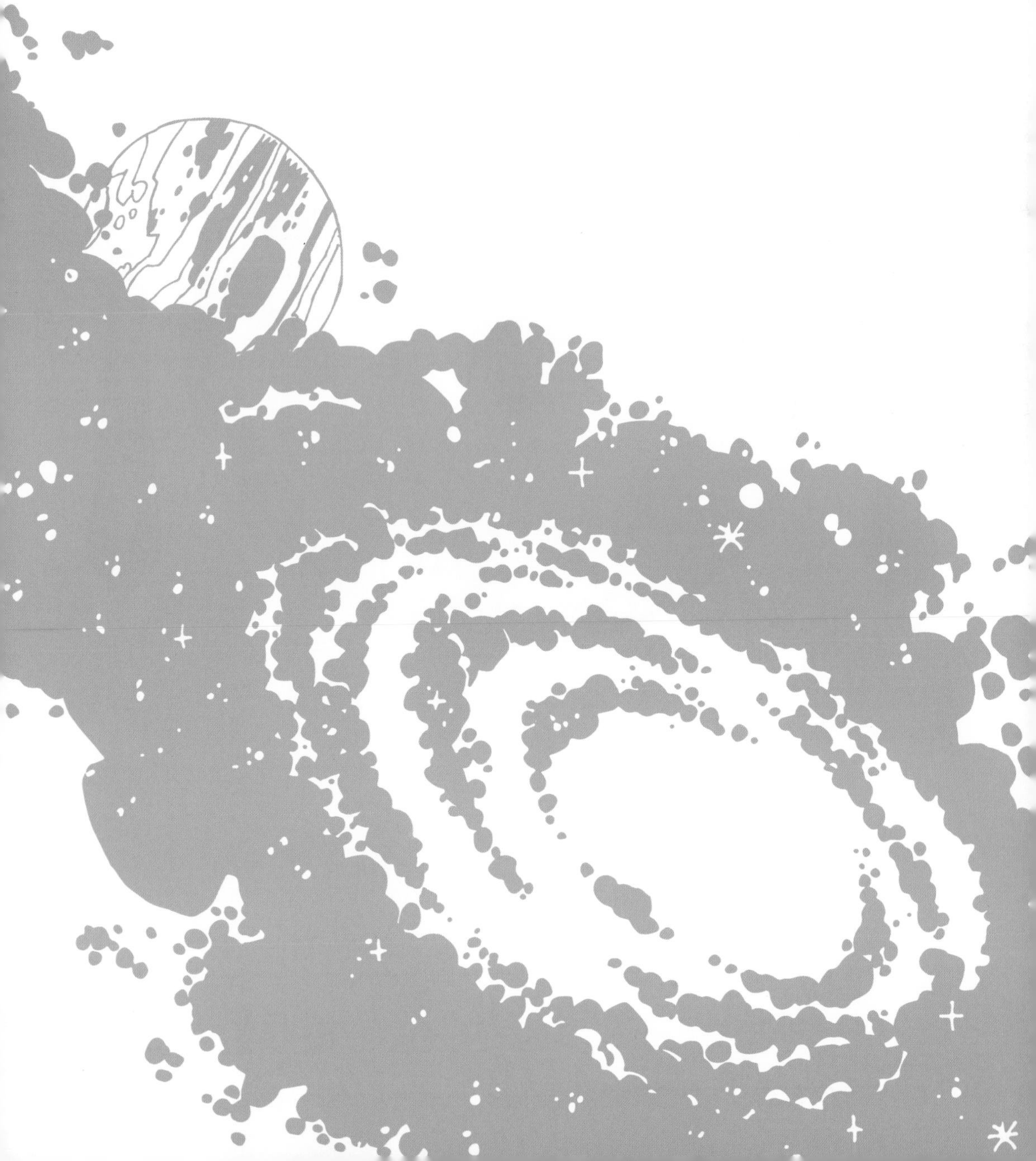

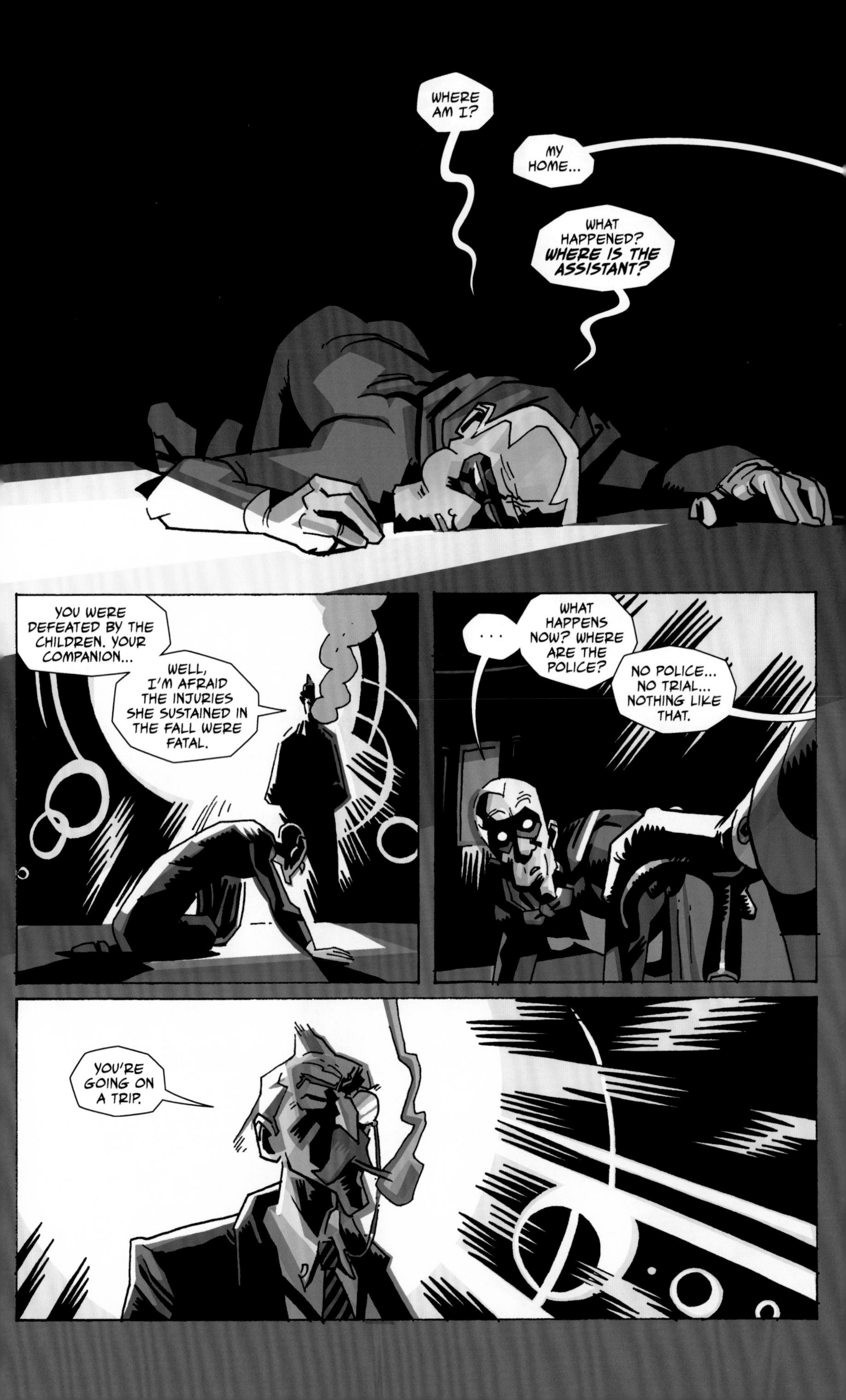
WHERE AM I?
MY HOME...
WHAT HAPPENED? WHERE IS THE ASSISTANT?
YOU WERE DEFEATED BY THE CHILDREN. YOUR COMPANION...
WELL, I'M AFRAID THE INJURIES SHE SUSTAINED IN THE FALL WERE FATAL.
. . .
WHAT HAPPENS NOW? WHERE ARE THE POLICE?
NO POLICE... NO TRIAL... NOTHING LIKE THAT.
YOU'RE GOING ON A TRIP.

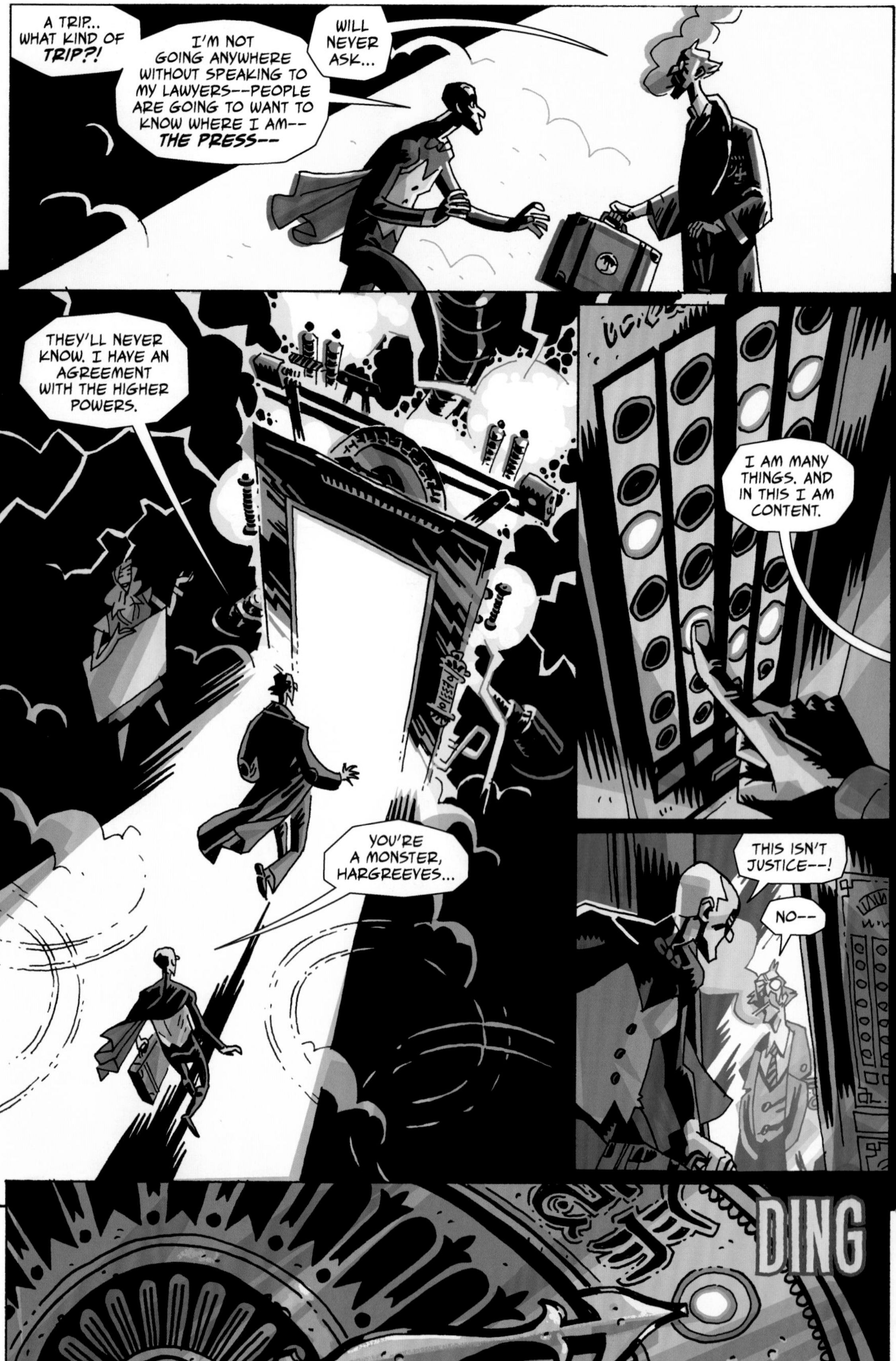
A TRIP... WHAT KIND OF TRIP?!
I'M NOT GOING ANYWHERE WITHOUT SPEAKING TO MY LAWYERS--PEOPLE ARE GOING TO WANT TO KNOW WHERE I AM-- THE PRESS--
WILL NEVER ASK...
THEY'LL NEVER KNOW. I HAVE AN AGREEMENT WITH THE HIGHER POWERS.
YOU'RE A MONSTER, HARGREEVES...
I AM MANY THINGS. AND IN THIS I AM CONTENT.
THIS ISN'T JUSTICE--!
NO--
DING

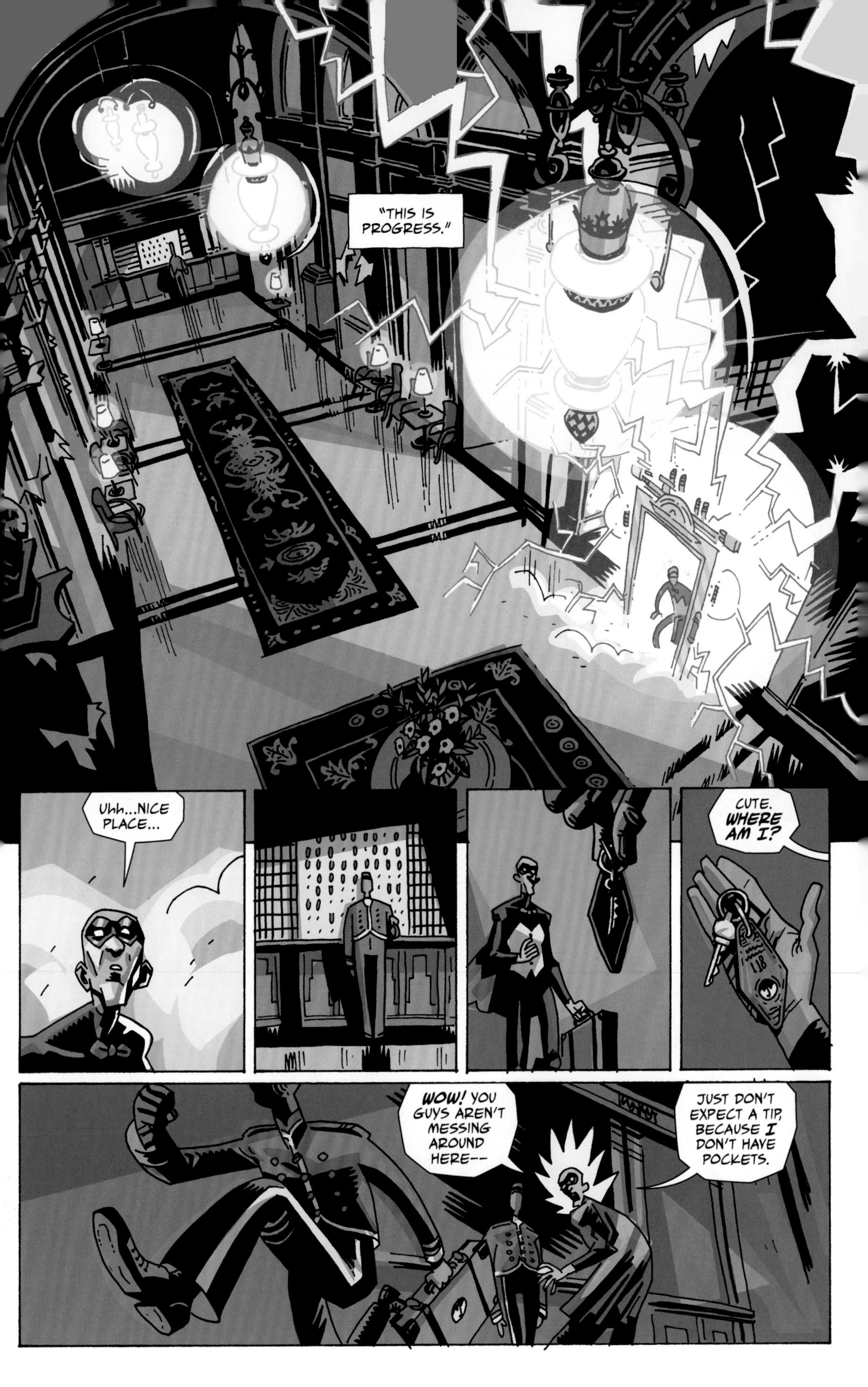
"THIS IS PROGRESS."
Uhh...NICE PLACE...
CUTE. WHERE AM I?
WOW! YOU GUYS AREN'T MESSING AROUND HERE--
JUST DON'T EXPECT A TIP, BECAUSE I DON'T HAVE POCKETS.

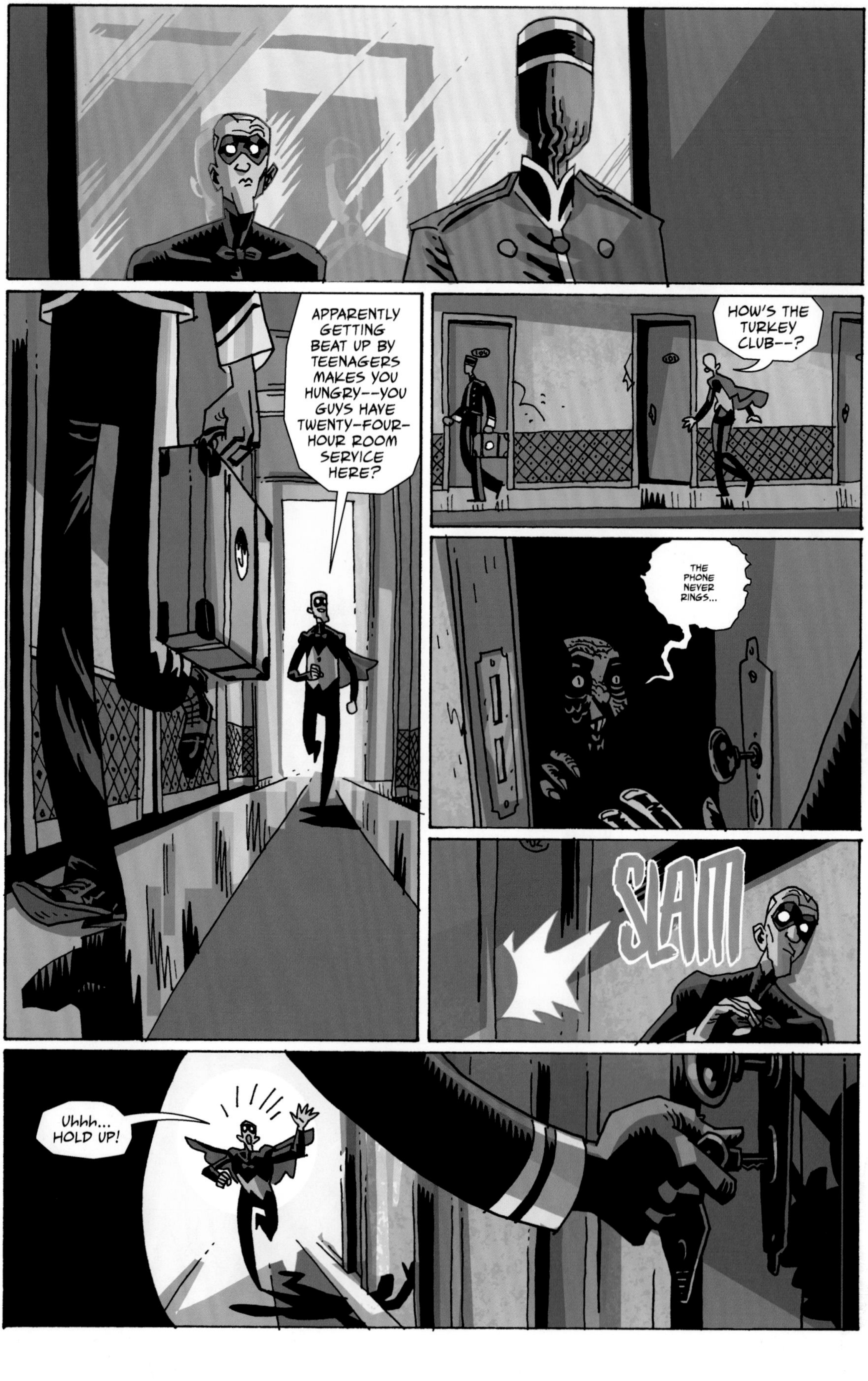

APPARENTLY GETTING BEAT UP BY TEENAGERS MAKES YOU HUNGRY--YOU GUYS HAVE TWENTY-FOUR-HOUR ROOM SERVICE HERE?
HOW'S THE TURKEY CLUB--?
THE PHONE NEVER RINGS...
SLAM
Uhhh... HOLD UP!

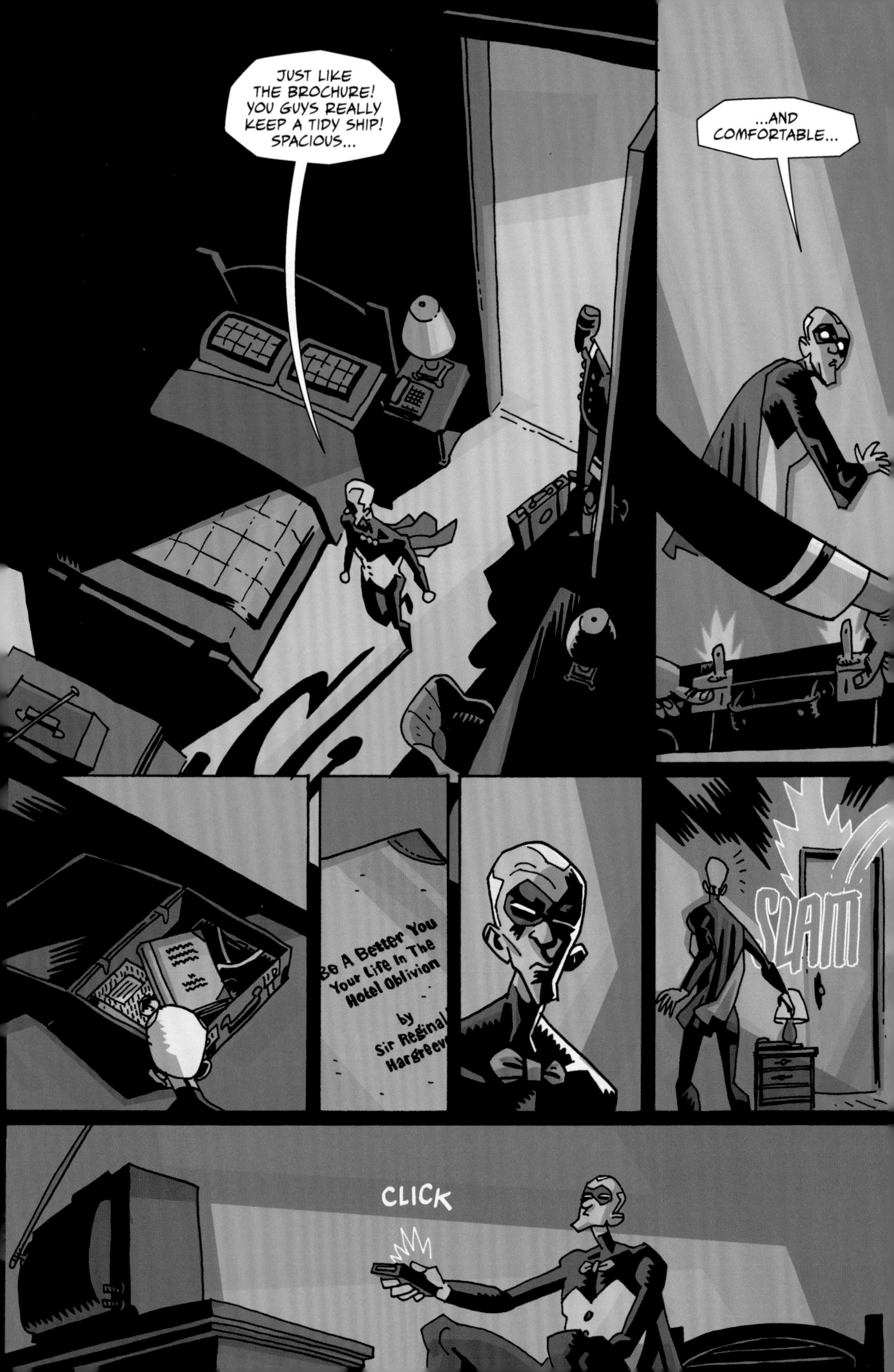
JUST LIKE THE BROCHURE! YOU GUYS REALLY KEEP A TIDY SHIP! SPACIOUS...
...AND COMFORTABLE...
Be A Better You
Your Life In The
Hotel Oblivion
by
Sir Reginal
Hargreev
SLAM
CLICK

OBLIVION

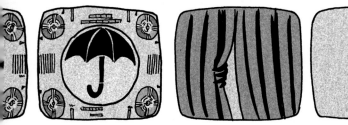

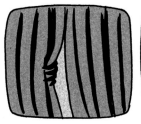

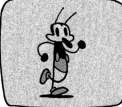

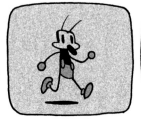

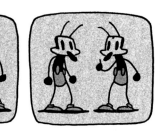

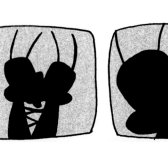

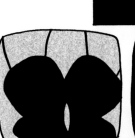

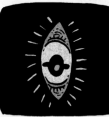

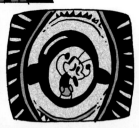

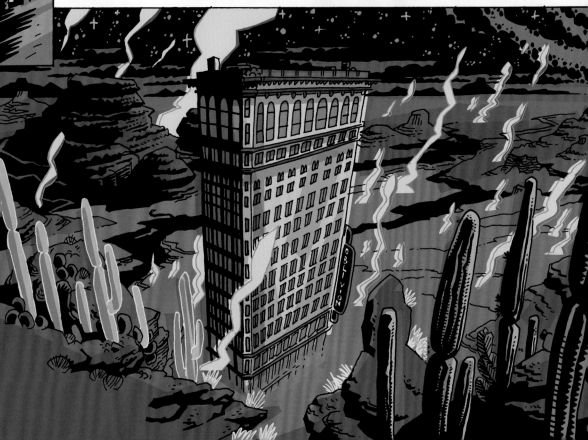

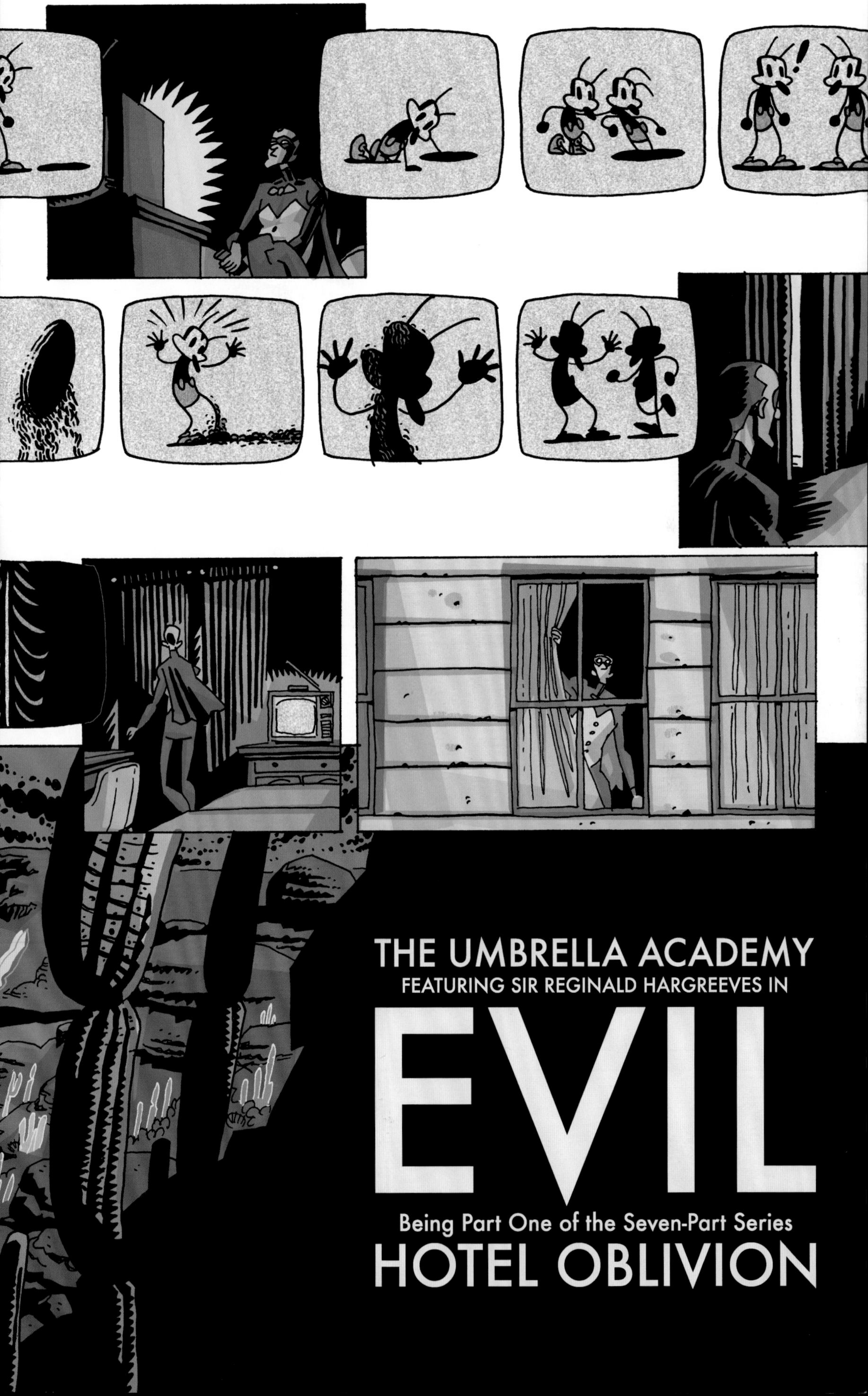
THE UMBRELLA ACADEMY
FEATURING SIR REGINALD HARGREEVES IN
EVIL
Being Part One of the Seven-Part Series
HOTEL OBLIVION

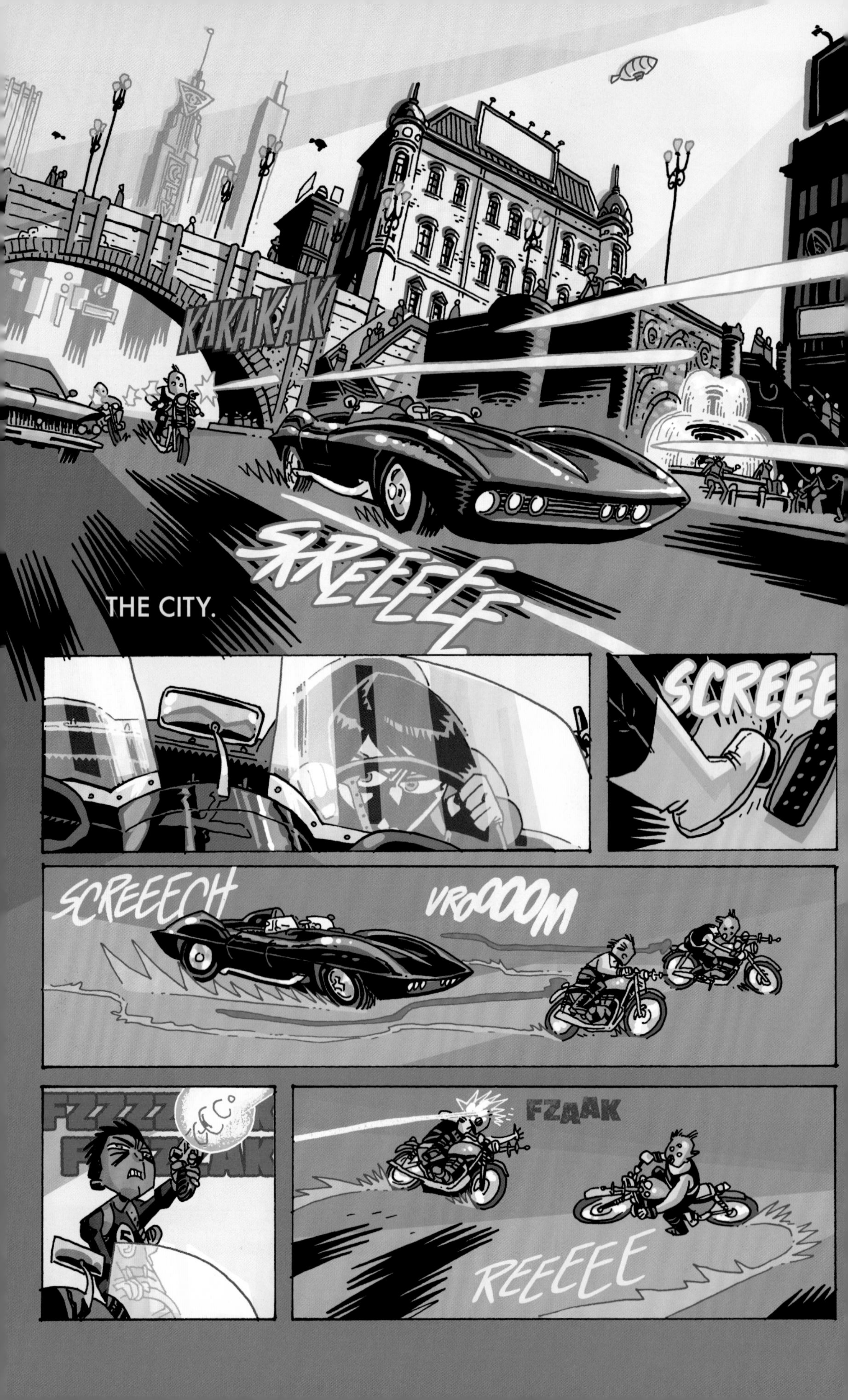
KAKAKAK
SKREEEEE
THE CITY.
SCREEE
SCREEECH
VROOOOM
FZAAK
REEEEE

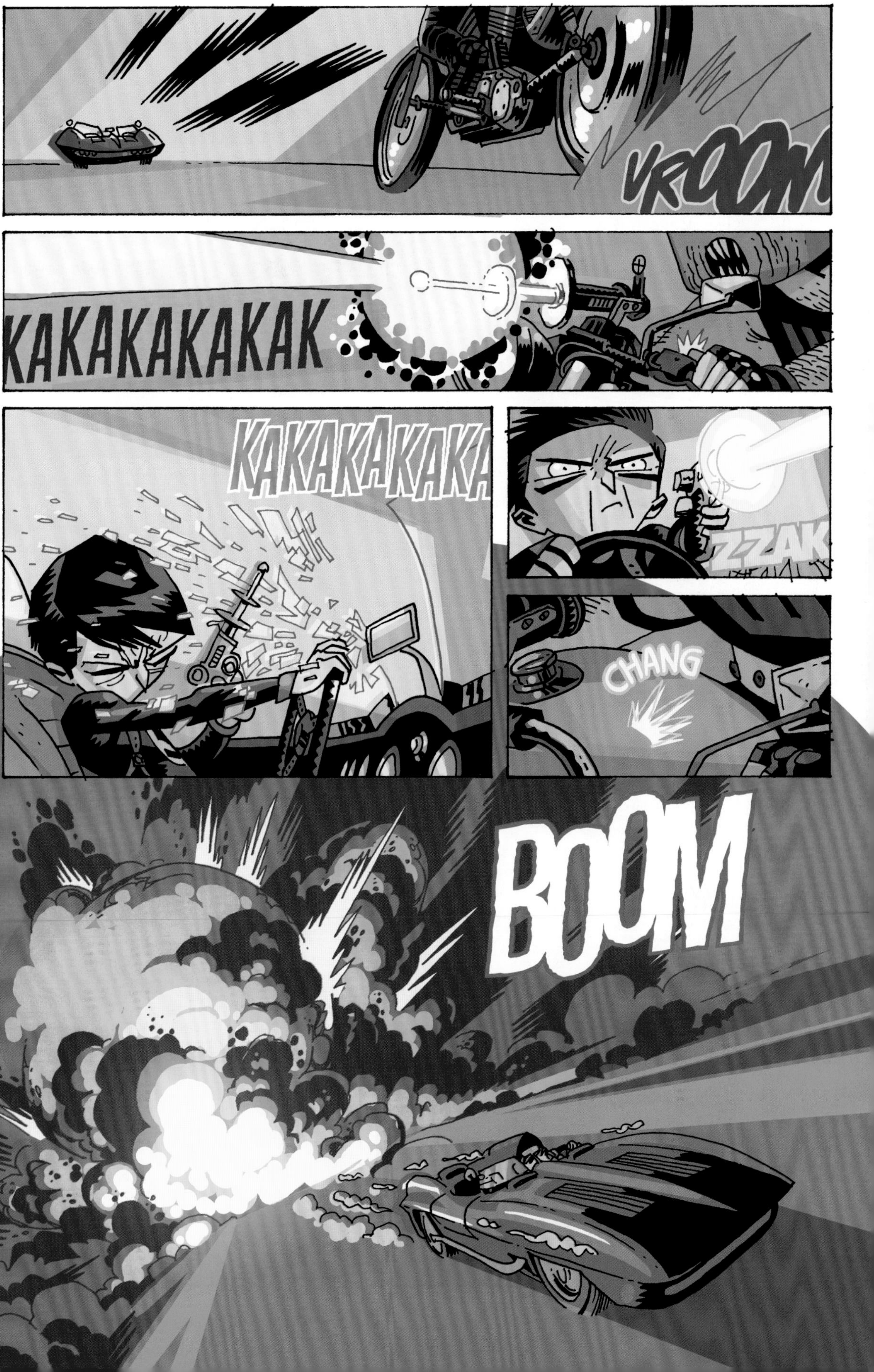
VROOM
KAKAKAKAKAKAK
KAKAKAKAKAKA
ZZAK
CHANG
BOOM

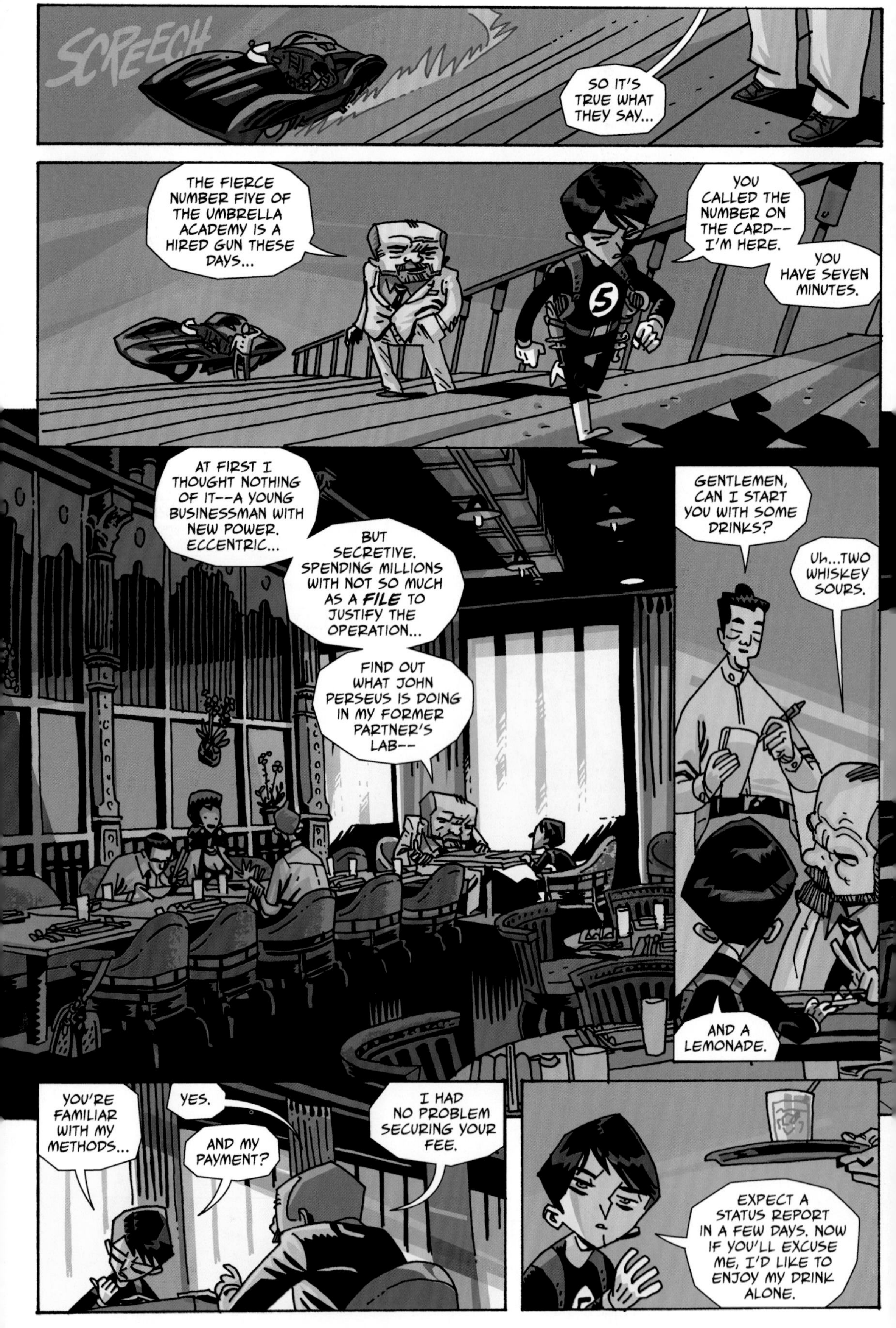
SCREECH
SO IT'S TRUE WHAT THEY SAY...
THE FIERCE NUMBER FIVE OF THE UMBRELLA ACADEMY IS A HIRED GUN THESE DAYS...
YOU CALLED THE NUMBER ON THE CARD-- I'M HERE.
YOU HAVE SEVEN MINUTES.
AT FIRST I THOUGHT NOTHING OF IT--A YOUNG BUSINESSMAN WITH NEW POWER. ECCENTRIC...
BUT SECRETIVE. SPENDING MILLIONS WITH NOT SO MUCH AS A *FILE* TO JUSTIFY THE OPERATION...
FIND OUT WHAT JOHN PERSEUS IS DOING IN MY FORMER PARTNER'S LAB--
GENTLEMEN, CAN I START YOU WITH SOME DRINKS?
Uh...TWO WHISKEY SOURS.
AND A LEMONADE.
YOU'RE FAMILIAR WITH MY METHODS...
YES.
AND MY PAYMENT?
I HAD NO PROBLEM SECURING YOUR FEE.
EXPECT A STATUS REPORT IN A FEW DAYS. NOW IF YOU'LL EXCUSE ME, I'D LIKE TO ENJOY MY DRINK ALONE.

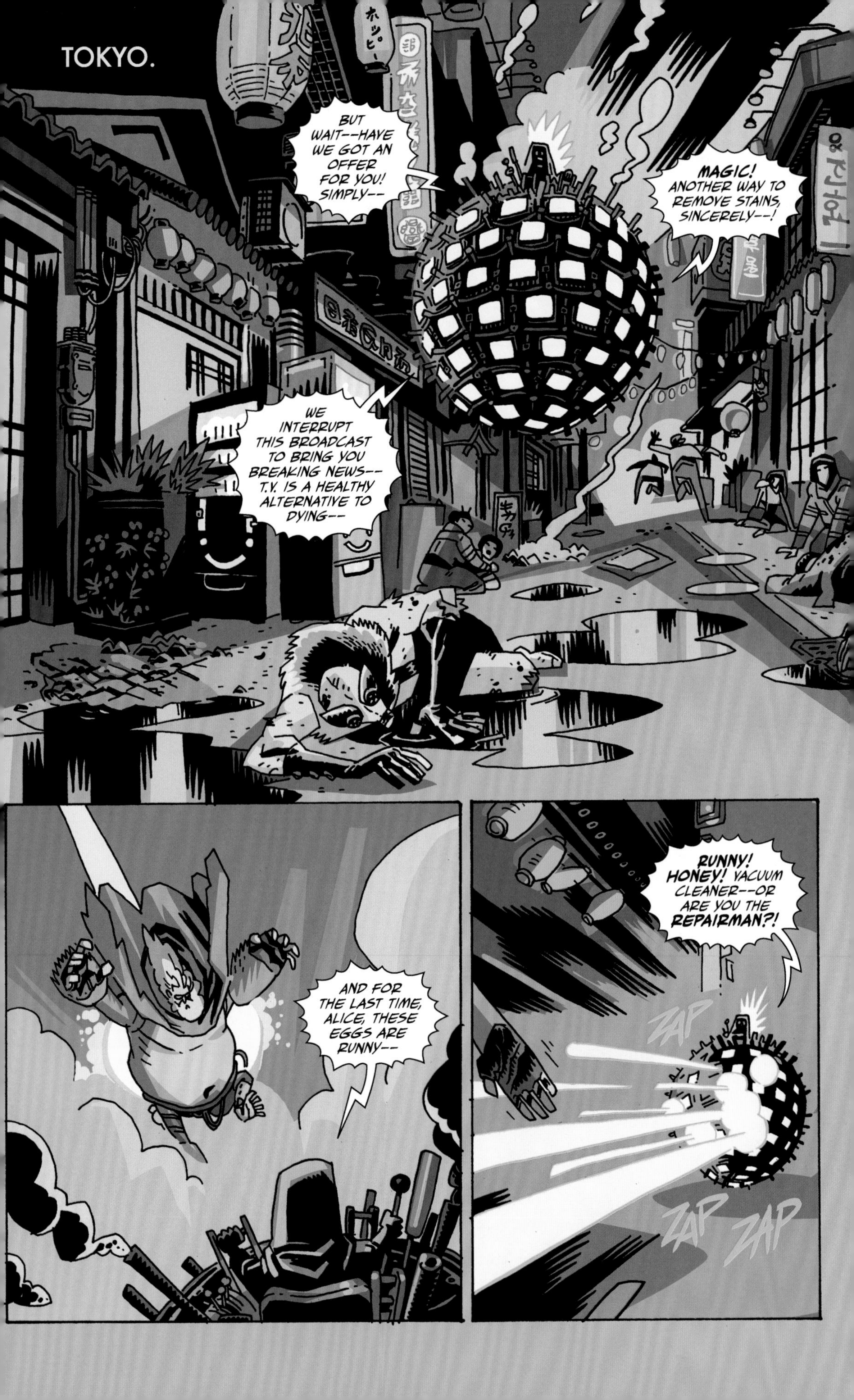
TOKYO.
BUT WAIT--HAVE WE GOT AN OFFER FOR YOU! SIMPLY--
MAGIC! ANOTHER WAY TO REMOVE STAINS, SINCERELY--!
WE INTERRUPT THIS BROADCAST TO BRING YOU BREAKING NEWS-- T.V. IS A HEALTHY ALTERNATIVE TO DYING--
AND FOR THE LAST TIME, ALICE, THESE EGGS ARE RUNNY--
RUNNY! HONEY! VACUUM CLEANER--OR ARE YOU THE REPAIRMAN?!
ZAP
ZAP ZAP

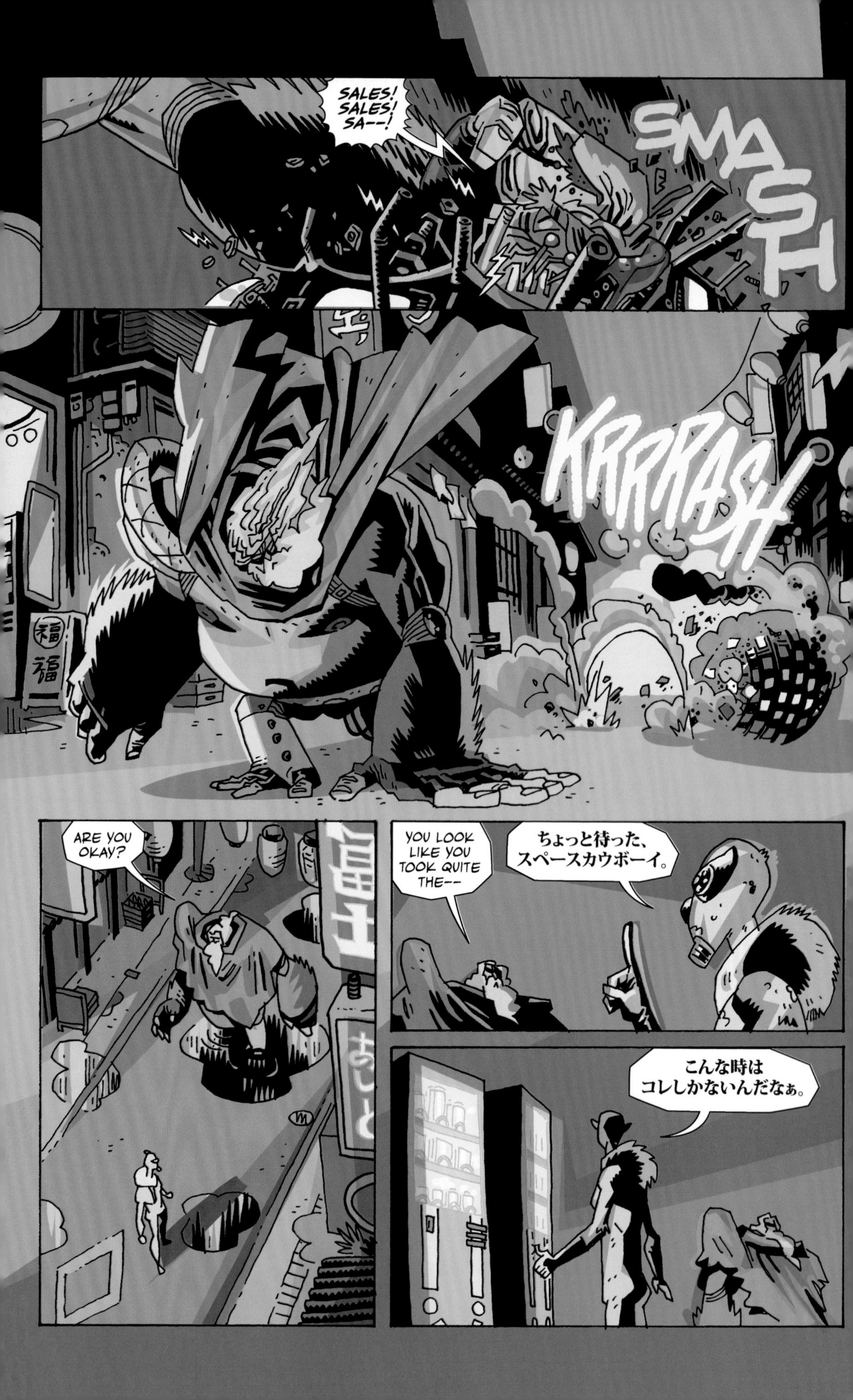
SALES! SALES! SA--!
SMASH
KRRRASH
ARE YOU OKAY?
YOU LOOK LIKE YOU TOOK QUITE THE--
ちょっと待った、スペースカウボーイ。
こんな時はコレしかないんだなぁ。

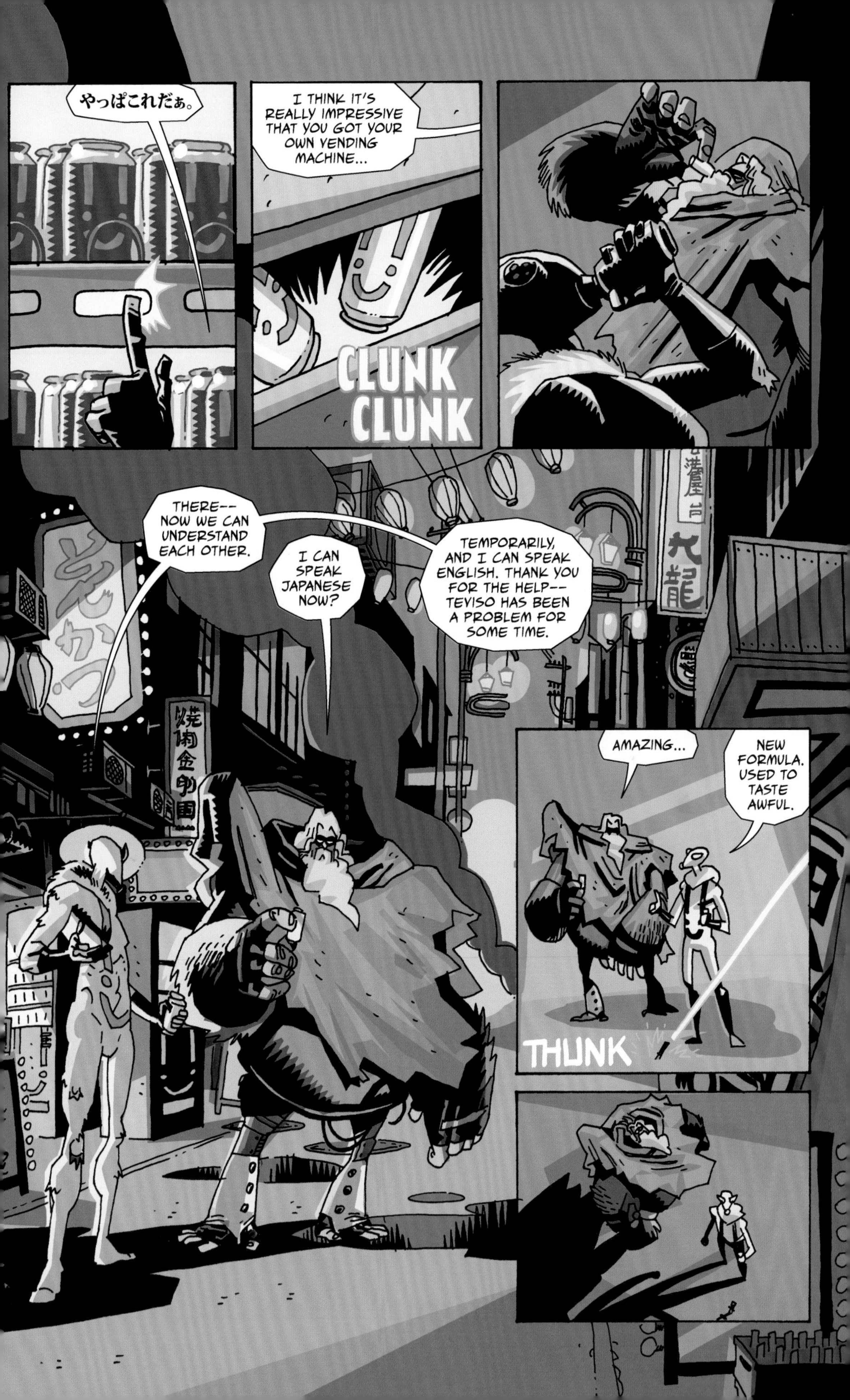
やっぱこれだぁ。
I THINK IT'S REALLY IMPRESSIVE THAT YOU GOT YOUR OWN VENDING MACHINE...
CLUNK
CLUNK
THERE-- NOW WE CAN UNDERSTAND EACH OTHER.
I CAN SPEAK JAPANESE NOW?
TEMPORARILY, AND I CAN SPEAK ENGLISH. THANK YOU FOR THE HELP-- TEVISO HAS BEEN A PROBLEM FOR SOME TIME.
AMAZING...
NEW FORMULA. USED TO TASTE AWFUL.
THUNK

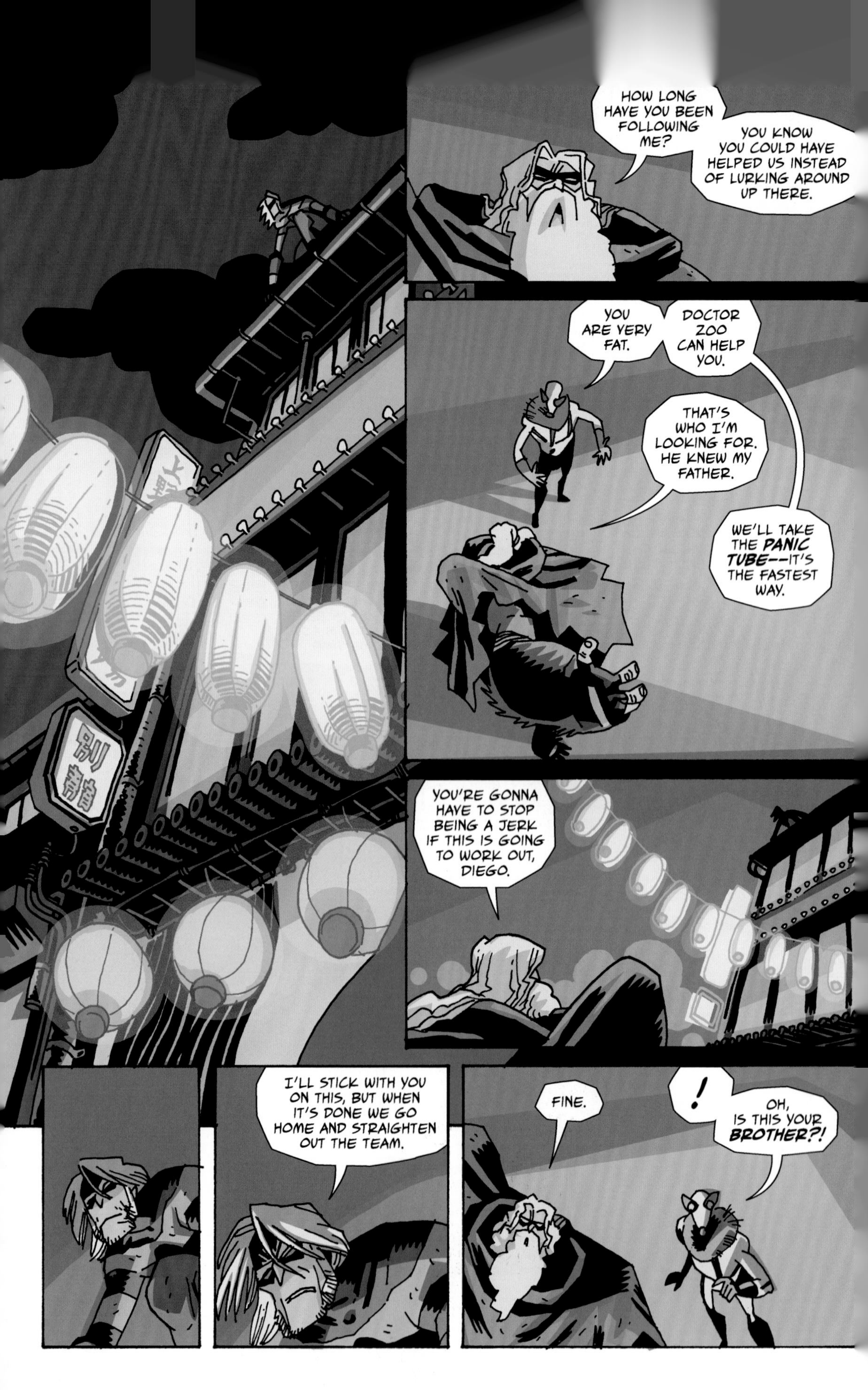

HOW LONG HAVE YOU BEEN FOLLOWING ME?
YOU KNOW YOU COULD HAVE HELPED US INSTEAD OF LURKING AROUND UP THERE.
YOU ARE VERY FAT.
DOCTOR ZOO CAN HELP YOU.
THAT'S WHO I'M LOOKING FOR. HE KNEW MY FATHER.
WE'LL TAKE THE PANIC TUBE--IT'S THE FASTEST WAY.
YOU'RE GONNA HAVE TO STOP BEING A JERK IF THIS IS GOING TO WORK OUT, DIEGO.
I'LL STICK WITH YOU ON THIS, BUT WHEN IT'S DONE WE GO HOME AND STRAIGHTEN OUT THE TEAM.
FINE.
!
OH, IS THIS YOUR BROTHER?!

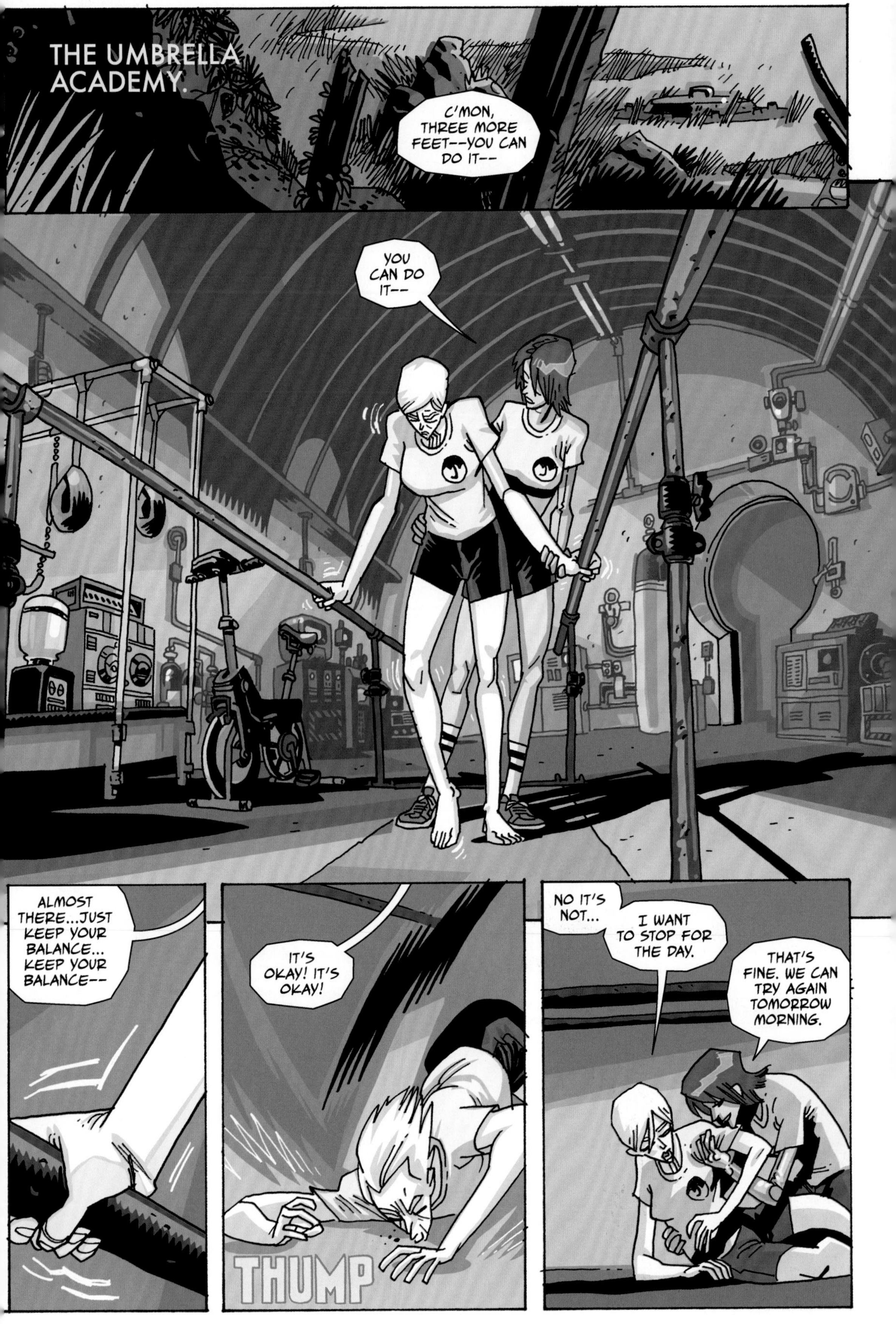
THE UMBRELLA ACADEMY.
C'MON, THREE MORE FEET--YOU CAN DO IT--
YOU CAN DO IT--
ALMOST THERE...JUST KEEP YOUR BALANCE... KEEP YOUR BALANCE--
IT'S OKAY! IT'S OKAY!
THUMP
NO IT'S NOT...
I WANT TO STOP FOR THE DAY.
THAT'S FINE. WE CAN TRY AGAIN TOMORROW MORNING.

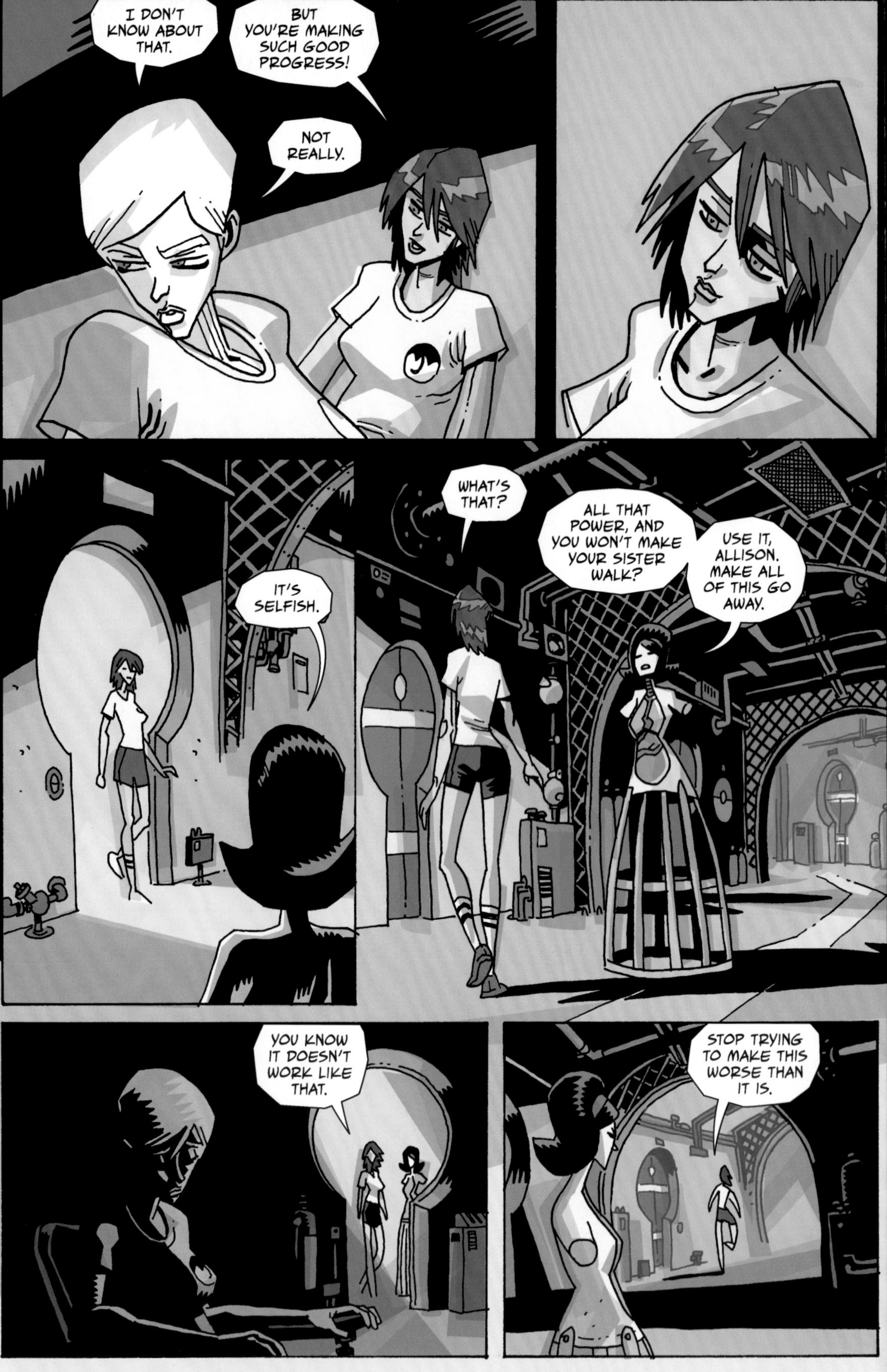
I DON'T KNOW ABOUT THAT.
BUT YOU'RE MAKING SUCH GOOD PROGRESS!
NOT REALLY.
IT'S SELFISH.
WHAT'S THAT?
ALL THAT POWER, AND YOU WON'T MAKE YOUR SISTER WALK?
USE IT, ALLISON. MAKE ALL OF THIS GO AWAY.
YOU KNOW IT DOESN'T WORK LIKE THAT.
STOP TRYING TO MAKE THIS WORSE THAN IT IS.

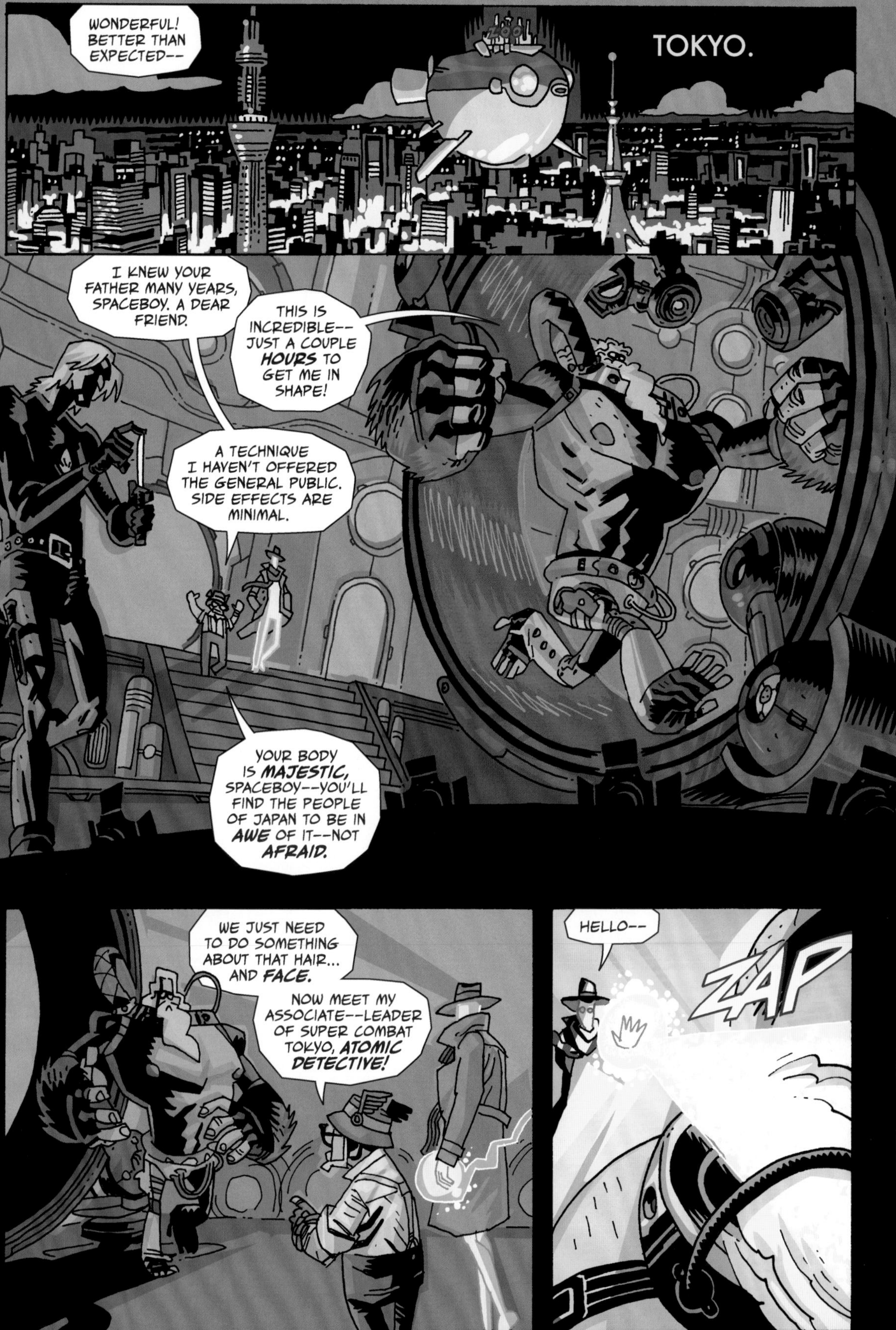
WONDERFUL! BETTER THAN EXPECTED--
TOKYO.
ZOO
I KNEW YOUR FATHER MANY YEARS, SPACEBOY. A DEAR FRIEND.
THIS IS INCREDIBLE-- JUST A COUPLE HOURS TO GET ME IN SHAPE!
A TECHNIQUE I HAVEN'T OFFERED THE GENERAL PUBLIC. SIDE EFFECTS ARE MINIMAL.
YOUR BODY IS MAJESTIC, SPACEBOY--YOU'LL FIND THE PEOPLE OF JAPAN TO BE IN AWE OF IT--NOT AFRAID.
WE JUST NEED TO DO SOMETHING ABOUT THAT HAIR... AND FACE.
NOW MEET MY ASSOCIATE--LEADER OF SUPER COMBAT TOKYO, ATOMIC DETECTIVE!
HELLO--
ZAP

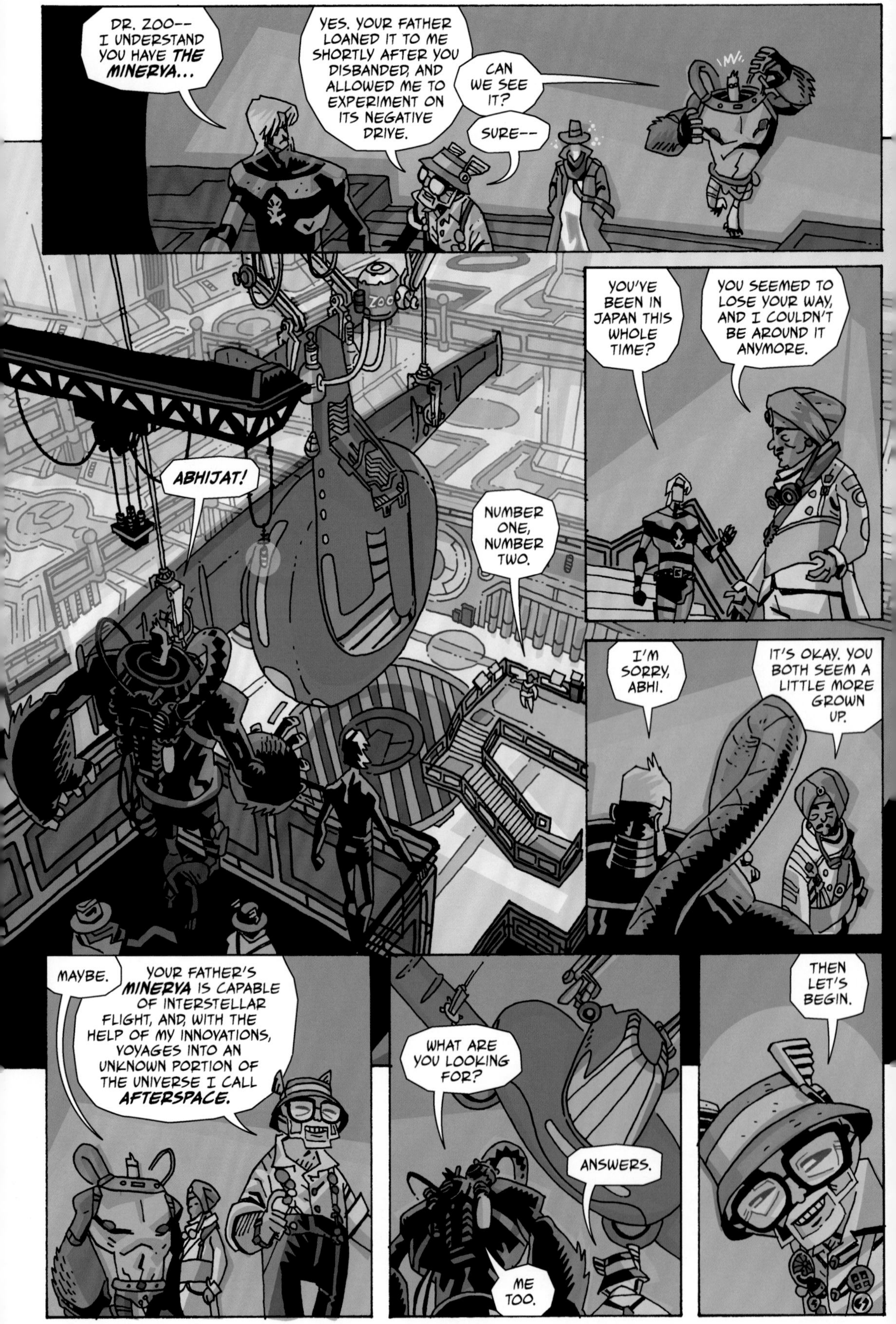
DR. ZOO--
I UNDERSTAND
YOU HAVE THE
MINERVA...
YES. YOUR FATHER LOANED IT TO ME SHORTLY AFTER YOU DISBANDED, AND ALLOWED ME TO EXPERIMENT ON ITS NEGATIVE DRIVE.
CAN WE SEE IT?
SURE--
ZOO
ABHIJAT!
NUMBER ONE, NUMBER TWO.
YOU'VE BEEN IN JAPAN THIS WHOLE TIME?
YOU SEEMED TO LOSE YOUR WAY, AND I COULDN'T BE AROUND IT ANYMORE.
I'M SORRY, ABHI.
IT'S OKAY. YOU BOTH SEEM A LITTLE MORE GROWN UP.
MAYBE.
YOUR FATHER'S MINERVA IS CAPABLE OF INTERSTELLAR FLIGHT, AND, WITH THE HELP OF MY INNOVATIONS, VOYAGES INTO AN UNKNOWN PORTION OF THE UNIVERSE I CALL AFTERSPACE.
WHAT ARE YOU LOOKING FOR?
ANSWERS.
ME TOO.
THEN LET'S BEGIN.

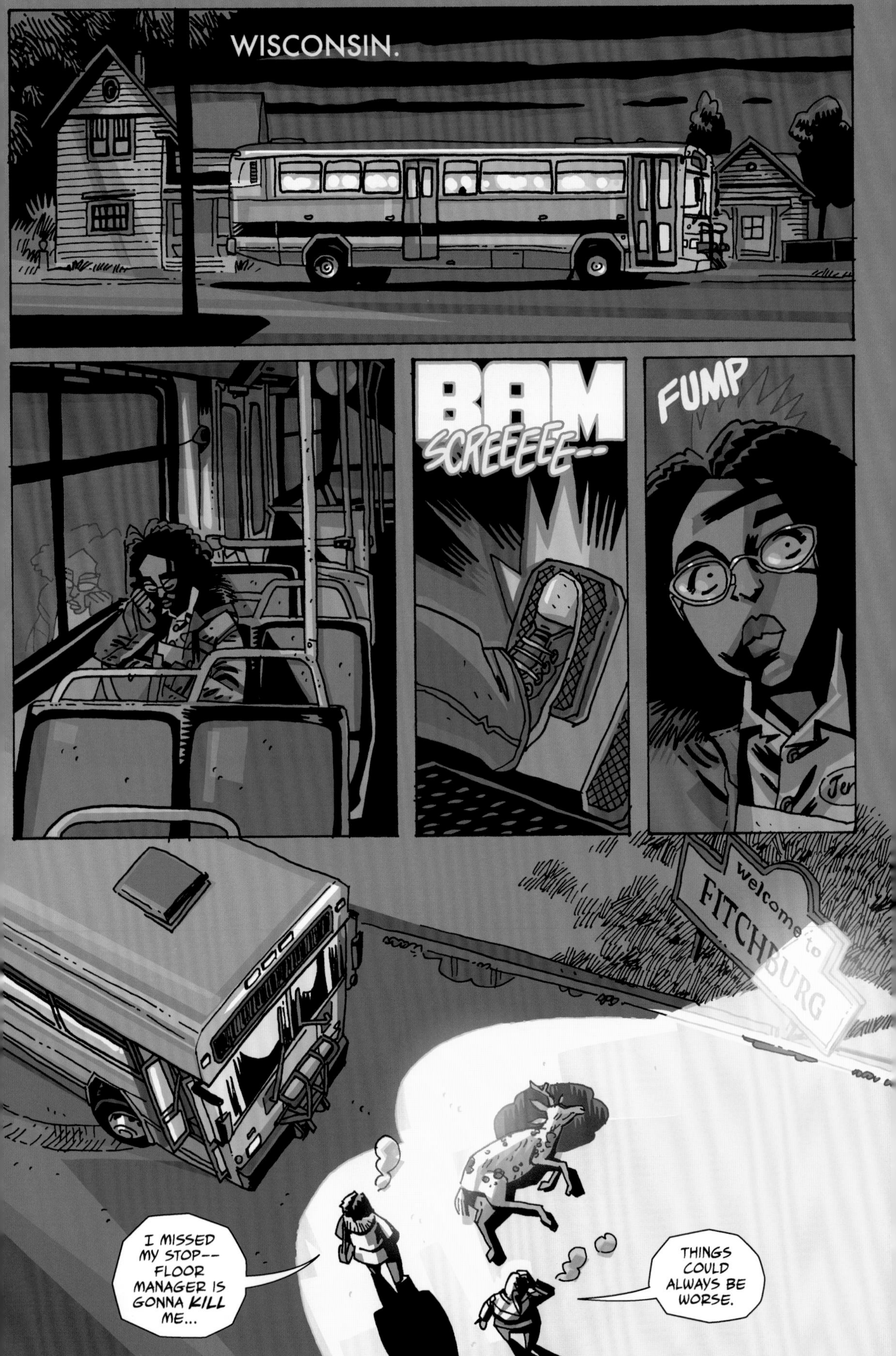
WISCONSIN.
BAM
SCREEEEEE--
FUMP
Jer
welcome to
FITCHBURG
I MISSED MY STOP-- FLOOR MANAGER IS GONNA KILL ME...
THINGS COULD ALWAYS BE WORSE.

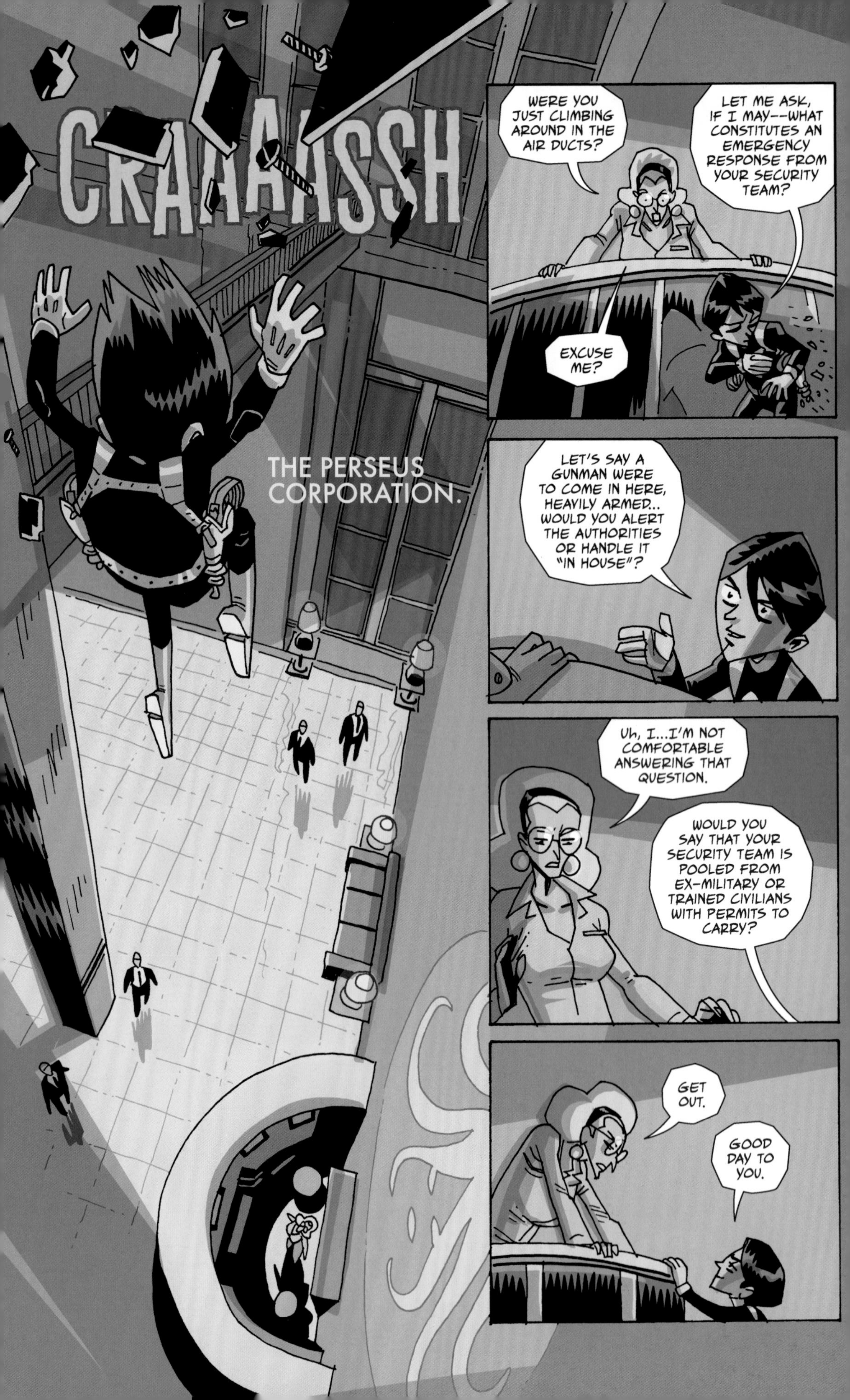
CRAAASSH
THE PERSEUS CORPORATION.
WERE YOU JUST CLIMBING AROUND IN THE AIR DUCTS?
LET ME ASK, IF I MAY--WHAT CONSTITUTES AN EMERGENCY RESPONSE FROM YOUR SECURITY TEAM?
EXCUSE ME?
LET'S SAY A GUNMAN WERE TO COME IN HERE, HEAVILY ARMED... WOULD YOU ALERT THE AUTHORITIES OR HANDLE IT "IN HOUSE"?
Uh, I...I'M NOT COMFORTABLE ANSWERING THAT QUESTION.
WOULD YOU SAY THAT YOUR SECURITY TEAM IS POOLED FROM EX-MILITARY OR TRAINED CIVILIANS WITH PERMITS TO CARRY?
GET OUT.
GOOD DAY TO YOU.

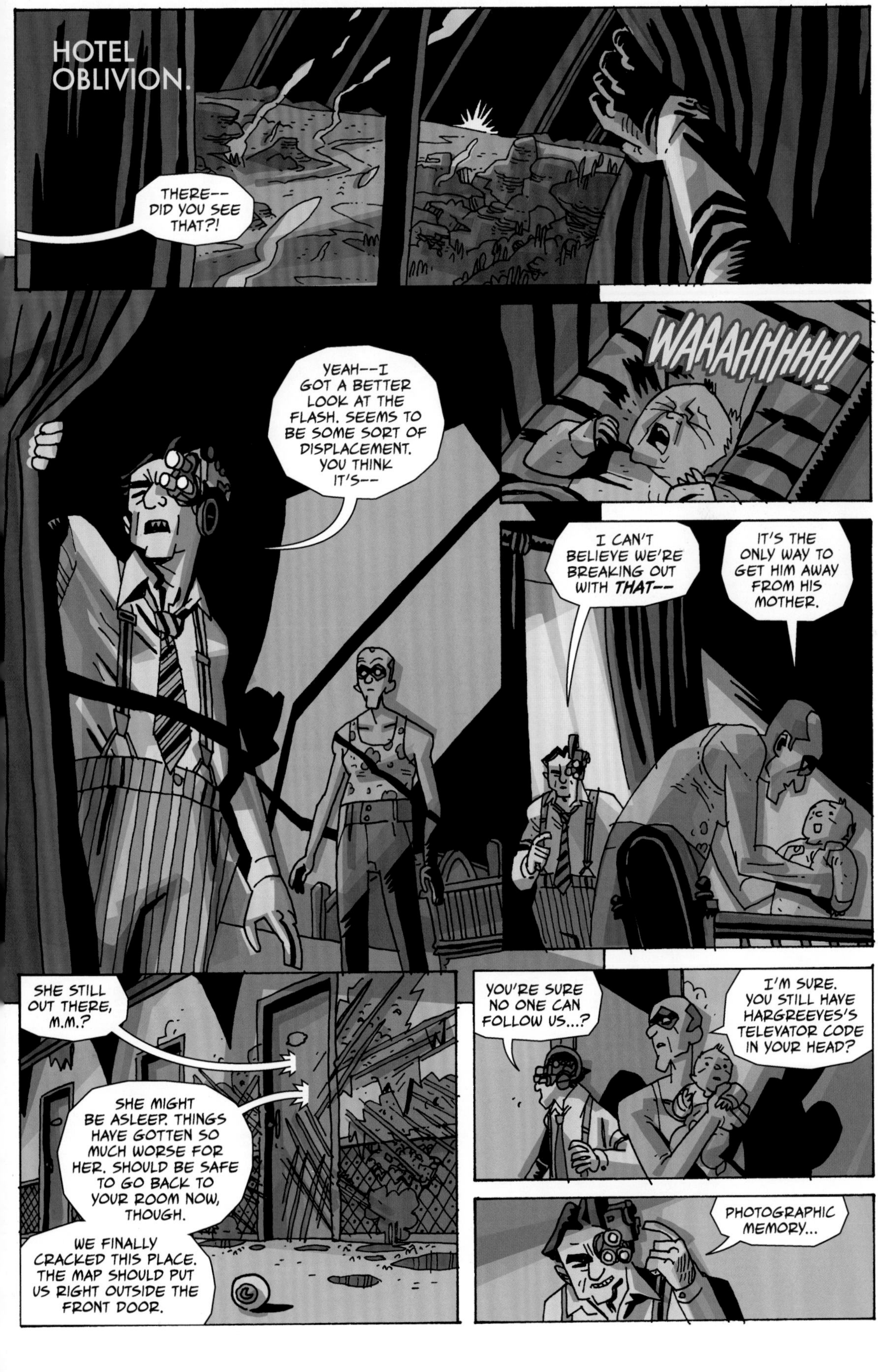
HOTEL OBLIVION.
THERE--DID YOU SEE THAT?!
YEAH--I GOT A BETTER LOOK AT THE FLASH. SEEMS TO BE SOME SORT OF DISPLACEMENT. YOU THINK IT'S--
WAAAHHHHH!
I CAN'T BELIEVE WE'RE BREAKING OUT WITH THAT--
IT'S THE ONLY WAY TO GET HIM AWAY FROM HIS MOTHER.
SHE STILL OUT THERE, M.M.?
SHE MIGHT BE ASLEEP. THINGS HAVE GOTTEN SO MUCH WORSE FOR HER. SHOULD BE SAFE TO GO BACK TO YOUR ROOM NOW, THOUGH.
WE FINALLY CRACKED THIS PLACE. THE MAP SHOULD PUT US RIGHT OUTSIDE THE FRONT DOOR.
YOU'RE SURE NO ONE CAN FOLLOW US...?
I'M SURE. YOU STILL HAVE HARGREEVES'S TELEVATOR CODE IN YOUR HEAD?
PHOTOGRAPHIC MEMORY...

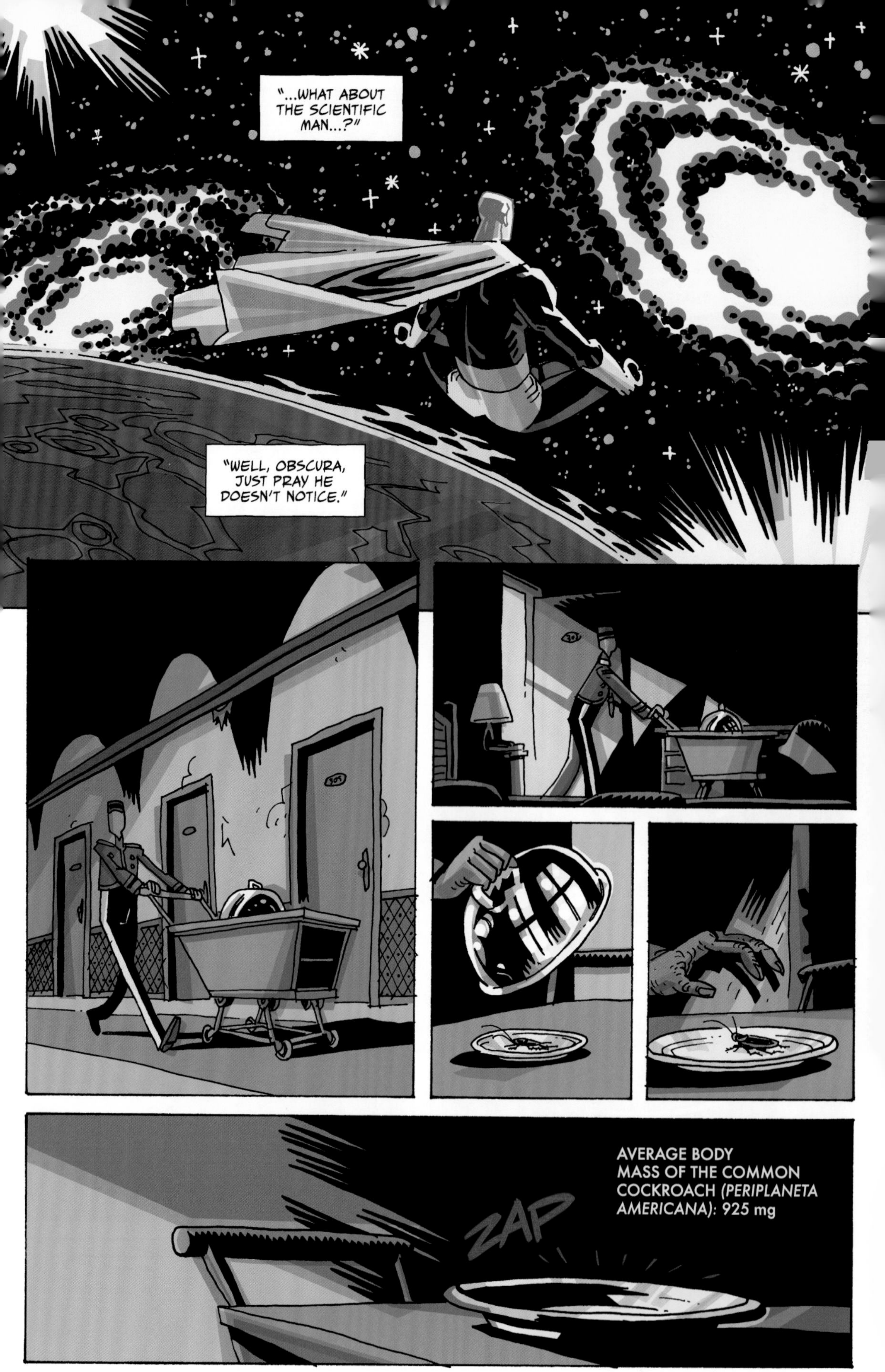
"...WHAT ABOUT THE SCIENTIFIC MAN...?"
"WELL, OBSCURA, JUST PRAY HE DOESN'T NOTICE."
AVERAGE BODY MASS OF THE COMMON COCKROACH (PERIPLANETA AMERICANA): 925 mg
ZAP

CHAPTER TWO

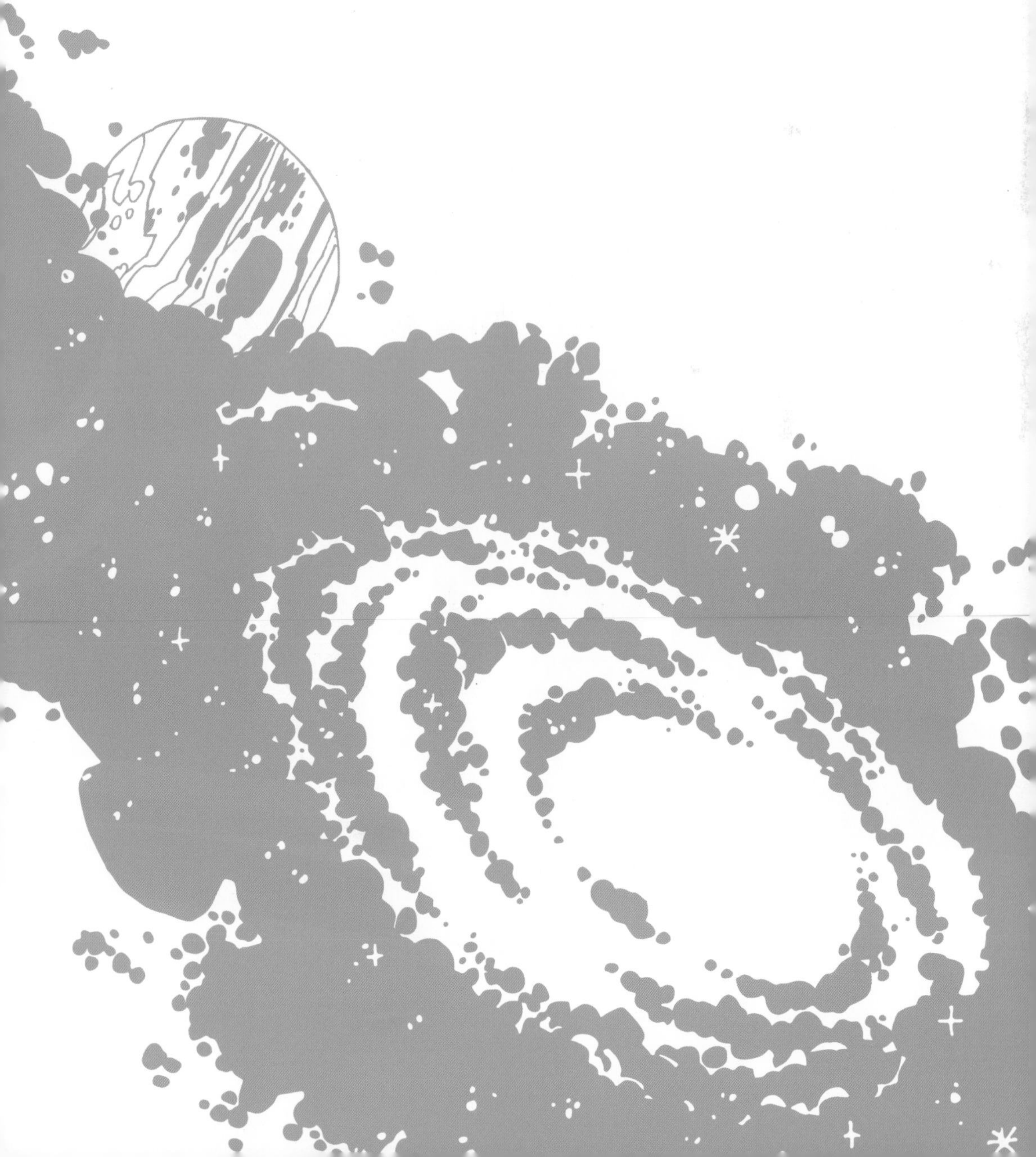

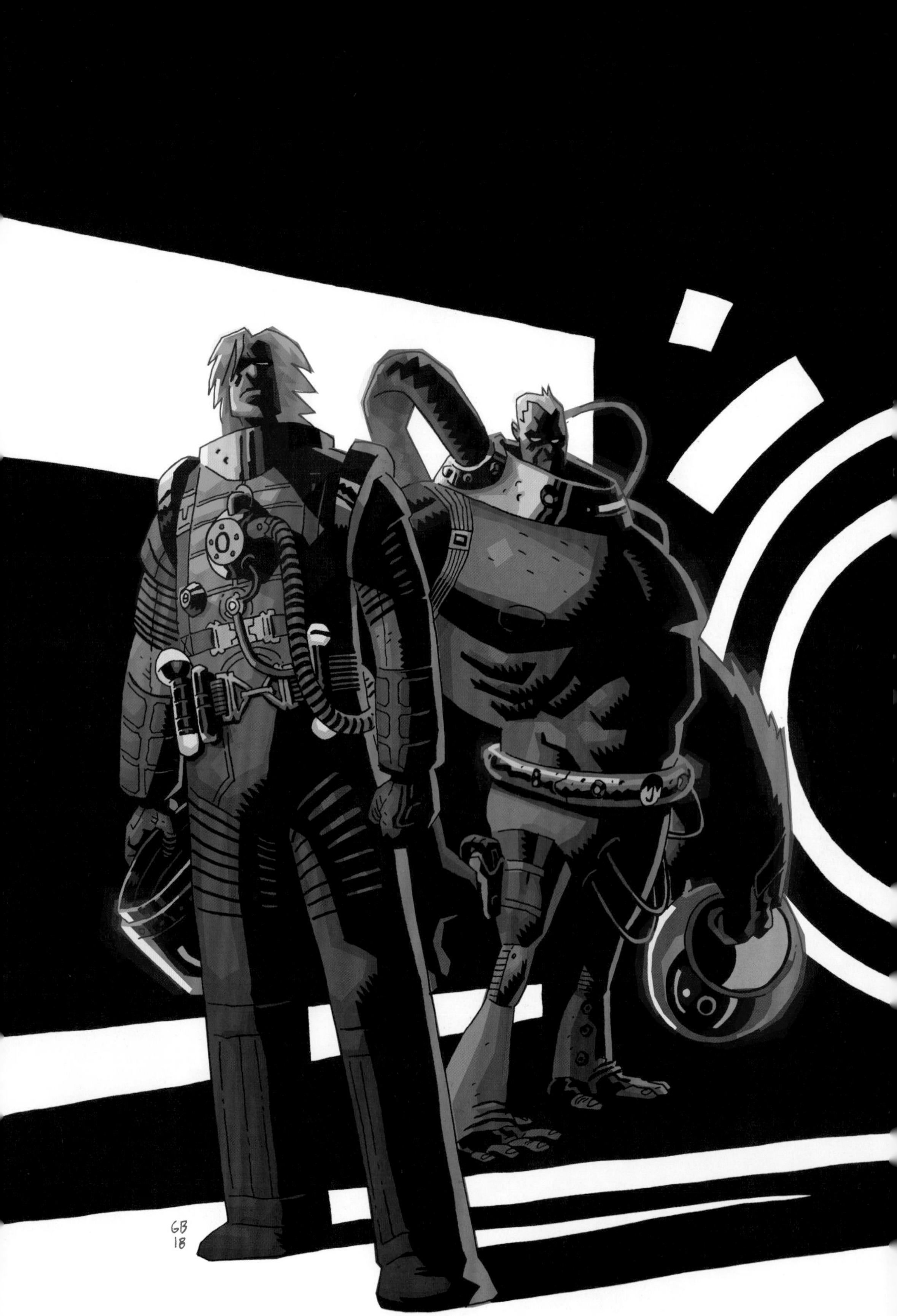
GB
18

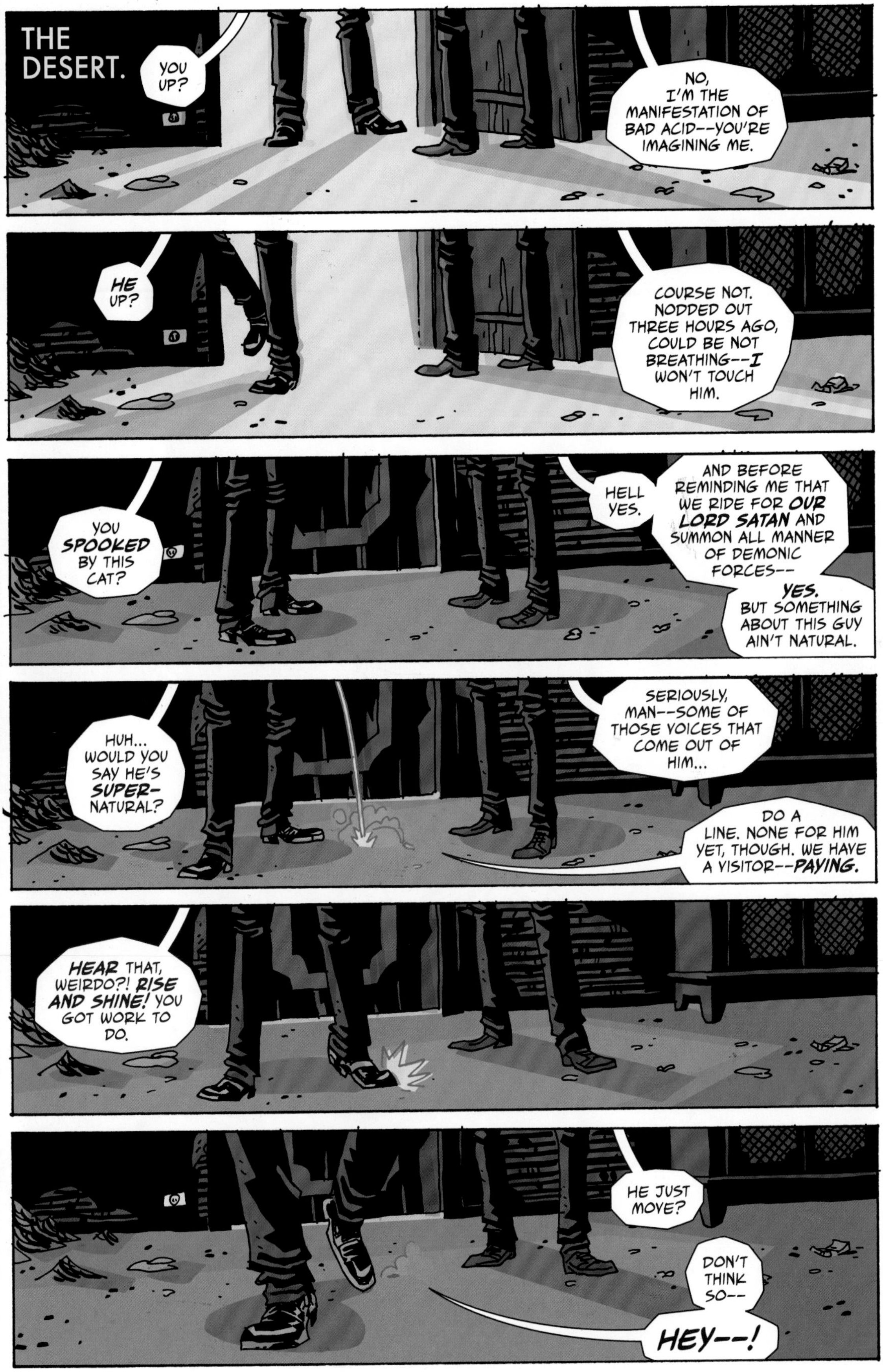
THE DESERT.
YOU UP?
NO, I'M THE MANIFESTATION OF BAD ACID--YOU'RE IMAGINING ME.
HE UP?
COURSE NOT. NODDED OUT THREE HOURS AGO, COULD BE NOT BREATHING--I WON'T TOUCH HIM.
YOU SPOOKED BY THIS CAT?
HELL YES.
AND BEFORE REMINDING ME THAT WE RIDE FOR OUR LORD SATAN AND SUMMON ALL MANNER OF DEMONIC FORCES--
YES. BUT SOMETHING ABOUT THIS GUY AIN'T NATURAL.
HUH... WOULD YOU SAY HE'S SUPER-NATURAL?
SERIOUSLY, MAN--SOME OF THOSE VOICES THAT COME OUT OF HIM...
DO A LINE. NONE FOR HIM YET, THOUGH. WE HAVE A VISITOR--PAYING.
HEAR THAT, WEIRDO?! RISE AND SHINE! YOU GOT WORK TO DO.
HE JUST MOVE?
DON'T THINK SO--
HEY--!

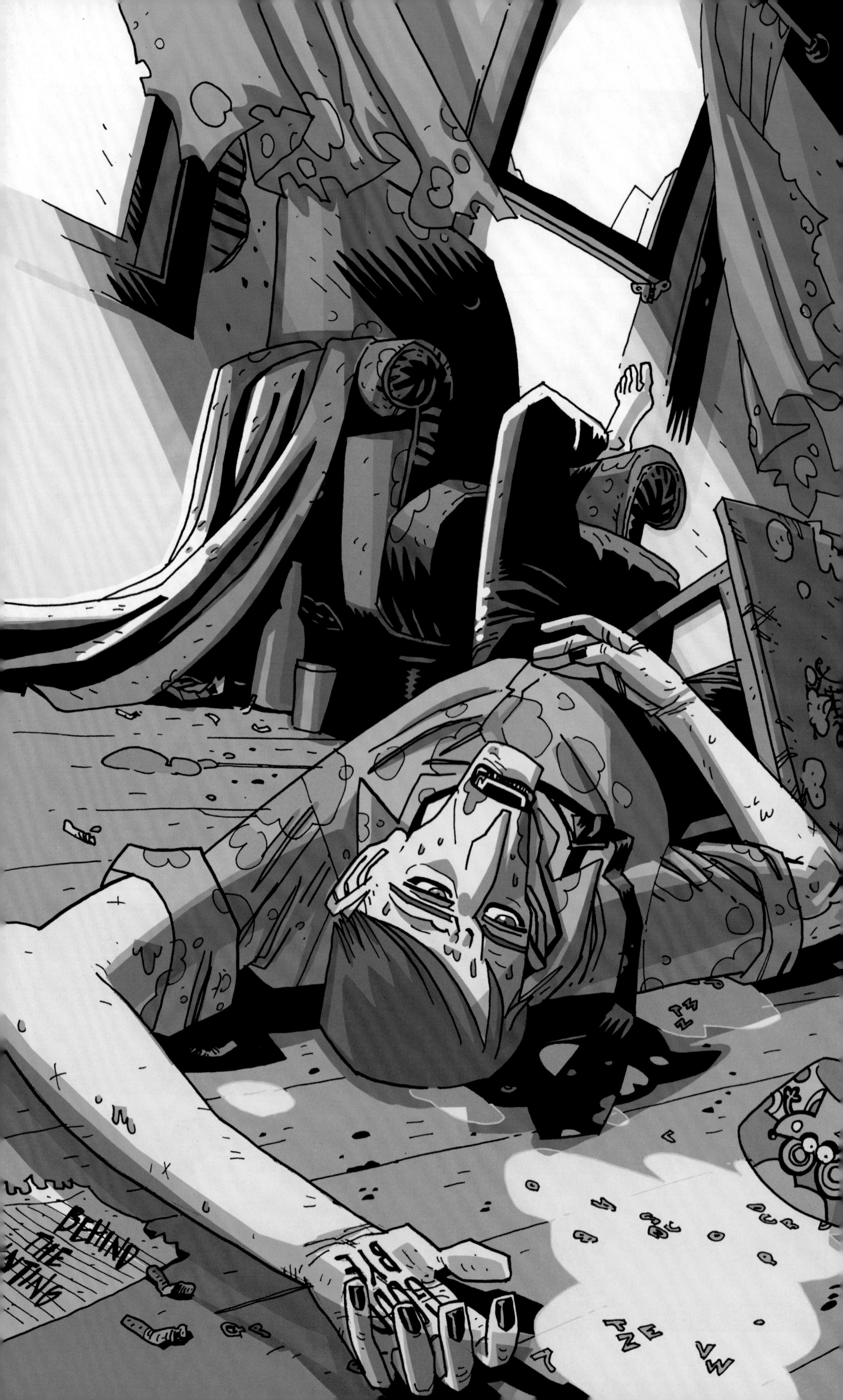

BEHIND
THE
GOOD BYE

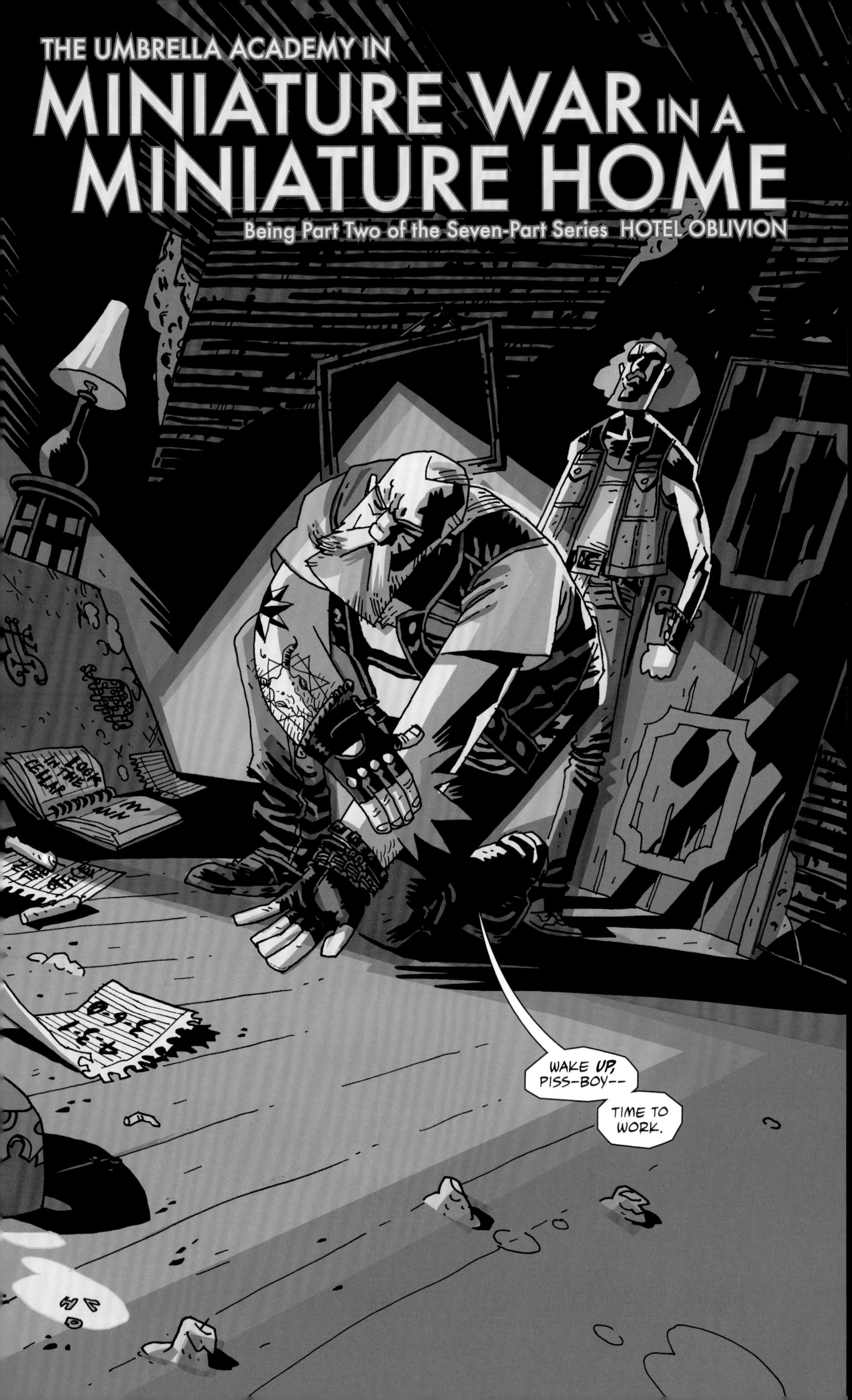
THE UMBRELLA ACADEMY IN
MINIATURE WAR IN A MINIATURE HOME
Being Part Two of the Seven-Part Series HOTEL OBLIVION
WAKE UP, PISS-BOY--
TIME TO WORK.

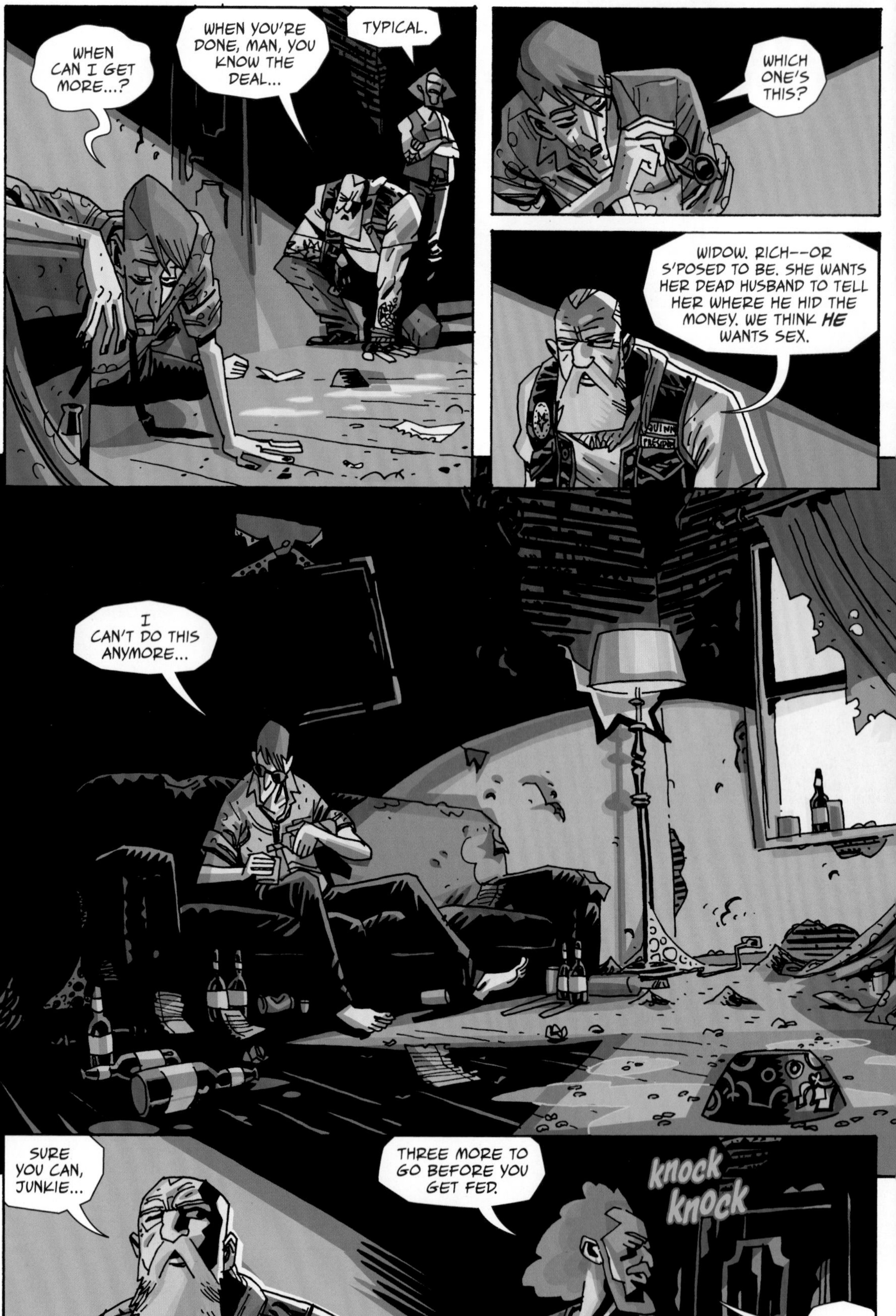
WHEN CAN I GET MORE...?
WHEN YOU'RE DONE, MAN, YOU KNOW THE DEAL...
TYPICAL.
WHICH ONE'S THIS?
WIDOW. RICH--OR S'POSED TO BE. SHE WANTS HER DEAD HUSBAND TO TELL HER WHERE HE HID THE MONEY. WE THINK HE WANTS SEX.
I CAN'T DO THIS ANYMORE...
SURE YOU CAN, JUNKIE...
THREE MORE TO GO BEFORE YOU GET FED.
knock knock
COME IN...

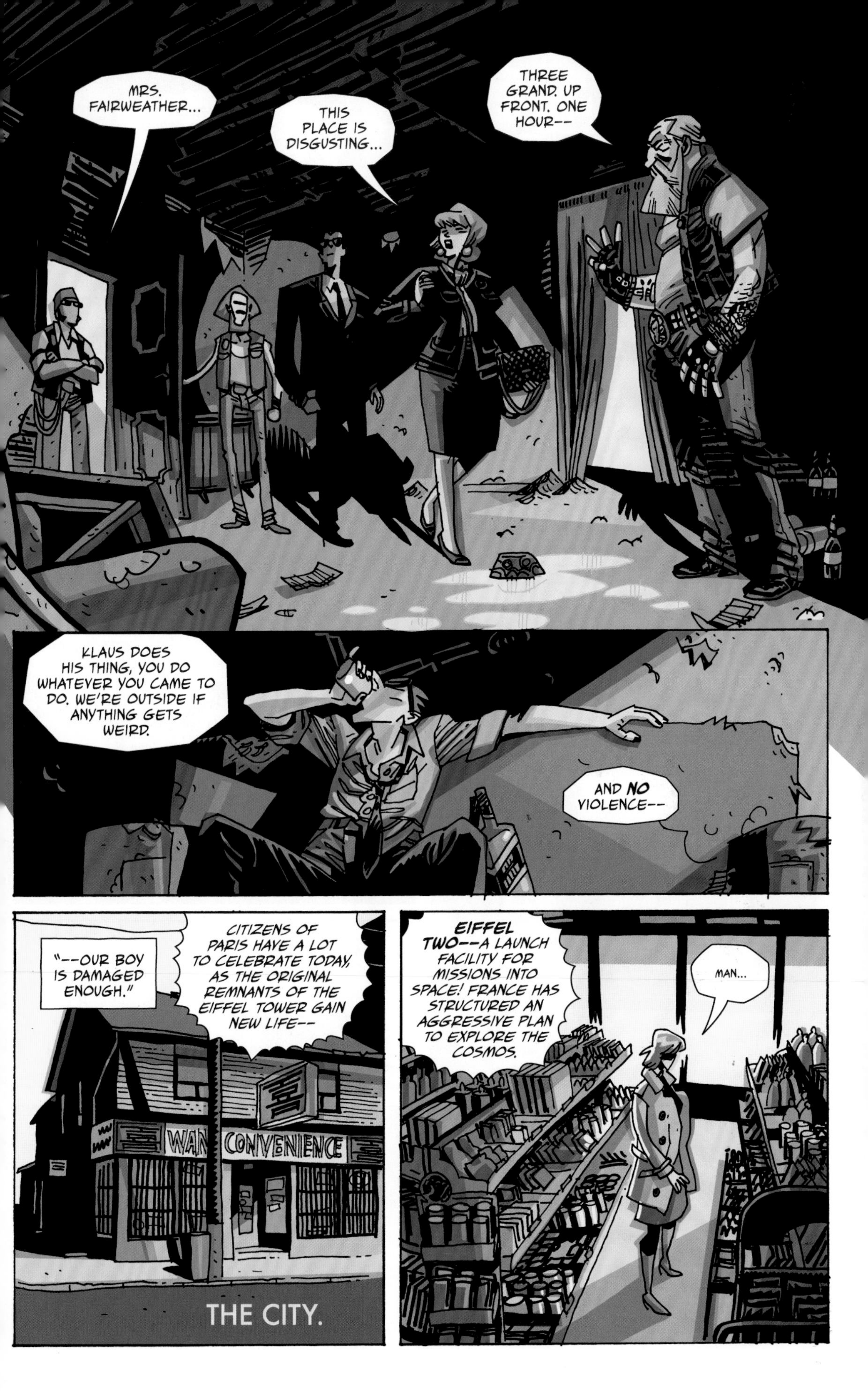
MRS. FAIRWEATHER...
THIS PLACE IS DISGUSTING...
THREE GRAND. UP FRONT. ONE HOUR--
KLAUS DOES HIS THING, YOU DO WHATEVER YOU CAME TO DO. WE'RE OUTSIDE IF ANYTHING GETS WEIRD.
AND **NO** VIOLENCE--
"--OUR BOY IS DAMAGED ENOUGH."
CITIZENS OF PARIS HAVE A LOT TO CELEBRATE TODAY, AS THE ORIGINAL REMNANTS OF THE EIFFEL TOWER GAIN NEW LIFE--
WAN CONVENIENCE
THE CITY.
EIFFEL TWO--A LAUNCH FACILITY FOR MISSIONS INTO SPACE! FRANCE HAS STRUCTURED AN AGGRESSIVE PLAN TO EXPLORE THE COSMOS.
MAN...

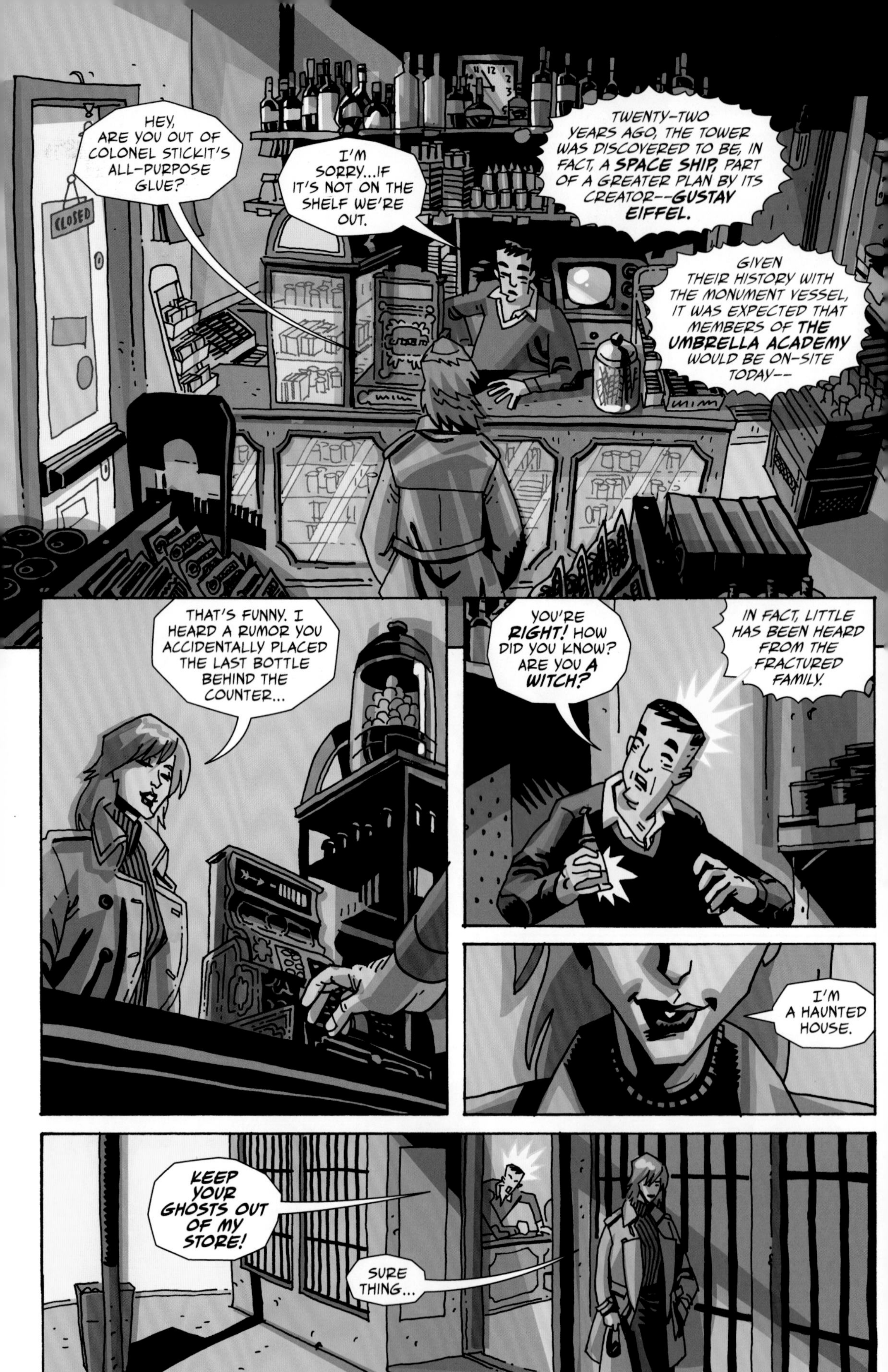
HEY, ARE YOU OUT OF COLONEL STICKIT'S ALL-PURPOSE GLUE?
I'M SORRY...IF IT'S NOT ON THE SHELF WE'RE OUT.
TWENTY-TWO YEARS AGO, THE TOWER WAS DISCOVERED TO BE, IN FACT, A SPACE SHIP, PART OF A GREATER PLAN BY ITS CREATOR--GUSTAV EIFFEL.
GIVEN THEIR HISTORY WITH THE MONUMENT VESSEL, IT WAS EXPECTED THAT MEMBERS OF THE UMBRELLA ACADEMY WOULD BE ON-SITE TODAY--
CLOSED
THAT'S FUNNY. I HEARD A RUMOR YOU ACCIDENTALLY PLACED THE LAST BOTTLE BEHIND THE COUNTER...
YOU'RE RIGHT! HOW DID YOU KNOW? ARE YOU A WITCH?
IN FACT, LITTLE HAS BEEN HEARD FROM THE FRACTURED FAMILY.
I'M A HAUNTED HOUSE.
KEEP YOUR GHOSTS OUT OF MY STORE!
SURE THING...

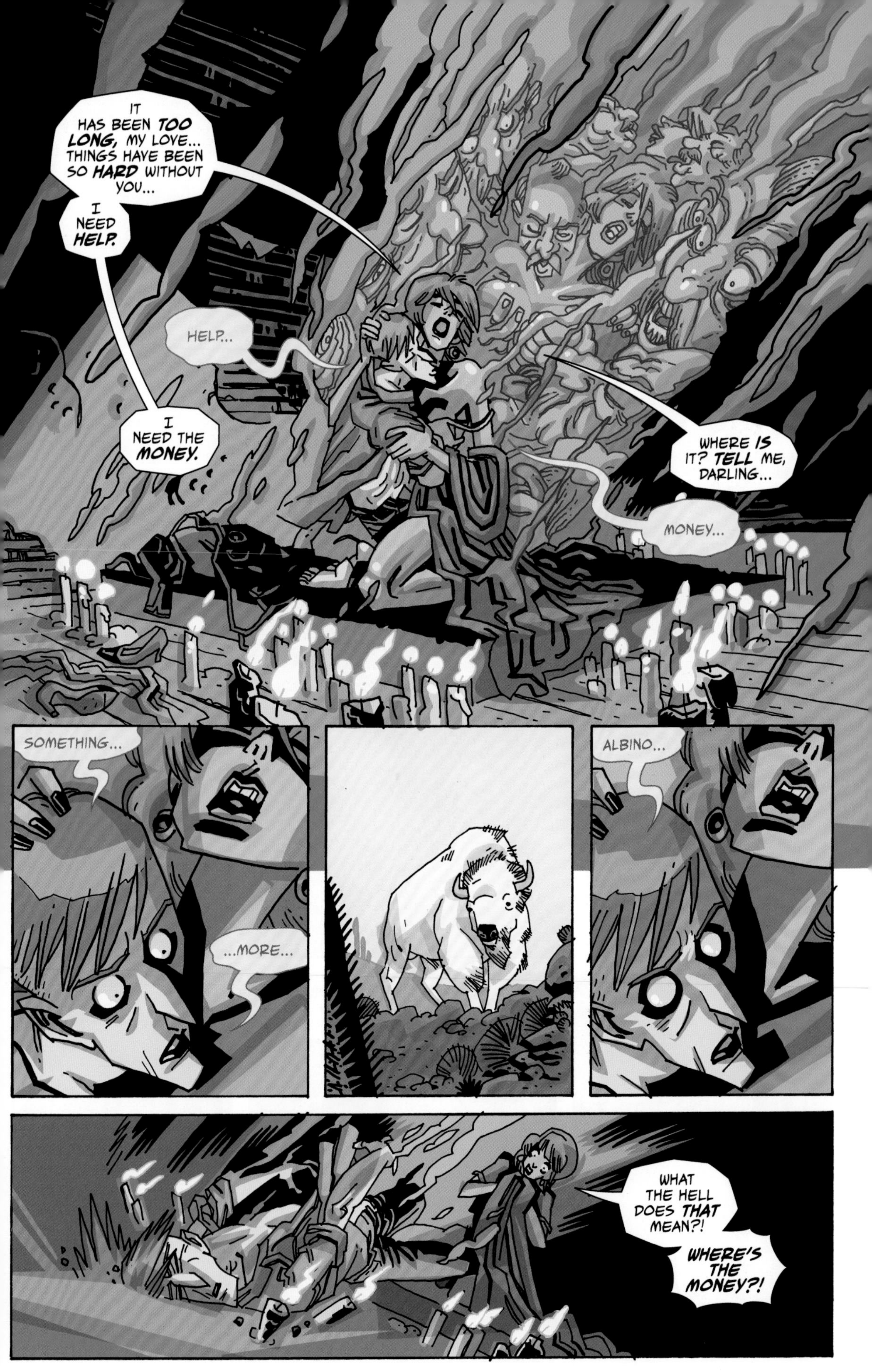
IT HAS BEEN TOO LONG, MY LOVE... THINGS HAVE BEEN SO HARD WITHOUT YOU...
I NEED HELP.
HELP...
I NEED THE MONEY.
WHERE IS IT? TELL ME, DARLING...
MONEY...
SOMETHING...
...MORE...
ALBINO...
WHAT THE HELL DOES THAT MEAN?!
WHERE'S THE MONEY?!

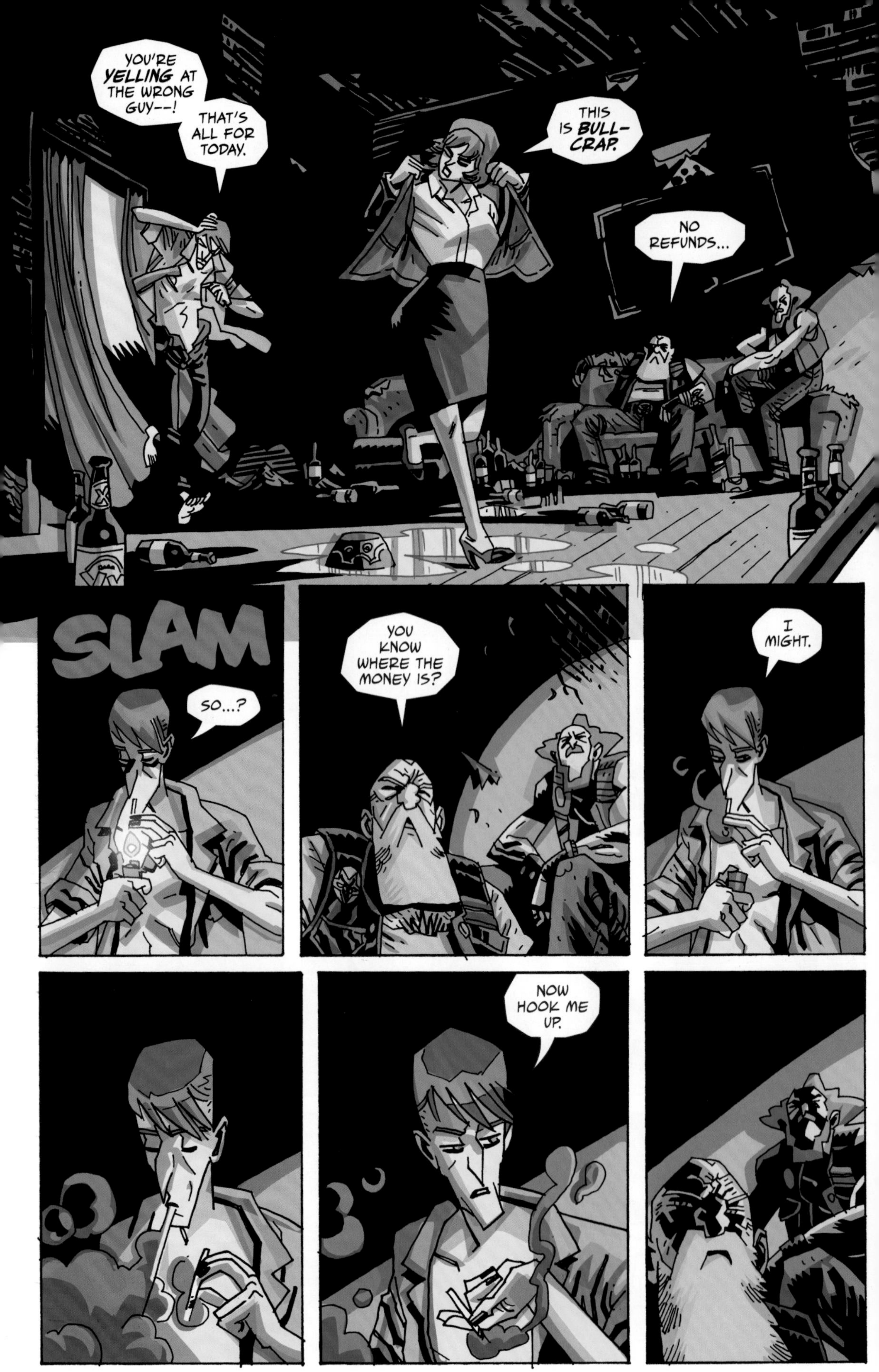

YOU'RE YELLING AT THE WRONG GUY--!
THAT'S ALL FOR TODAY.
THIS IS BULL-CRAP.
NO REFUNDS...
SLAM
SO...?
YOU KNOW WHERE THE MONEY IS?
I MIGHT.
NOW HOOK ME UP.

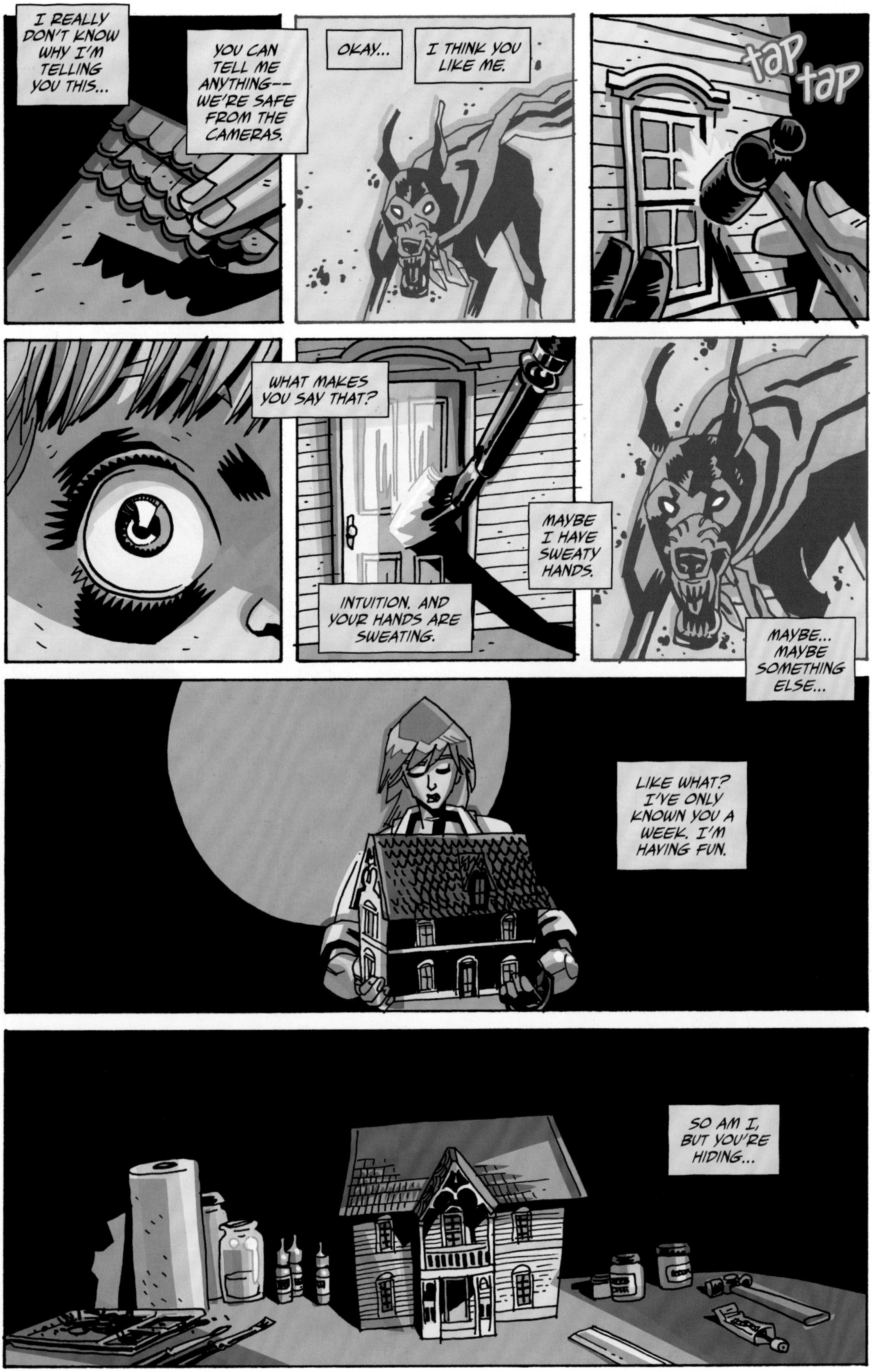
I REALLY DON'T KNOW WHY I'M TELLING YOU THIS...
YOU CAN TELL ME ANYTHING-- WE'RE SAFE FROM THE CAMERAS.
OKAY...
I THINK YOU LIKE ME.
tap tap
WHAT MAKES YOU SAY THAT?
INTUITION. AND YOUR HANDS ARE SWEATING.
MAYBE I HAVE SWEATY HANDS.
MAYBE... MAYBE SOMETHING ELSE...
LIKE WHAT? I'VE ONLY KNOWN YOU A WEEK. I'M HAVING FUN.
SO AM I, BUT YOU'RE HIDING...

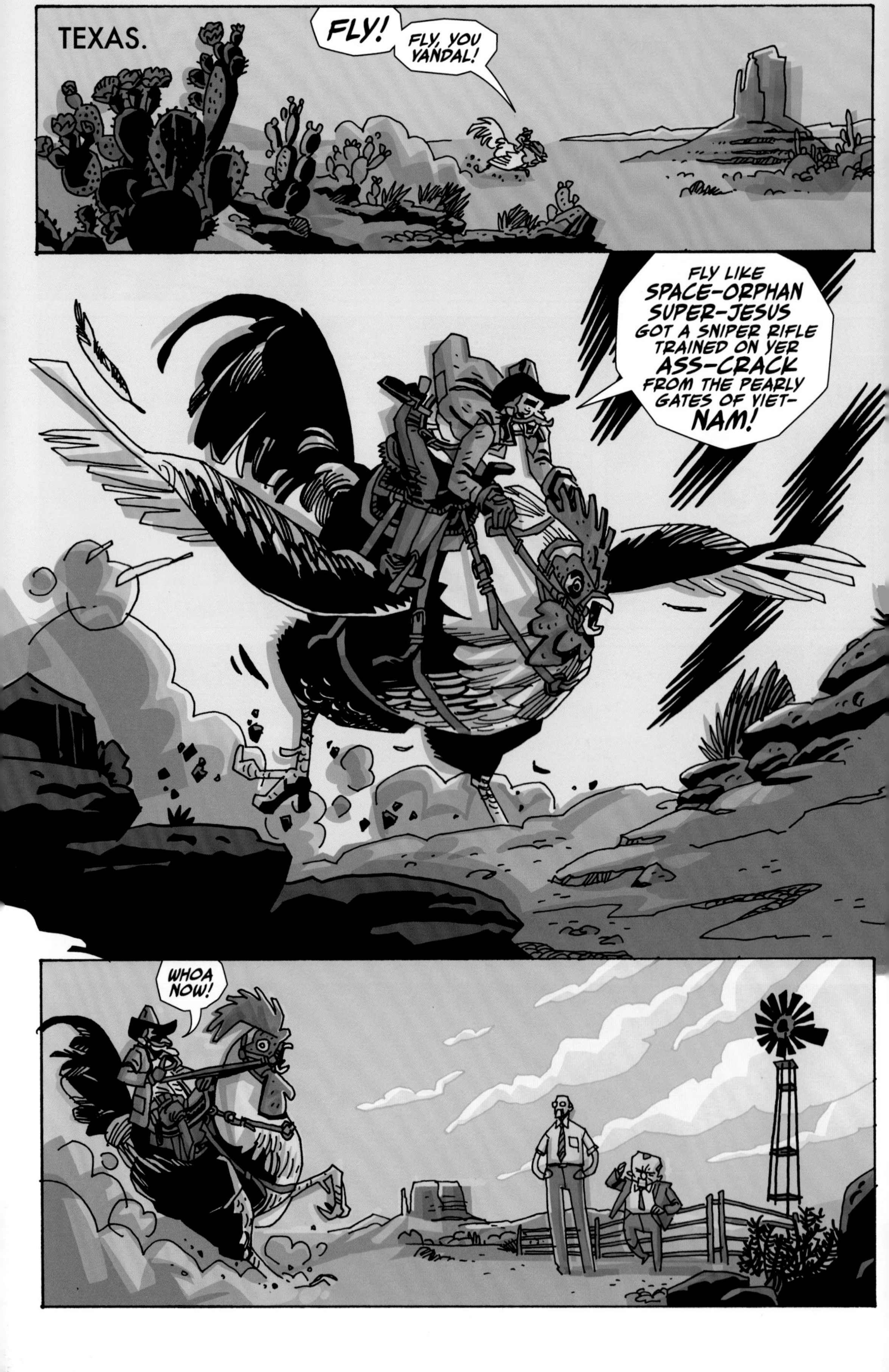
TEXAS.
FLY!
FLY, YOU VANDAL!
FLY LIKE SPACE-ORPHAN SUPER-JESUS GOT A SNIPER RIFLE TRAINED ON YER ASS-CRACK FROM THE PEARLY GATES OF VIET-NAM!
WHOA NOW!

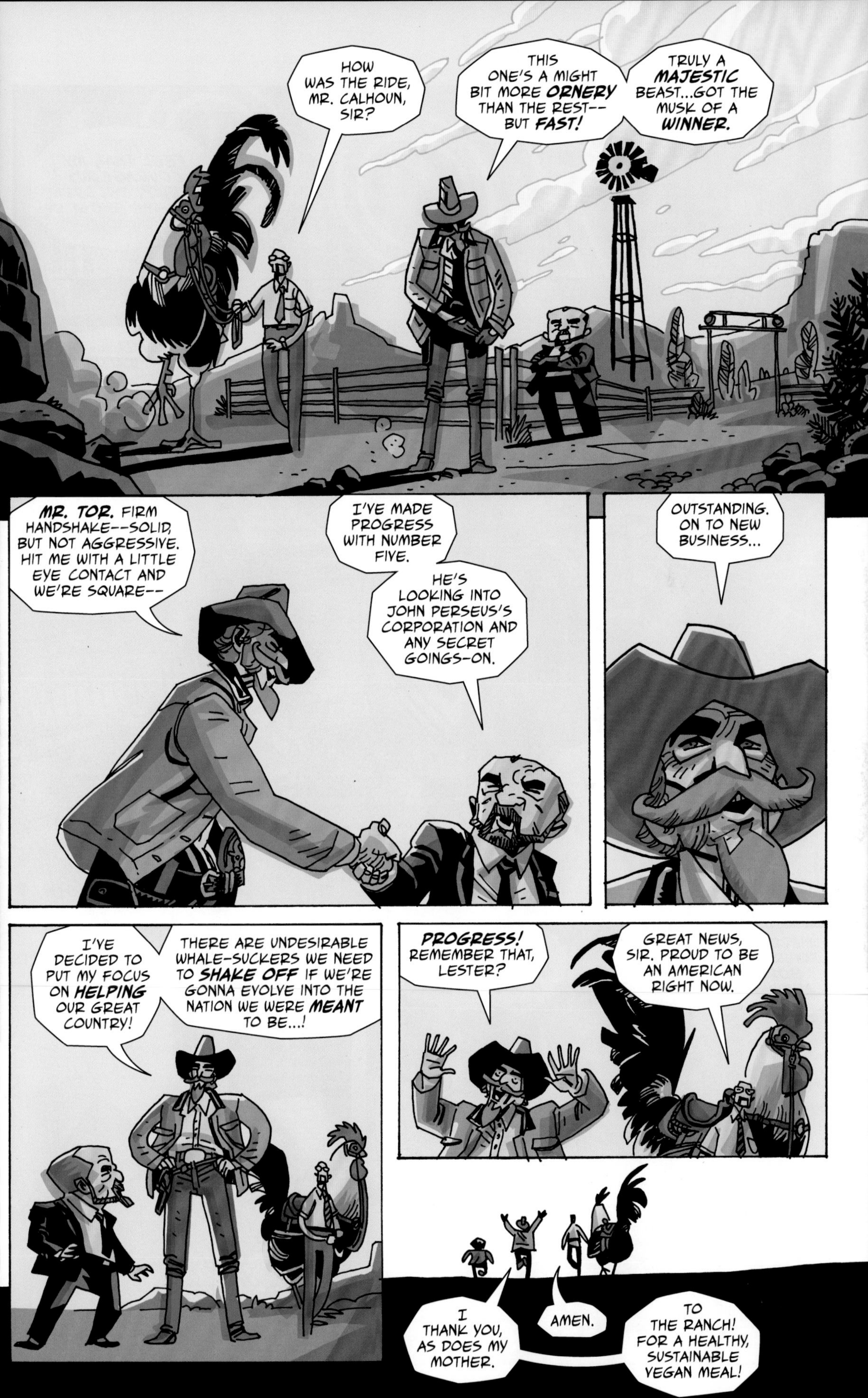
HOW WAS THE RIDE, MR. CALHOUN, SIR?
THIS ONE'S A MIGHT BIT MORE ORNERY THAN THE REST--BUT FAST!
TRULY A MAJESTIC BEAST...GOT THE MUSK OF A WINNER.
MR. TOR. FIRM HANDSHAKE--SOLID, BUT NOT AGGRESSIVE. HIT ME WITH A LITTLE EYE CONTACT AND WE'RE SQUARE--
I'VE MADE PROGRESS WITH NUMBER FIVE.
HE'S LOOKING INTO JOHN PERSEUS'S CORPORATION AND ANY SECRET GOINGS-ON.
OUTSTANDING. ON TO NEW BUSINESS...
I'VE DECIDED TO PUT MY FOCUS ON HELPING OUR GREAT COUNTRY!
THERE ARE UNDESIRABLE WHALE-SUCKERS WE NEED TO SHAKE OFF IF WE'RE GONNA EVOLVE INTO THE NATION WE WERE MEANT TO BE...!
PROGRESS! REMEMBER THAT, LESTER?
GREAT NEWS, SIR. PROUD TO BE AN AMERICAN RIGHT NOW.
I THANK YOU, AS DOES MY MOTHER.
AMEN.
TO THE RANCH! FOR A HEALTHY, SUSTAINABLE VEGAN MEAL!

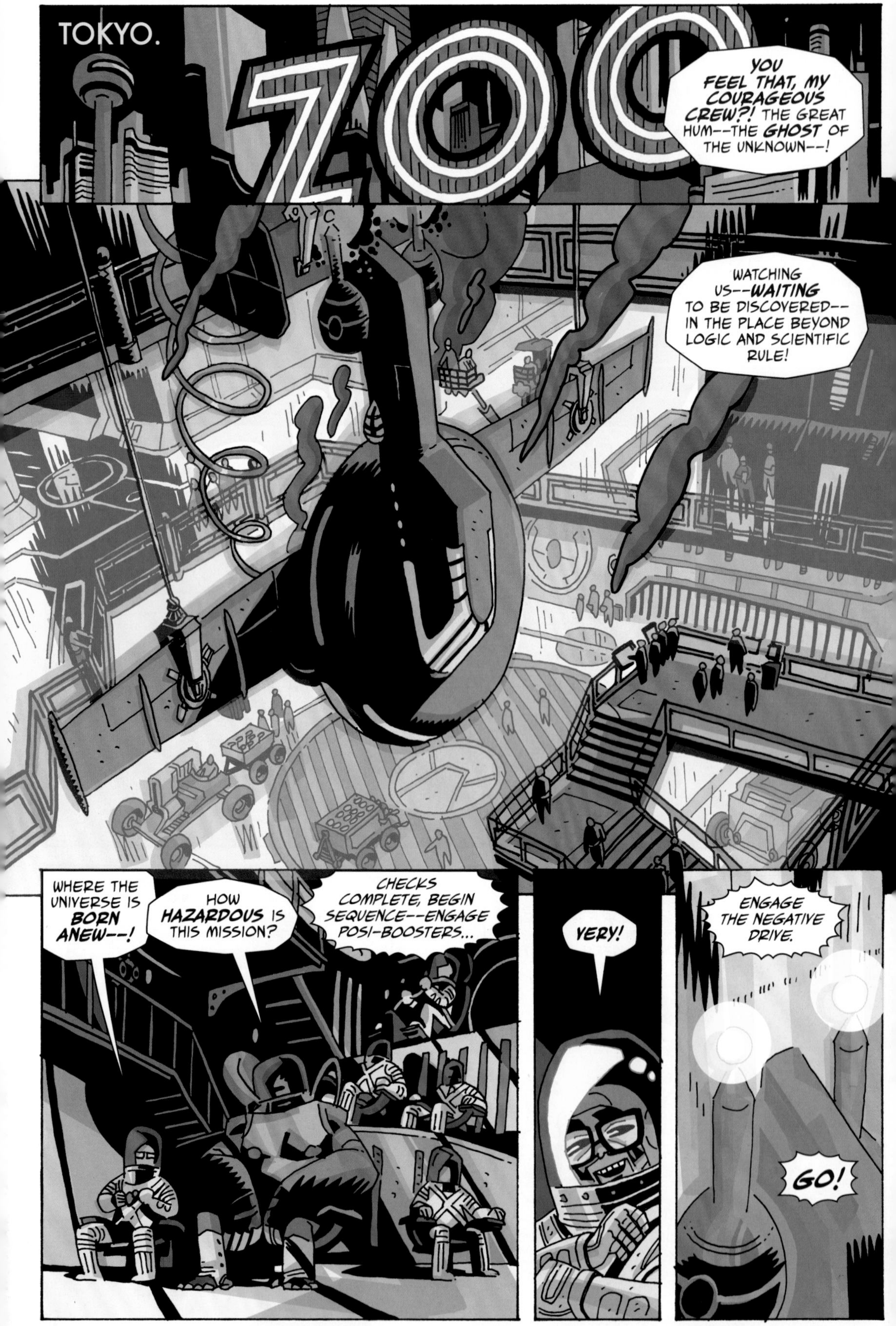
TOKYO.
ZOO
YOU FEEL THAT, MY COURAGEOUS CREW?! THE GREAT HUM--THE GHOST OF THE UNKNOWN--!
WATCHING US--WAITING TO BE DISCOVERED--IN THE PLACE BEYOND LOGIC AND SCIENTIFIC RULE!
WHERE THE UNIVERSE IS BORN ANEW--!
HOW HAZARDOUS IS THIS MISSION?
CHECKS COMPLETE, BEGIN SEQUENCE--ENGAGE POSI-BOOSTERS...
VERY!
ENGAGE THE NEGATIVE DRIVE.
GO!

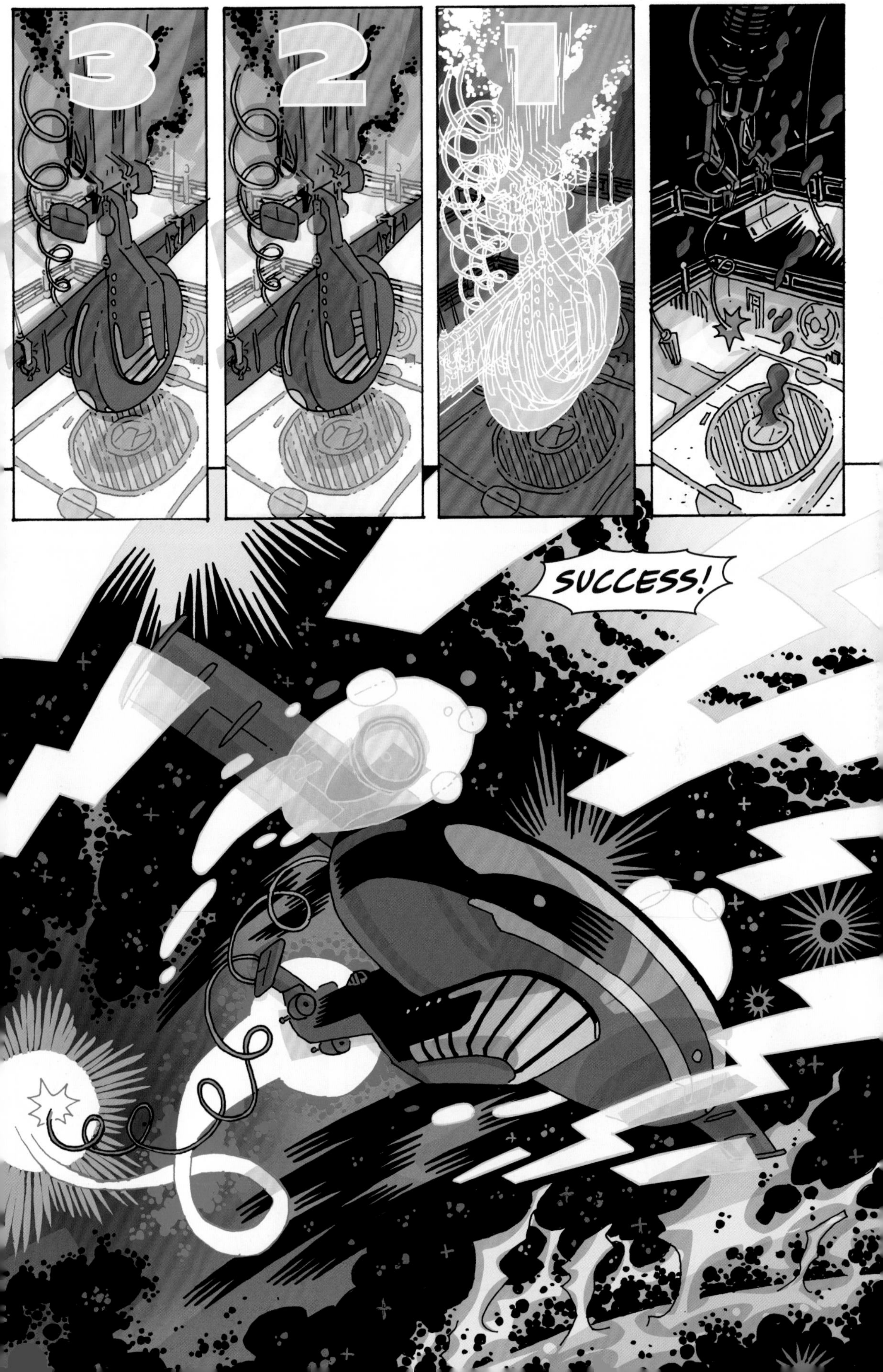
3
2
1
SUCCESS!

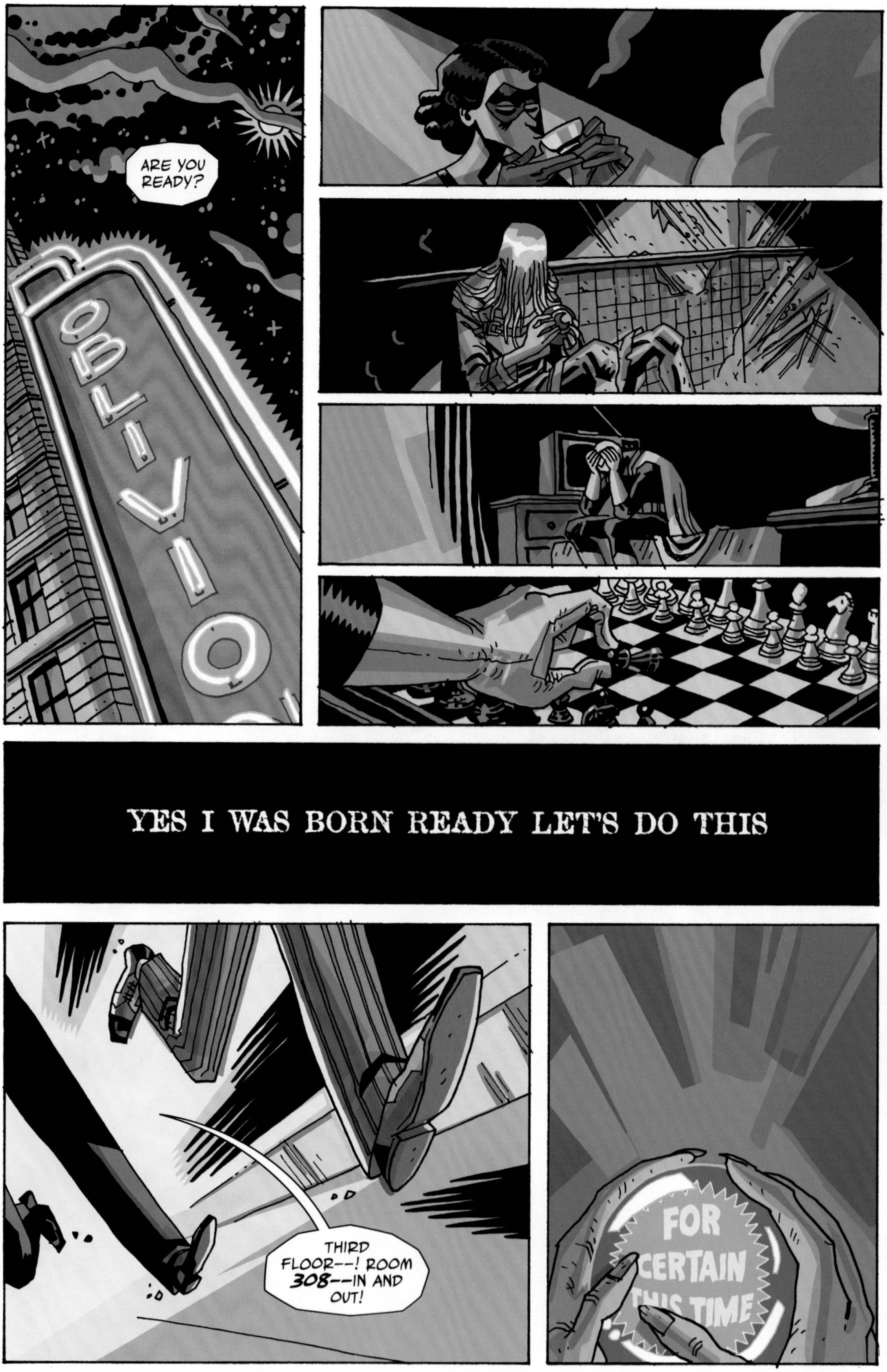
ARE YOU READY?
OBLIVION
YES I WAS BORN READY LET'S DO THIS
THIRD FLOOR--! ROOM 308--IN AND OUT!
FOR CERTAIN THIS TIME

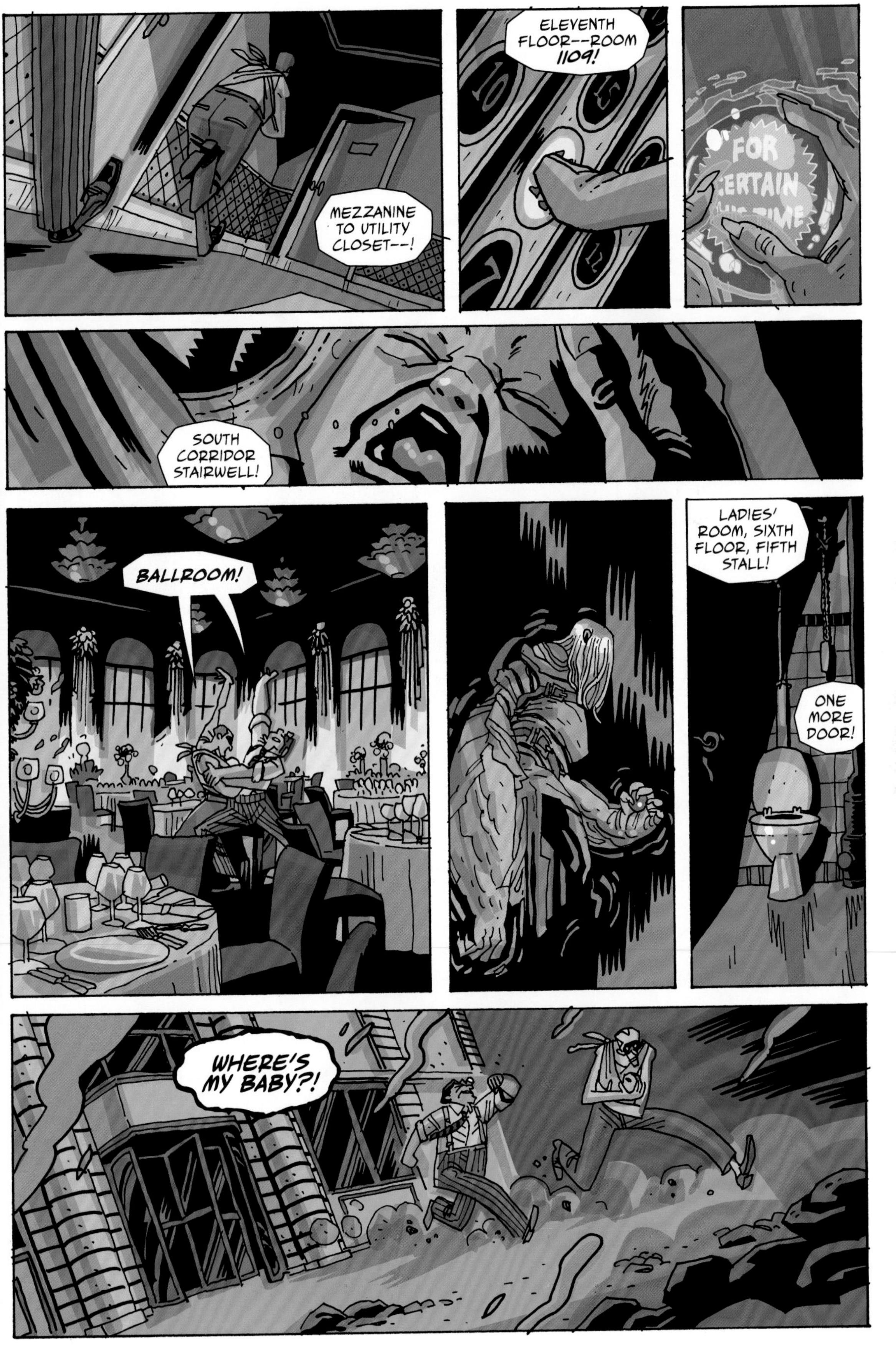
MEZZANINE TO UTILITY CLOSET--!
ELEVENTH FLOOR--ROOM 1109!
FOR CERTAIN
SOUTH CORRIDOR STAIRWELL!
BALLROOM!
LADIES' ROOM, SIXTH FLOOR, FIFTH STALL!
ONE MORE DOOR!
WHERE'S MY BABY?!

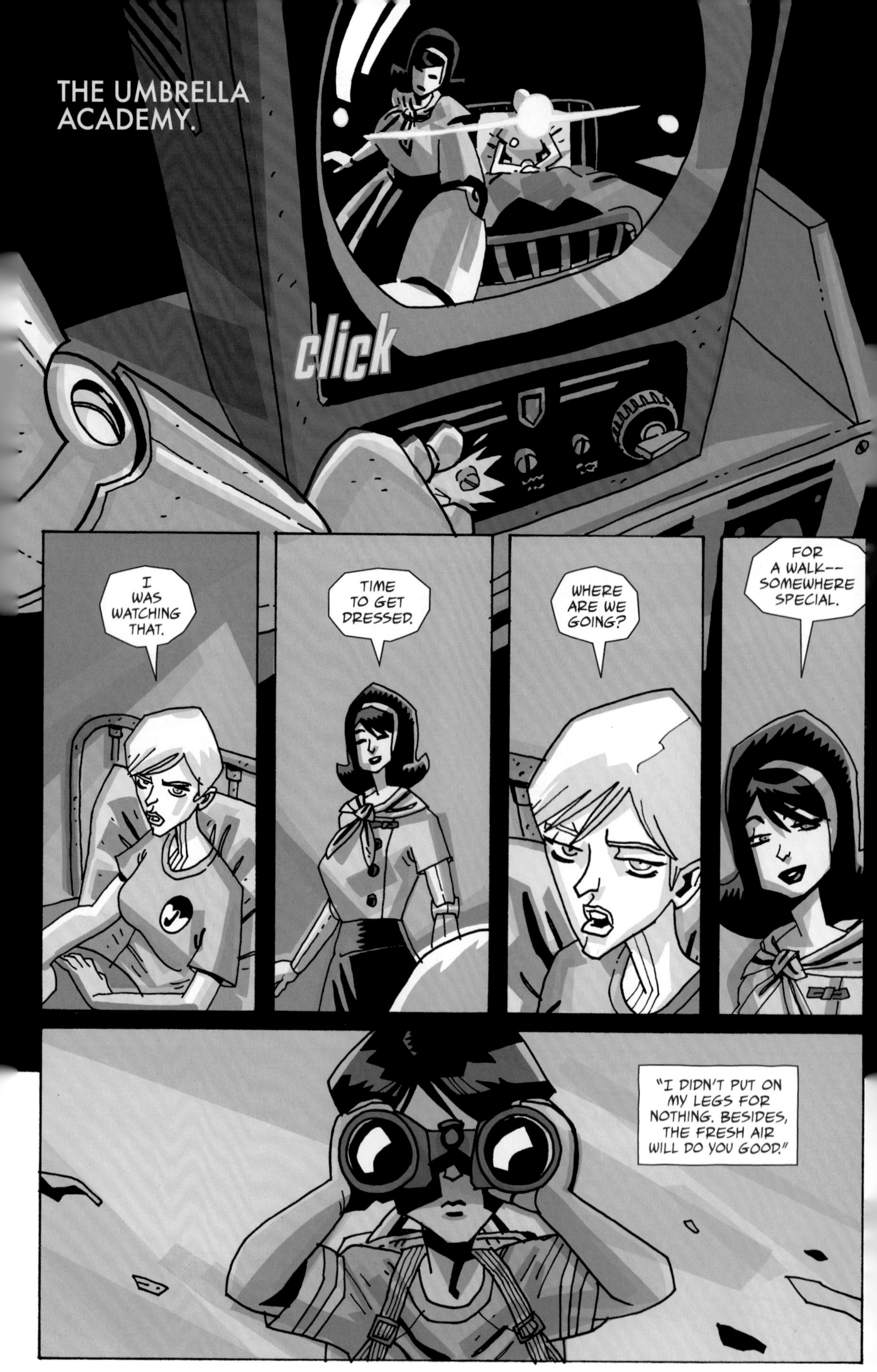
THE UMBRELLA ACADEMY.
click
I WAS WATCHING THAT.
TIME TO GET DRESSED.
WHERE ARE WE GOING?
FOR A WALK-- SOMEWHERE SPECIAL.
"I DIDN'T PUT ON MY LEGS FOR NOTHING. BESIDES, THE FRESH AIR WILL DO YOU GOOD."

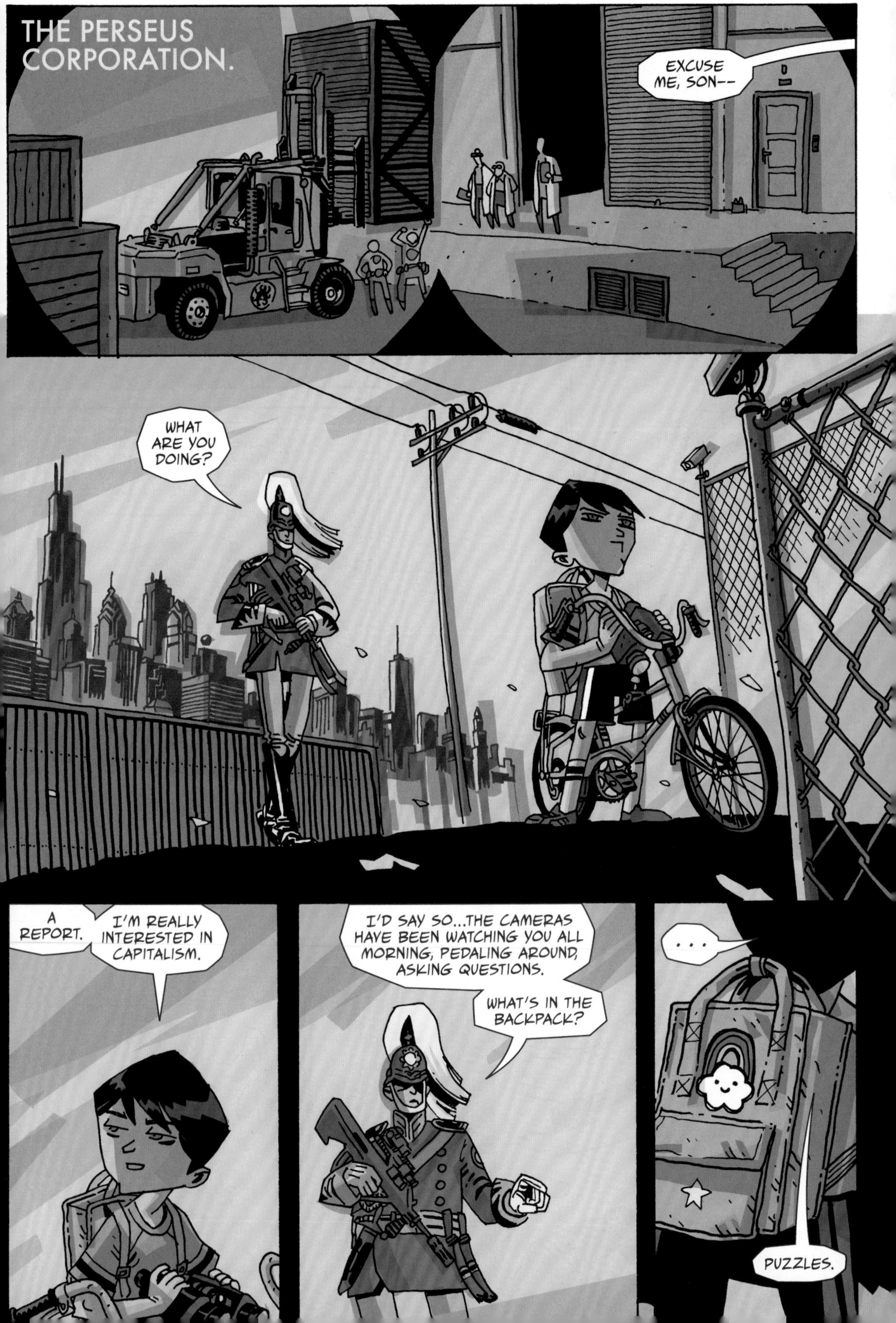
THE PERSEUS CORPORATION.
EXCUSE ME, SON--
WHAT ARE YOU DOING?
A REPORT.
I'M REALLY INTERESTED IN CAPITALISM.
I'D SAY SO...THE CAMERAS HAVE BEEN WATCHING YOU ALL MORNING, PEDALING AROUND, ASKING QUESTIONS.
WHAT'S IN THE BACKPACK?
...
PUZZLES.

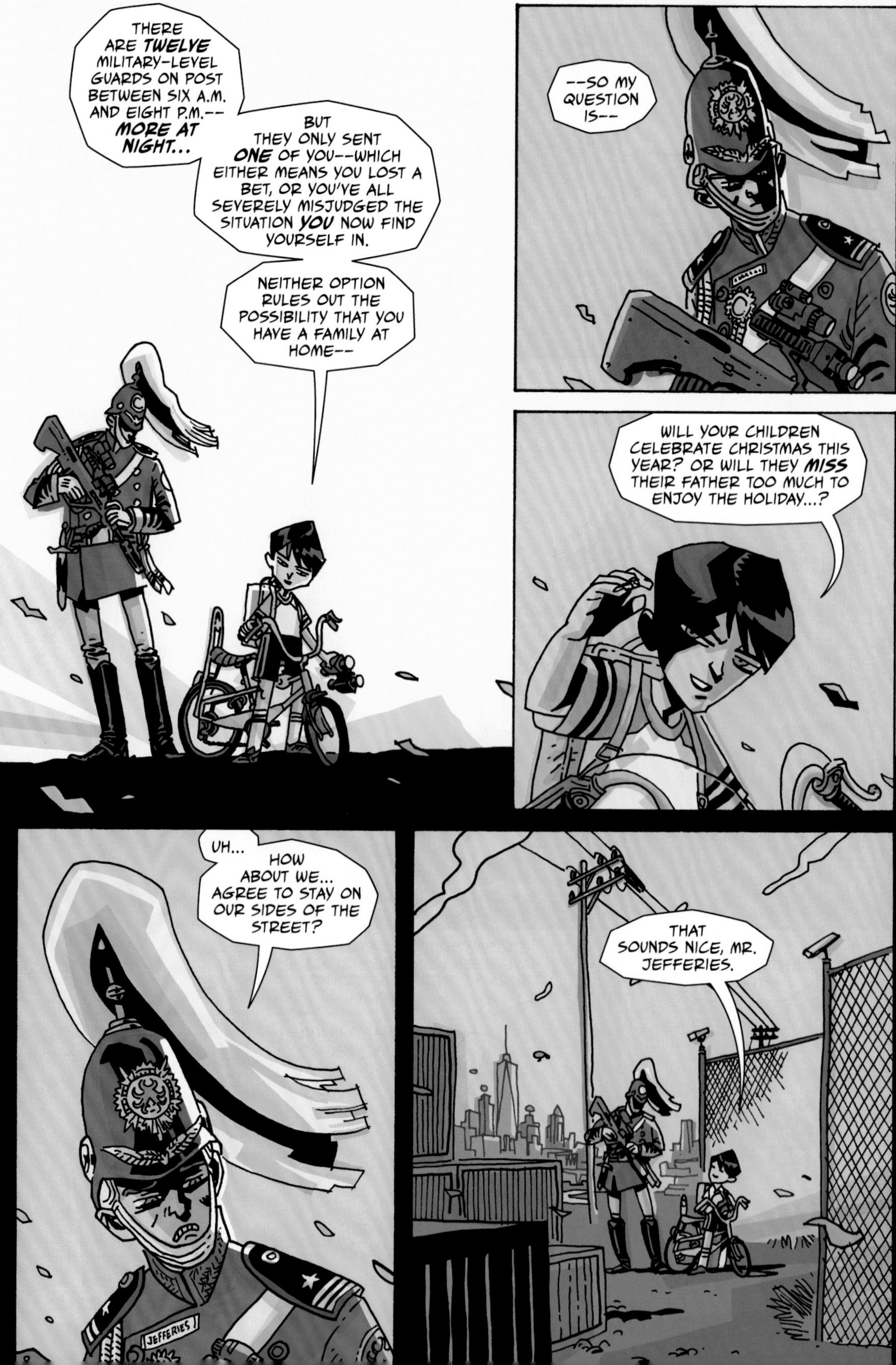
THERE ARE TWELVE MILITARY-LEVEL GUARDS ON POST BETWEEN SIX A.M. AND EIGHT P.M.-- MORE AT NIGHT...
BUT THEY ONLY SENT ONE OF YOU--WHICH EITHER MEANS YOU LOST A BET, OR YOU'VE ALL SEVERELY MISJUDGED THE SITUATION YOU NOW FIND YOURSELF IN.
NEITHER OPTION RULES OUT THE POSSIBILITY THAT YOU HAVE A FAMILY AT HOME--
--SO MY QUESTION IS--
WILL YOUR CHILDREN CELEBRATE CHRISTMAS THIS YEAR? OR WILL THEY MISS THEIR FATHER TOO MUCH TO ENJOY THE HOLIDAY...?
UH... HOW ABOUT WE... AGREE TO STAY ON OUR SIDES OF THE STREET?
JEFFERIES
THAT SOUNDS NICE, MR. JEFFERIES.

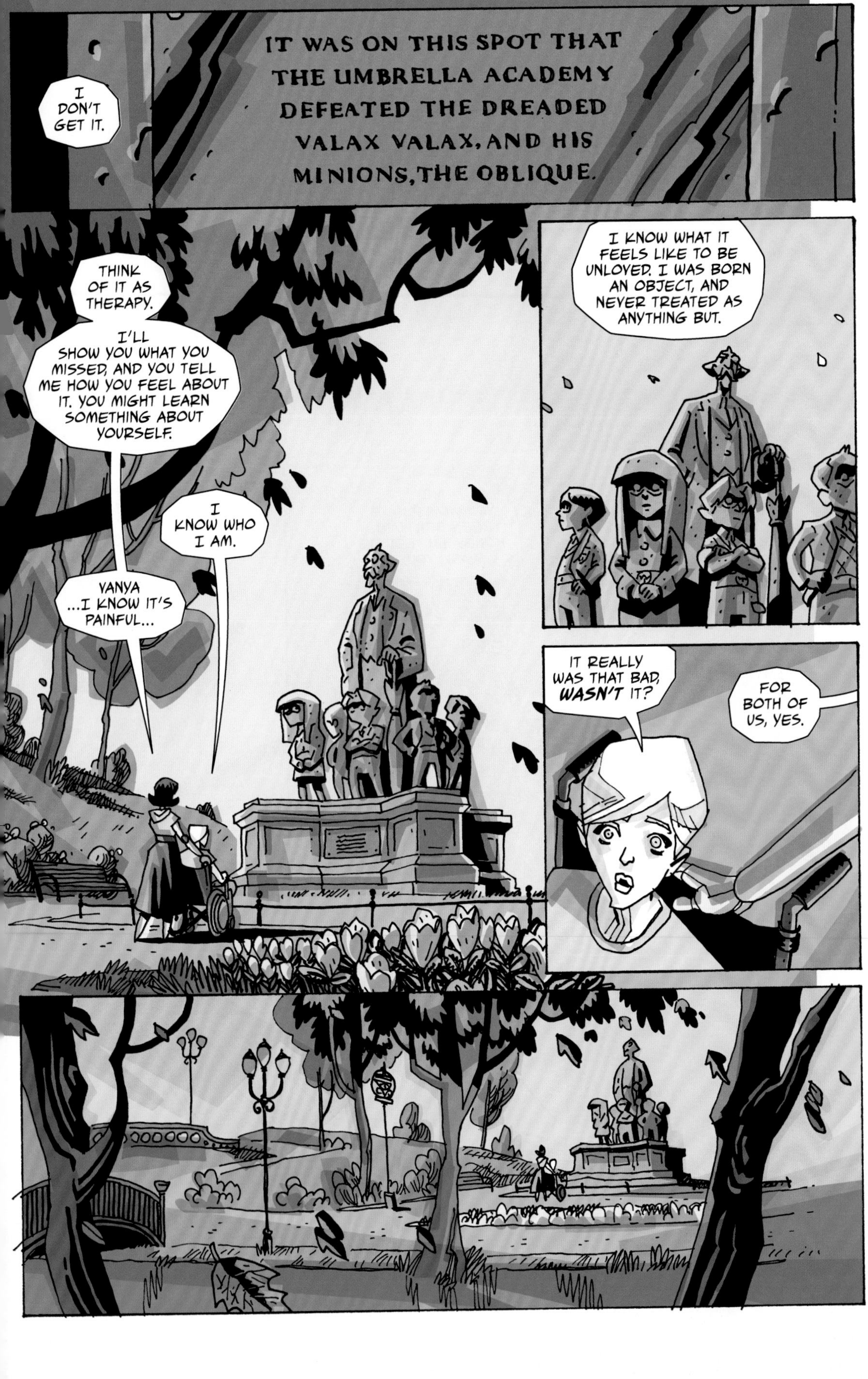
IT WAS ON THIS SPOT THAT THE UMBRELLA ACADEMY DEFEATED THE DREADED VALAX VALAX, AND HIS MINIONS, THE OBLIQUE.
I DON'T GET IT.
THINK OF IT AS THERAPY.
I'LL SHOW YOU WHAT YOU MISSED, AND YOU TELL ME HOW YOU FEEL ABOUT IT. YOU MIGHT LEARN SOMETHING ABOUT YOURSELF.
I KNOW WHO I AM.
VANYA ...I KNOW IT'S PAINFUL...
I KNOW WHAT IT FEELS LIKE TO BE UNLOVED. I WAS BORN AN OBJECT, AND NEVER TREATED AS ANYTHING BUT.
IT REALLY WAS THAT BAD, WASN'T IT?
FOR BOTH OF US, YES.

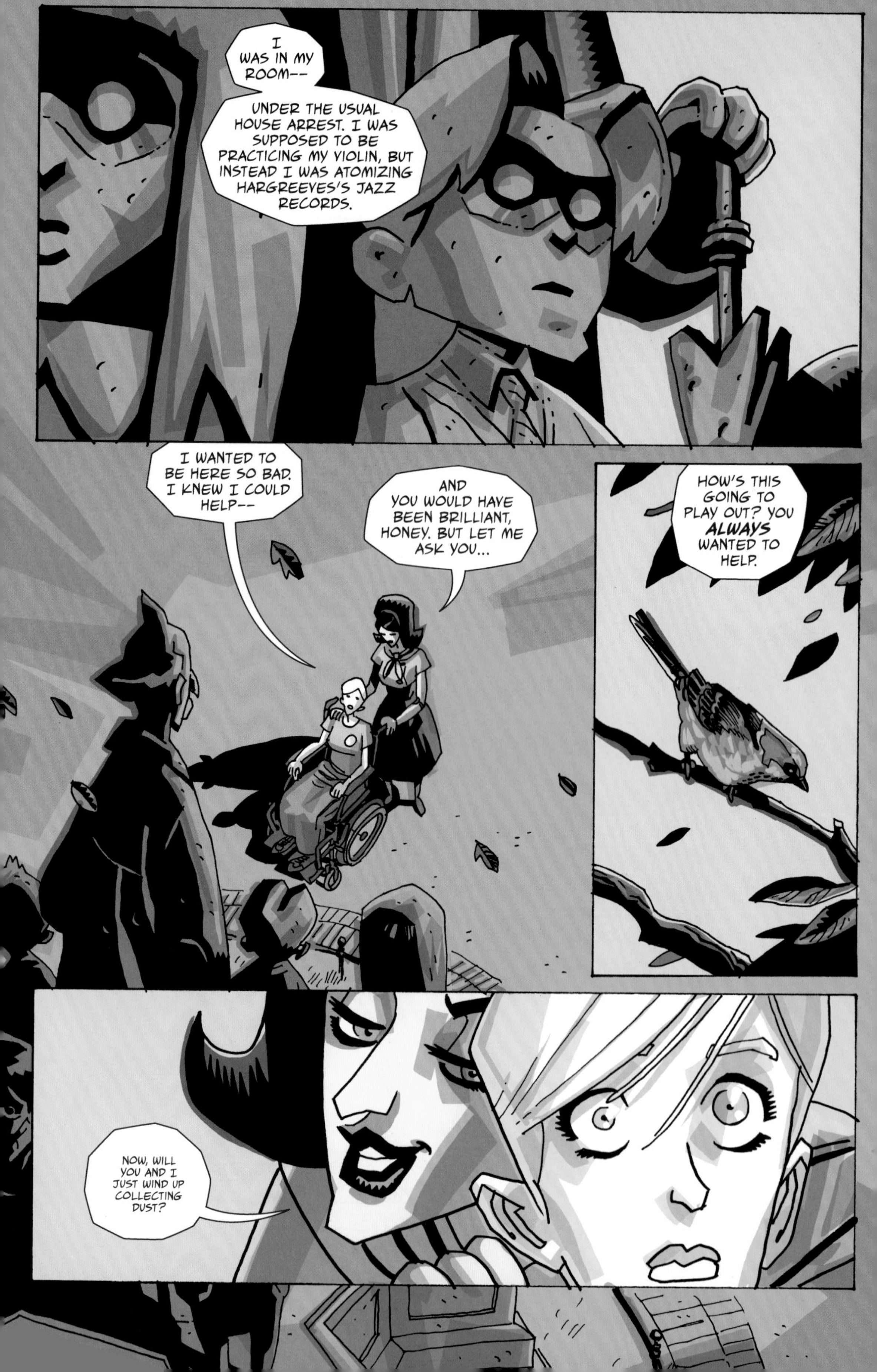
I WAS IN MY ROOM--
UNDER THE USUAL HOUSE ARREST. I WAS SUPPOSED TO BE PRACTICING MY VIOLIN, BUT INSTEAD I WAS ATOMIZING HARGREEVES'S JAZZ RECORDS.
I WANTED TO BE HERE SO BAD. I KNEW I COULD HELP--
AND YOU WOULD HAVE BEEN BRILLIANT, HONEY. BUT LET ME ASK YOU...
HOW'S THIS GOING TO PLAY OUT? YOU **ALWAYS** WANTED TO HELP.
NOW, WILL YOU AND I JUST WIND UP COLLECTING DUST?

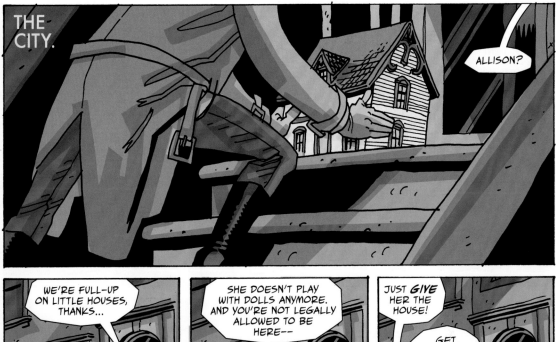

ALLISON?

WE'RE FULL-UP ON LITTLE HOUSES, THANKS...

CLAIRE'S BIRTHDAY IS COMING, SO--

SHE DOESN'T PLAY WITH DOLLS ANYMORE. AND YOU'RE NOT LEGALLY ALLOWED TO BE HERE--

CAN'T YOU JUST GIVE HER THE HOUSE?

NO. YOU NEED TO GO.

JUST *GIVE* HER THE HOUSE!

GET OUT OF OUR LIVES!

YOU CAN'T MAKE ME DISAPPEAR. *WE* HAPPENED-- *WE USED TO LOVE EACH OTHER!*

YOU MADE THAT PART *UP*, REMEMBER?!

I DON'T THINK I DID!

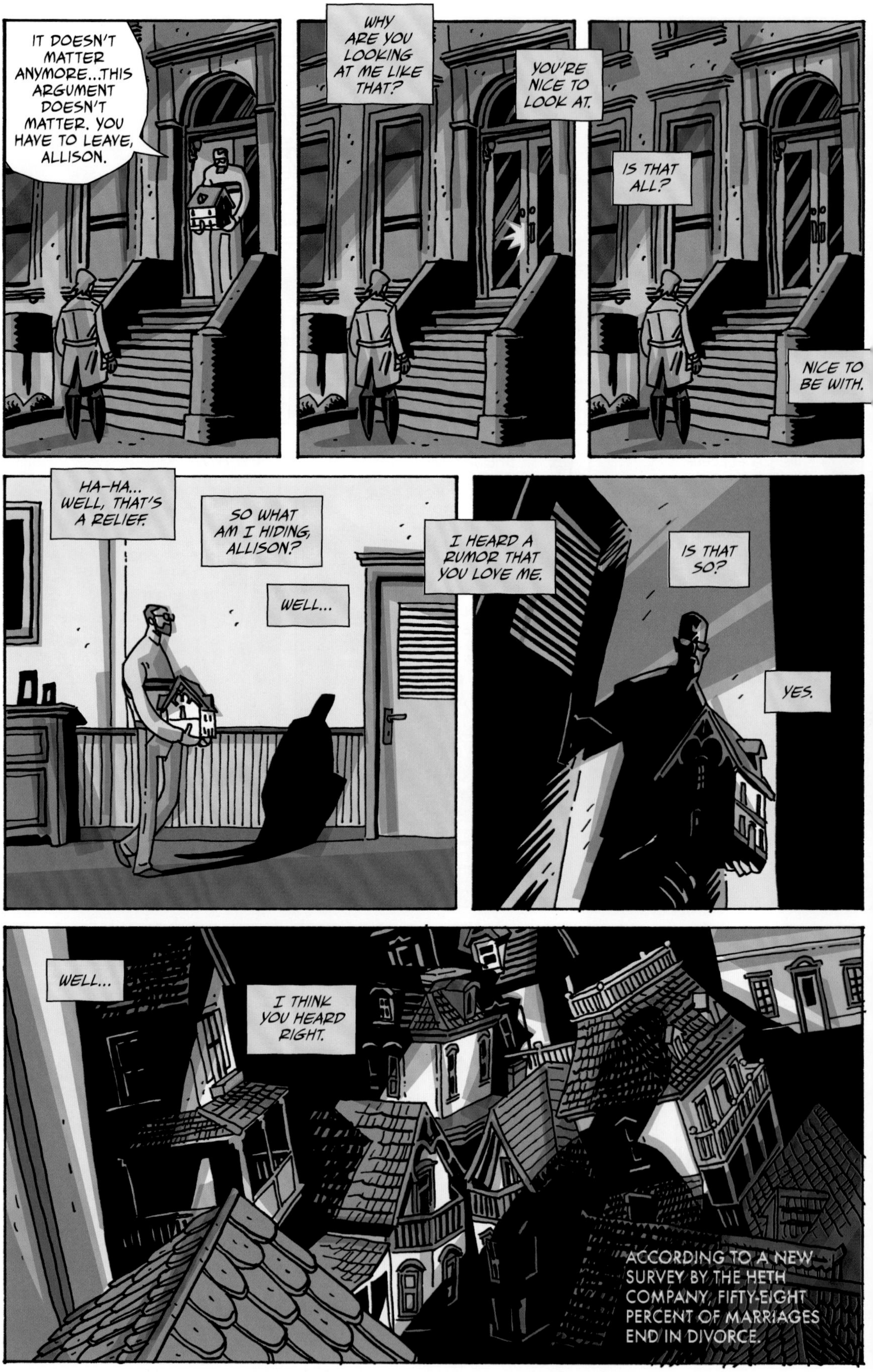
IT DOESN'T MATTER ANYMORE...THIS ARGUMENT DOESN'T MATTER. YOU HAVE TO LEAVE, ALLISON.
WHY ARE YOU LOOKING AT ME LIKE THAT?
YOU'RE NICE TO LOOK AT.
IS THAT ALL?
NICE TO BE WITH.
HA-HA... WELL, THAT'S A RELIEF.
SO WHAT AM I HIDING, ALLISON?
WELL...
I HEARD A RUMOR THAT YOU LOVE ME.
IS THAT SO?
YES.
WELL...
I THINK YOU HEARD RIGHT.
ACCORDING TO A NEW SURVEY BY THE HETH COMPANY, FIFTY-EIGHT PERCENT OF MARRIAGES END IN DIVORCE.

CHAPTER THREE

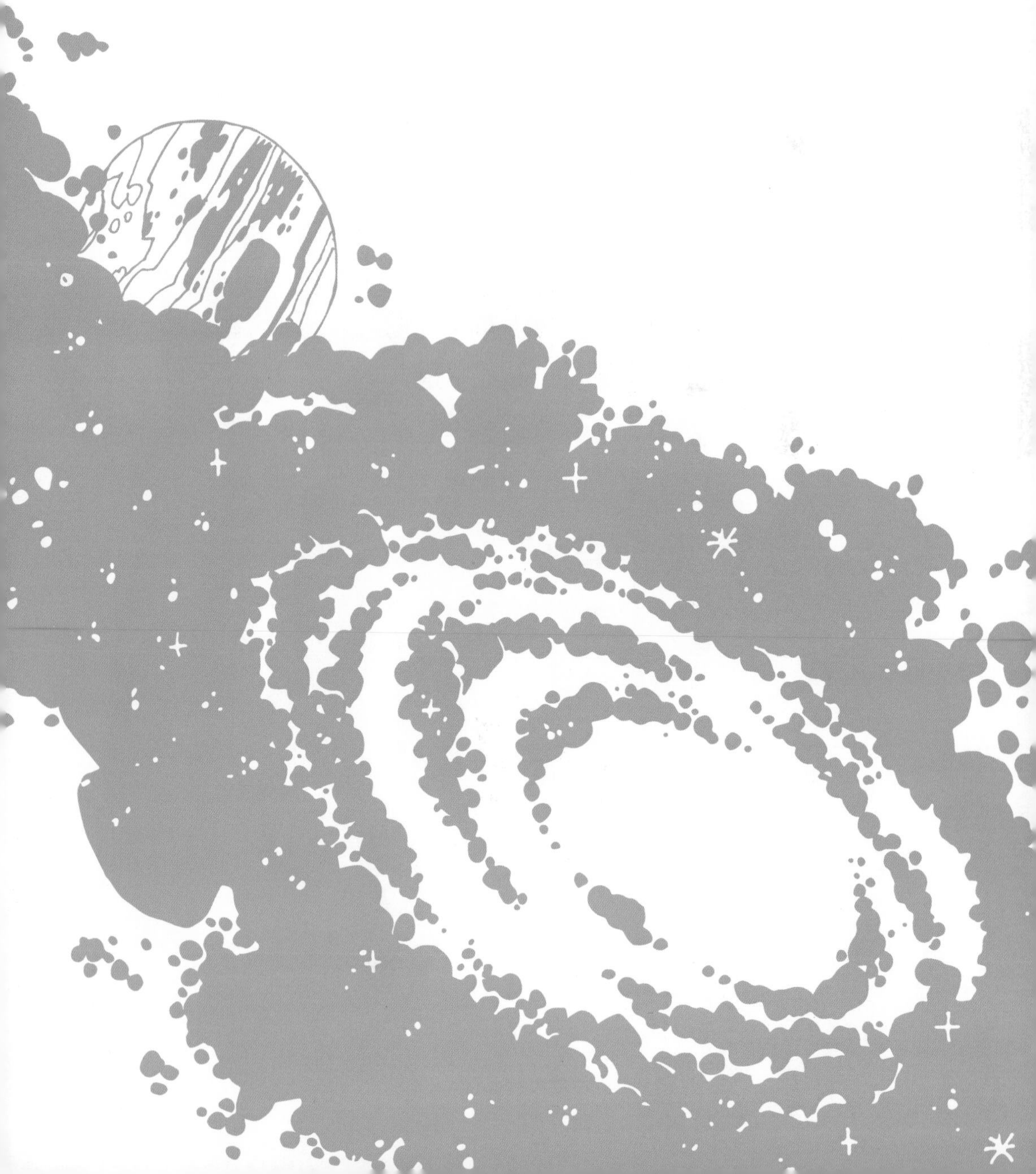

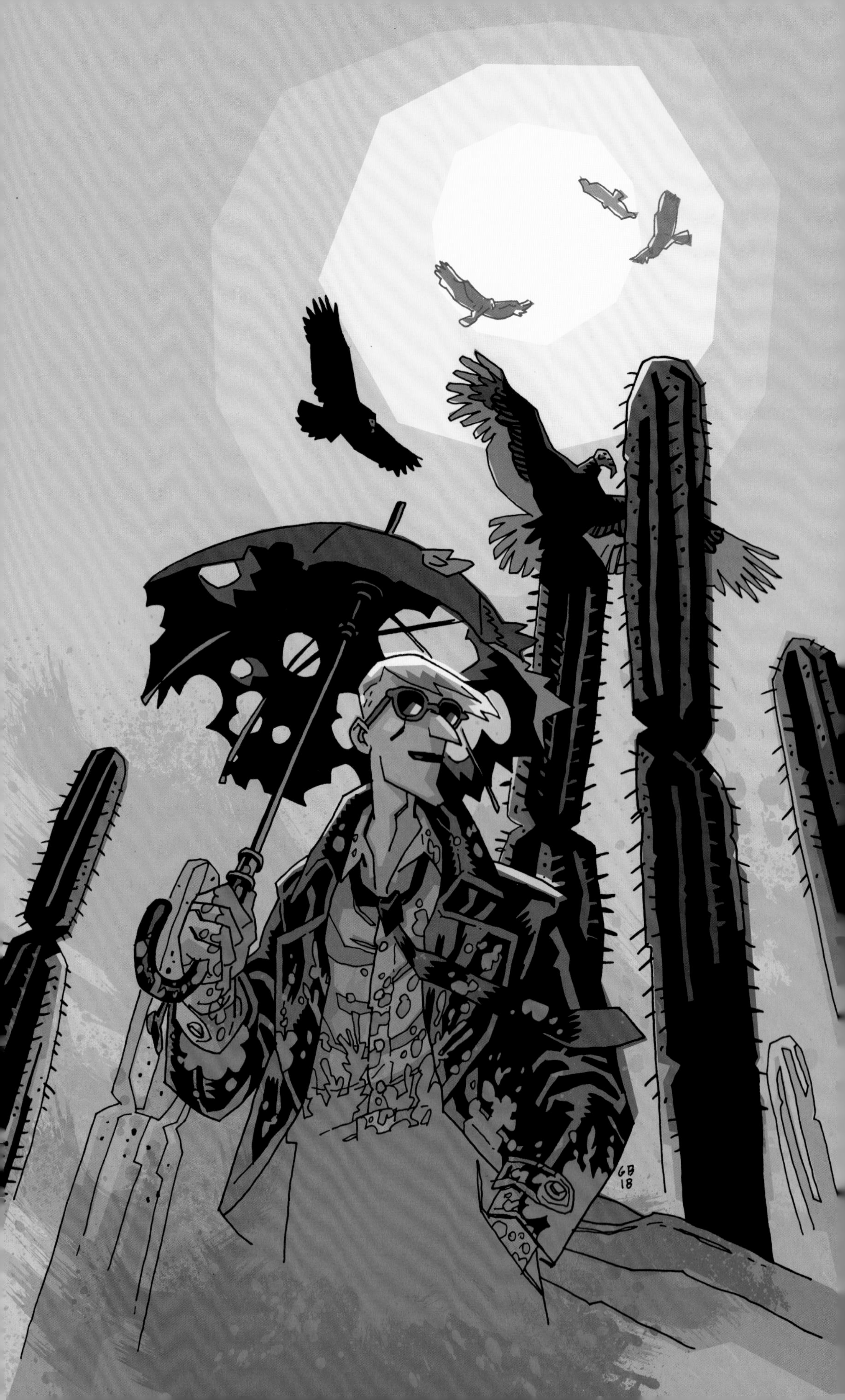
GB
18

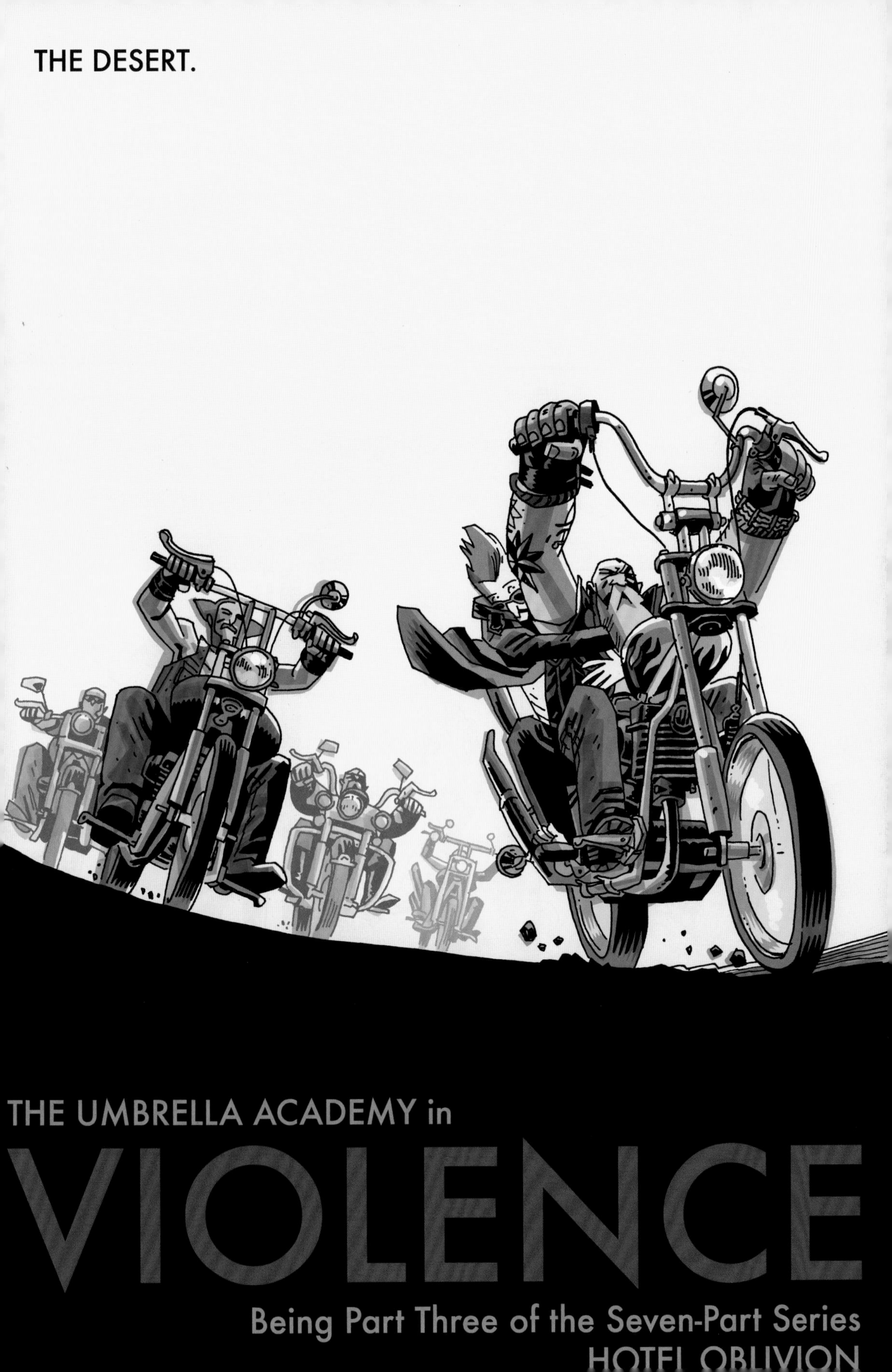
THE DESERT.
THE UMBRELLA ACADEMY in
VIOLENCE
Being Part Three of the Seven-Part Series
HOTEL OBLIVION

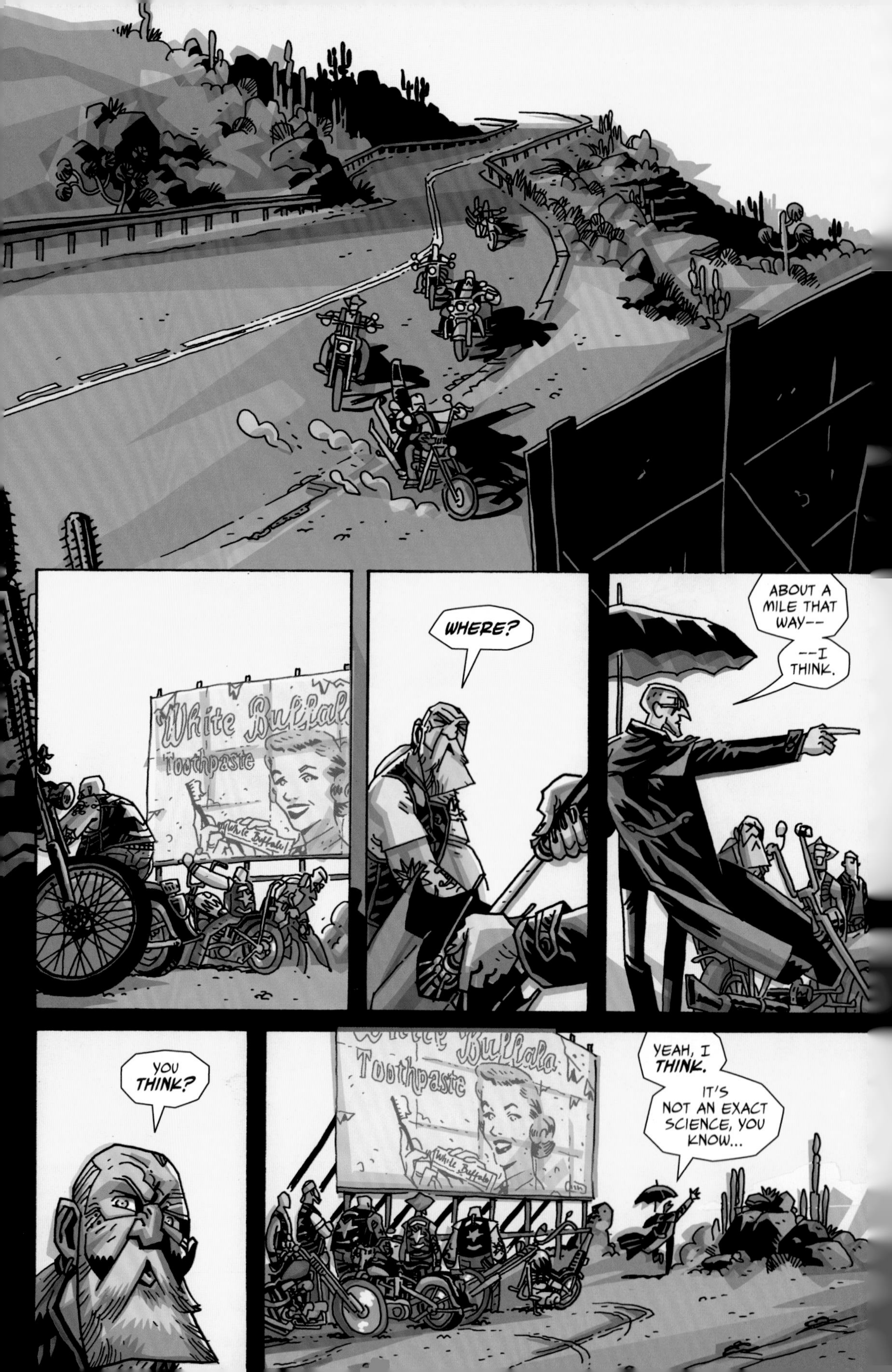
White Buffalo Toothpaste
WHERE?
ABOUT A MILE THAT WAY--
--I THINK.
YOU THINK?
White Buffalo Toothpaste
YEAH, I THINK.
IT'S NOT AN EXACT SCIENCE, YOU KNOW...

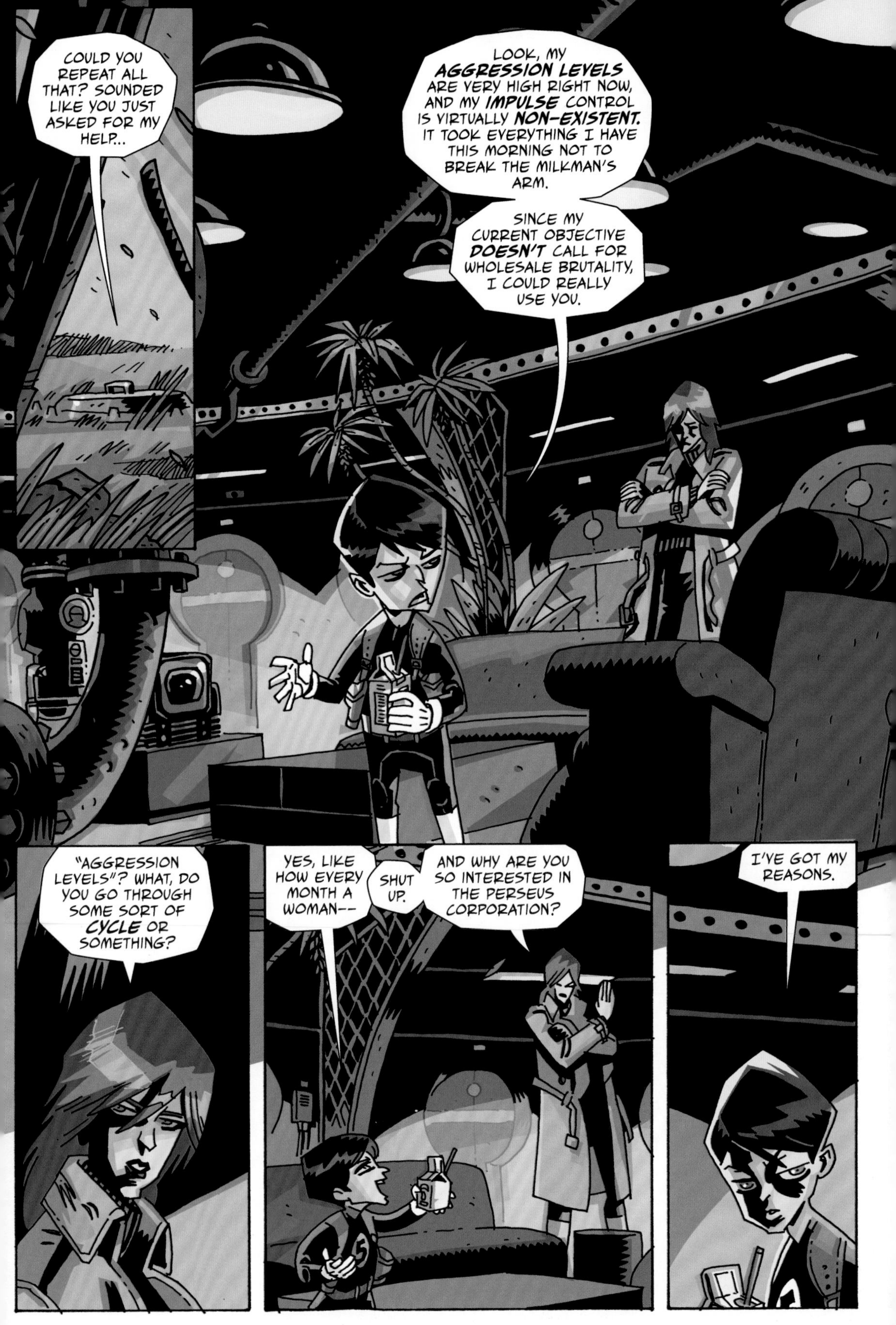
COULD YOU REPEAT ALL THAT? SOUNDED LIKE YOU JUST ASKED FOR MY HELP...
LOOK, MY AGGRESSION LEVELS ARE VERY HIGH RIGHT NOW, AND MY IMPULSE CONTROL IS VIRTUALLY NON-EXISTENT. IT TOOK EVERYTHING I HAVE THIS MORNING NOT TO BREAK THE MILKMAN'S ARM.
SINCE MY CURRENT OBJECTIVE DOESN'T CALL FOR WHOLESALE BRUTALITY, I COULD REALLY USE YOU.
"AGGRESSION LEVELS"? WHAT, DO YOU GO THROUGH SOME SORT OF CYCLE OR SOMETHING?
YES, LIKE HOW EVERY MONTH A WOMAN--
SHUT UP.
AND WHY ARE YOU SO INTERESTED IN THE PERSEUS CORPORATION?
I'VE GOT MY REASONS.

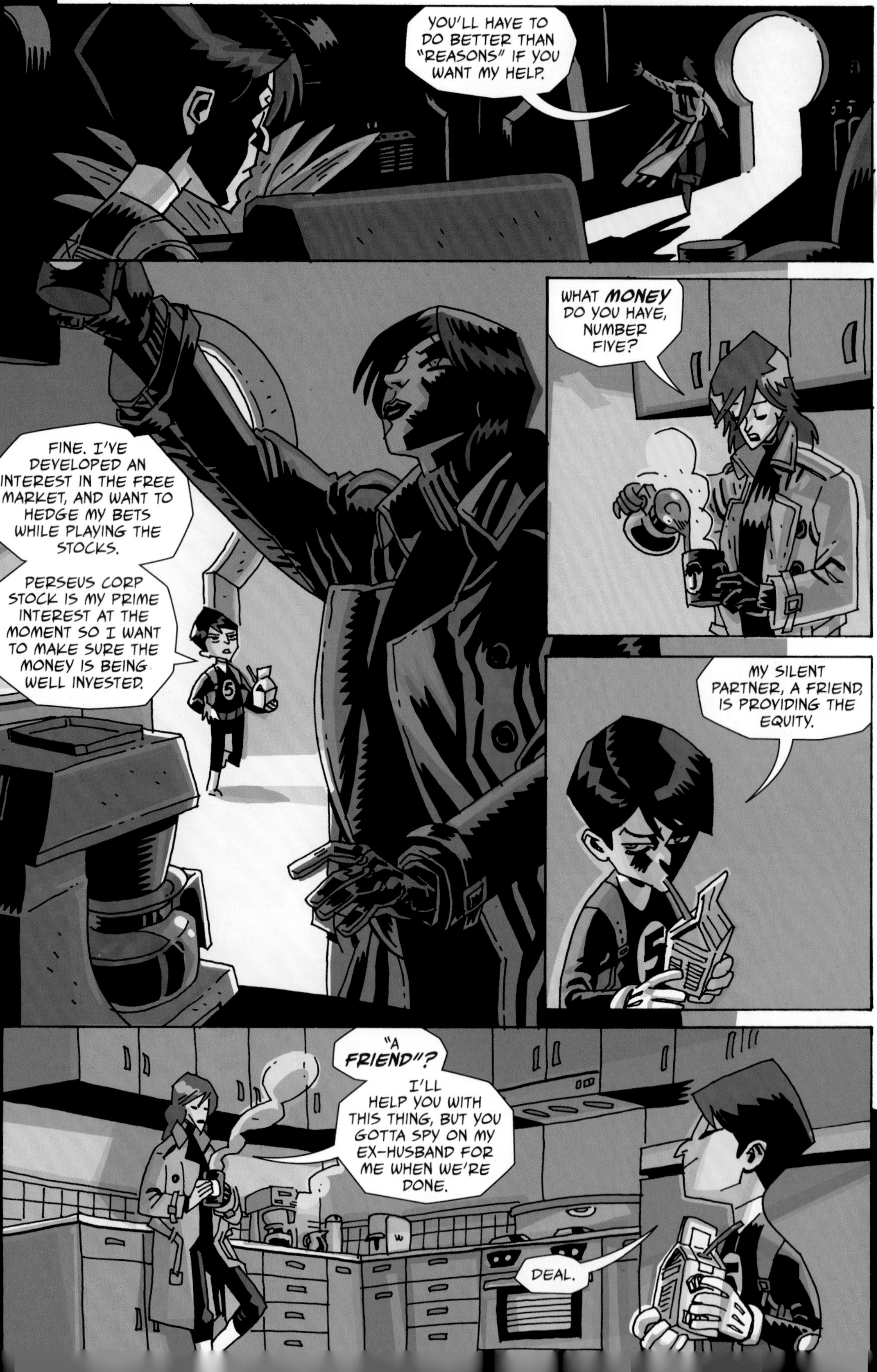
YOU'LL HAVE TO DO BETTER THAN "REASONS" IF YOU WANT MY HELP.
WHAT MONEY DO YOU HAVE, NUMBER FIVE?
FINE. I'VE DEVELOPED AN INTEREST IN THE FREE MARKET, AND WANT TO HEDGE MY BETS WHILE PLAYING THE STOCKS.
PERSEUS CORP STOCK IS MY PRIME INTEREST AT THE MOMENT SO I WANT TO MAKE SURE THE MONEY IS BEING WELL INVESTED.
MY SILENT PARTNER, A FRIEND, IS PROVIDING THE EQUITY.
"A FRIEND"?
I'LL HELP YOU WITH THIS THING, BUT YOU GOTTA SPY ON MY EX-HUSBAND FOR ME WHEN WE'RE DONE.
DEAL.

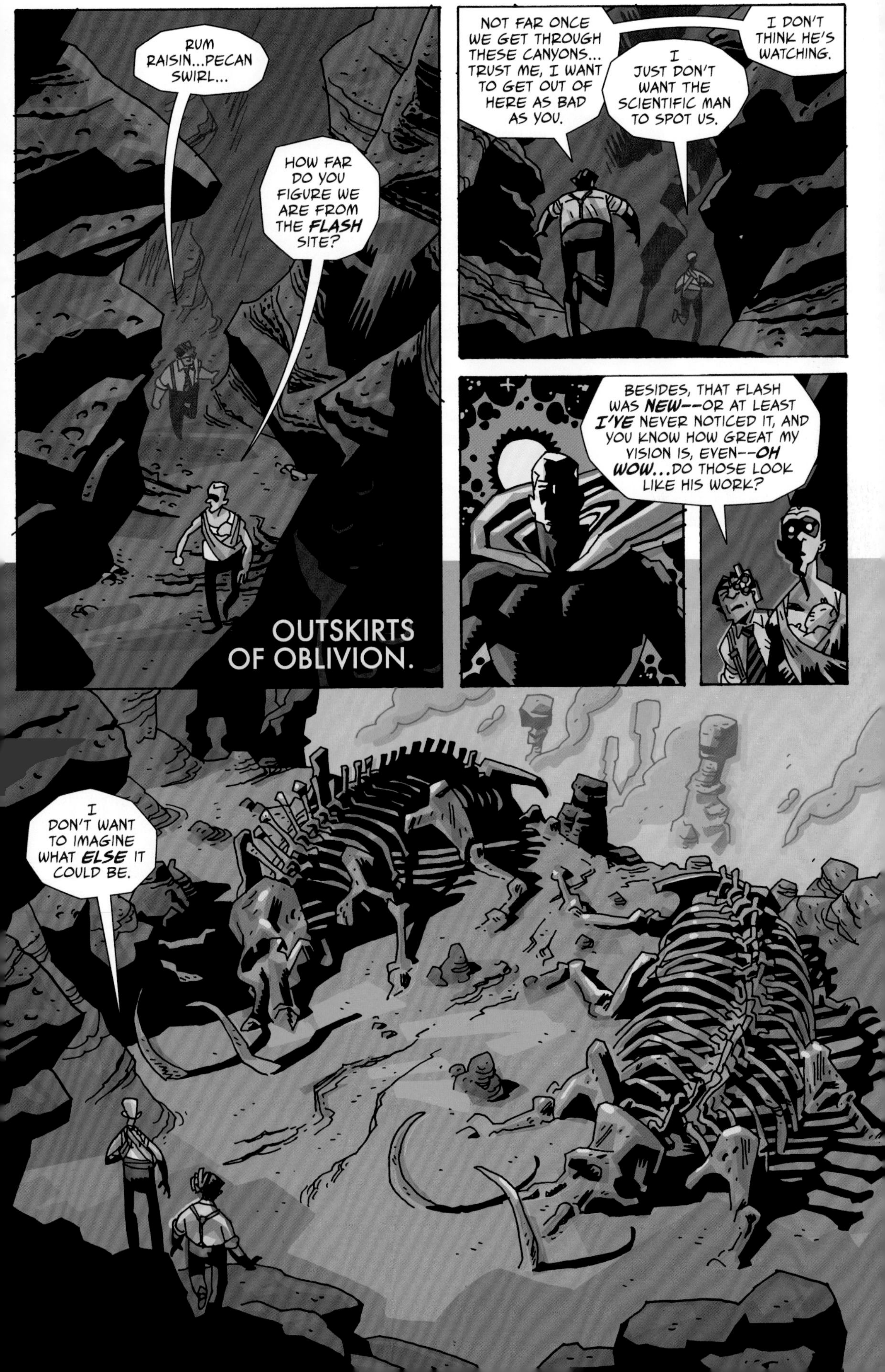
RUM RAISIN...PECAN SWIRL...
HOW FAR DO YOU FIGURE WE ARE FROM THE FLASH SITE?
OUTSKIRTS OF OBLIVION.
NOT FAR ONCE WE GET THROUGH THESE CANYONS... TRUST ME, I WANT TO GET OUT OF HERE AS BAD AS YOU.
I DON'T THINK HE'S WATCHING.
I JUST DON'T WANT THE SCIENTIFIC MAN TO SPOT US.
BESIDES, THAT FLASH WAS NEW--OR AT LEAST I'VE NEVER NOTICED IT, AND YOU KNOW HOW GREAT MY VISION IS, EVEN--OH WOW...DO THOSE LOOK LIKE HIS WORK?
I DON'T WANT TO IMAGINE WHAT ELSE IT COULD BE.

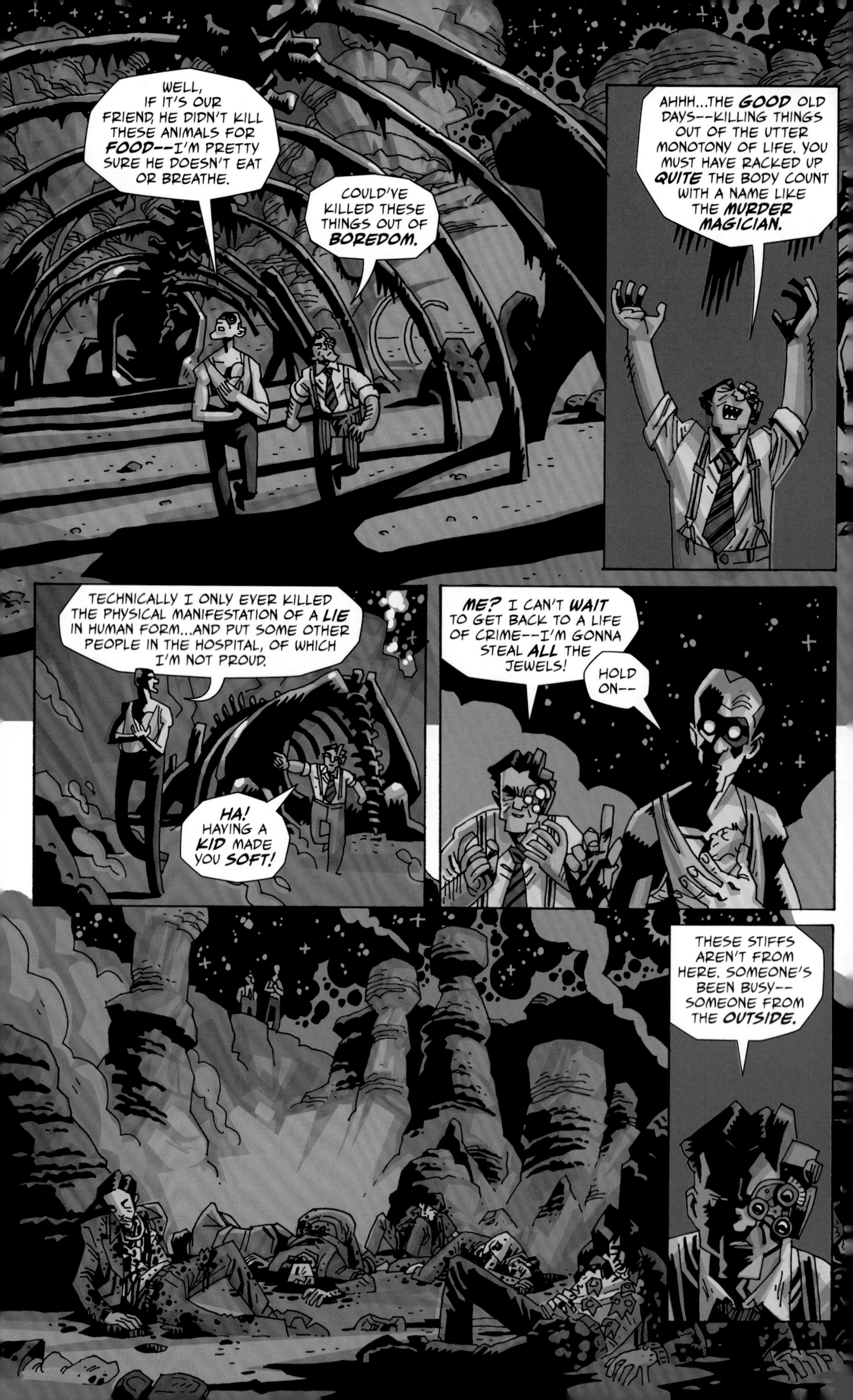
WELL, IF IT'S OUR FRIEND, HE DIDN'T KILL THESE ANIMALS FOR FOOD--I'M PRETTY SURE HE DOESN'T EAT OR BREATHE.
COULD'VE KILLED THESE THINGS OUT OF BOREDOM.
AHHH...THE GOOD OLD DAYS--KILLING THINGS OUT OF THE UTTER MONOTONY OF LIFE. YOU MUST HAVE RACKED UP QUITE THE BODY COUNT WITH A NAME LIKE THE MURDER MAGICIAN.
TECHNICALLY I ONLY EVER KILLED THE PHYSICAL MANIFESTATION OF A LIE IN HUMAN FORM...AND PUT SOME OTHER PEOPLE IN THE HOSPITAL, OF WHICH I'M NOT PROUD.
HA! HAVING A KID MADE YOU SOFT!
ME? I CAN'T WAIT TO GET BACK TO A LIFE OF CRIME--I'M GONNA STEAL ALL THE JEWELS!
HOLD ON--
THESE STIFFS AREN'T FROM HERE. SOMEONE'S BEEN BUSY--SOMEONE FROM THE OUTSIDE.

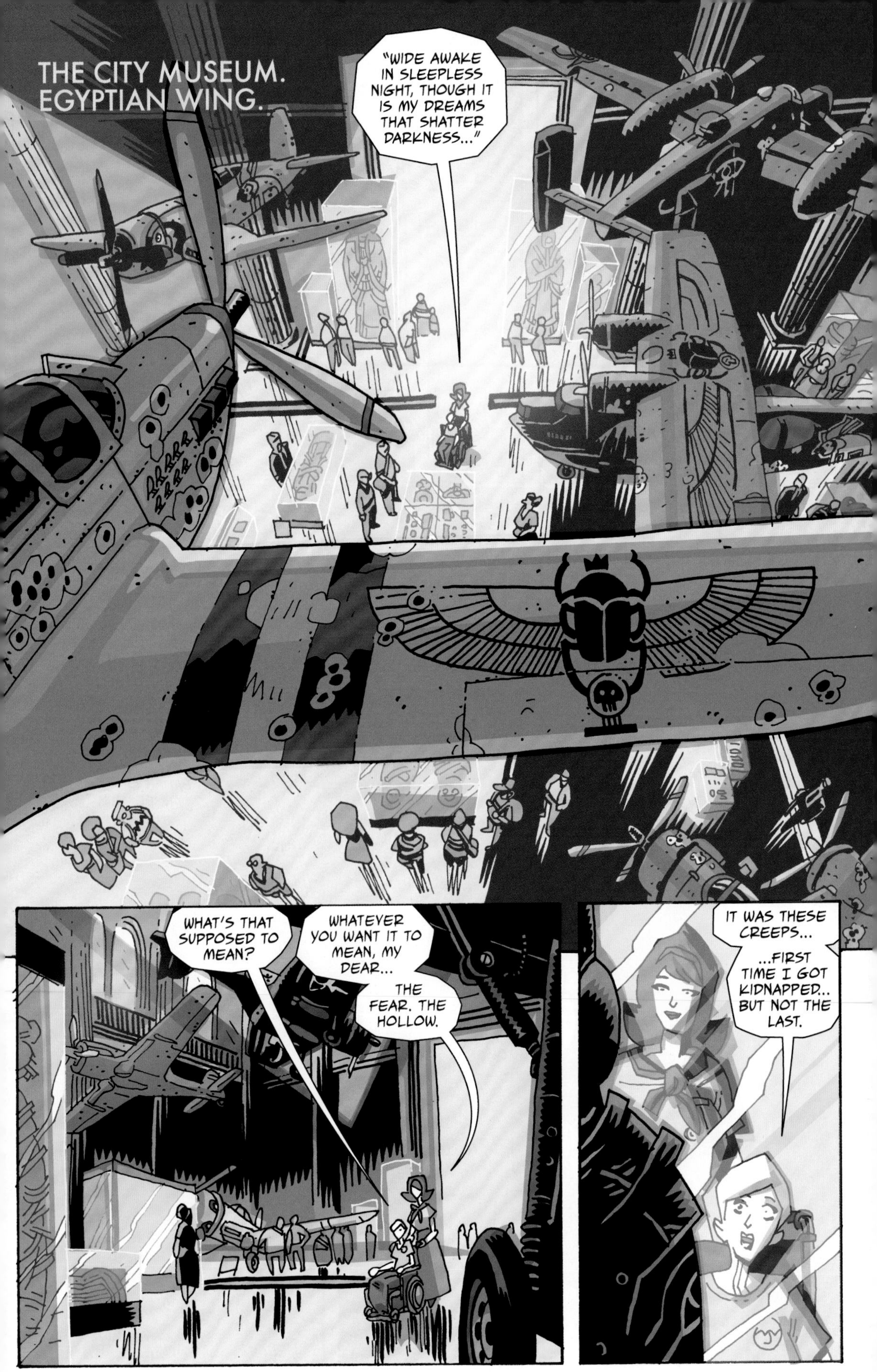
THE CITY MUSEUM. EGYPTIAN WING.
"WIDE AWAKE IN SLEEPLESS NIGHT, THOUGH IT IS MY DREAMS THAT SHATTER DARKNESS..."
WHAT'S THAT SUPPOSED TO MEAN?
WHATEVER YOU WANT IT TO MEAN, MY DEAR...
THE FEAR. THE HOLLOW.
IT WAS THESE CREEPS...
...FIRST TIME I GOT KIDNAPPED... BUT NOT THE LAST.

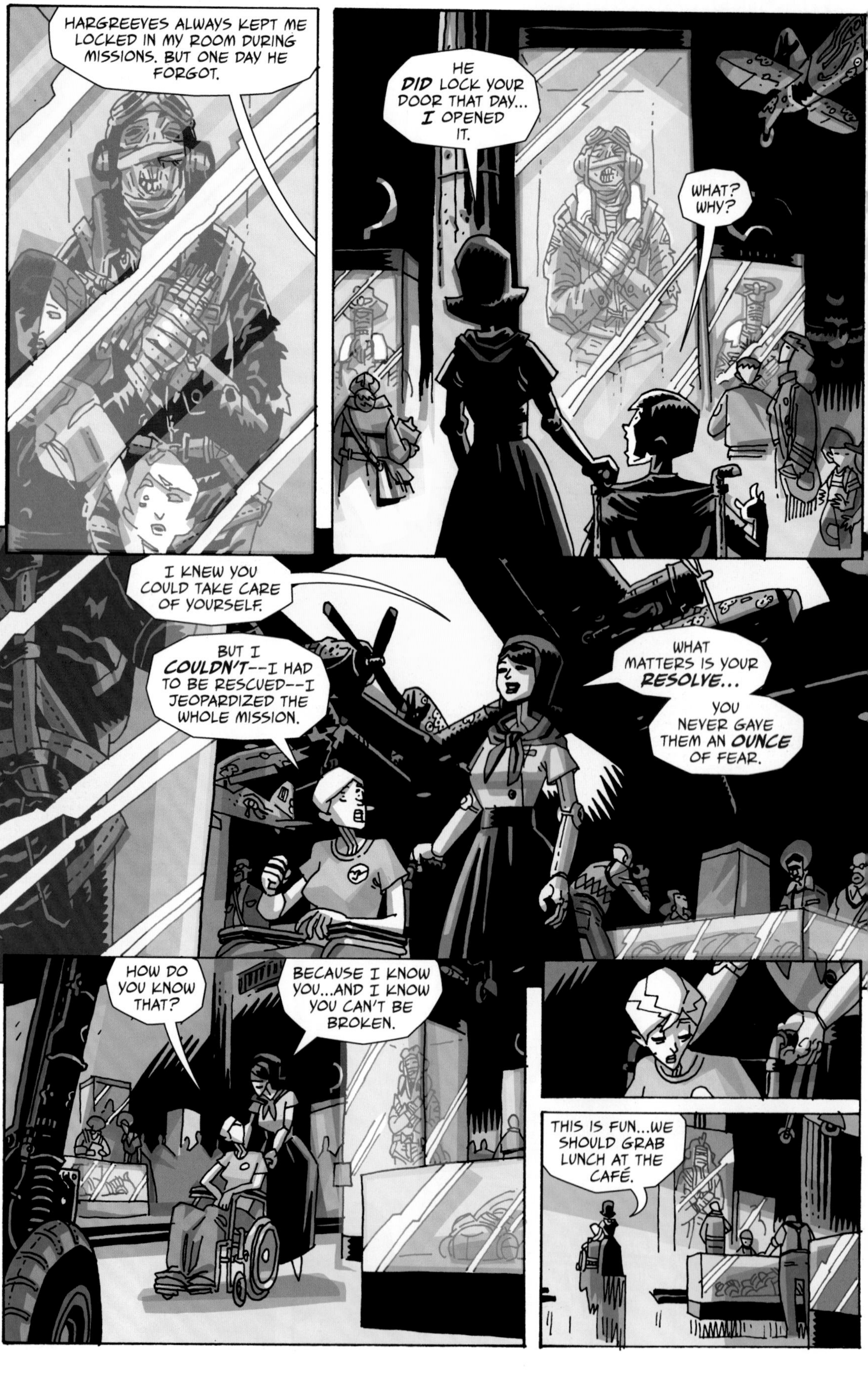
HARGREEVES ALWAYS KEPT ME LOCKED IN MY ROOM DURING MISSIONS. BUT ONE DAY HE FORGOT.
HE *DID* LOCK YOUR DOOR THAT DAY... *I* OPENED IT.
WHAT? WHY?
I KNEW YOU COULD TAKE CARE OF YOURSELF.
BUT I *COULDN'T*--I HAD TO BE RESCUED--I JEOPARDIZED THE WHOLE MISSION.
WHAT MATTERS IS YOUR *RESOLVE...*
YOU NEVER GAVE THEM AN *OUNCE* OF FEAR.
HOW DO YOU KNOW THAT?
BECAUSE I KNOW YOU...AND I KNOW YOU CAN'T BE BROKEN.
THIS IS FUN...WE SHOULD GRAB LUNCH AT THE CAFÉ.

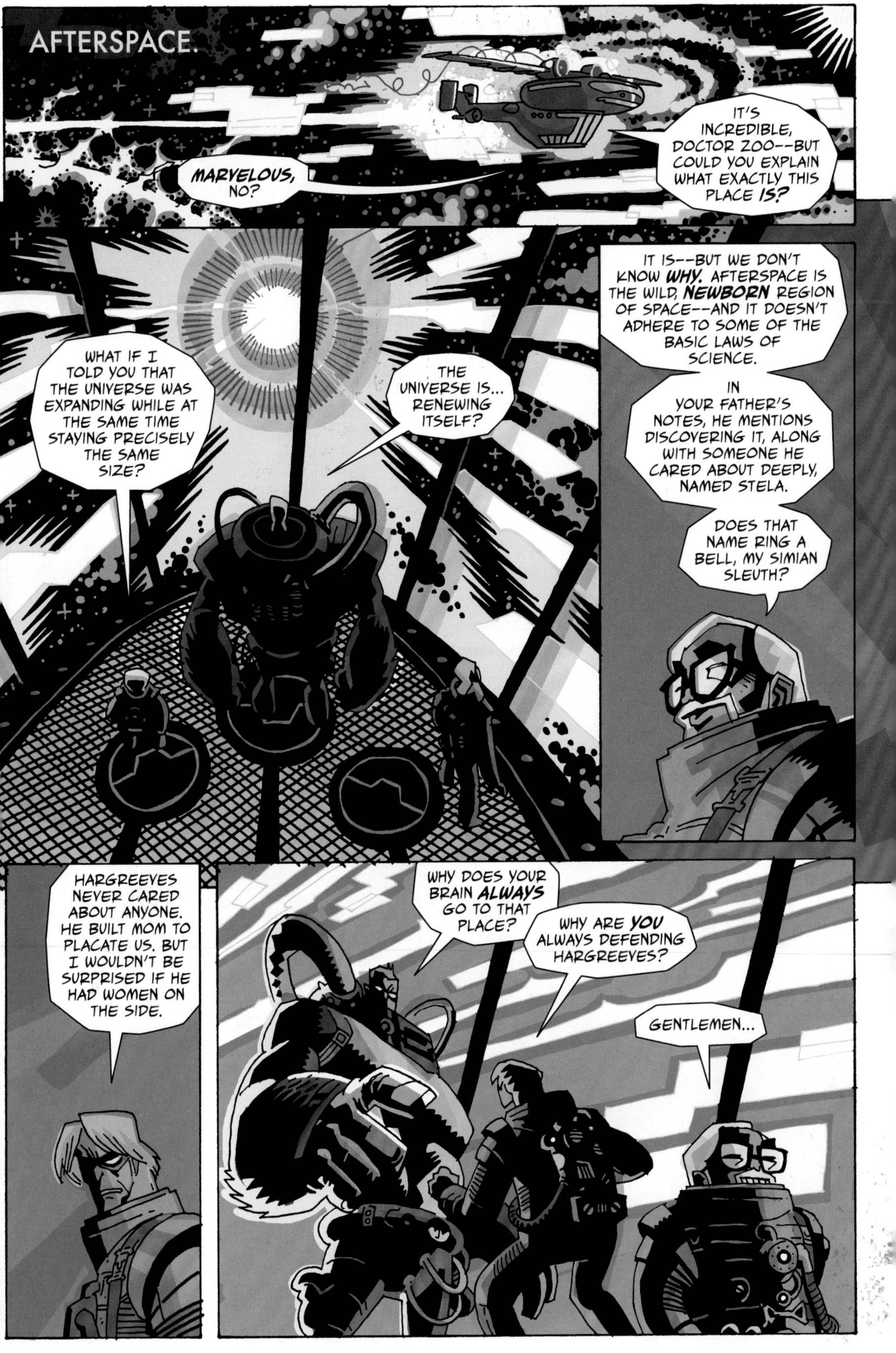
AFTERSPACE.
MARVELOUS, NO?
IT'S INCREDIBLE, DOCTOR ZOO--BUT COULD YOU EXPLAIN WHAT EXACTLY THIS PLACE IS?
WHAT IF I TOLD YOU THAT THE UNIVERSE WAS EXPANDING WHILE AT THE SAME TIME STAYING PRECISELY THE SAME SIZE?
THE UNIVERSE IS... RENEWING ITSELF?
IT IS--BUT WE DON'T KNOW WHY. AFTERSPACE IS THE WILD, NEWBORN REGION OF SPACE--AND IT DOESN'T ADHERE TO SOME OF THE BASIC LAWS OF SCIENCE.
IN YOUR FATHER'S NOTES, HE MENTIONS DISCOVERING IT, ALONG WITH SOMEONE HE CARED ABOUT DEEPLY, NAMED STELA.
DOES THAT NAME RING A BELL, MY SIMIAN SLEUTH?
HARGREEVES NEVER CARED ABOUT ANYONE. HE BUILT MOM TO PLACATE US. BUT I WOULDN'T BE SURPRISED IF HE HAD WOMEN ON THE SIDE.
WHY DOES YOUR BRAIN ALWAYS GO TO THAT PLACE?
WHY ARE YOU ALWAYS DEFENDING HARGREEVES?
GENTLEMEN...

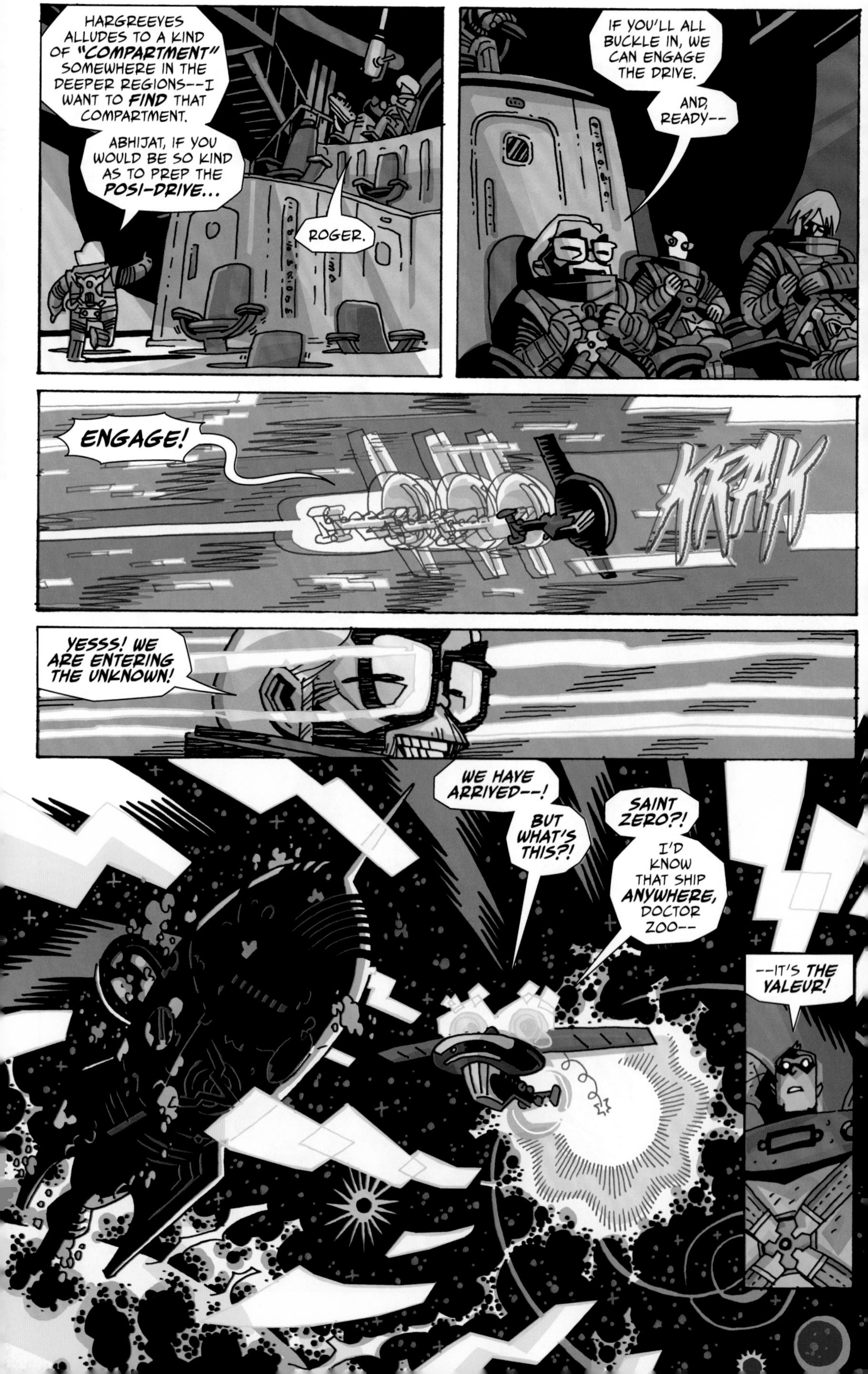
HARGREEVES ALLUDES TO A KIND OF "COMPARTMENT" SOMEWHERE IN THE DEEPER REGIONS--I WANT TO FIND THAT COMPARTMENT.
ABHIJAT, IF YOU WOULD BE SO KIND AS TO PREP THE POSI-DRIVE...
ROGER.
IF YOU'LL ALL BUCKLE IN, WE CAN ENGAGE THE DRIVE.
AND, READY--
ENGAGE!
KRAK
YESSS! WE ARE ENTERING THE UNKNOWN!
WE HAVE ARRIVED--!
BUT WHAT'S THIS?!
SAINT ZERO?!
I'D KNOW THAT SHIP ANYWHERE, DOCTOR ZOO--
--IT'S THE VALEUR!

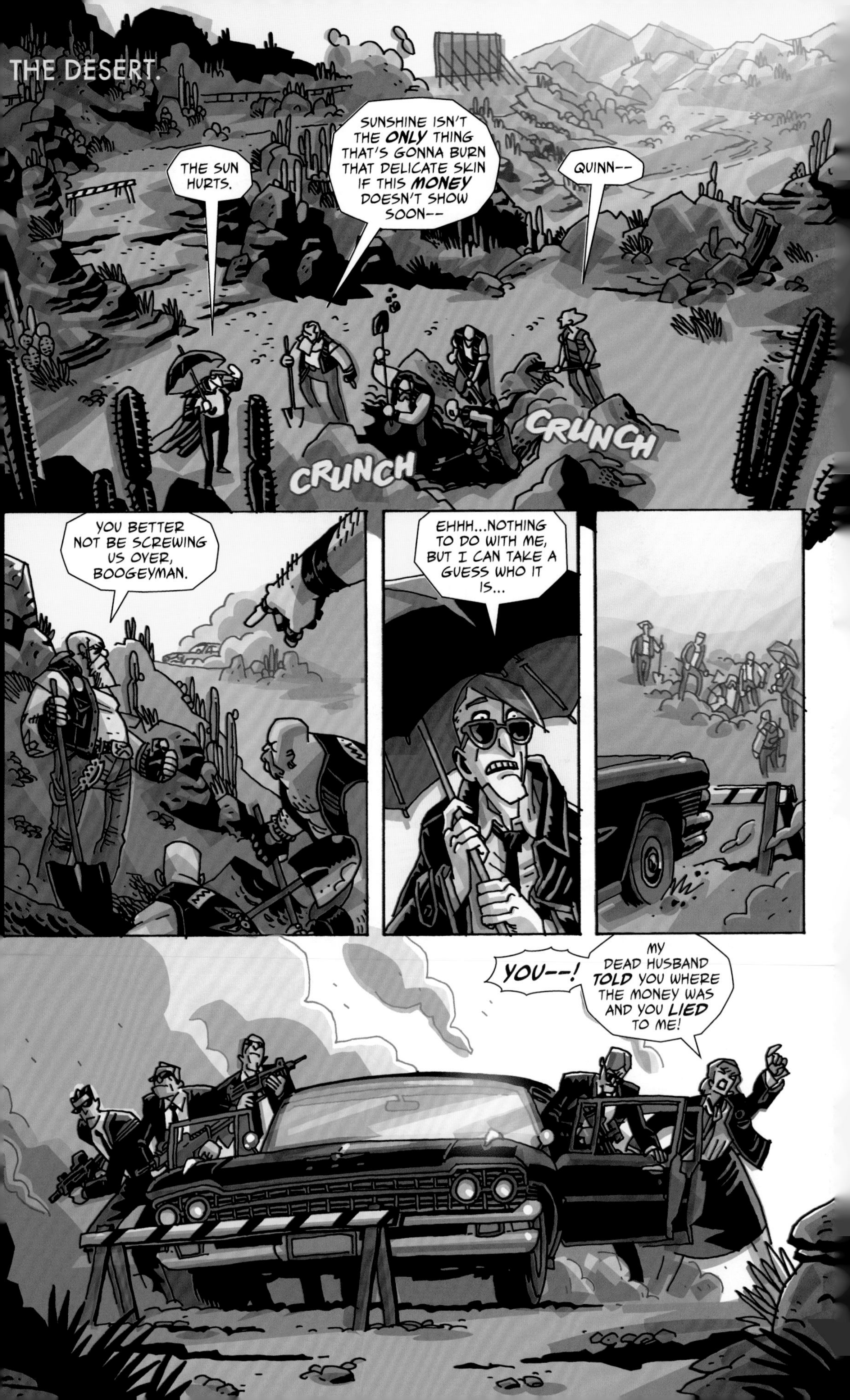
THE DESERT.
THE SUN HURTS.
SUNSHINE ISN'T THE ONLY THING THAT'S GONNA BURN THAT DELICATE SKIN IF THIS MONEY DOESN'T SHOW SOON--
QUINN--
CRUNCH
CRUNCH
YOU BETTER NOT BE SCREWING US OVER, BOOGEYMAN.
EHHH...NOTHING TO DO WITH ME, BUT I CAN TAKE A GUESS WHO IT IS...
YOU--!
MY DEAD HUSBAND TOLD YOU WHERE THE MONEY WAS AND YOU LIED TO ME!

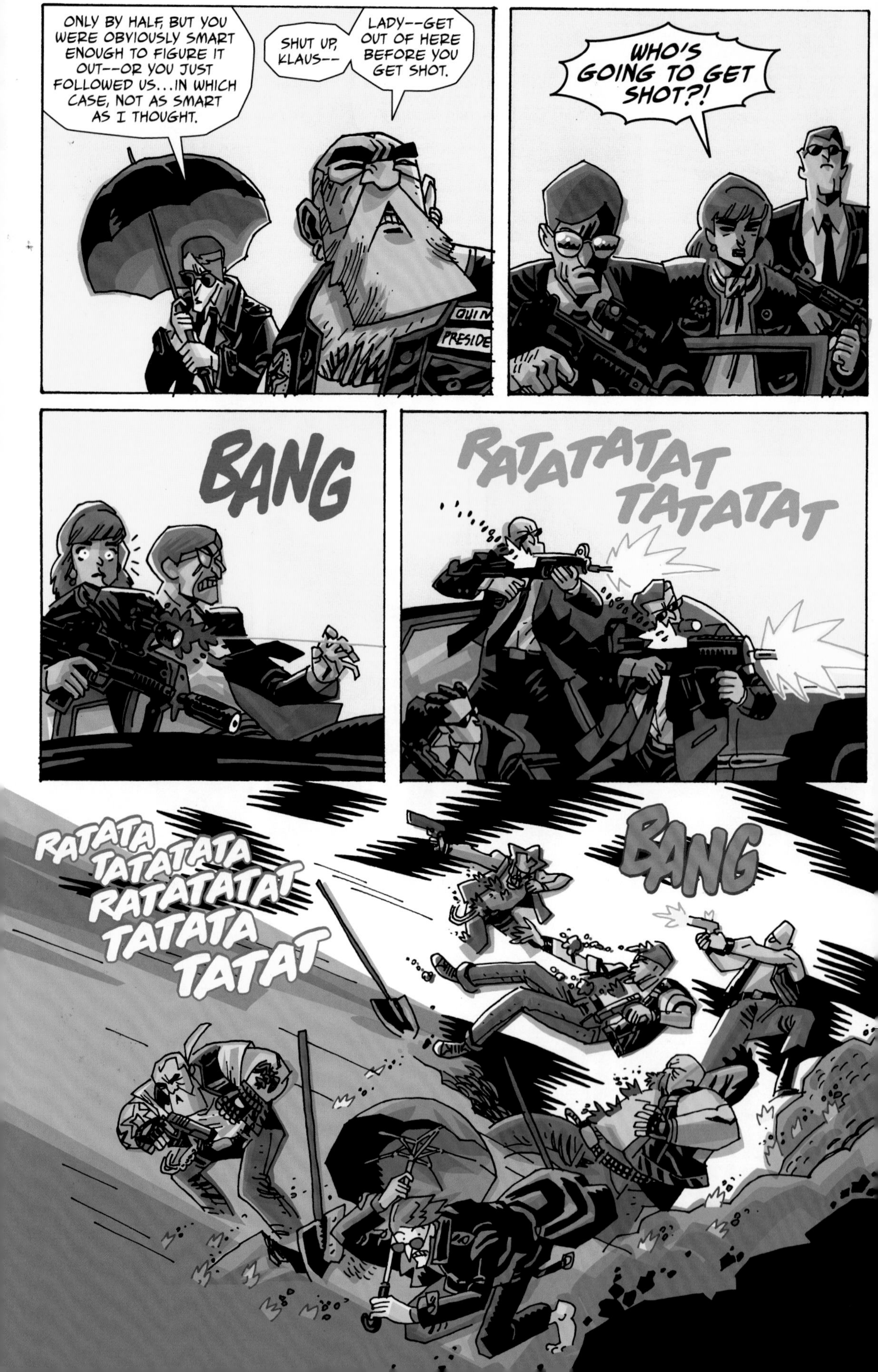
ONLY BY HALF, BUT YOU WERE OBVIOUSLY SMART ENOUGH TO FIGURE IT OUT--OR YOU JUST FOLLOWED US...IN WHICH CASE, NOT AS SMART AS I THOUGHT.
SHUT UP, KLAUS--
LADY--GET OUT OF HERE BEFORE YOU GET SHOT.
QUIN
PRESIDE
WHO'S GOING TO GET SHOT?!
BANG
RATATATAT TATATAT
RATATA TATATATA RATATATAT TATATA TATAT
BANG

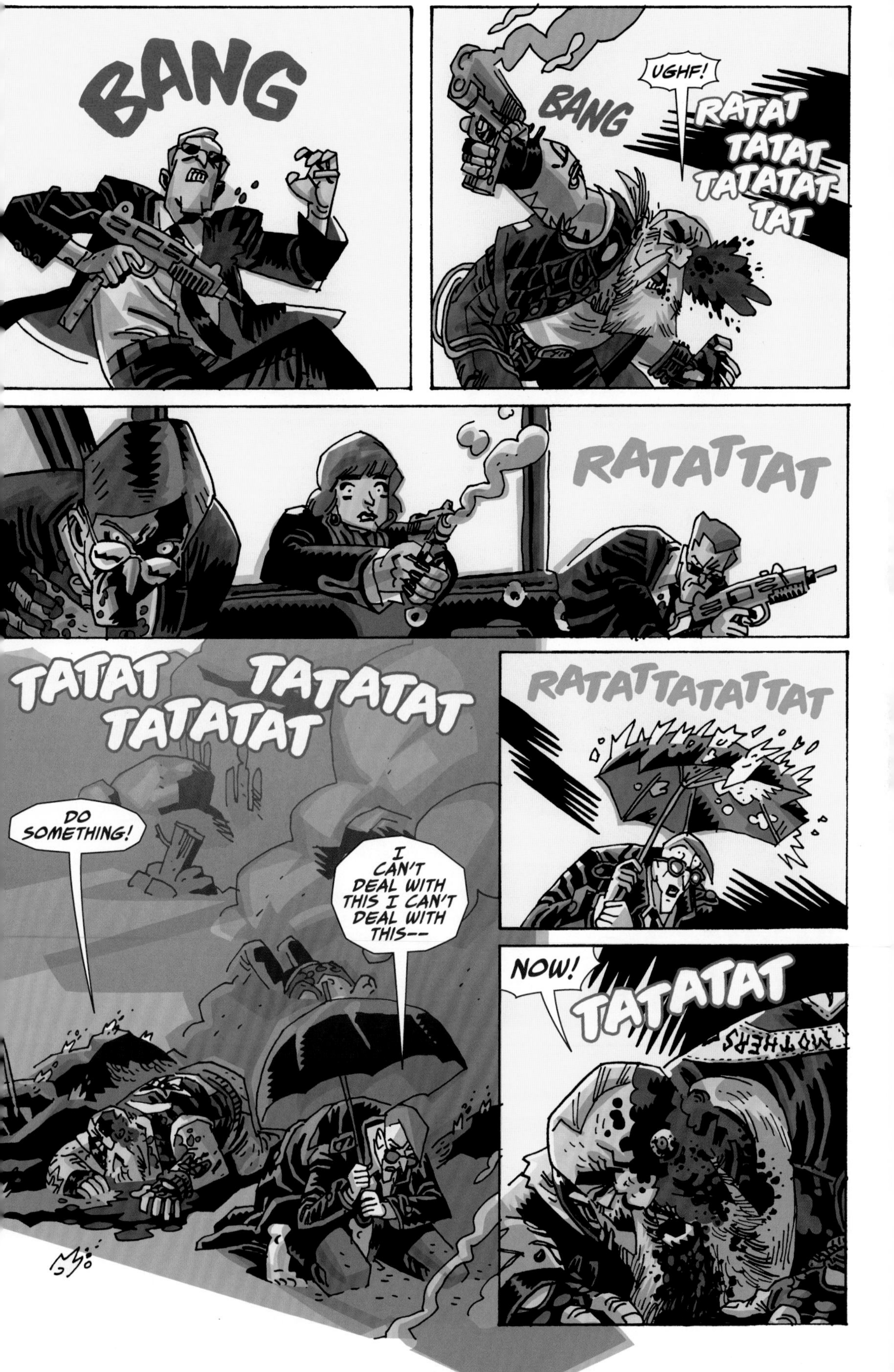
BANG
BANG
UGHF!
RATAT TATAT TATATAT TAT
RATATTAT
TATAT TATATAT TATATAT
DO SOMETHING!
I CAN'T DEAL WITH THIS I CAN'T DEAL WITH THIS--
RATATTATATTAT
NOW!
TATATAT
MOTHERS

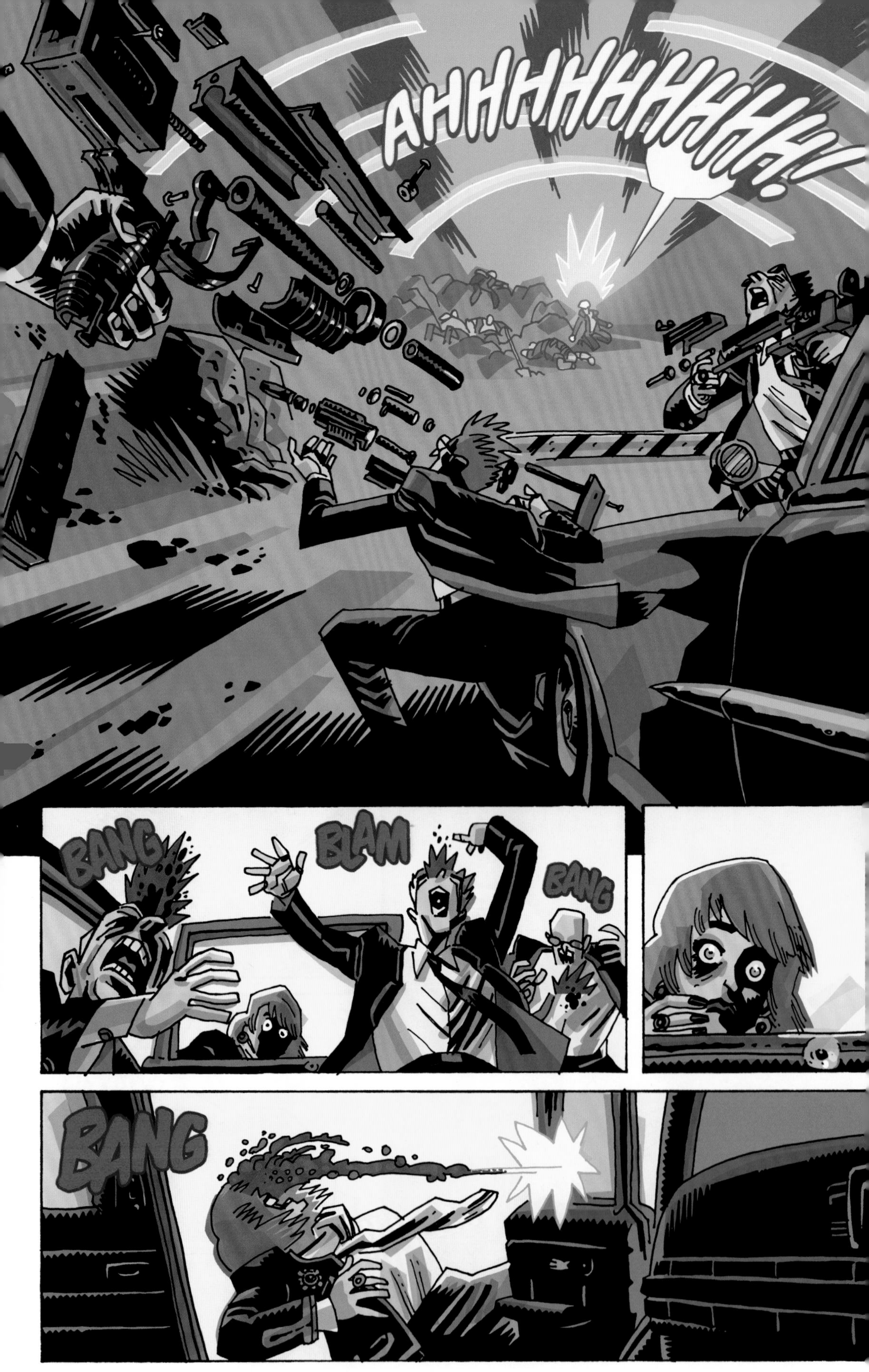
AHHHHHHHHH!!
BANG
BLAM
BANG
BANG

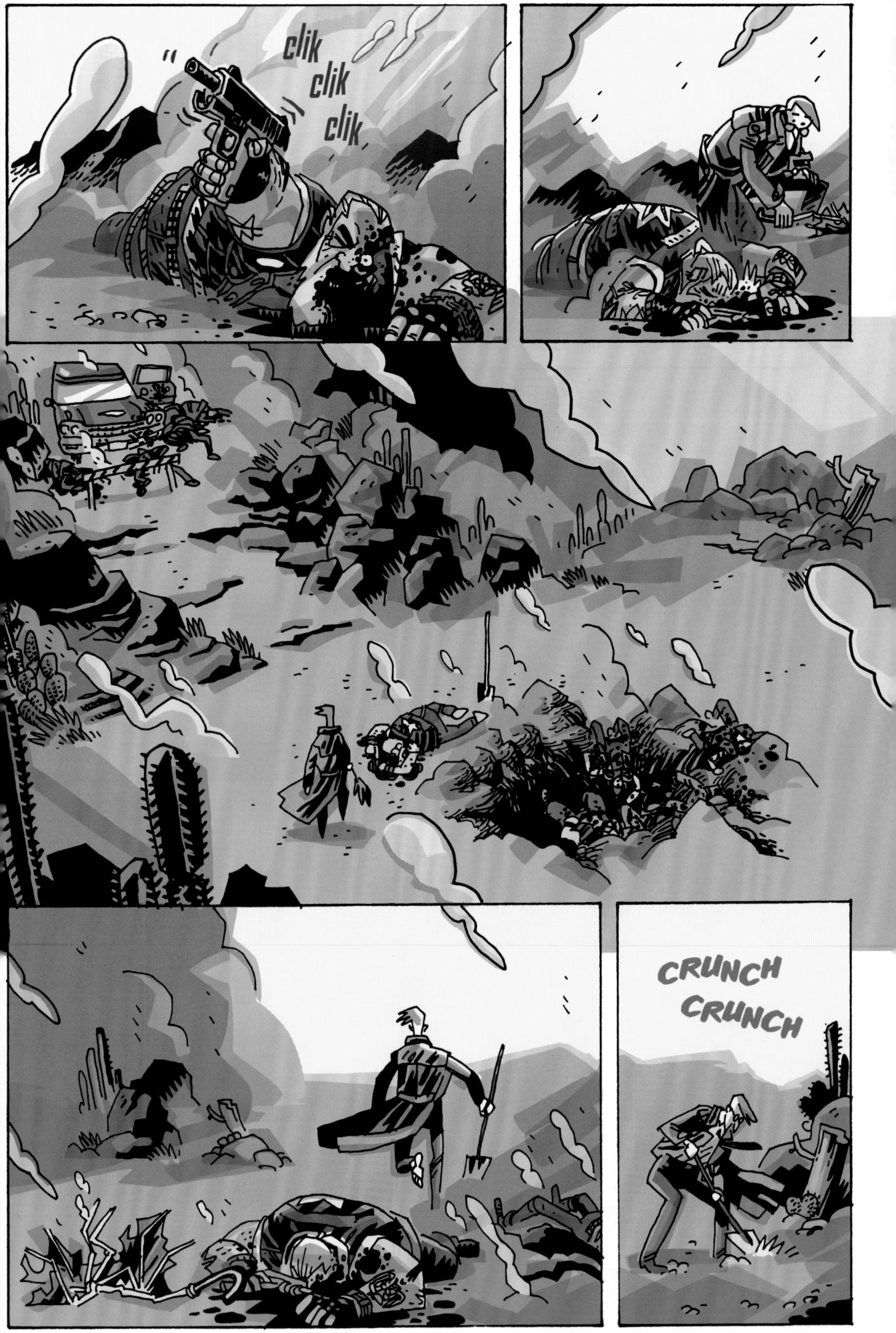
clik
clik
clik
CRUNCH
CRUNCH

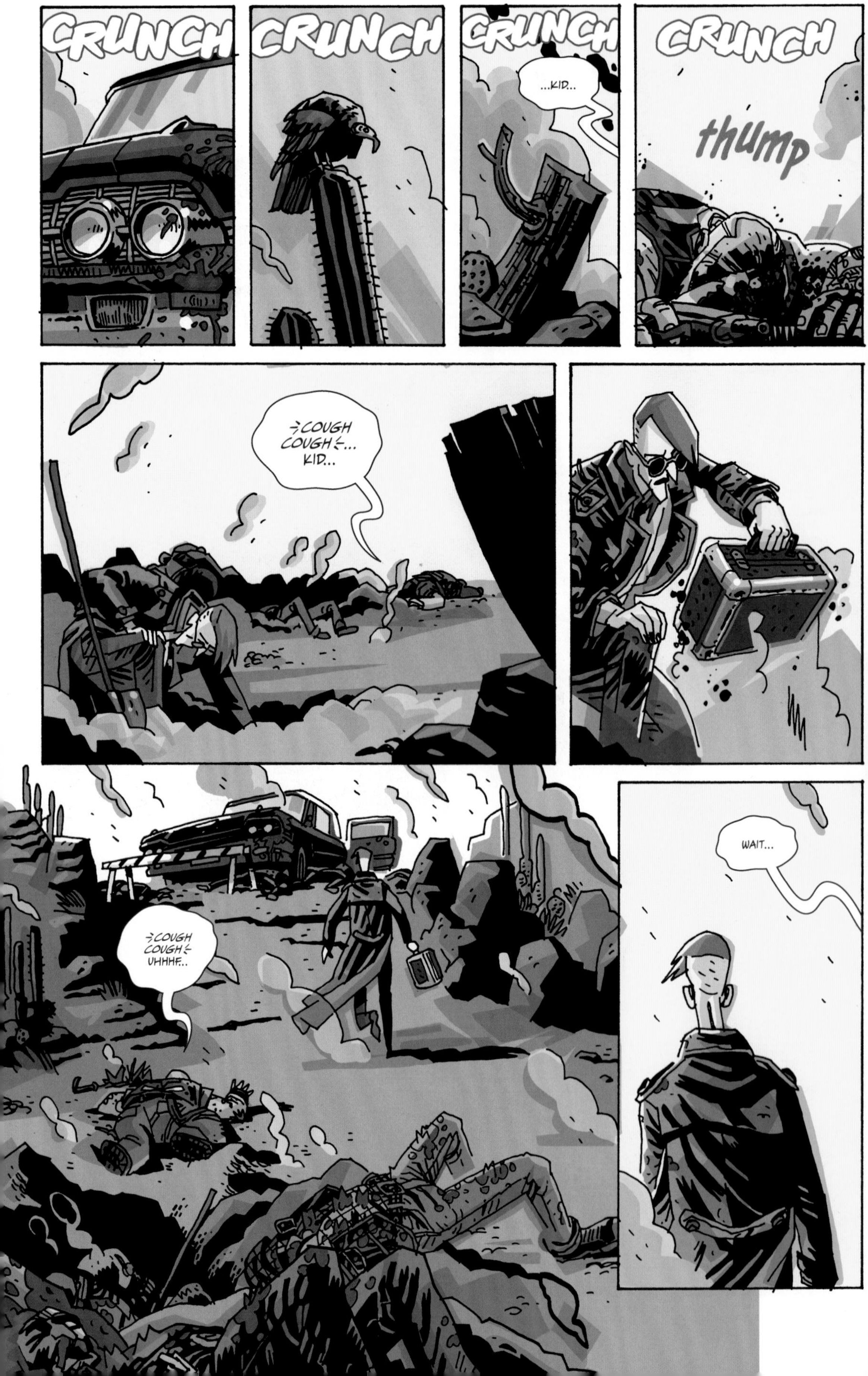
CRUNCH
CRUNCH
CRUNCH
...KID...
CRUNCH
thump
COUGH COUGH... KID...
COUGH COUGH UHHHF...
WAIT...

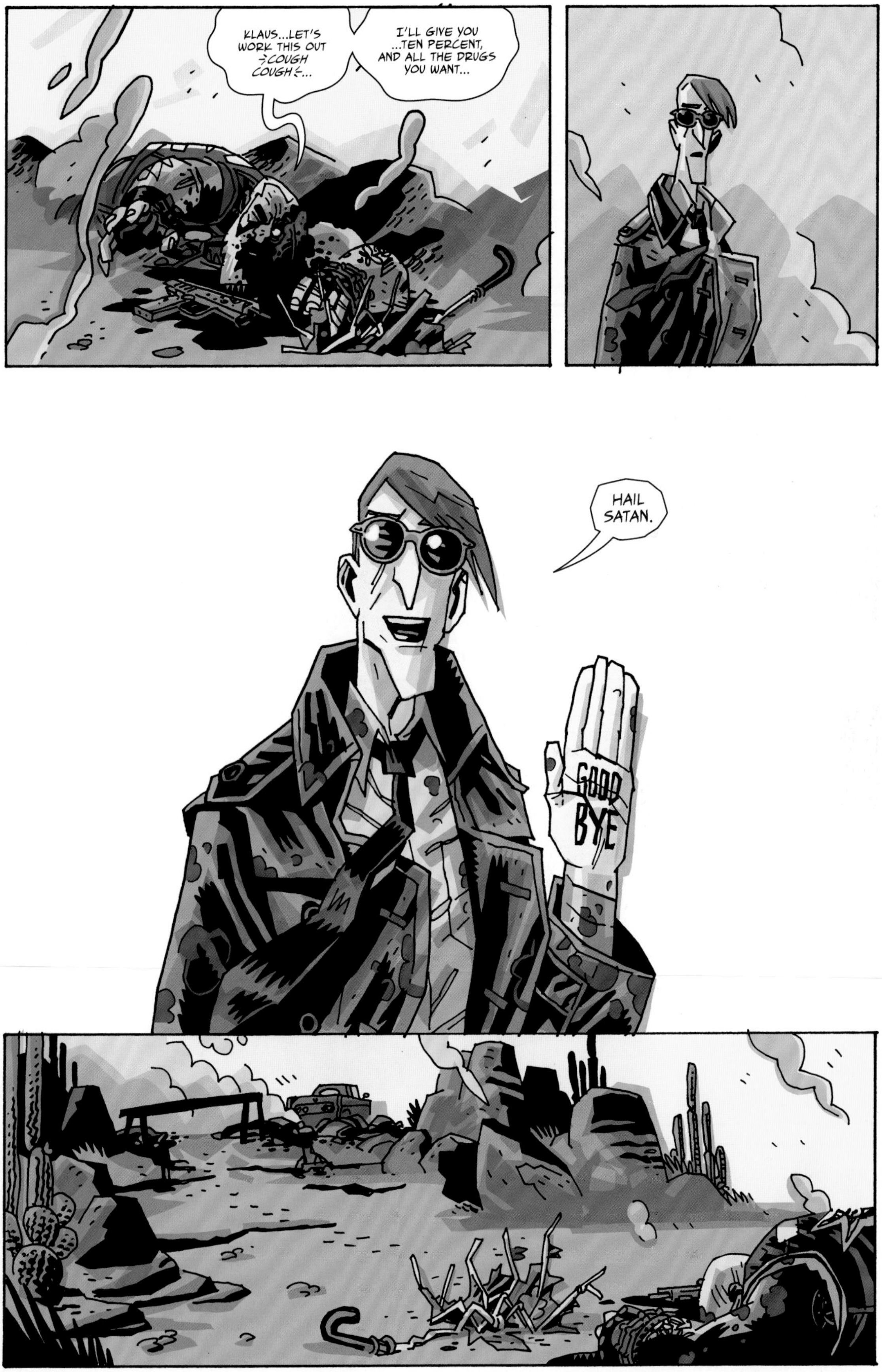
KLAUS...LET'S WORK THIS OUT ≻COUGH COUGH≺...
I'LL GIVE YOU ...TEN PERCENT, AND ALL THE DRUGS YOU WANT...
HAIL SATAN.
GOOD BYE

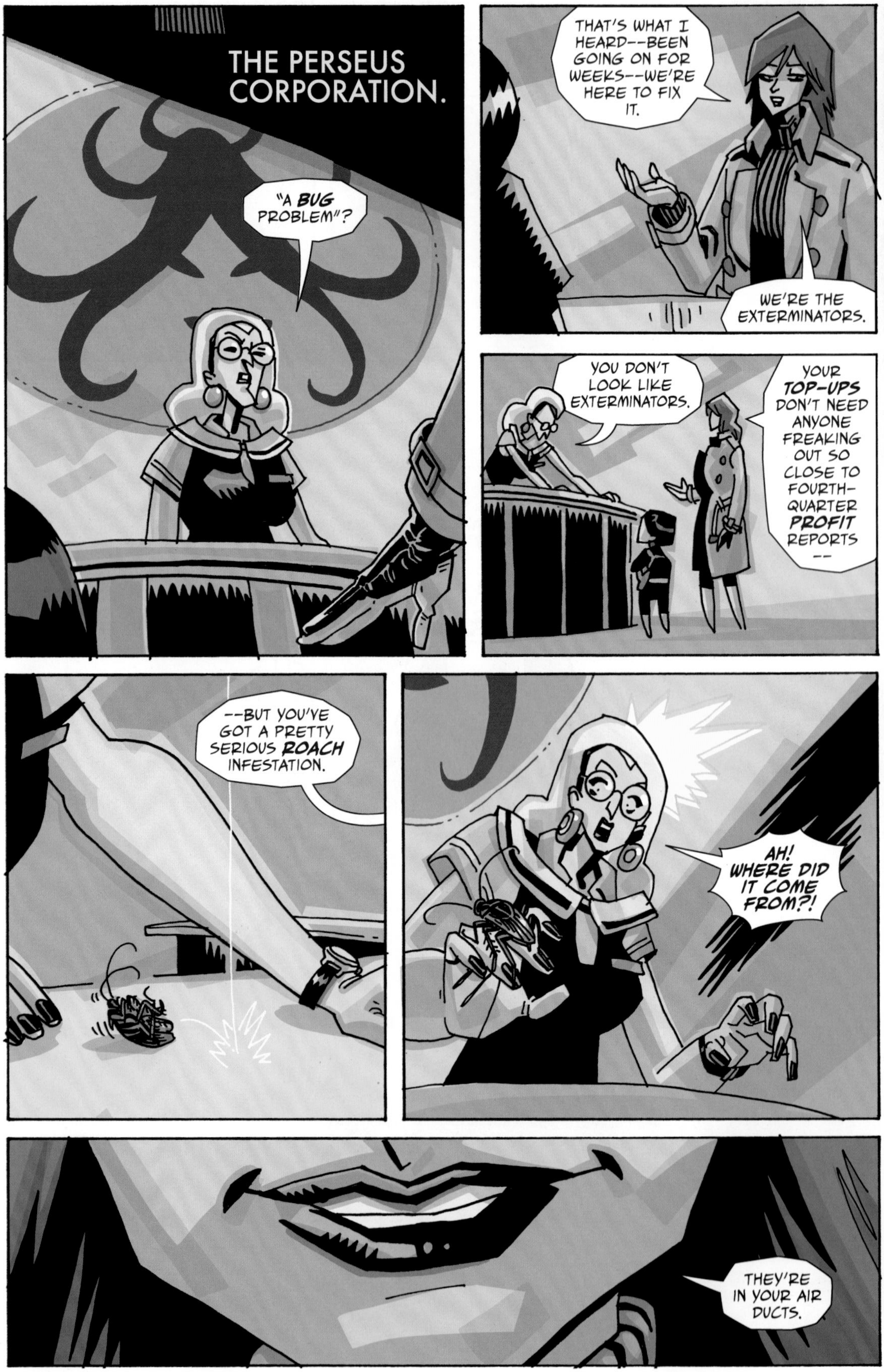

THE PERSEUS CORPORATION.
"A BUG PROBLEM"?
THAT'S WHAT I HEARD--BEEN GOING ON FOR WEEKS--WE'RE HERE TO FIX IT.
WE'RE THE EXTERMINATORS.
YOU DON'T LOOK LIKE EXTERMINATORS.
YOUR TOP-UPS DON'T NEED ANYONE FREAKING OUT SO CLOSE TO FOURTH-QUARTER PROFIT REPORTS --
--BUT YOU'VE GOT A PRETTY SERIOUS ROACH INFESTATION.
AH! WHERE DID IT COME FROM?!
THEY'RE IN YOUR AIR DUCTS.

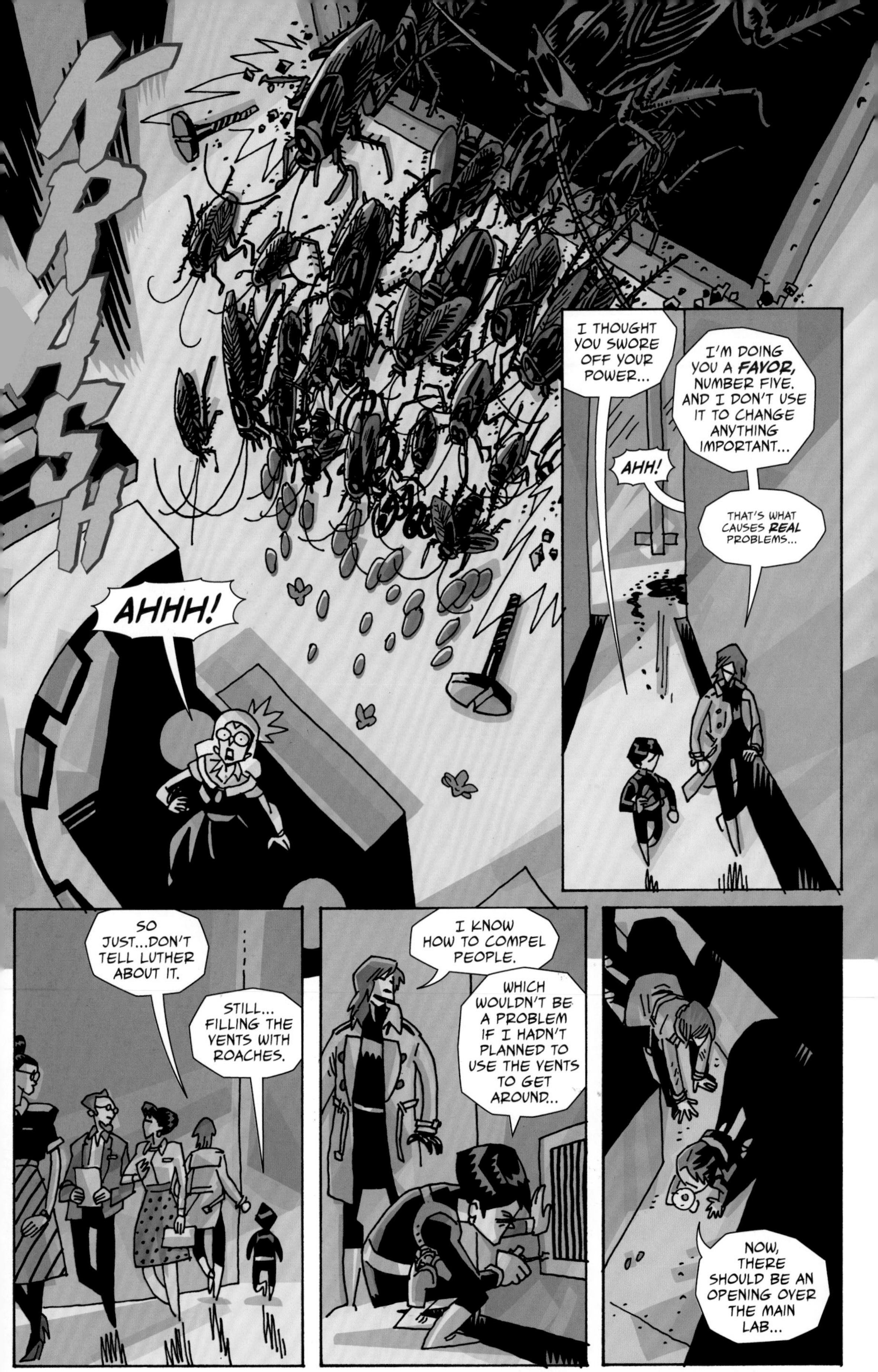
KRASH
AHHH!
I THOUGHT YOU SWORE OFF YOUR POWER...
I'M DOING YOU A **FAVOR,** NUMBER FIVE. AND I DON'T USE IT TO CHANGE ANYTHING IMPORTANT...
AHH!
THAT'S WHAT CAUSES **REAL** PROBLEMS...
SO JUST...DON'T TELL LUTHER ABOUT IT.
STILL... FILLING THE VENTS WITH ROACHES.
I KNOW HOW TO COMPEL PEOPLE.
WHICH WOULDN'T BE A PROBLEM IF I HADN'T PLANNED TO USE THE VENTS TO GET AROUND...
NOW, THERE SHOULD BE AN OPENING OVER THE MAIN LAB...

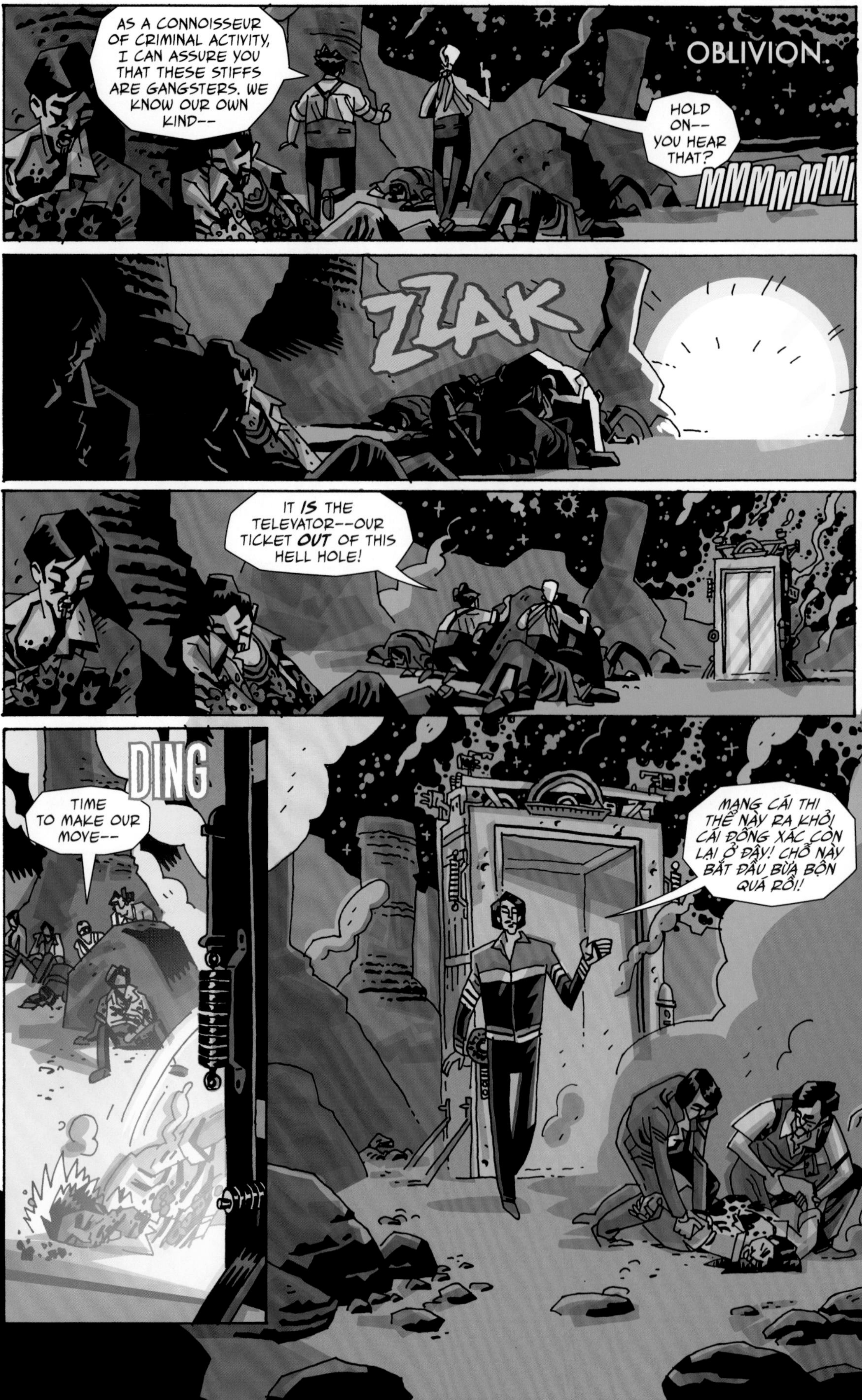

AS A CONNOISSEUR OF CRIMINAL ACTIVITY, I CAN ASSURE YOU THAT THESE STIFFS ARE GANGSTERS. WE KNOW OUR OWN KIND--
OBLIVION.
HOLD ON-- YOU HEAR THAT?
MMMMMMMM
ZZAK
IT *IS* THE TELEVATOR--OUR TICKET *OUT* OF THIS HELL HOLE!
DING
TIME TO MAKE OUR MOVE--
MANG CÁI THI THỂ NÀY RA KHỎI CÁI ĐỐNG XÁC CÒN LẠI Ở ĐÂY! CHỖ NÀY BẮT ĐẦU BỪA BỘN QUÁ RỒI!

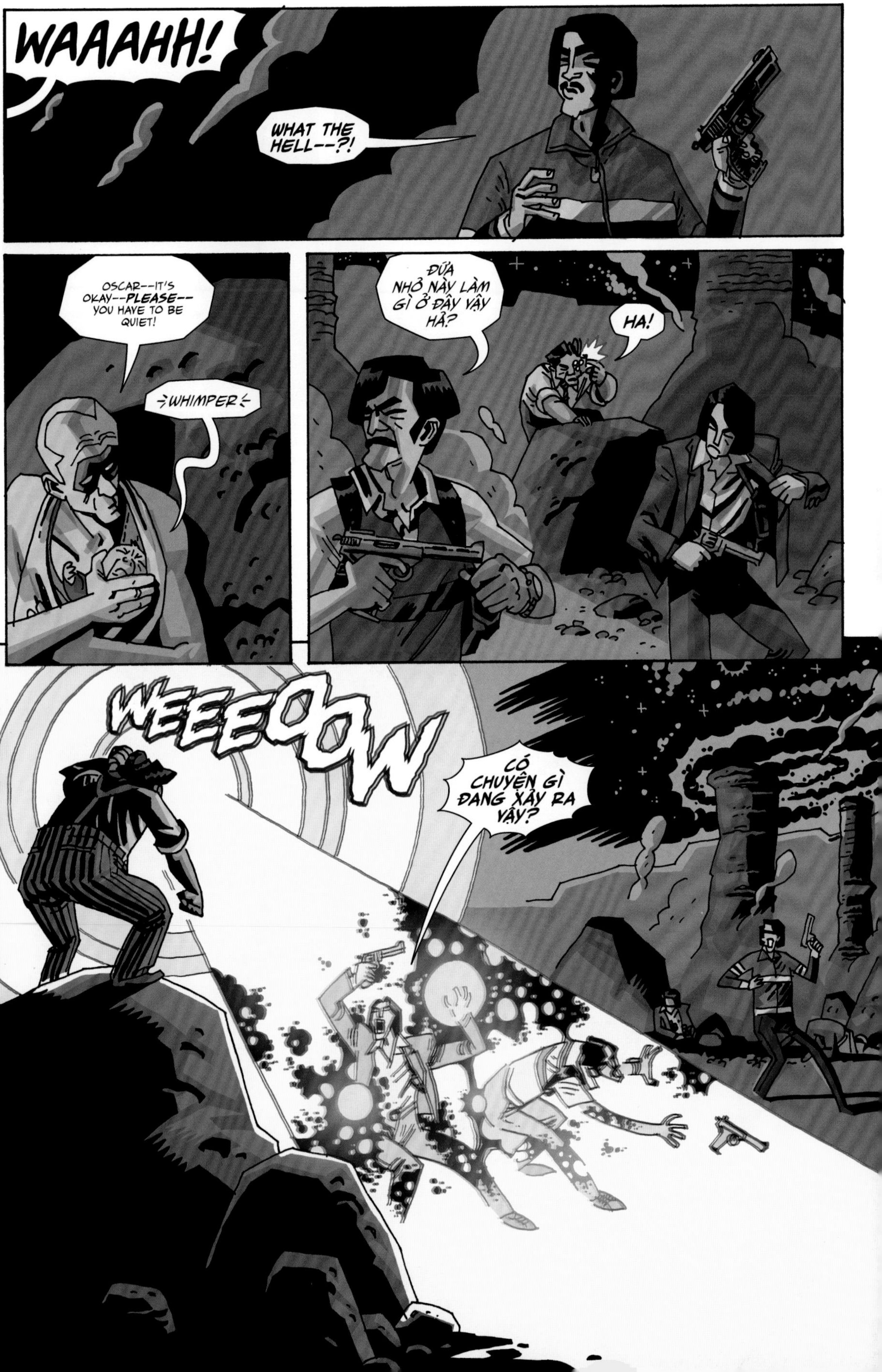

WAAAHH!
WHAT THE HELL--?!
OSCAR--IT'S OKAY--**PLEASE**--YOU HAYE TO BE QUIET!
WHIMPER
ĐỨA NHỎ NÀY LÀM GÌ Ở ĐÂY VẬY HẢ?
HA!
WEEEOOW
CÓ CHUYỆN GÌ ĐANG XẢY RA VẬY?

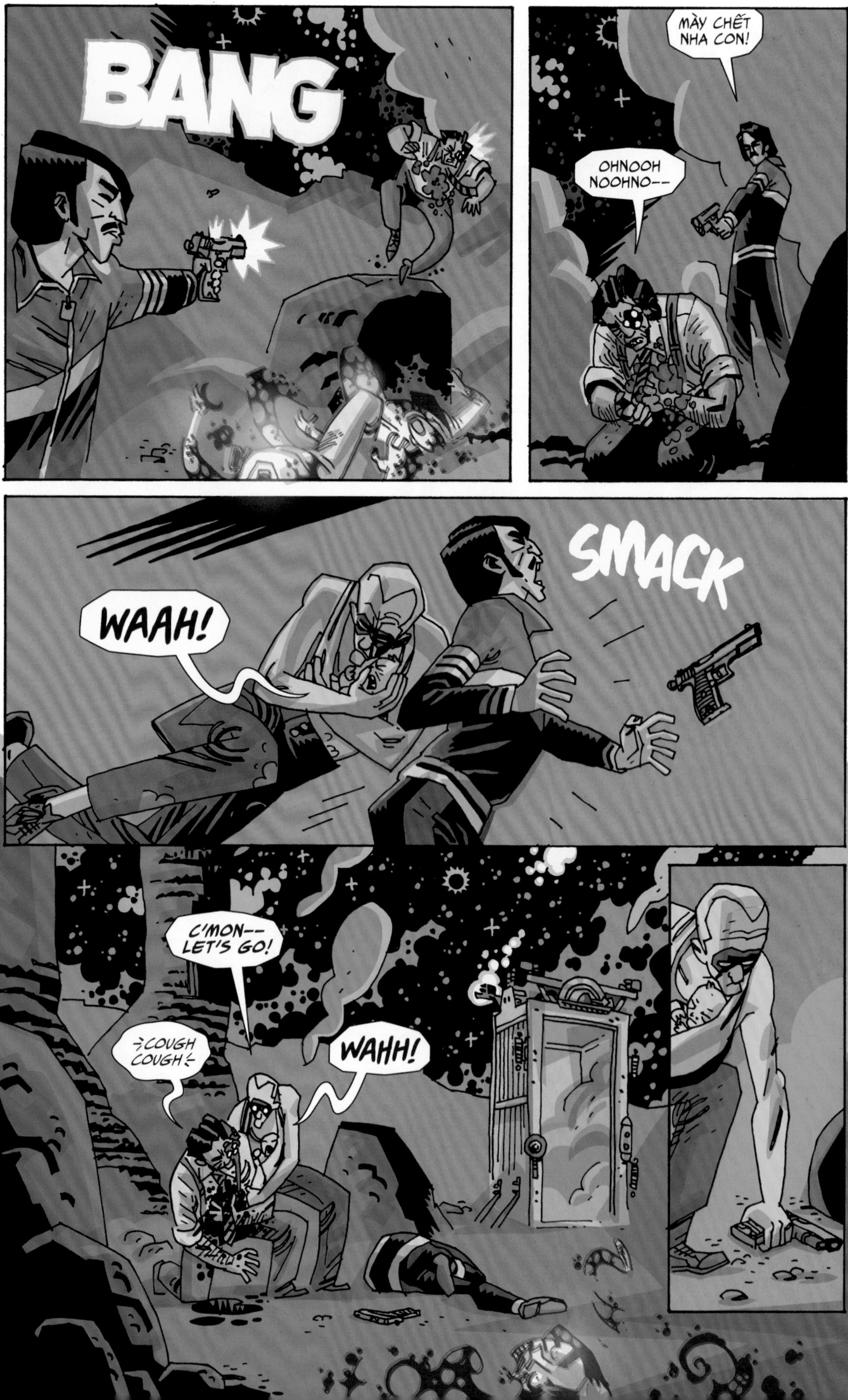
BANG
MÀY CHẾT NHA CON!
OHNOOH NOOHNO--
SMACK
WAAH!
C'MON-- LET'S GO!
COUGH COUGH
WAHH!

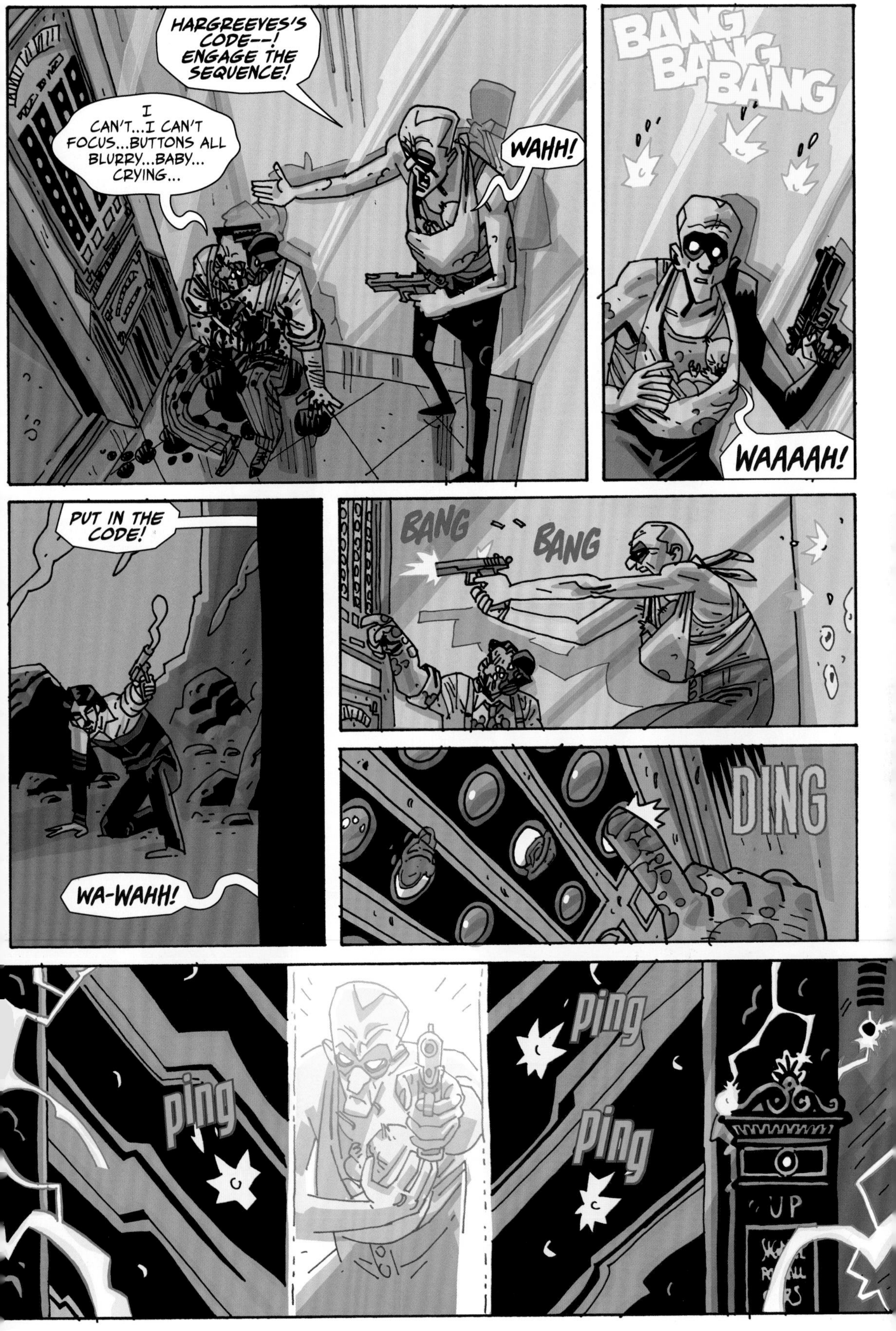
HARGREEVES'S CODE--! ENGAGE THE SEQUENCE!
I CAN'T...I CAN'T FOCUS...BUTTONS ALL BLURRY...BABY... CRYING...
WAHH!
BANG BANG BANG
WAAAAH!
PUT IN THE CODE!
WA-WAHH!
BANG
BANG
DING
ping
ping
ping
UP

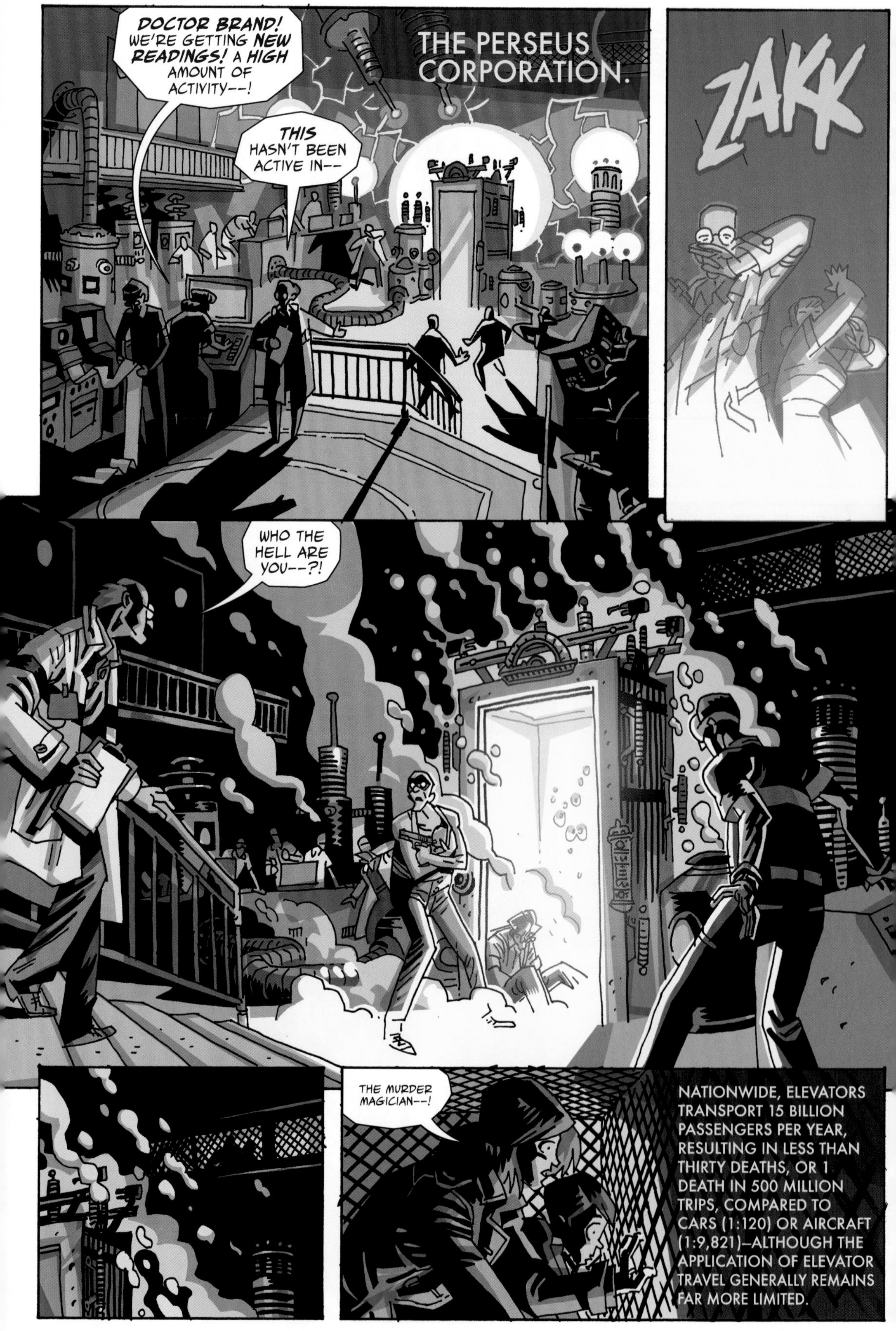
THE PERSEUS CORPORATION.
DOCTOR BRAND! WE'RE GETTING NEW READINGS! A HIGH AMOUNT OF ACTIVITY--!
THIS HASN'T BEEN ACTIVE IN--
ZAKK
WHO THE HELL ARE YOU--?!
THE MURDER MAGICIAN--!
NATIONWIDE, ELEVATORS TRANSPORT 15 BILLION PASSENGERS PER YEAR, RESULTING IN LESS THAN THIRTY DEATHS, OR 1 DEATH IN 500 MILLION TRIPS, COMPARED TO CARS (1:120) OR AIRCRAFT (1:9,821)—ALTHOUGH THE APPLICATION OF ELEVATOR TRAVEL GENERALLY REMAINS FAR MORE LIMITED.

CHAPTER FOUR

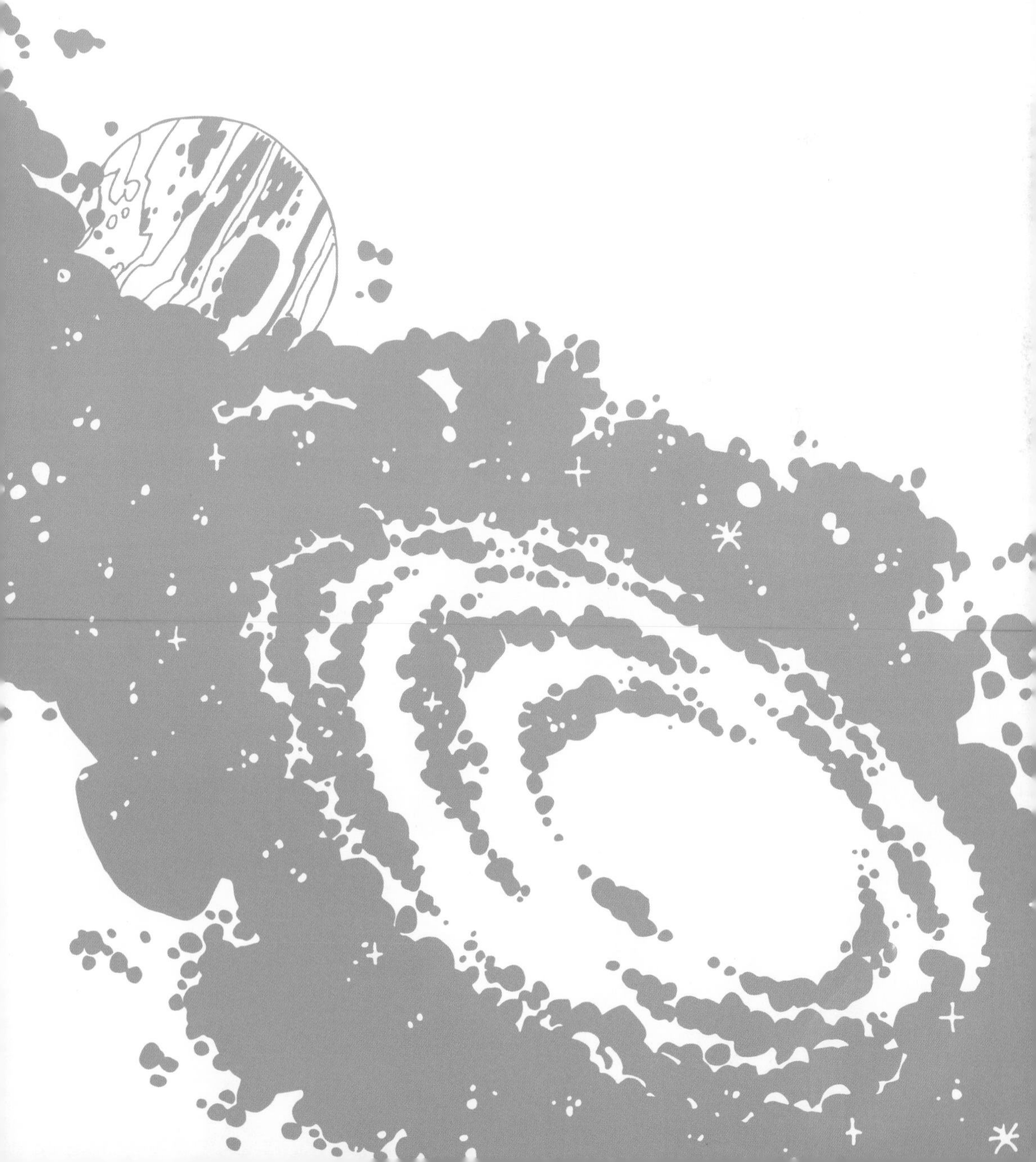

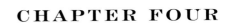

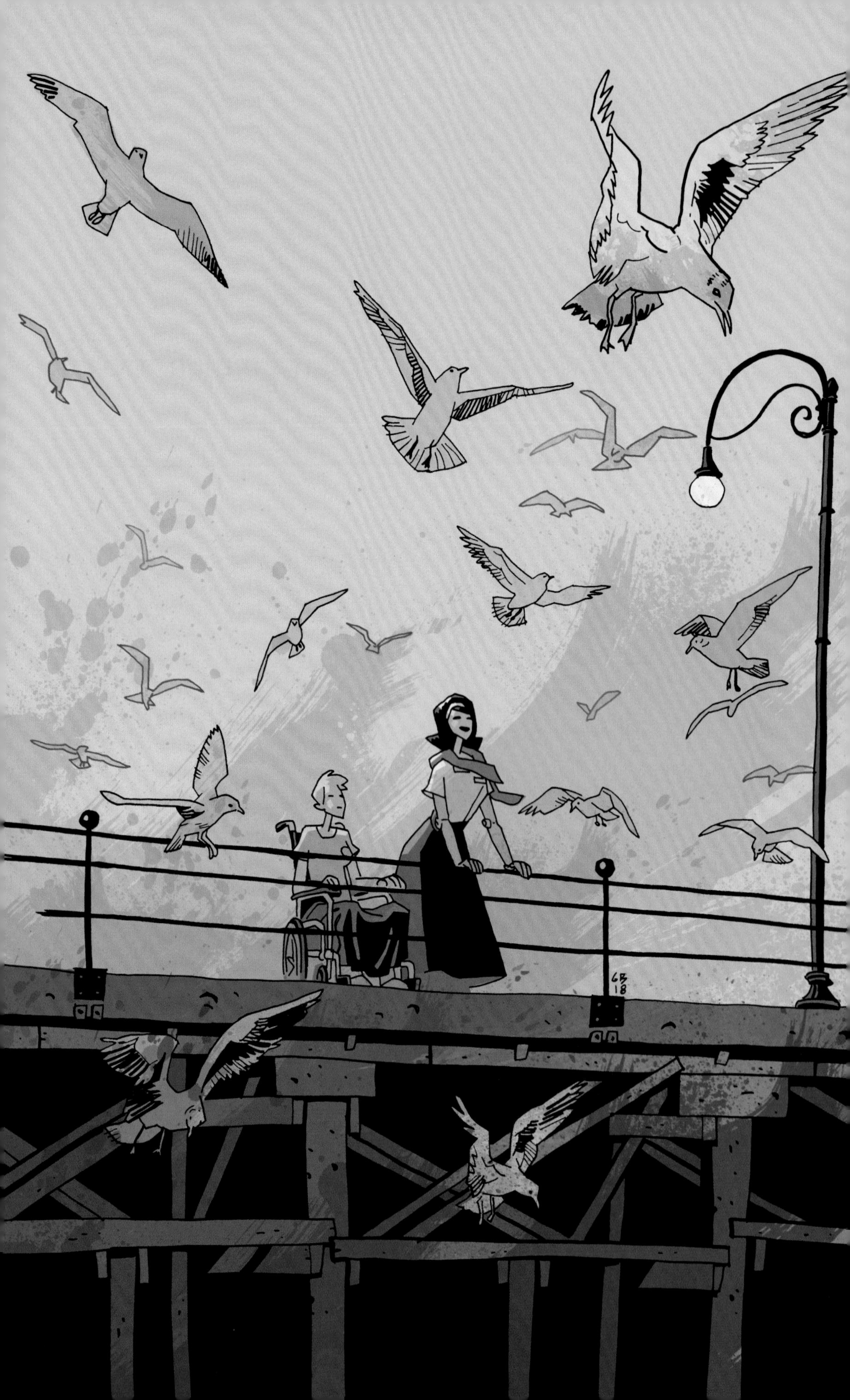
GB
18

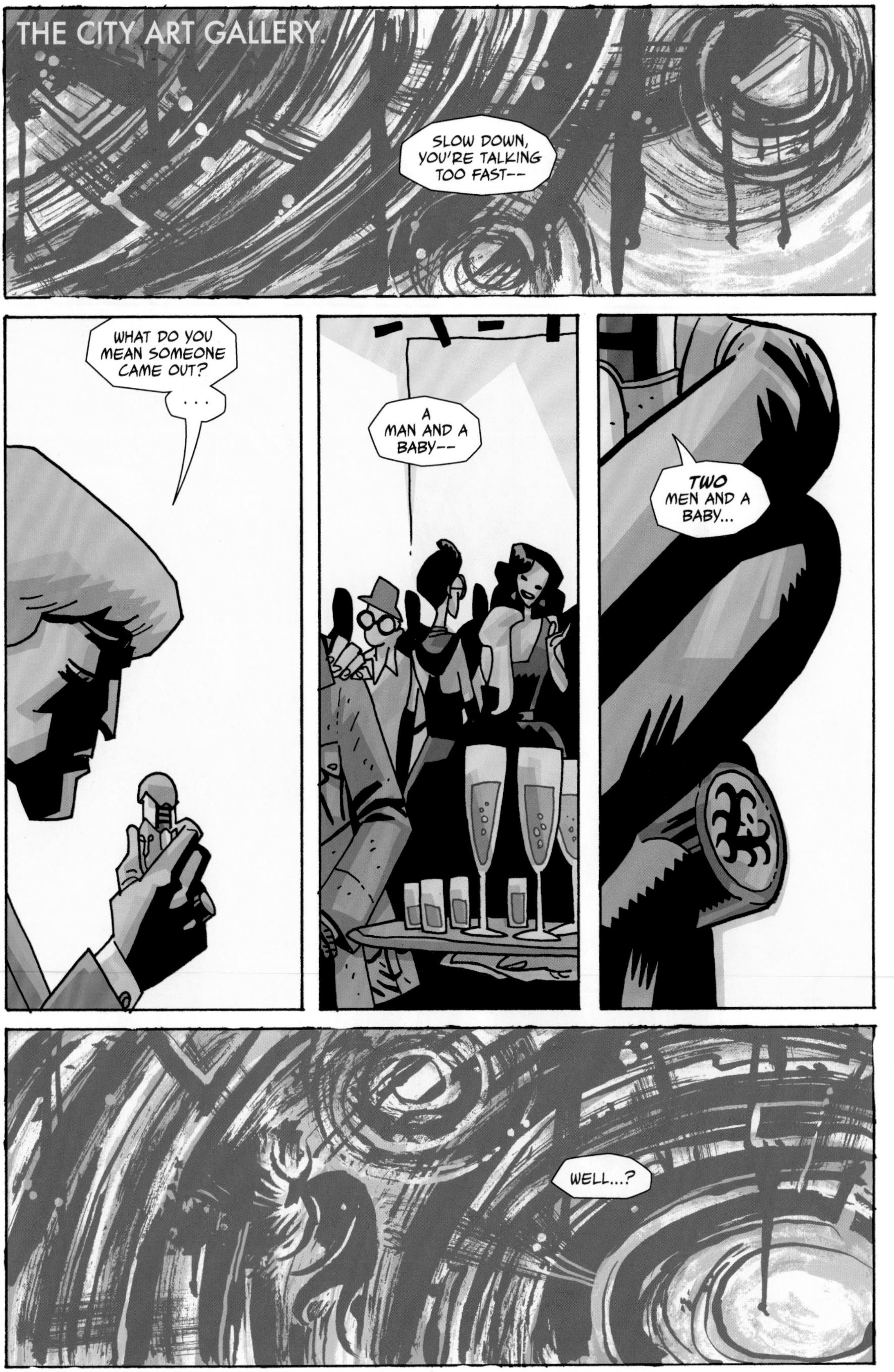
THE CITY ART GALLERY.
SLOW DOWN, YOU'RE TALKING TOO FAST--
WHAT DO YOU MEAN SOMEONE CAME OUT?
. . .
A MAN AND A BABY--
TWO MEN AND A BABY...
WELL...?

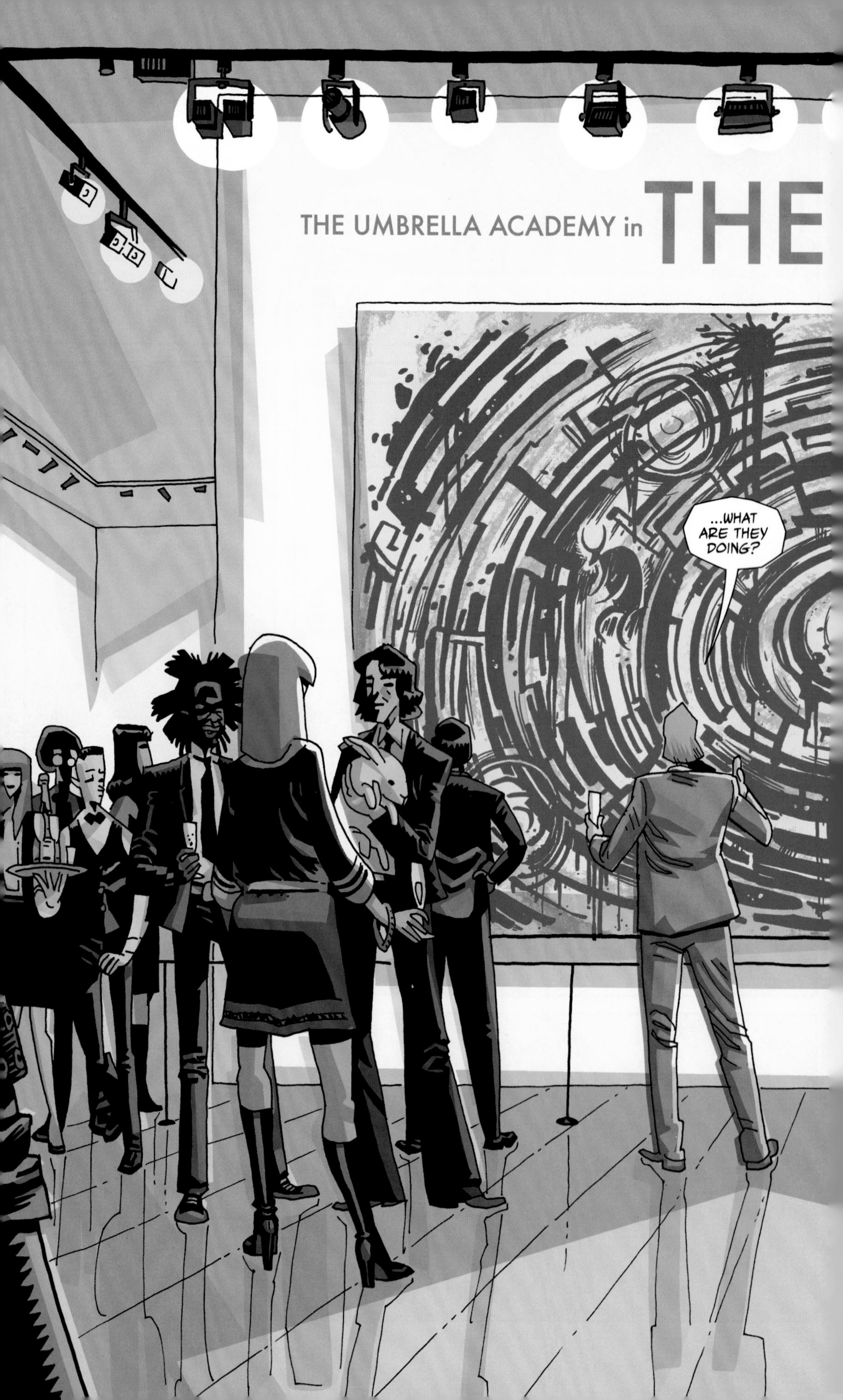
THE UMBRELLA ACADEMY in THE
...WHAT ARE THEY DOING?

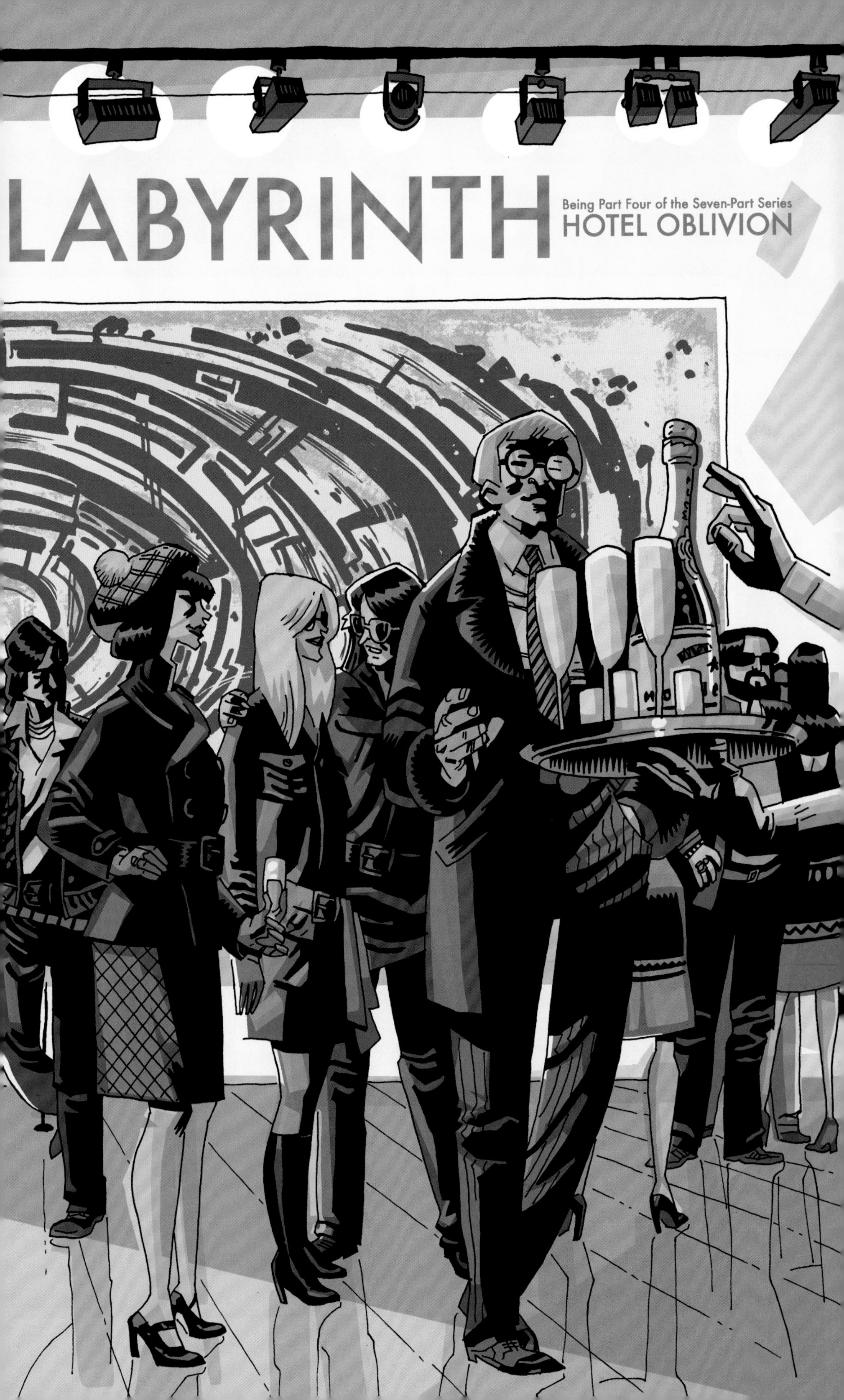
LABYRINTH
Being Part Four of the Seven-Part Series
HOTEL OBLIVION

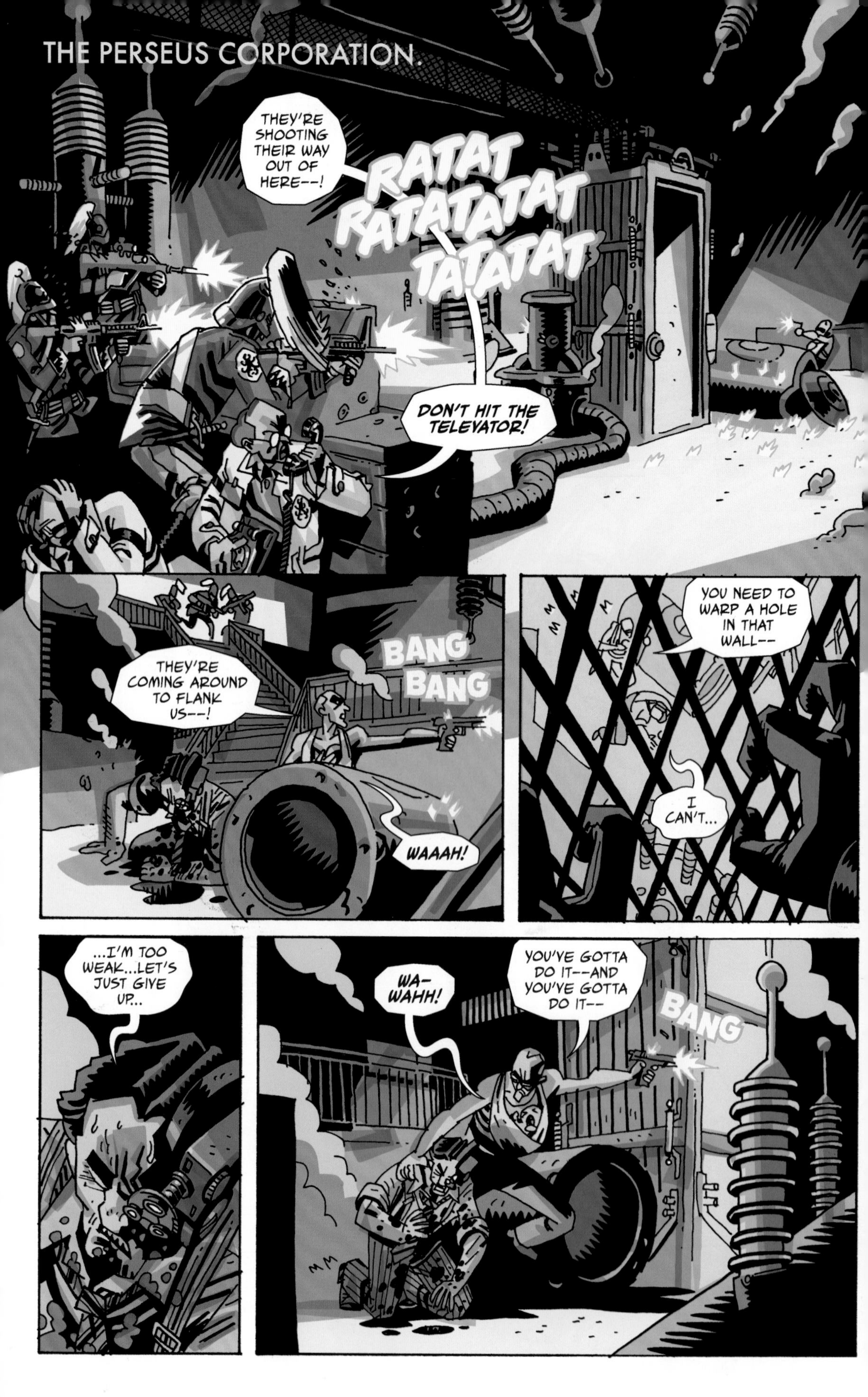
THE PERSEUS CORPORATION.
THEY'RE SHOOTING THEIR WAY OUT OF HERE--!
RATAT RATATATAT TATATAT
DON'T HIT THE TELEVATOR!
THEY'RE COMING AROUND TO FLANK US--!
BANG BANG
WAAAH!
YOU NEED TO WARP A HOLE IN THAT WALL--
I CAN'T...
...I'M TOO WEAK...LET'S JUST GIVE UP...
WA-WAHH!
YOU'VE GOTTA DO IT--AND YOU'VE GOTTA DO IT--
BANG

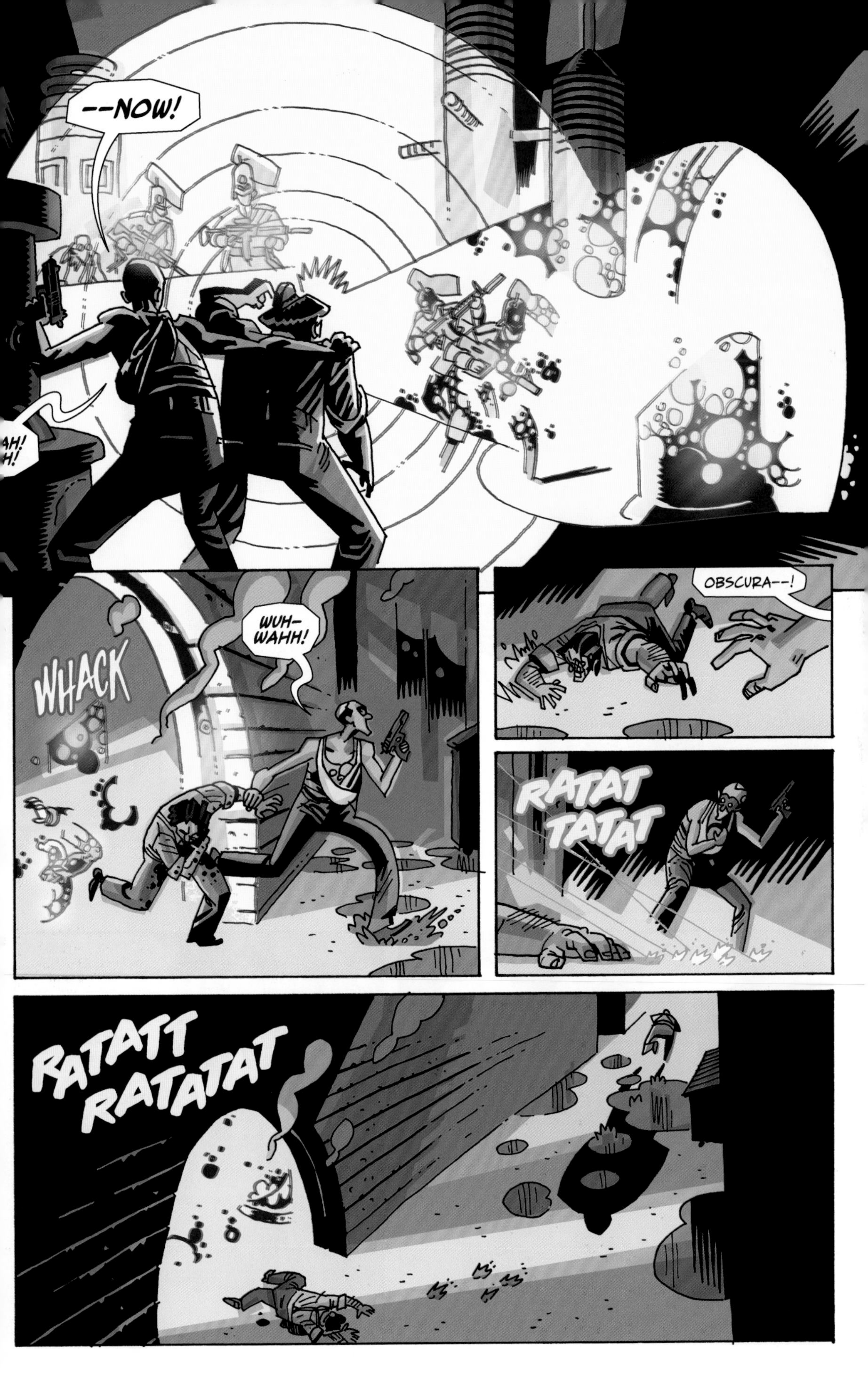
--NOW!
WHACK
WUH-WAHH!
OBSCURA--!
RATAT TATAT
RATATT RATATAT

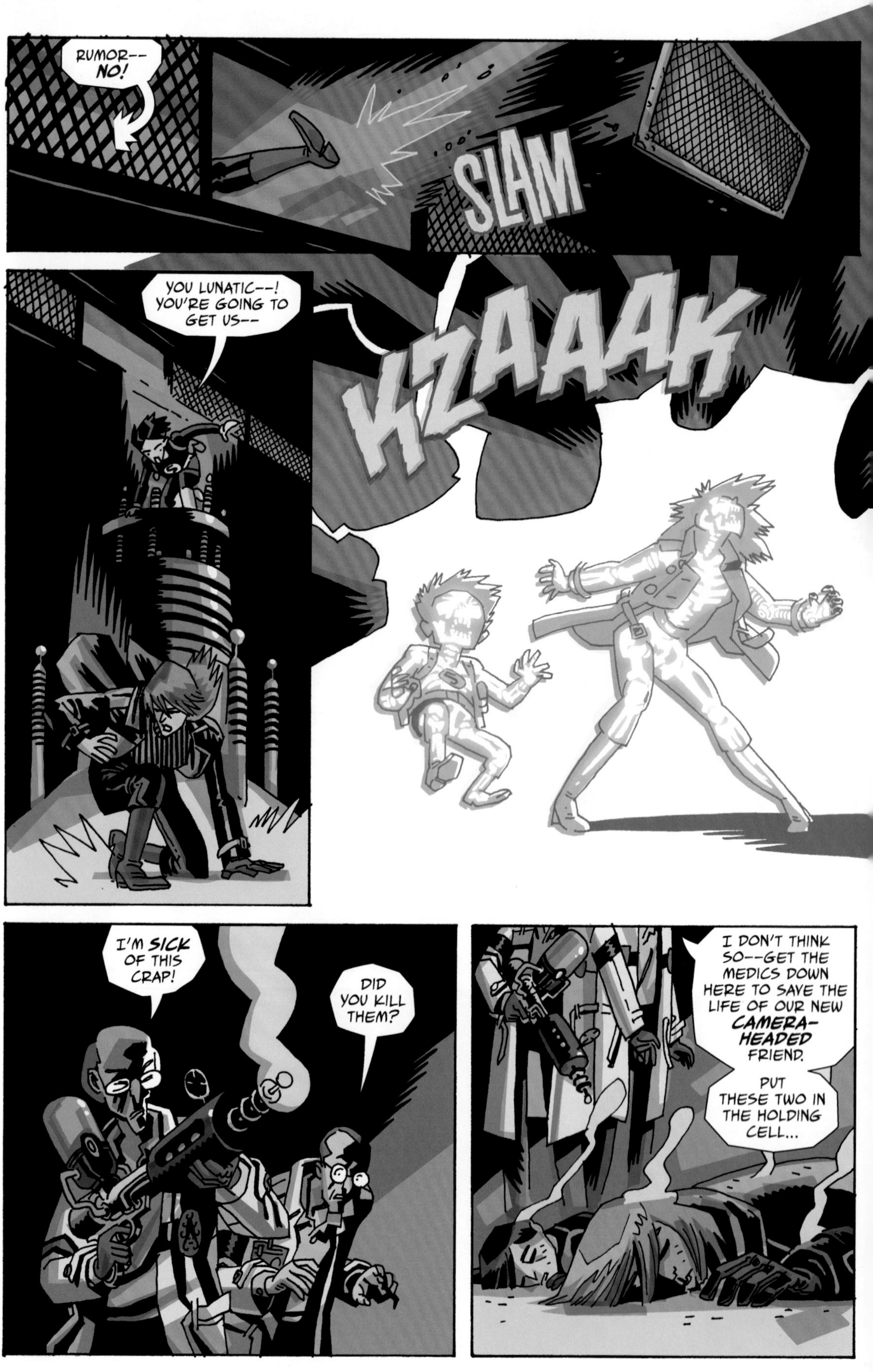
RUMOR-- NO!
SLAM
YOU LUNATIC--! YOU'RE GOING TO GET US--
KZAAAK
I'M SICK OF THIS CRAP!
DID YOU KILL THEM?
I DON'T THINK SO--GET THE MEDICS DOWN HERE TO SAVE THE LIFE OF OUR NEW CAMERA-HEADED FRIEND.
PUT THESE TWO IN THE HOLDING CELL...

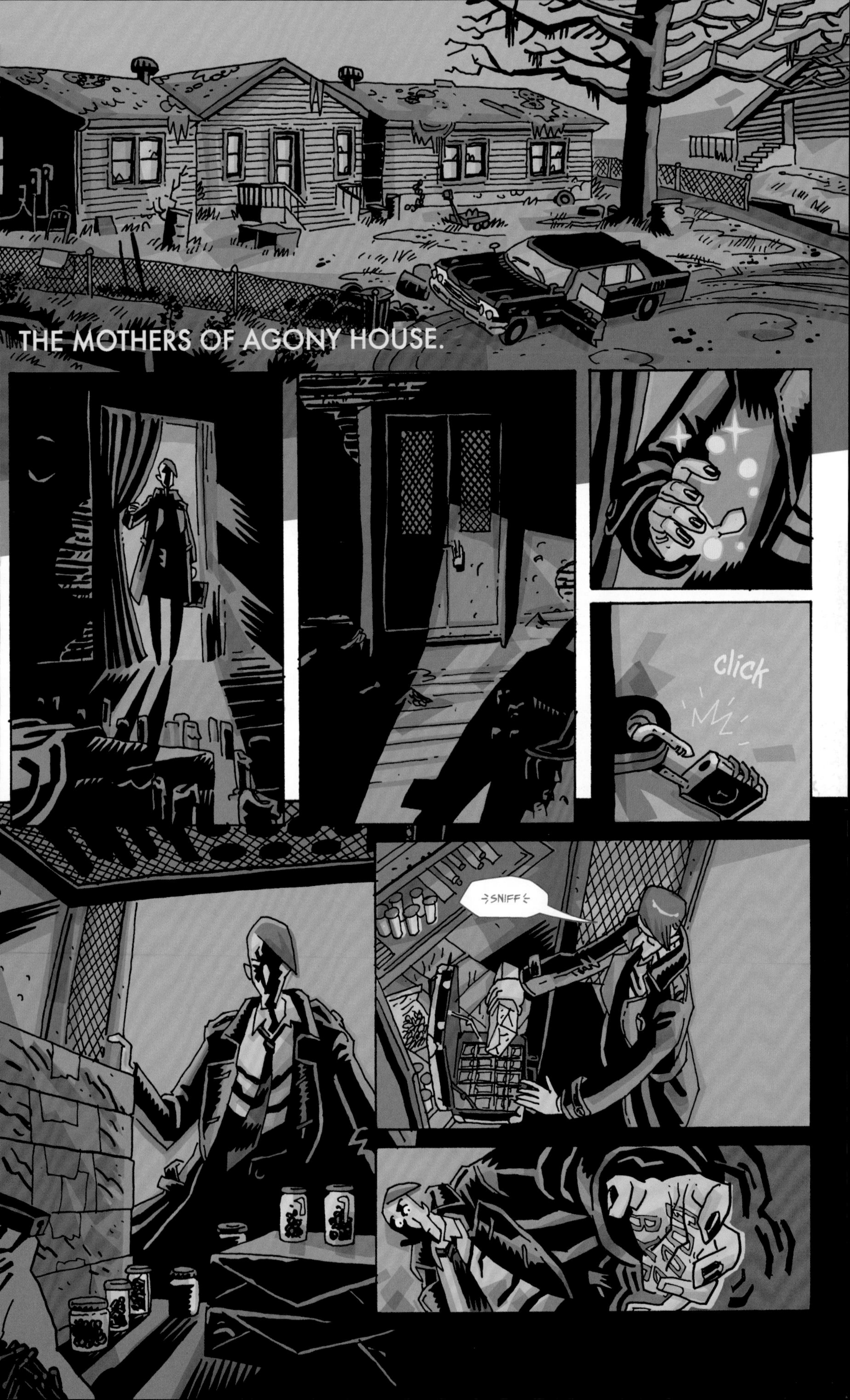
THE MOTHERS OF AGONY HOUSE.
click
SNIFF

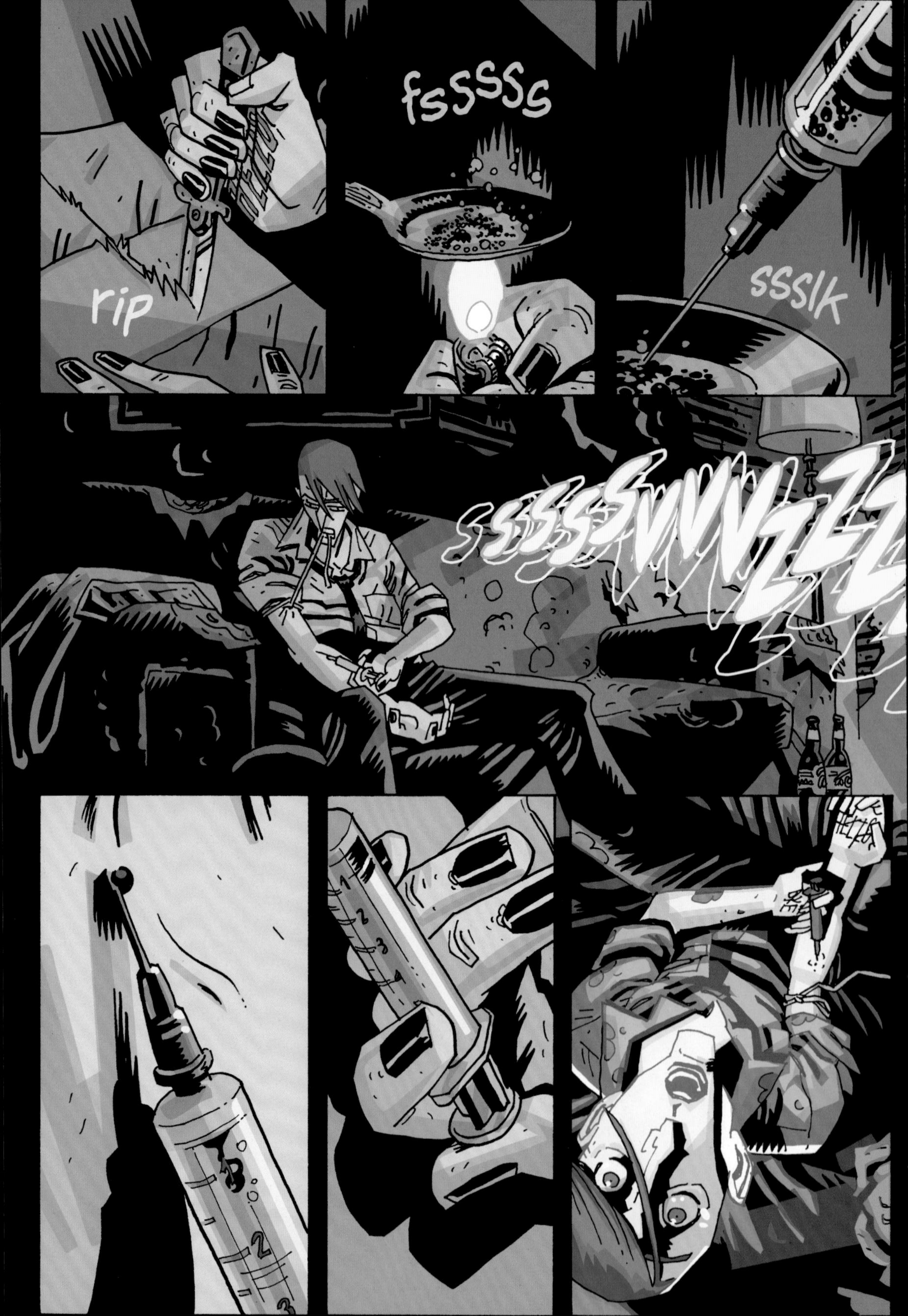
rip
fsSSSs
sssIk
sSSSSVVVNZZZ

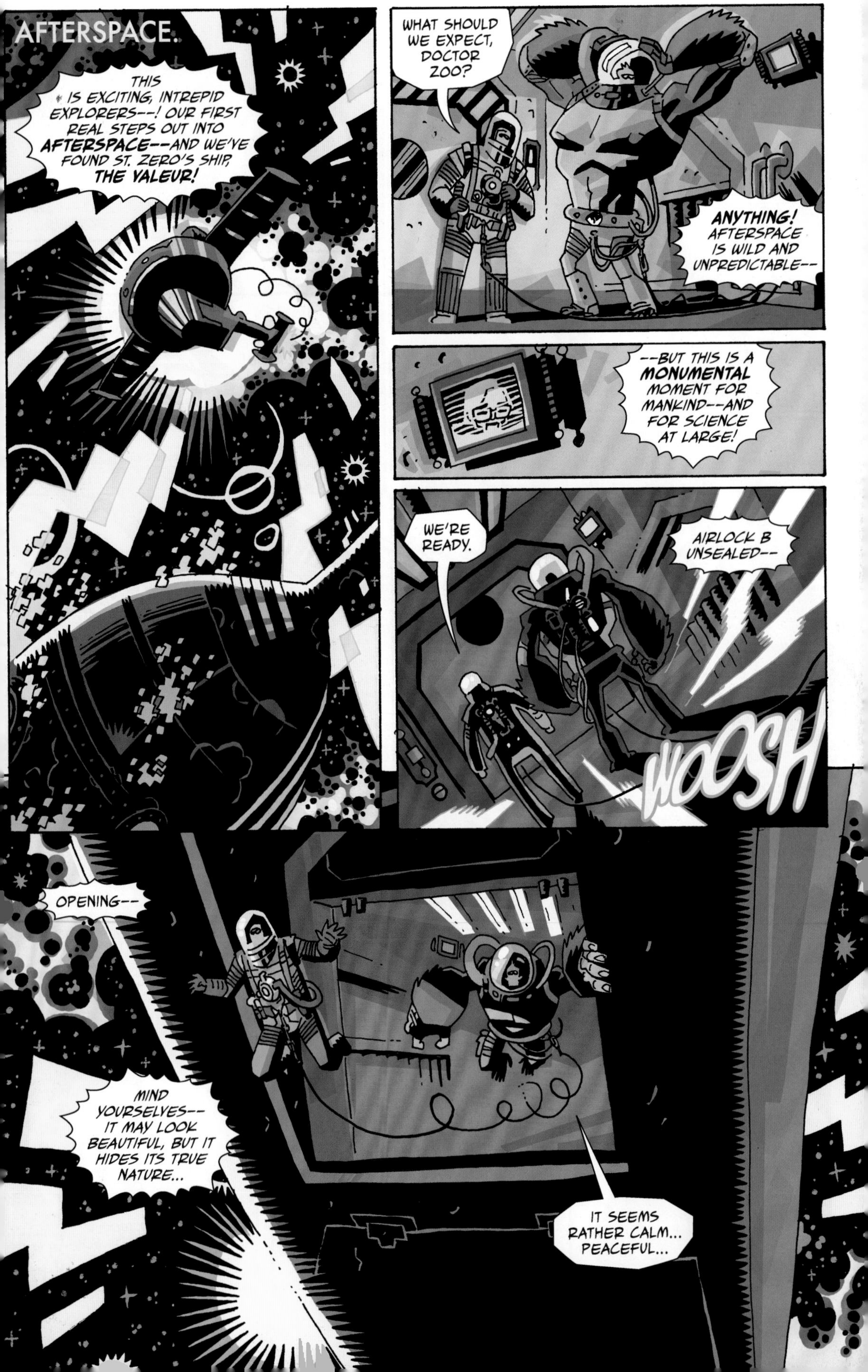
AFTERSPACE.
THIS IS EXCITING, INTREPID EXPLORERS--! OUR FIRST REAL STEPS OUT INTO AFTERSPACE--AND WE'VE FOUND ST. ZERO'S SHIP, THE VALEUR!
WHAT SHOULD WE EXPECT, DOCTOR ZOO?
ANYTHING! AFTERSPACE IS WILD AND UNPREDICTABLE--
--BUT THIS IS A MONUMENTAL MOMENT FOR MANKIND--AND FOR SCIENCE AT LARGE!
WE'RE READY.
AIRLOCK B UNSEALED--
WOOSH
OPENING--
MIND YOURSELVES-- IT MAY LOOK BEAUTIFUL, BUT IT HIDES ITS TRUE NATURE...
IT SEEMS RATHER CALM... PEACEFUL...

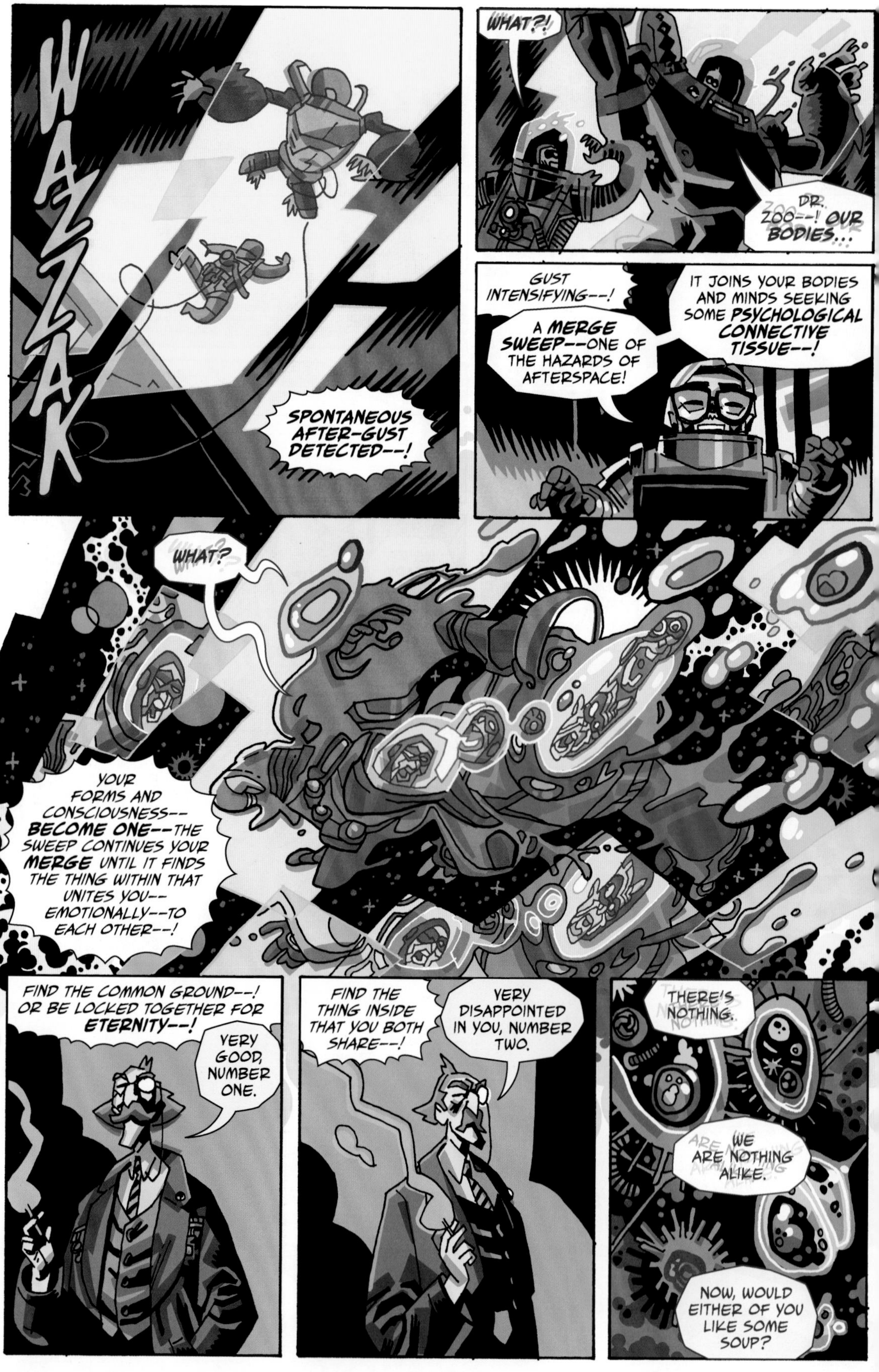
WAZZAK
SPONTANEOUS AFTER-GUST DETECTED--!
WHAT?!
DR. ZOO--! OUR BODIES...
GUST INTENSIFYING--!
A MERGE SWEEP--ONE OF THE HAZARDS OF AFTERSPACE!
IT JOINS YOUR BODIES AND MINDS SEEKING SOME PSYCHOLOGICAL CONNECTIVE TISSUE--!
WHAT?
YOUR FORMS AND CONSCIOUSNESS-- BECOME ONE--THE SWEEP CONTINUES YOUR MERGE UNTIL IT FINDS THE THING WITHIN THAT UNITES YOU-- EMOTIONALLY--TO EACH OTHER--!
FIND THE COMMON GROUND--! OR BE LOCKED TOGETHER FOR ETERNITY--!
VERY GOOD, NUMBER ONE.
FIND THE THING INSIDE THAT YOU BOTH SHARE--!
VERY DISAPPOINTED IN YOU, NUMBER TWO.
THERE'S NOTHING.
WE ARE NOTHING ALIKE.
NOW, WOULD EITHER OF YOU LIKE SOME SOUP?

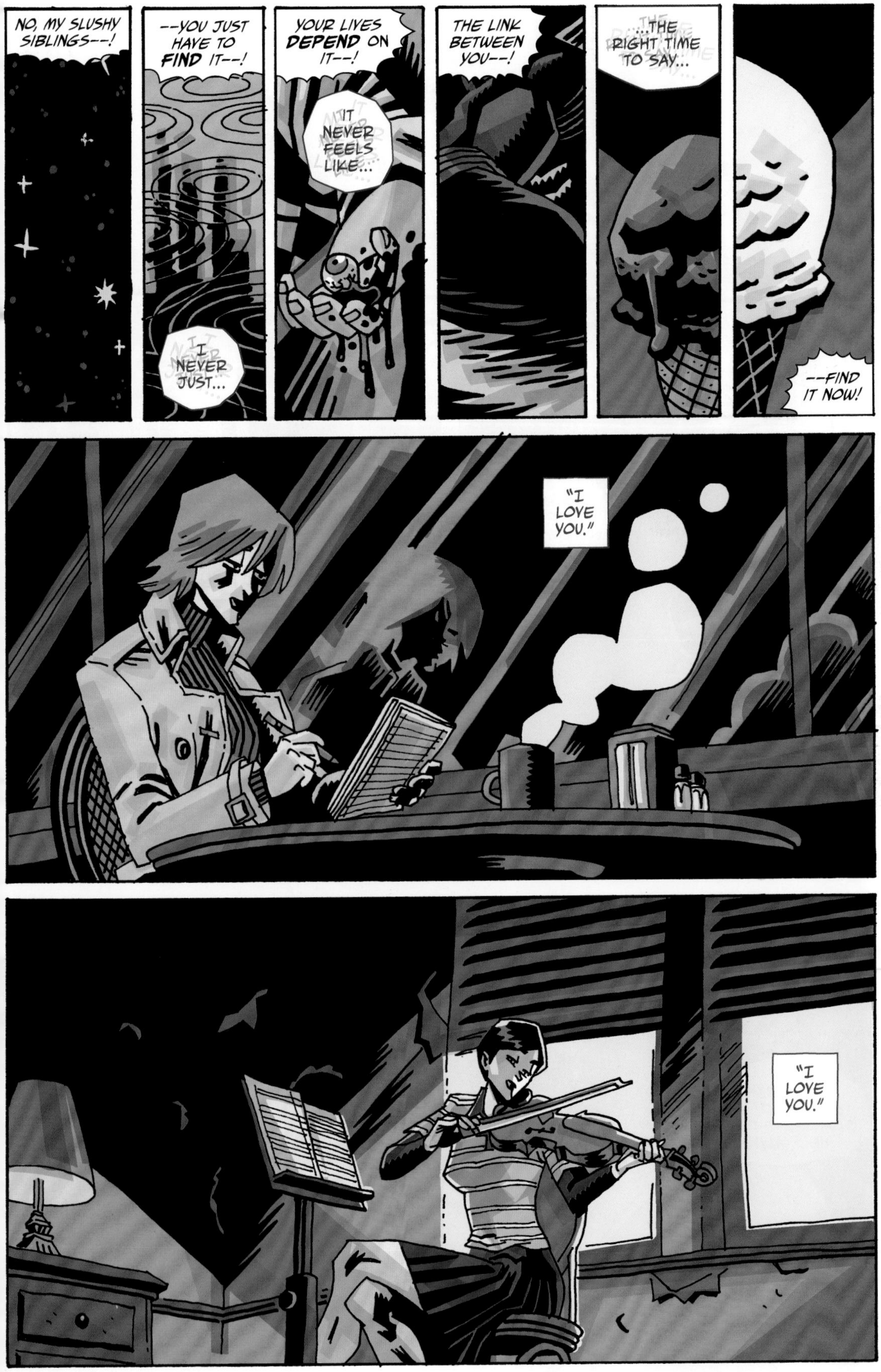
NO, MY SLUSHY SIBLINGS--!
--YOU JUST HAVE TO FIND IT--!
I NEVER JUST...
YOUR LIVES DEPEND ON IT--!
IT NEVER FEELS LIKE...
THE LINK BETWEEN YOU--!
...THE RIGHT TIME TO SAY...
--FIND IT NOW!
"I LOVE YOU."
"I LOVE YOU."

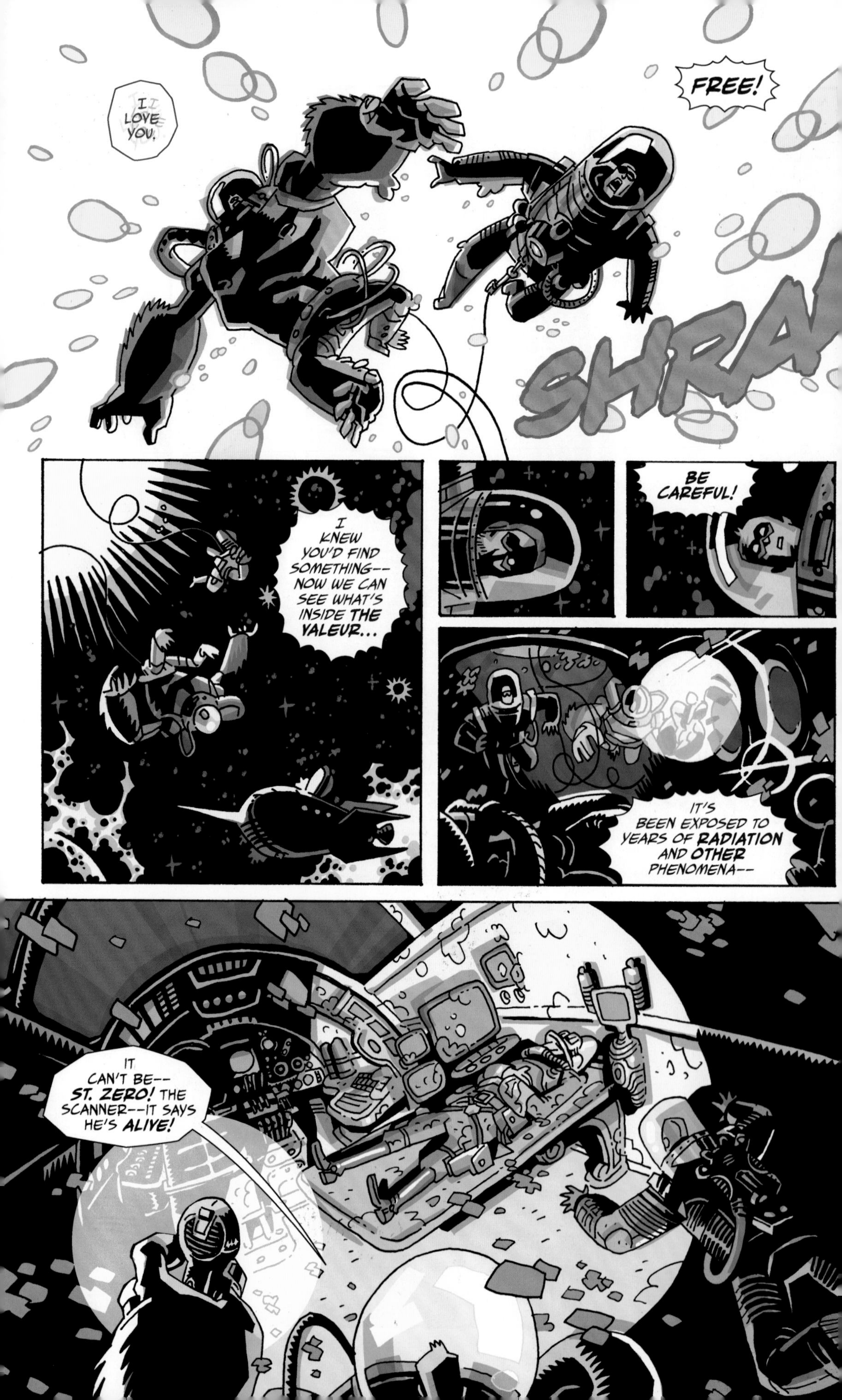

I LOVE YOU.
FREE!
SHRA
I KNEW YOU'D FIND SOMETHING-- NOW WE CAN SEE WHAT'S INSIDE THE VALEUR...
BE CAREFUL!
IT'S BEEN EXPOSED TO YEARS OF RADIATION AND OTHER PHENOMENA--
IT CAN'T BE-- ST. ZERO! THE SCANNER--IT SAYS HE'S ALIVE!

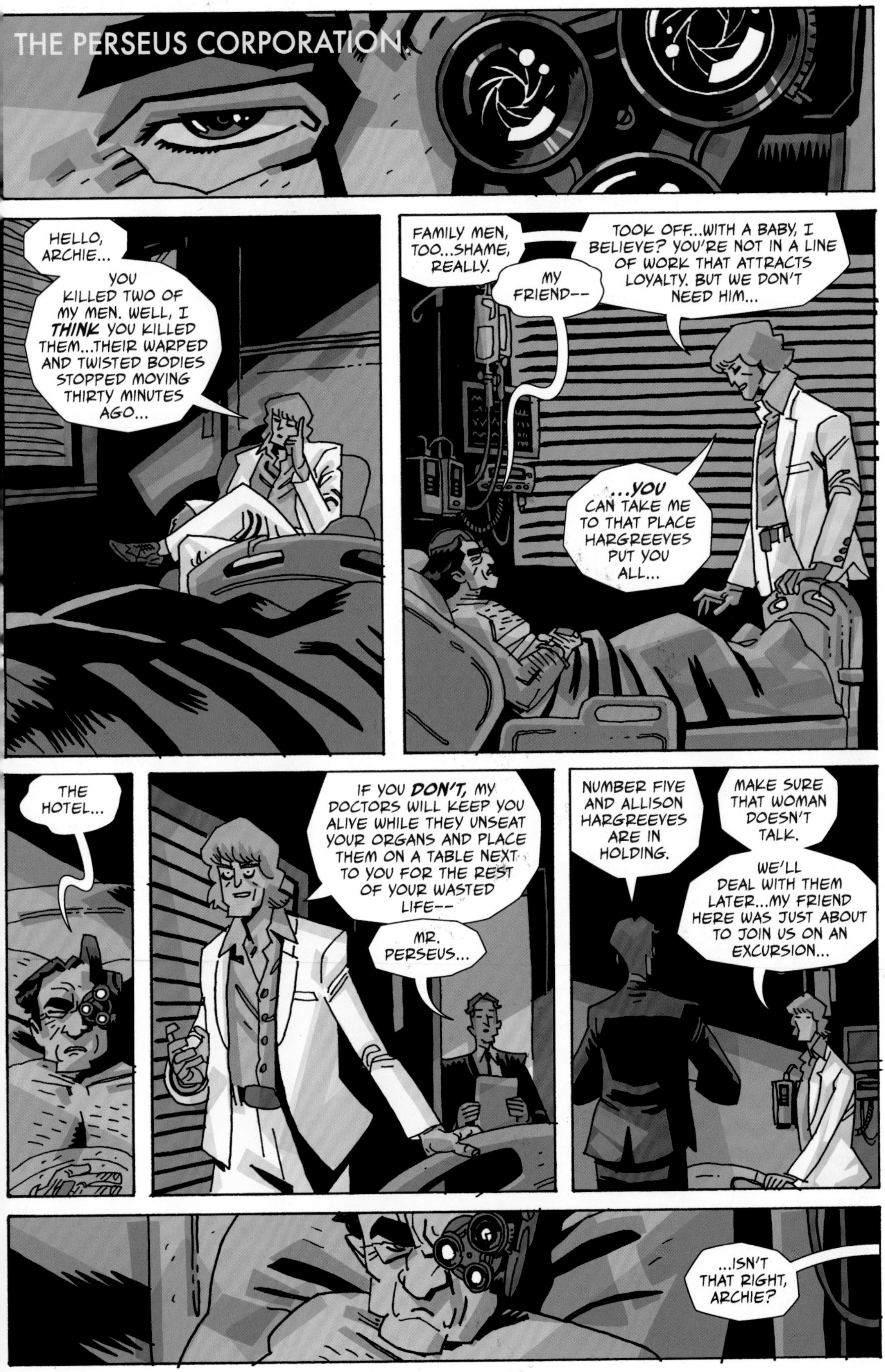
THE PERSEUS CORPORATION.
HELLO, ARCHIE...
YOU KILLED TWO OF MY MEN. WELL, I THINK YOU KILLED THEM...THEIR WARPED AND TWISTED BODIES STOPPED MOVING THIRTY MINUTES AGO...
FAMILY MEN, TOO...SHAME, REALLY.
MY FRIEND--
TOOK OFF...WITH A BABY, I BELIEVE? YOU'RE NOT IN A LINE OF WORK THAT ATTRACTS LOYALTY. BUT WE DON'T NEED HIM...
...YOU CAN TAKE ME TO THAT PLACE HARGREEVES PUT YOU ALL...
THE HOTEL...
IF YOU DON'T, MY DOCTORS WILL KEEP YOU ALIVE WHILE THEY UNSEAT YOUR ORGANS AND PLACE THEM ON A TABLE NEXT TO YOU FOR THE REST OF YOUR WASTED LIFE--
MR. PERSEUS...
NUMBER FIVE AND ALLISON HARGREEVES ARE IN HOLDING.
MAKE SURE THAT WOMAN DOESN'T TALK.
WE'LL DEAL WITH THEM LATER...MY FRIEND HERE WAS JUST ABOUT TO JOIN US ON AN EXCURSION...
...ISN'T THAT RIGHT, ARCHIE?

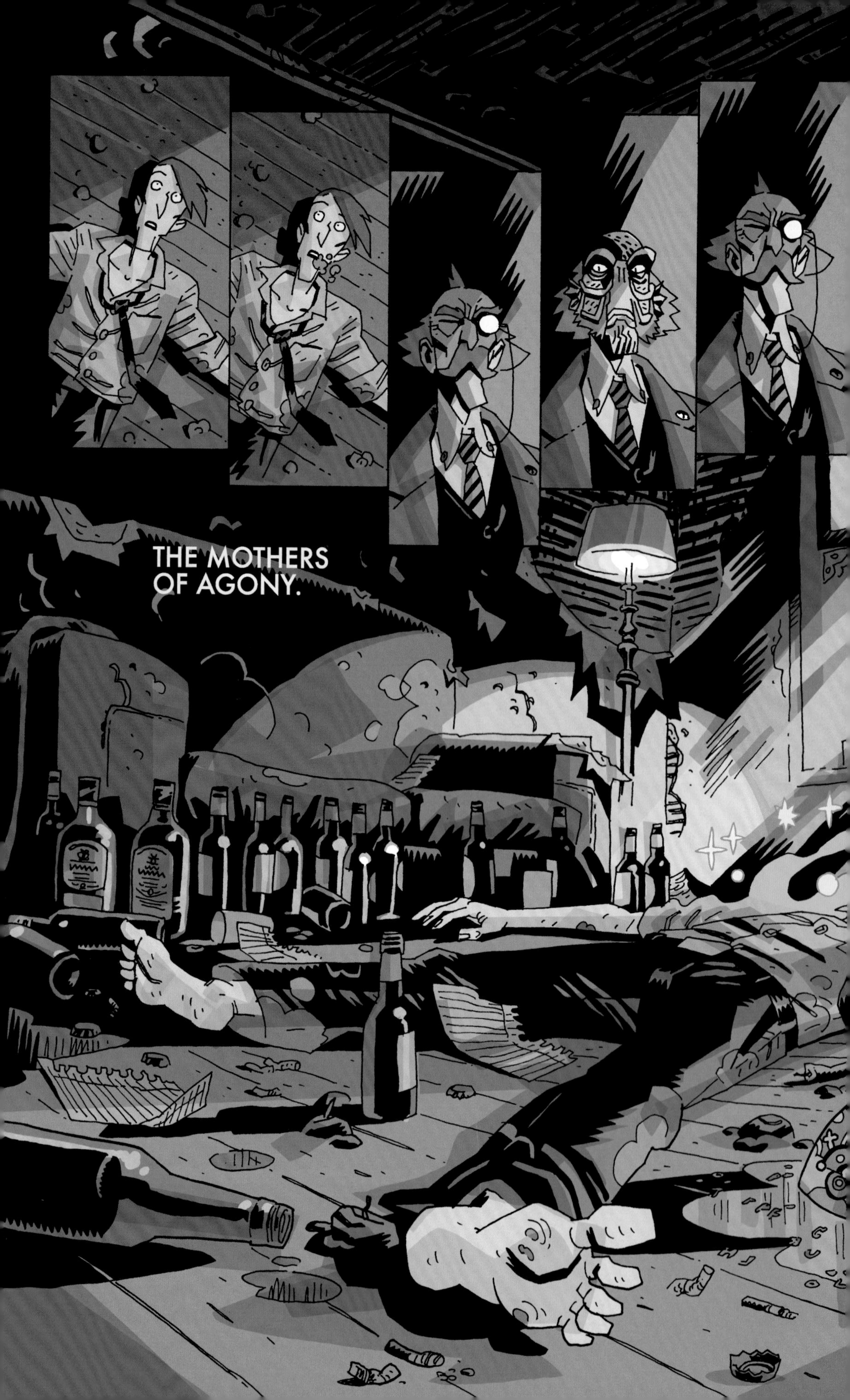
THE MOTHERS OF AGONY.

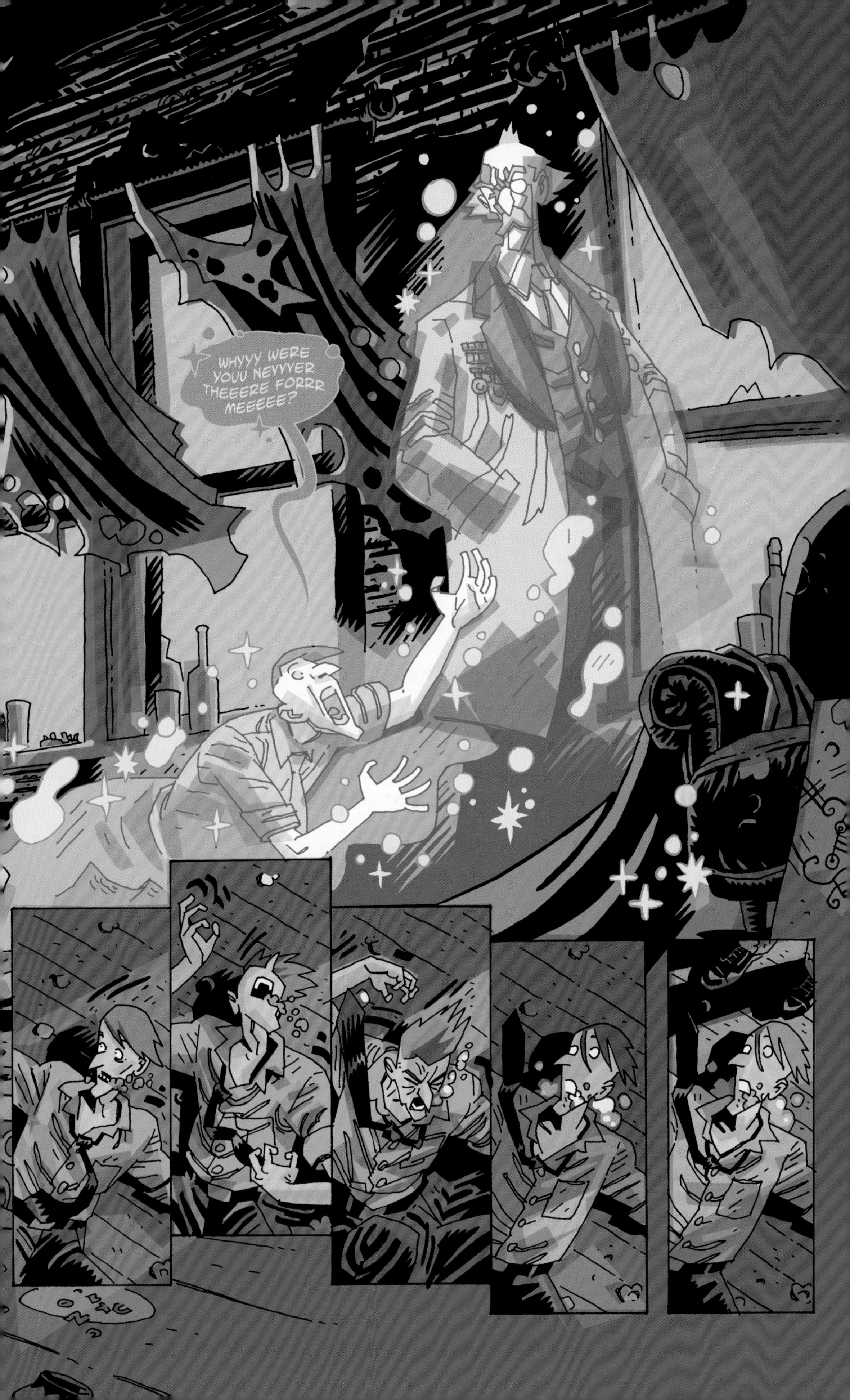
WHYYY WERE YOUU NEVYYER THEEERE FORRR MEEEEE?

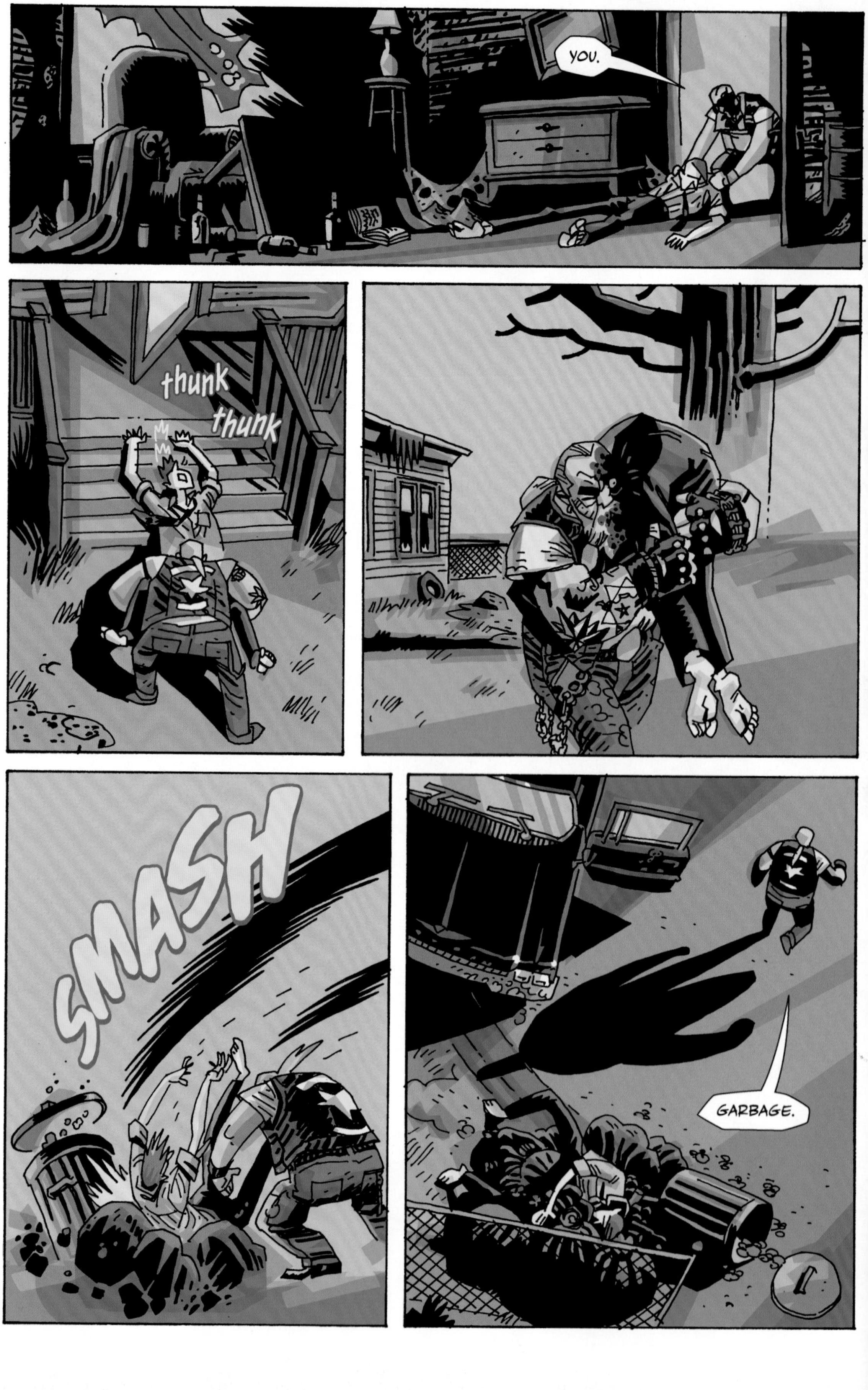
YOU.
thunk
thunk
SMASH
GARBAGE.

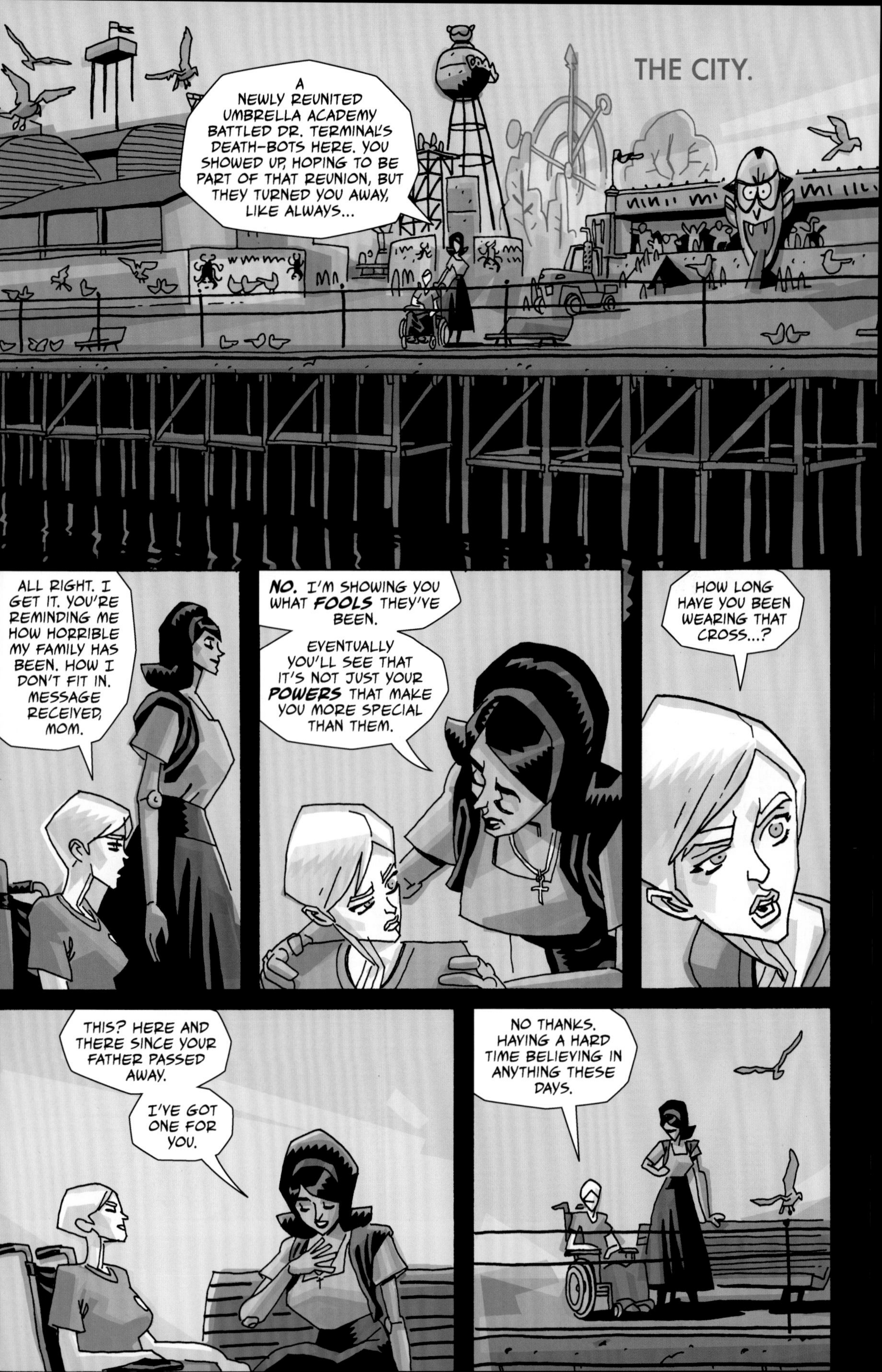
THE CITY.
A NEWLY REUNITED UMBRELLA ACADEMY BATTLED DR. TERMINAL'S DEATH-BOTS HERE. YOU SHOWED UP, HOPING TO BE PART OF THAT REUNION, BUT THEY TURNED YOU AWAY, LIKE ALWAYS...
ALL RIGHT. I GET IT. YOU'RE REMINDING ME HOW HORRIBLE MY FAMILY HAS BEEN. HOW I DON'T FIT IN. MESSAGE RECEIVED, MOM.
NO. I'M SHOWING YOU WHAT FOOLS THEY'VE BEEN.
EVENTUALLY YOU'LL SEE THAT IT'S NOT JUST YOUR POWERS THAT MAKE YOU MORE SPECIAL THAN THEM.
HOW LONG HAVE YOU BEEN WEARING THAT CROSS...?
THIS? HERE AND THERE SINCE YOUR FATHER PASSED AWAY.
I'VE GOT ONE FOR YOU.
NO THANKS. HAVING A HARD TIME BELIEVING IN ANYTHING THESE DAYS.

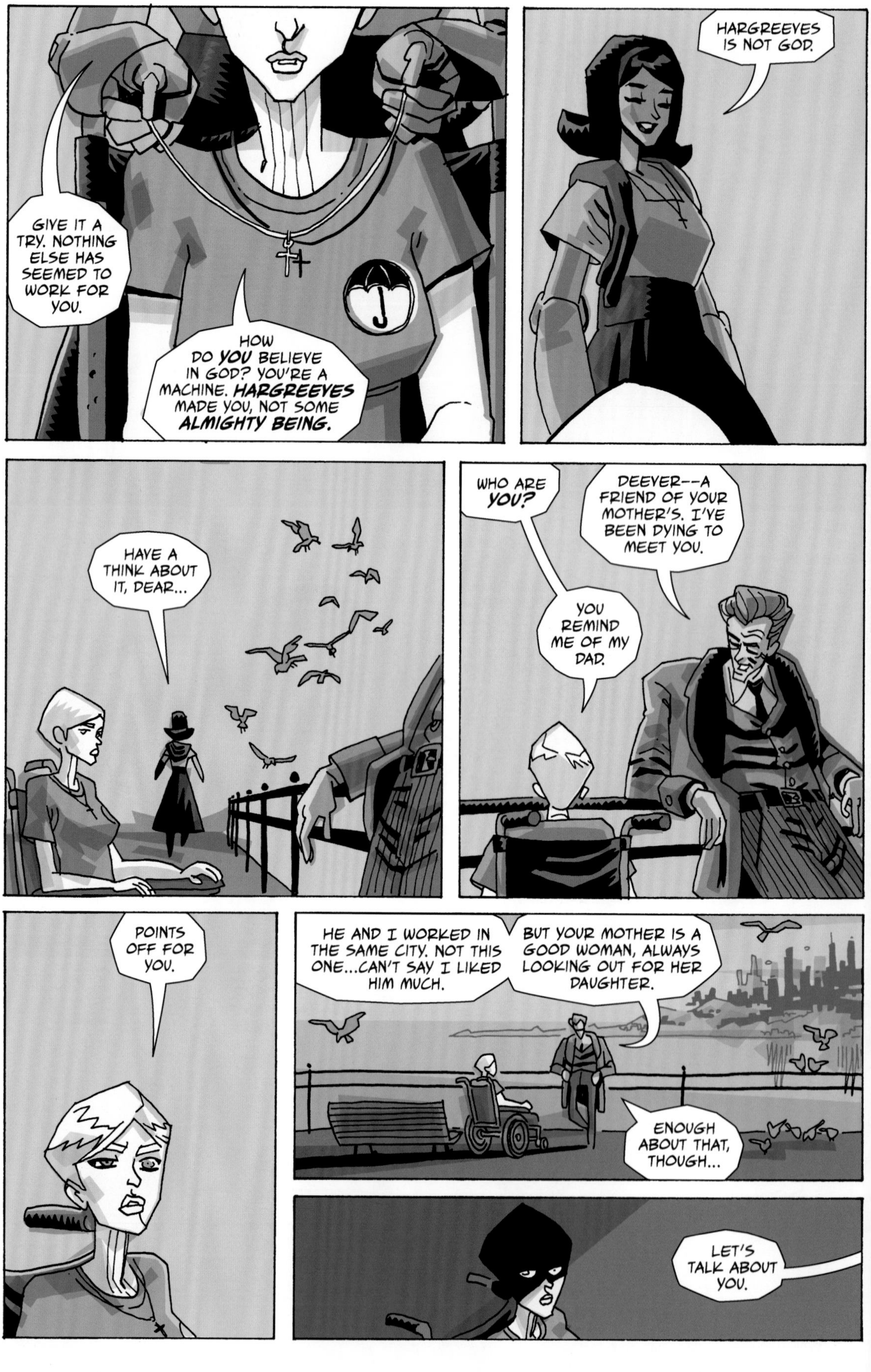
GIVE IT A TRY. NOTHING ELSE HAS SEEMED TO WORK FOR YOU.
HOW DO YOU BELIEVE IN GOD? YOU'RE A MACHINE. HARGREEVES MADE YOU, NOT SOME ALMIGHTY BEING.
HARGREEVES IS NOT GOD.
HAVE A THINK ABOUT IT, DEAR...
WHO ARE YOU?
DEEVER--A FRIEND OF YOUR MOTHER'S. I'VE BEEN DYING TO MEET YOU.
YOU REMIND ME OF MY DAD.
POINTS OFF FOR YOU.
HE AND I WORKED IN THE SAME CITY. NOT THIS ONE...CAN'T SAY I LIKED HIM MUCH.
BUT YOUR MOTHER IS A GOOD WOMAN, ALWAYS LOOKING OUT FOR HER DAUGHTER.
ENOUGH ABOUT THAT, THOUGH...
LET'S TALK ABOUT YOU.

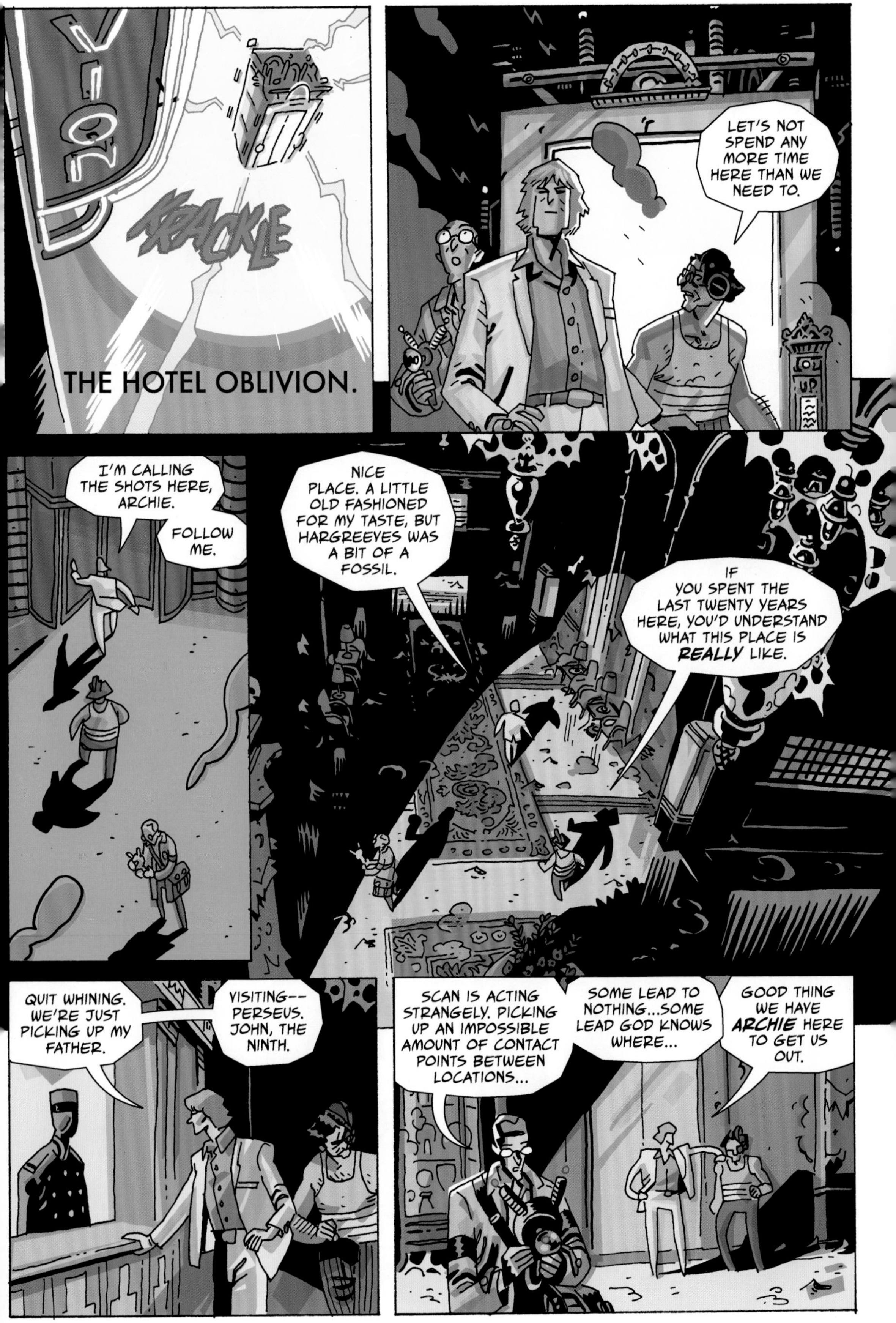
KRACKLE
THE HOTEL OBLIVION.
LET'S NOT SPEND ANY MORE TIME HERE THAN WE NEED TO.
I'M CALLING THE SHOTS HERE, ARCHIE.
FOLLOW ME.
NICE PLACE. A LITTLE OLD FASHIONED FOR MY TASTE, BUT HARGREEVES WAS A BIT OF A FOSSIL.
IF YOU SPENT THE LAST TWENTY YEARS HERE, YOU'D UNDERSTAND WHAT THIS PLACE IS **REALLY** LIKE.
QUIT WHINING. WE'RE JUST PICKING UP MY FATHER.
VISITING-- PERSEUS. JOHN, THE NINTH.
SCAN IS ACTING STRANGELY. PICKING UP AN IMPOSSIBLE AMOUNT OF CONTACT POINTS BETWEEN LOCATIONS...
SOME LEAD TO NOTHING...SOME LEAD GOD KNOWS WHERE...
GOOD THING WE HAVE **ARCHIE** HERE TO GET US OUT.

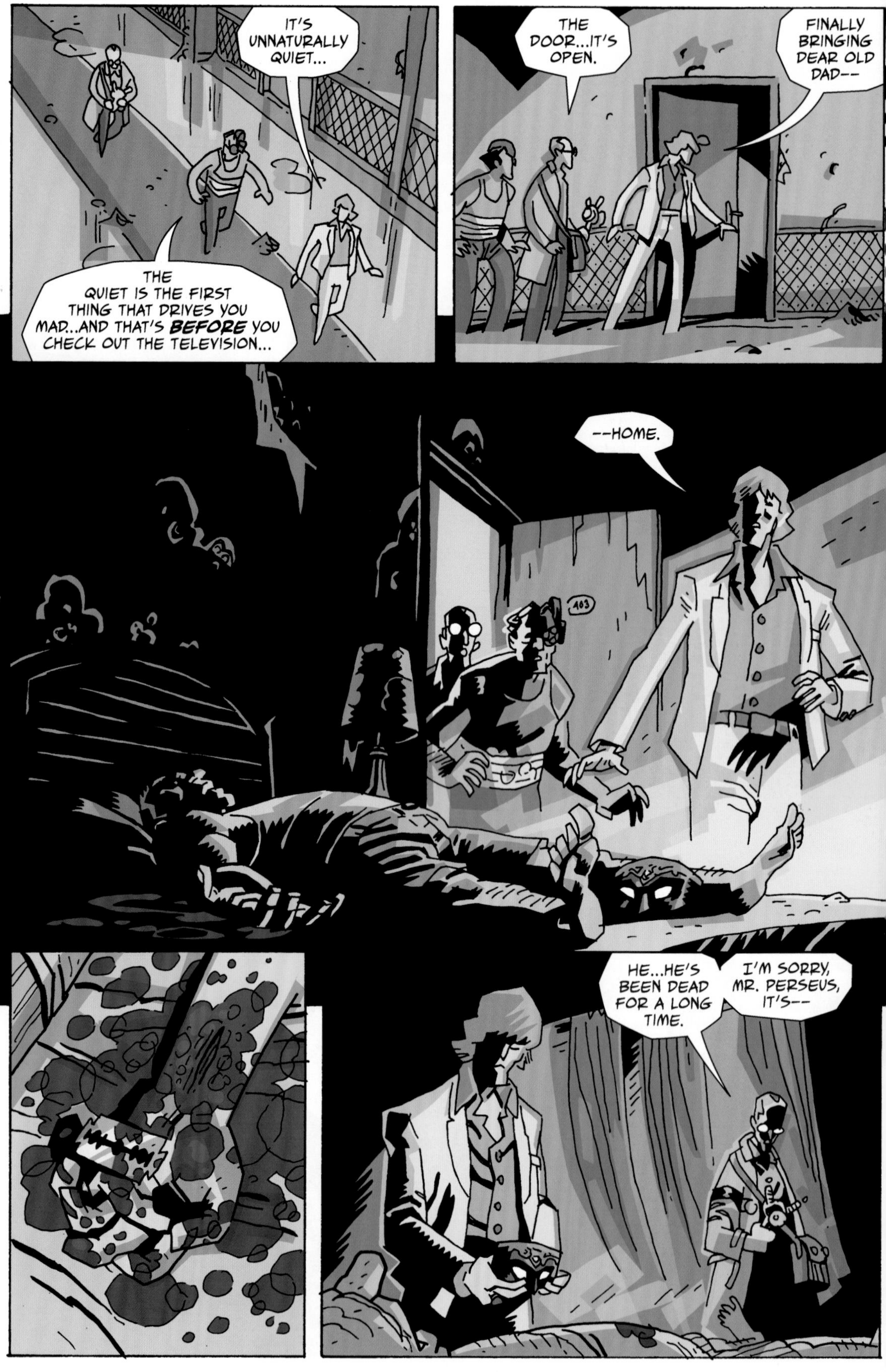
IT'S UNNATURALLY QUIET...
THE QUIET IS THE FIRST THING THAT DRIVES YOU MAD...AND THAT'S **BEFORE** YOU CHECK OUT THE TELEVISION...
THE DOOR...IT'S OPEN.
FINALLY BRINGING DEAR OLD DAD--
--HOME.
403
HE...HE'S BEEN DEAD FOR A LONG TIME.
I'M SORRY, MR. PERSEUS, IT'S--

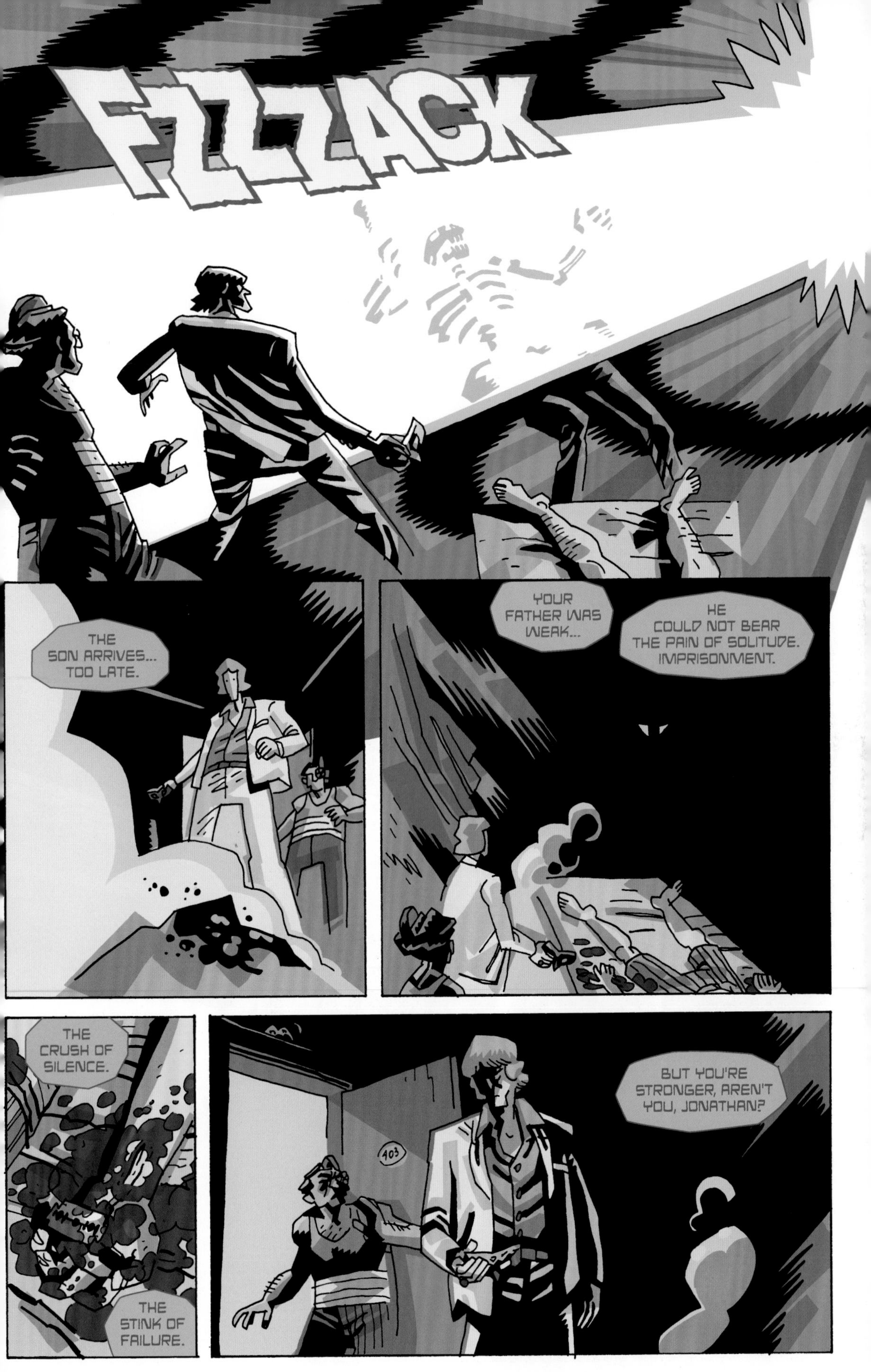
FZZACK
THE SON ARRIVES... TOO LATE.
YOUR FATHER WAS WEAK...
HE COULD NOT BEAR THE PAIN OF SOLITUDE. IMPRISONMENT.
THE CRUSH OF SILENCE.
THE STINK OF FAILURE.
403
BUT YOU'RE STRONGER, AREN'T YOU, JONATHAN?

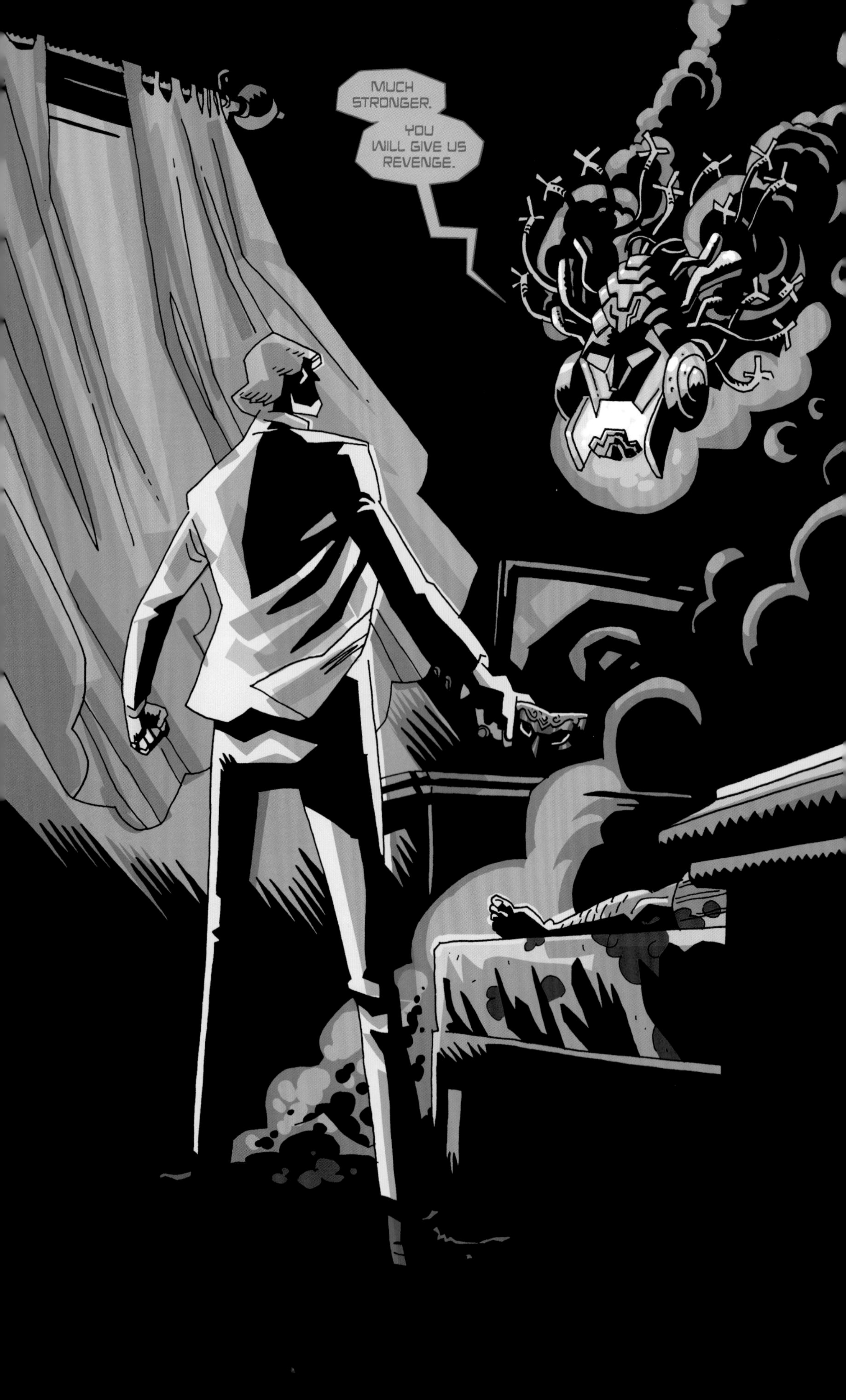
MUCH STRONGER.
YOU WILL GIVE US REVENGE.

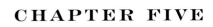

CHAPTER FIVE

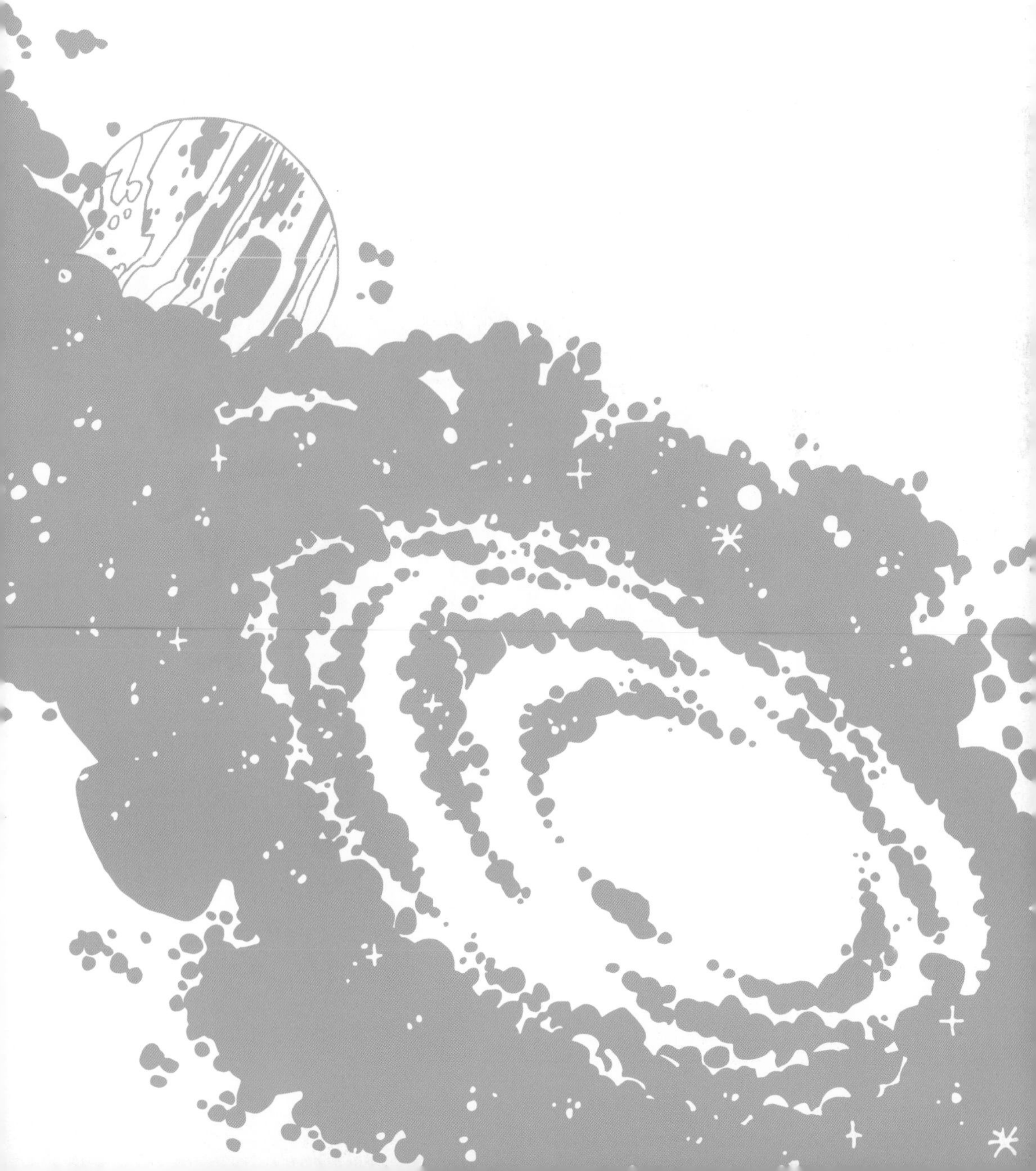

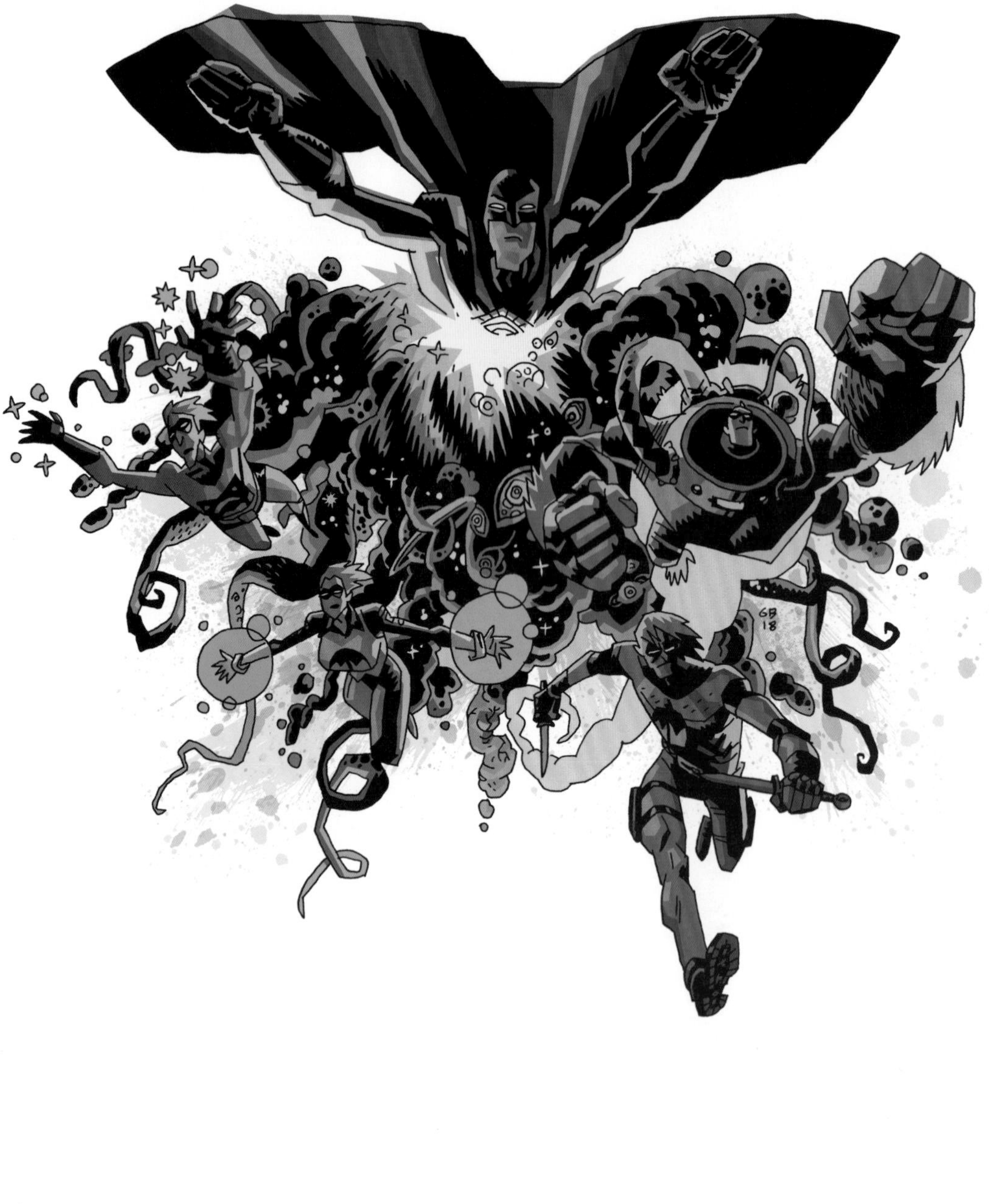
GB
18

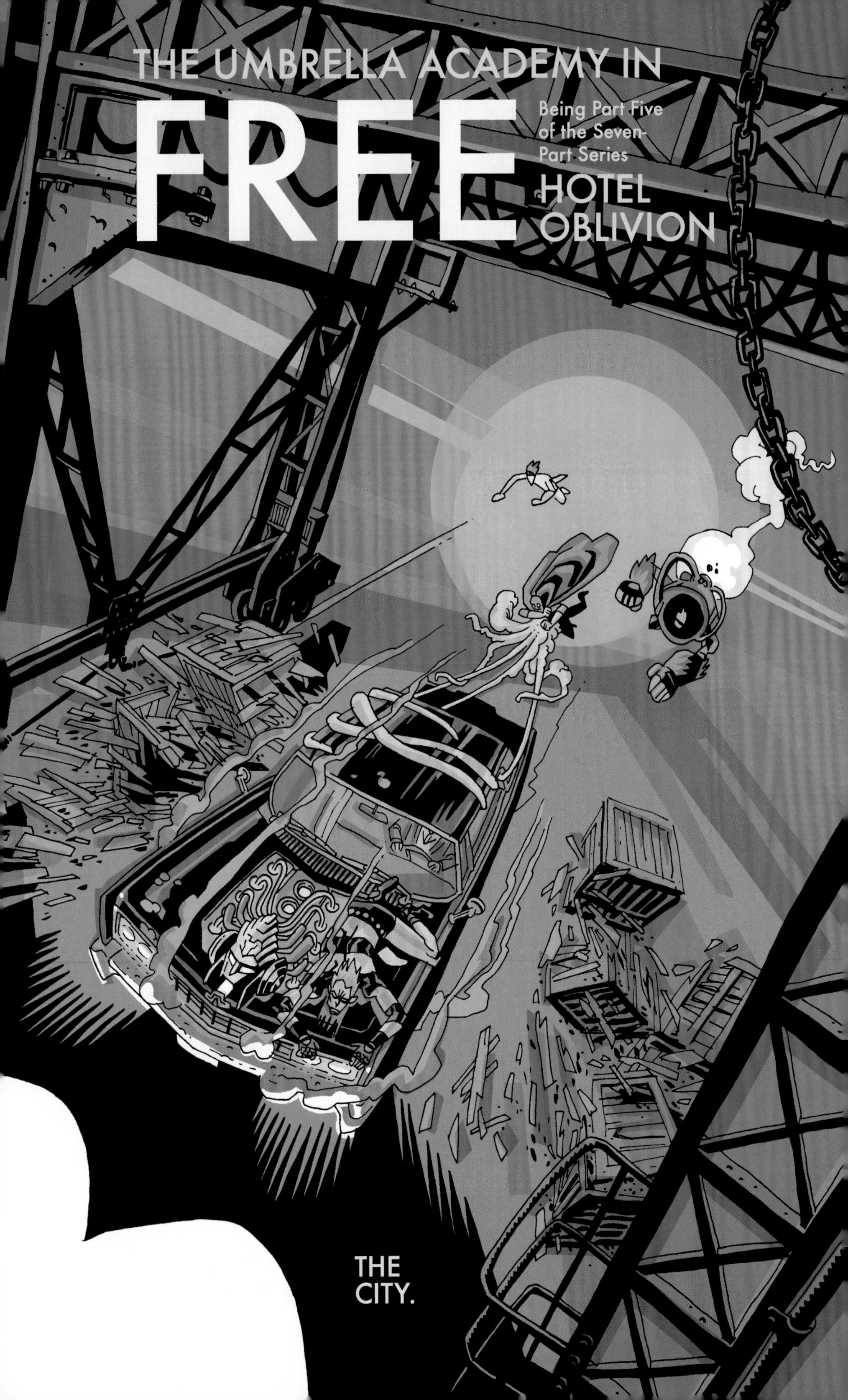
THE UMBRELLA ACADEMY IN
FREE
Being Part Five of the Seven-Part Series
HOTEL OBLIVION
THE CITY.

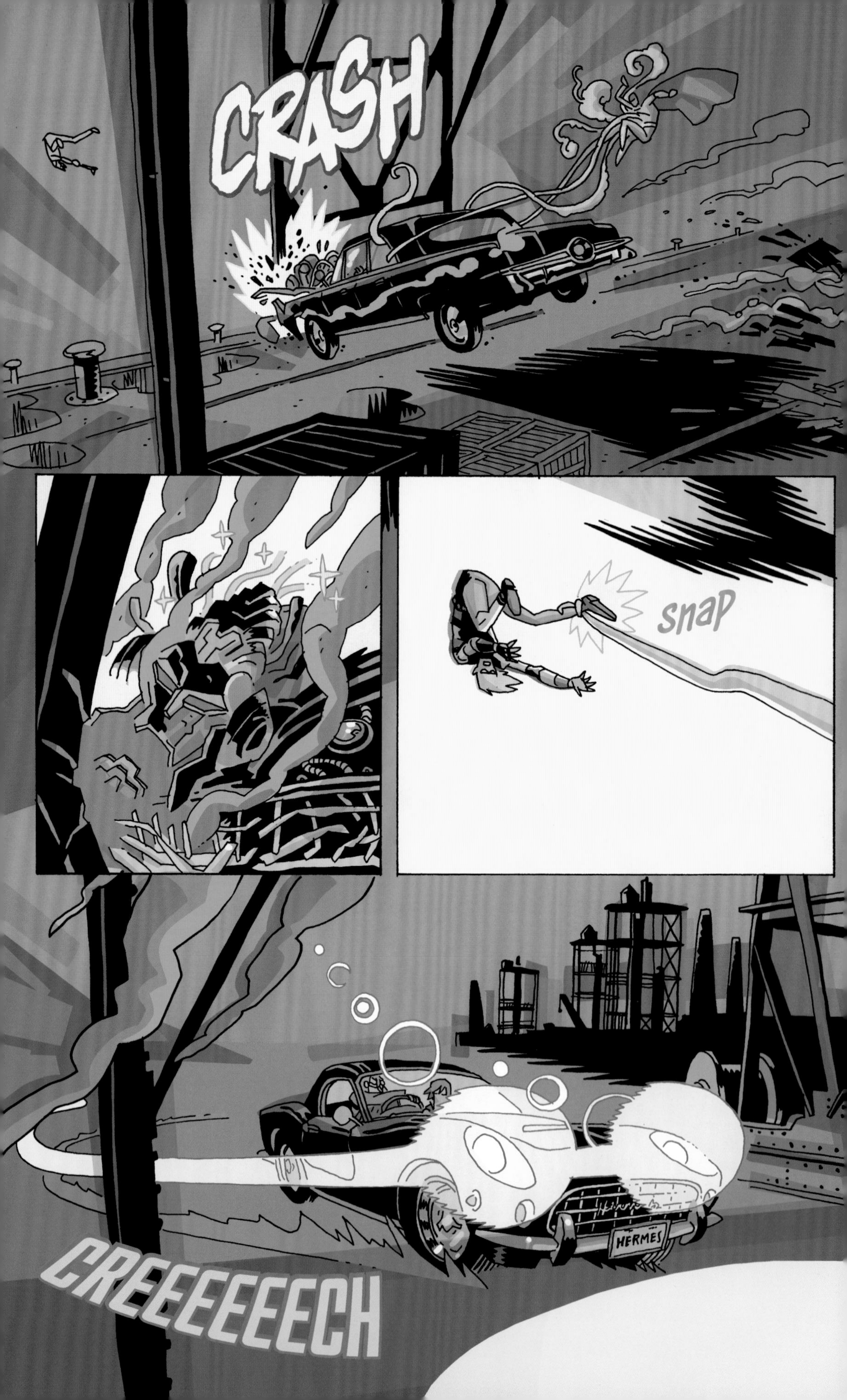
CRASH
SNAP
HERMES
CREEEEEEECH

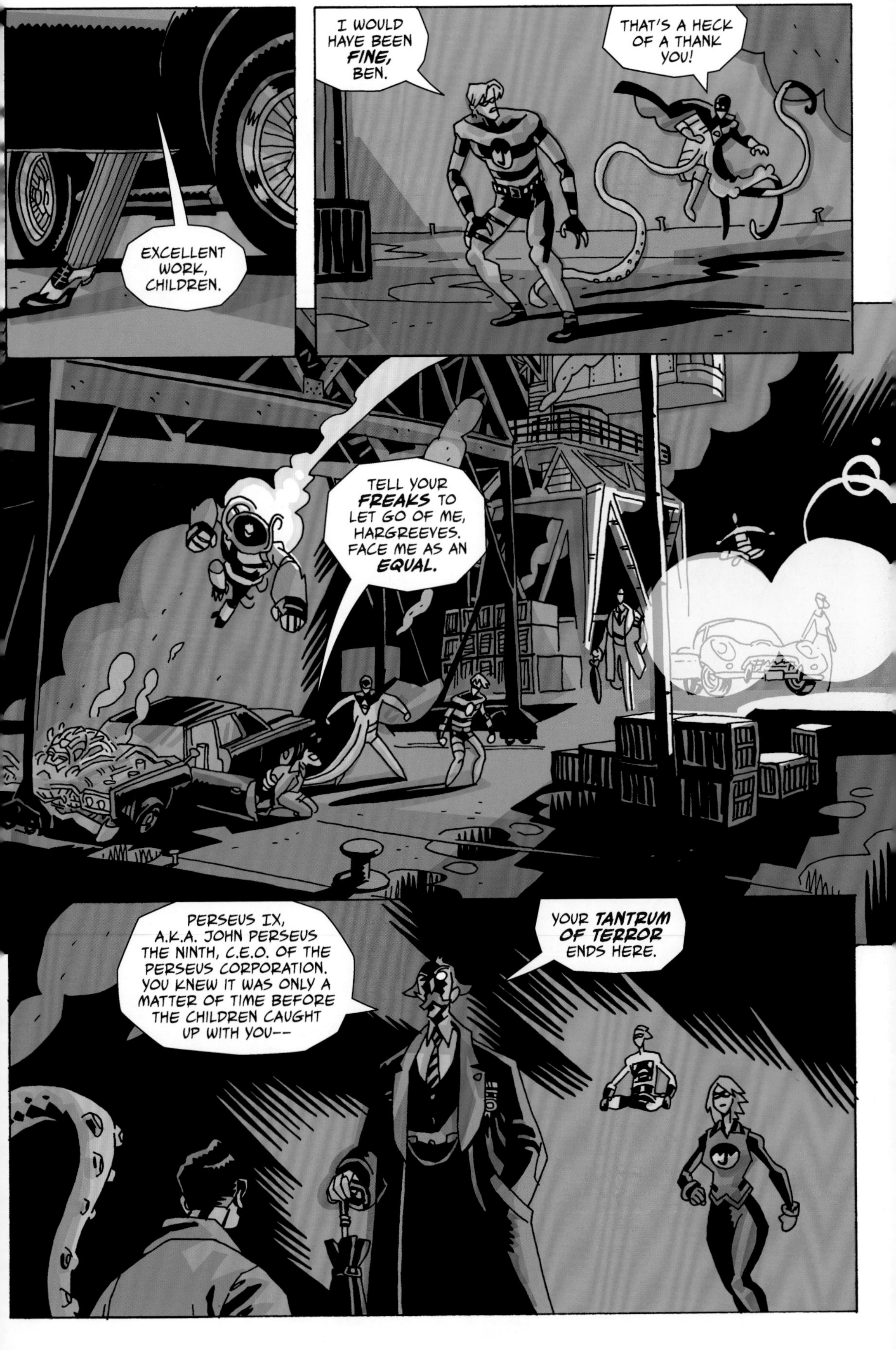
EXCELLENT WORK, CHILDREN.
I WOULD HAVE BEEN FINE, BEN.
THAT'S A HECK OF A THANK YOU!
TELL YOUR FREAKS TO LET GO OF ME, HARGREEVES. FACE ME AS AN EQUAL.
PERSEUS IX, A.K.A. JOHN PERSEUS THE NINTH, C.E.O. OF THE PERSEUS CORPORATION. YOU KNEW IT WAS ONLY A MATTER OF TIME BEFORE THE CHILDREN CAUGHT UP WITH YOU--
YOUR TANTRUM OF TERROR ENDS HERE.

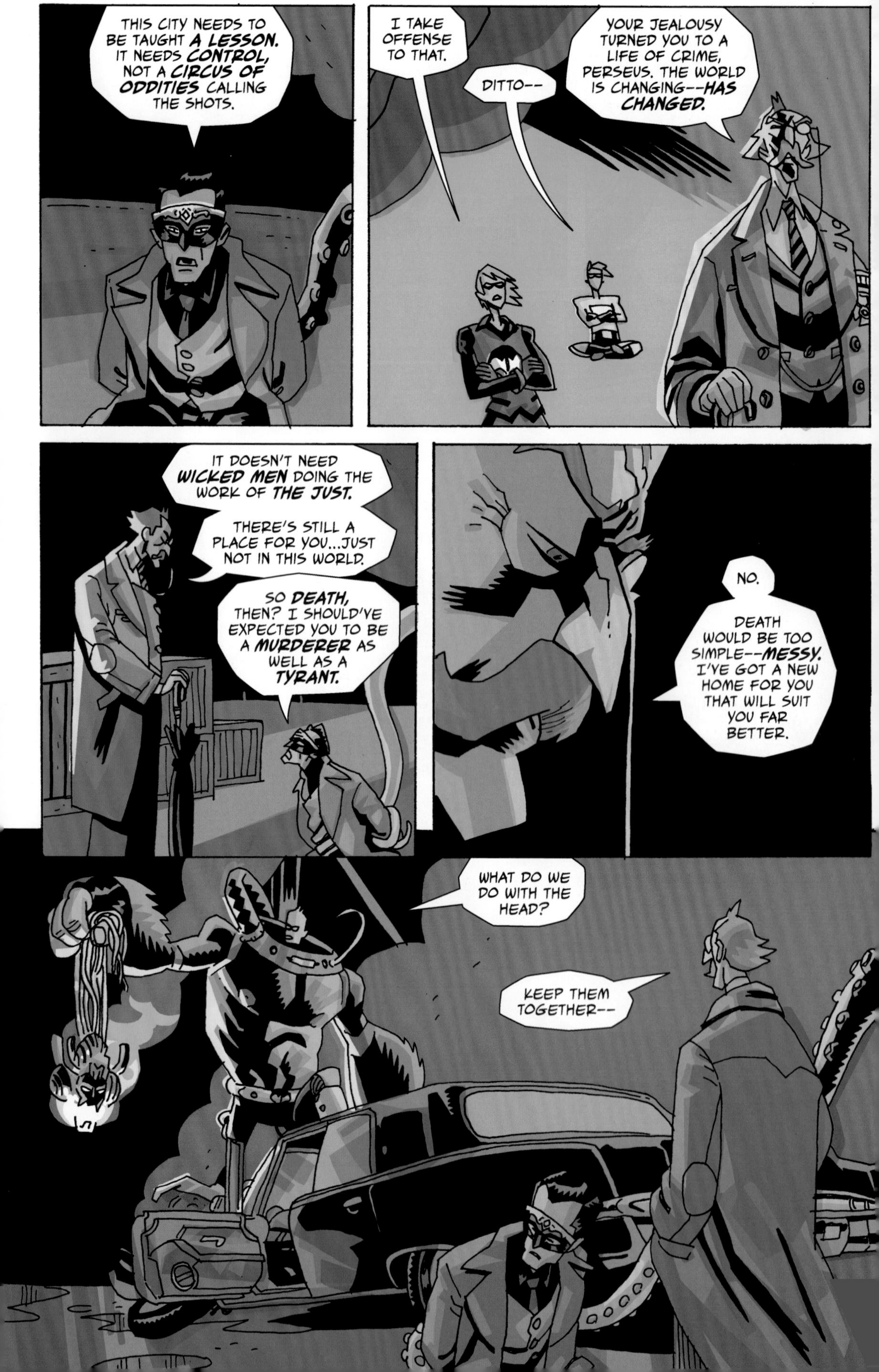
THIS CITY NEEDS TO BE TAUGHT A LESSON. IT NEEDS CONTROL, NOT A CIRCUS OF ODDITIES CALLING THE SHOTS.
I TAKE OFFENSE TO THAT.
DITTO--
YOUR JEALOUSY TURNED YOU TO A LIFE OF CRIME, PERSEUS. THE WORLD IS CHANGING--HAS CHANGED.
IT DOESN'T NEED WICKED MEN DOING THE WORK OF THE JUST.
THERE'S STILL A PLACE FOR YOU...JUST NOT IN THIS WORLD.
SO DEATH, THEN? I SHOULD'VE EXPECTED YOU TO BE A MURDERER AS WELL AS A TYRANT.
NO.
DEATH WOULD BE TOO SIMPLE--MESSY. I'VE GOT A NEW HOME FOR YOU THAT WILL SUIT YOU FAR BETTER.
WHAT DO WE DO WITH THE HEAD?
KEEP THEM TOGETHER--

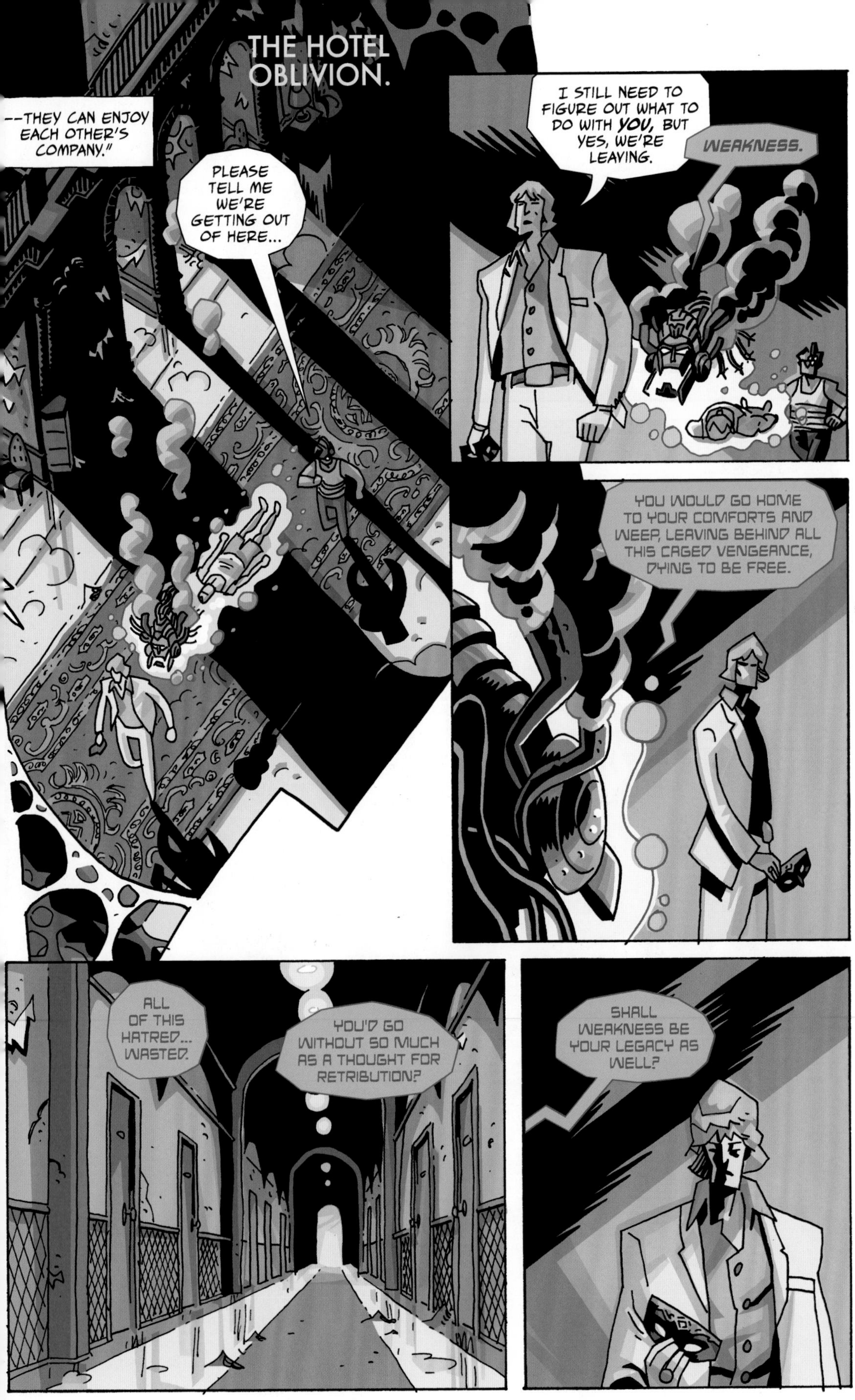
THE HOTEL OBLIVION.
--THEY CAN ENJOY EACH OTHER'S COMPANY."
PLEASE TELL ME WE'RE GETTING OUT OF HERE...
I STILL NEED TO FIGURE OUT WHAT TO DO WITH *YOU,* BUT YES, WE'RE LEAVING.
WEAKNESS.
YOU WOULD GO HOME TO YOUR COMFORTS AND WEEP, LEAVING BEHIND ALL THIS CAGED VENGEANCE, DYING TO BE FREE.
ALL OF THIS HATRED... WASTED.
YOU'D GO WITHOUT SO MUCH AS A THOUGHT FOR RETRIBUTION?
SHALL WEAKNESS BE YOUR LEGACY AS WELL?

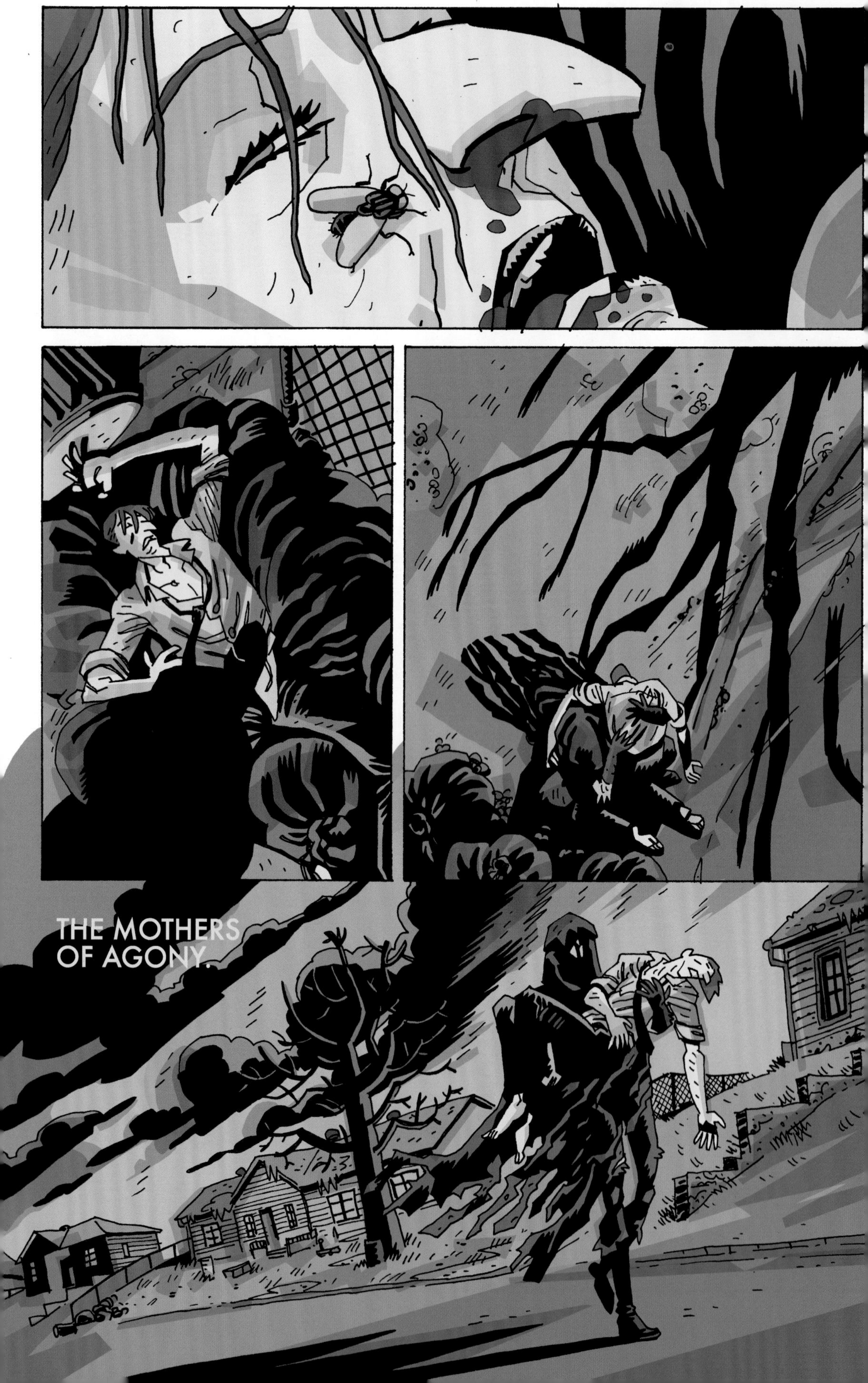
THE MOTHERS OF AGONY.

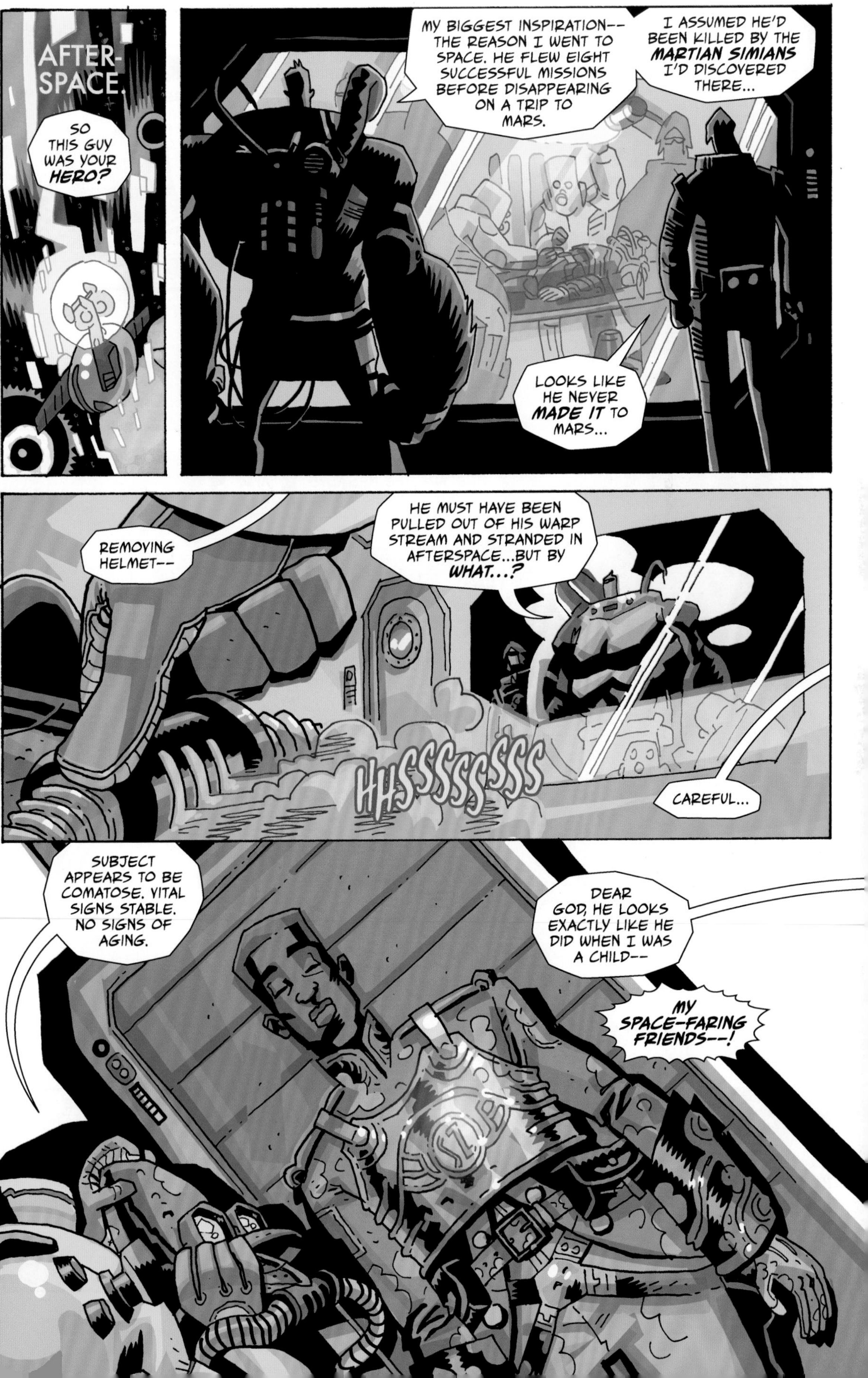
AFTER-SPACE.
SO THIS GUY WAS YOUR HERO?
MY BIGGEST INSPIRATION-- THE REASON I WENT TO SPACE. HE FLEW EIGHT SUCCESSFUL MISSIONS BEFORE DISAPPEARING ON A TRIP TO MARS.
I ASSUMED HE'D BEEN KILLED BY THE MARTIAN SIMIANS I'D DISCOVERED THERE...
LOOKS LIKE HE NEVER MADE IT TO MARS...
REMOVING HELMET--
HE MUST HAVE BEEN PULLED OUT OF HIS WARP STREAM AND STRANDED IN AFTERSPACE...BUT BY WHAT...?
HHSSSSSSSS
CAREFUL...
SUBJECT APPEARS TO BE COMATOSE. VITAL SIGNS STABLE. NO SIGNS OF AGING.
DEAR GOD, HE LOOKS EXACTLY LIKE HE DID WHEN I WAS A CHILD--
MY SPACE-FARING FRIENDS--!

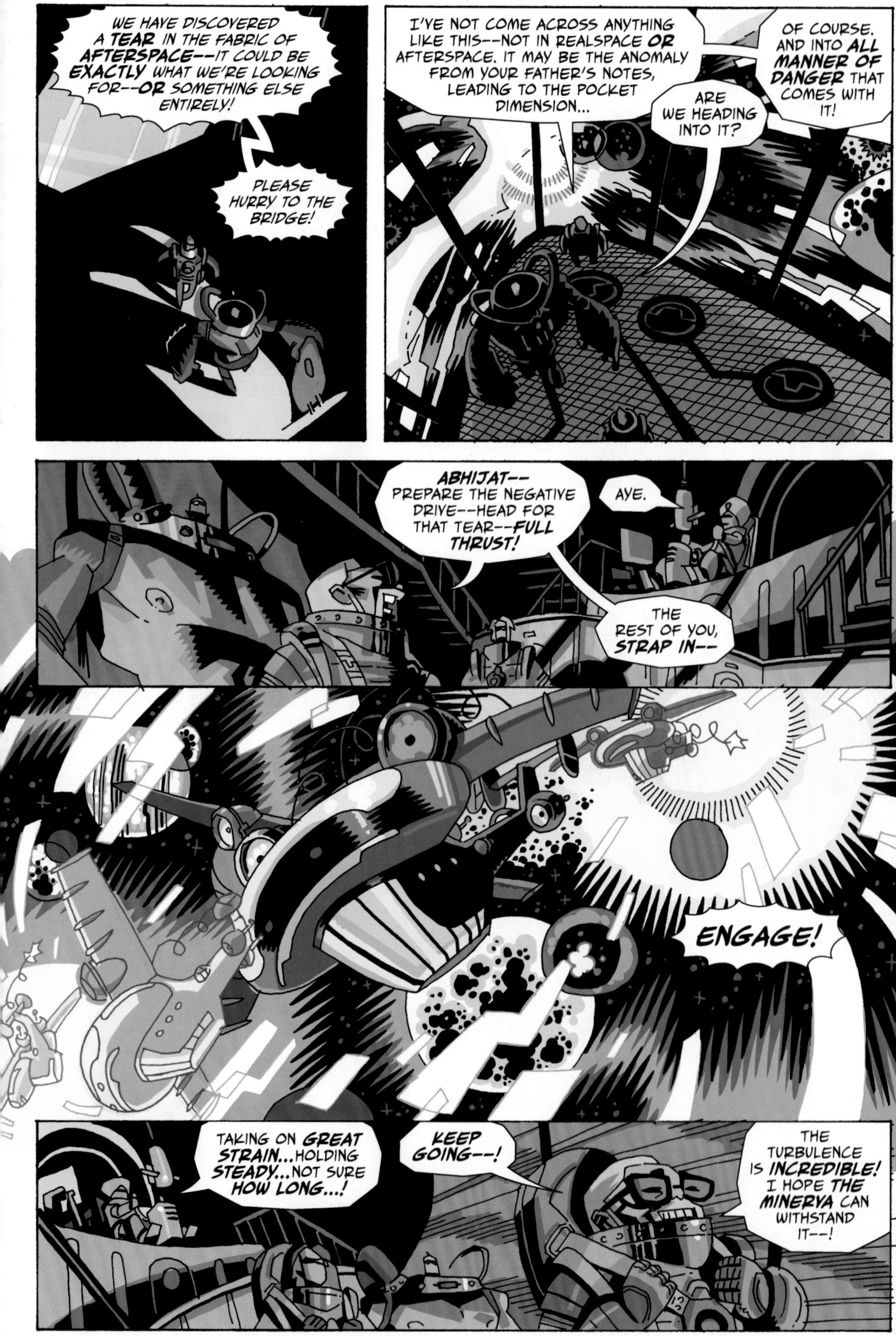
WE HAVE DISCOVERED A TEAR IN THE FABRIC OF AFTERSPACE--IT COULD BE EXACTLY WHAT WE'RE LOOKING FOR--OR SOMETHING ELSE ENTIRELY!
PLEASE HURRY TO THE BRIDGE!
I'VE NOT COME ACROSS ANYTHING LIKE THIS--NOT IN REALSPACE OR AFTERSPACE. IT MAY BE THE ANOMALY FROM YOUR FATHER'S NOTES, LEADING TO THE POCKET DIMENSION...
ARE WE HEADING INTO IT?
OF COURSE. AND INTO ALL MANNER OF DANGER THAT COMES WITH IT!
ABHIJAT-- PREPARE THE NEGATIVE DRIVE--HEAD FOR THAT TEAR--FULL THRUST!
AYE.
THE REST OF YOU, STRAP IN--
ENGAGE!
TAKING ON GREAT STRAIN...HOLDING STEADY...NOT SURE HOW LONG...!
KEEP GOING--!
THE TURBULENCE IS INCREDIBLE! I HOPE THE MINERVA CAN WITHSTAND IT--!

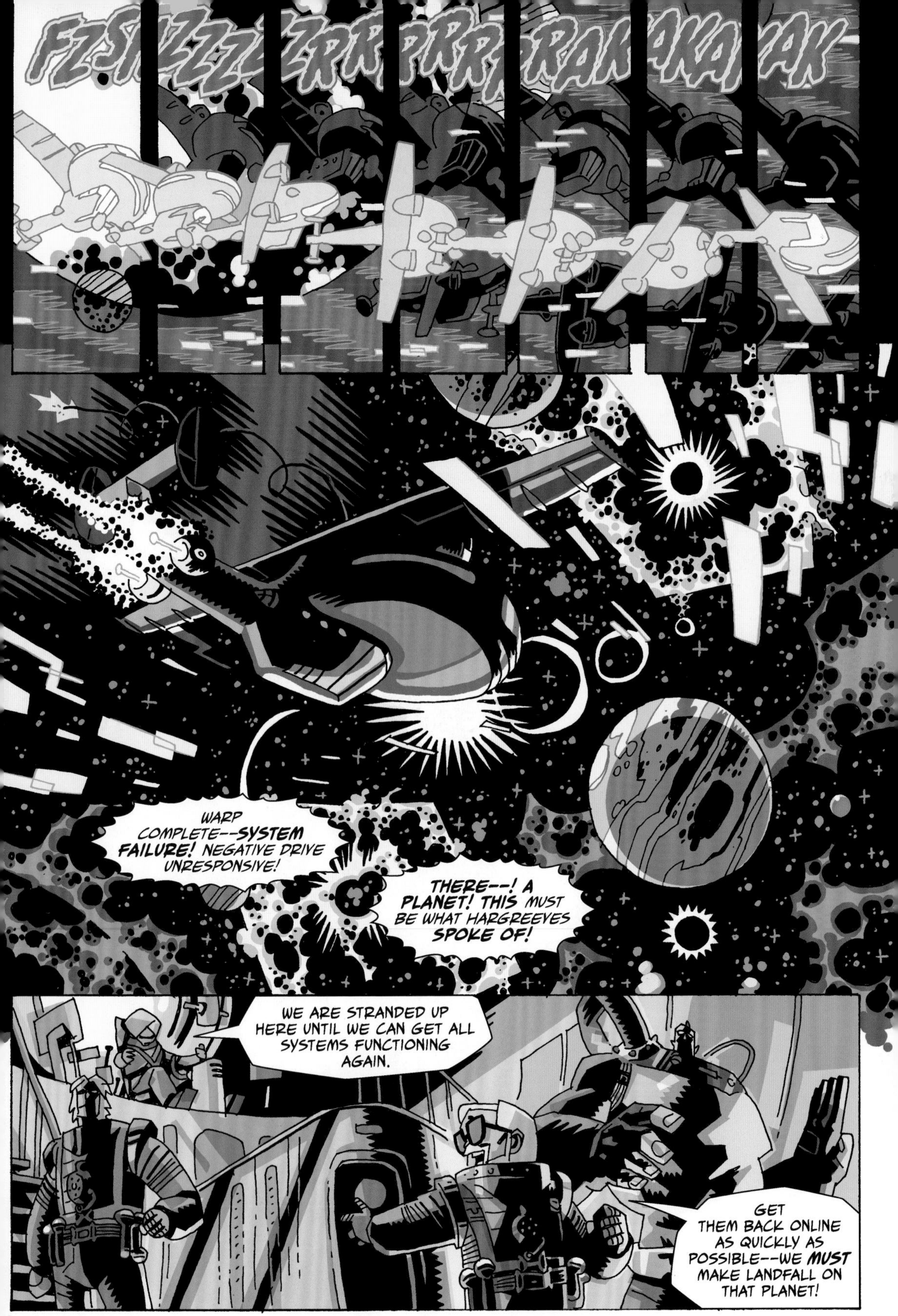
FZSHZZZZZZRRRRPRRRRAKAKAKAK
WARP COMPLETE--SYSTEM FAILURE! NEGATIVE DRIVE UNRESPONSIVE!
THERE--! A PLANET! THIS MUST BE WHAT HARGREEVES SPOKE OF!
WE ARE STRANDED UP HERE UNTIL WE CAN GET ALL SYSTEMS FUNCTIONING AGAIN.
GET THEM BACK ONLINE AS QUICKLY AS POSSIBLE--WE MUST MAKE LANDFALL ON THAT PLANET!

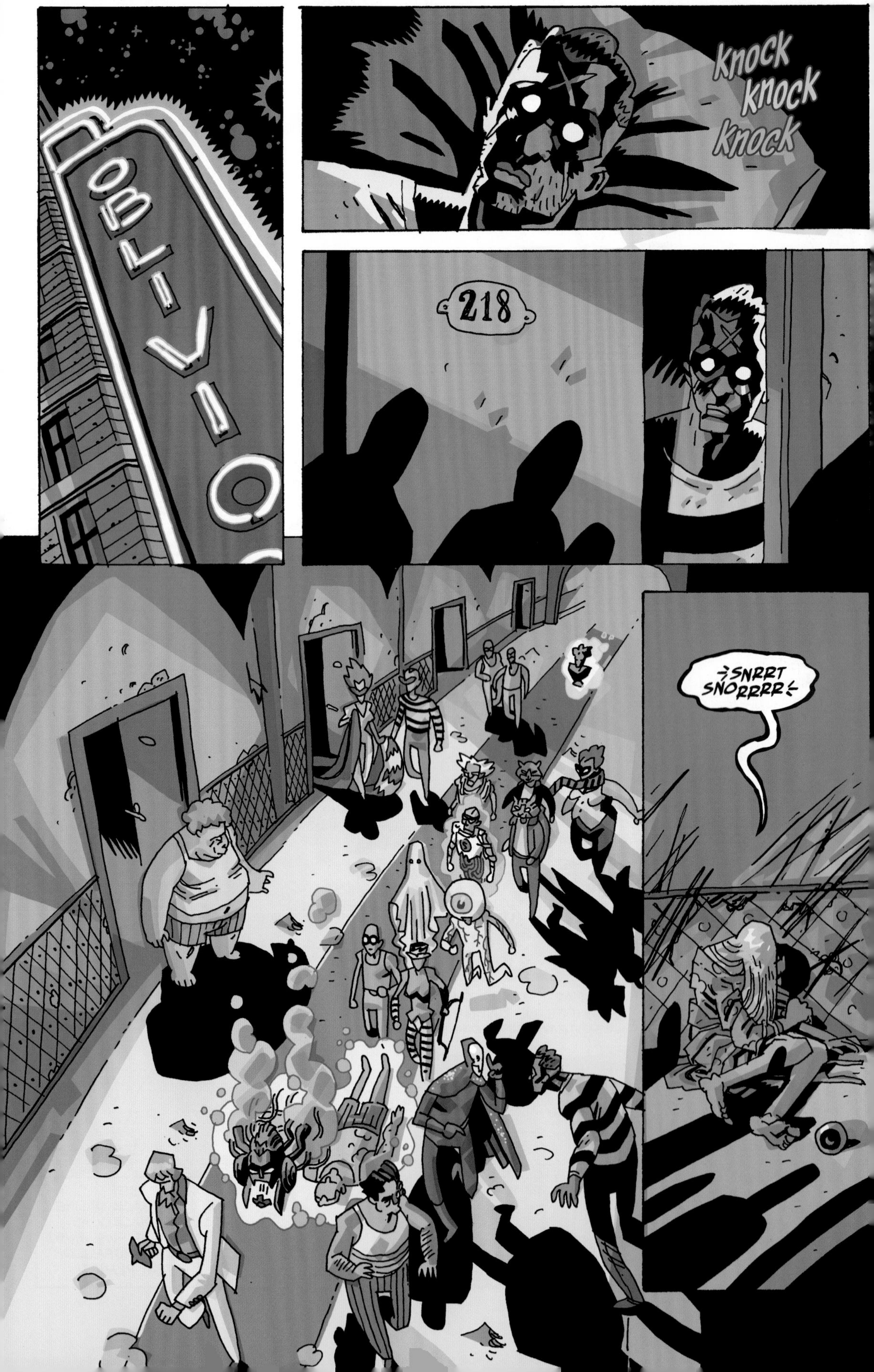
OBLIVIO
knock knock knock
218
SNRRT SNORRRR

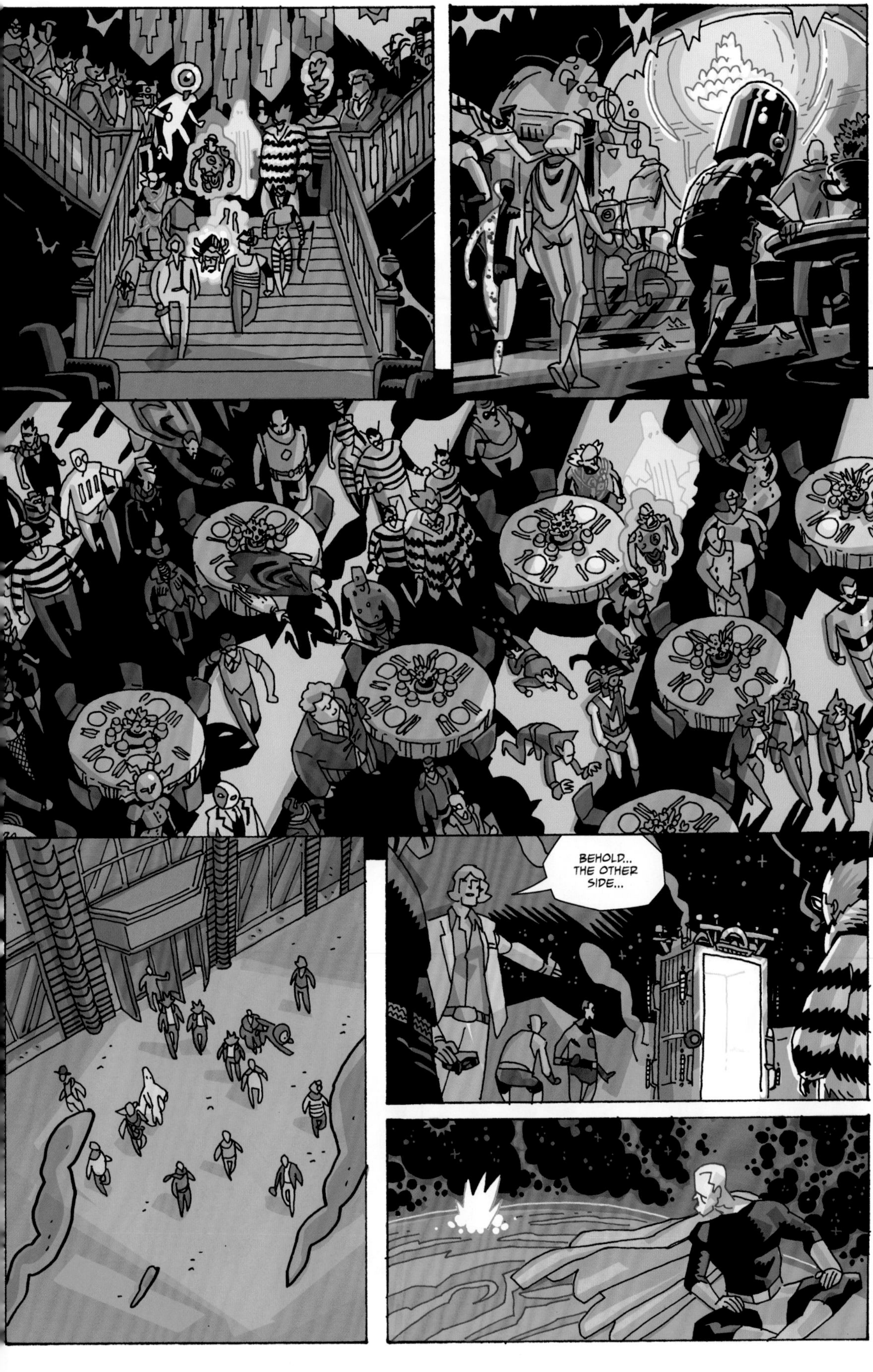
BEHOLD... THE OTHER SIDE...

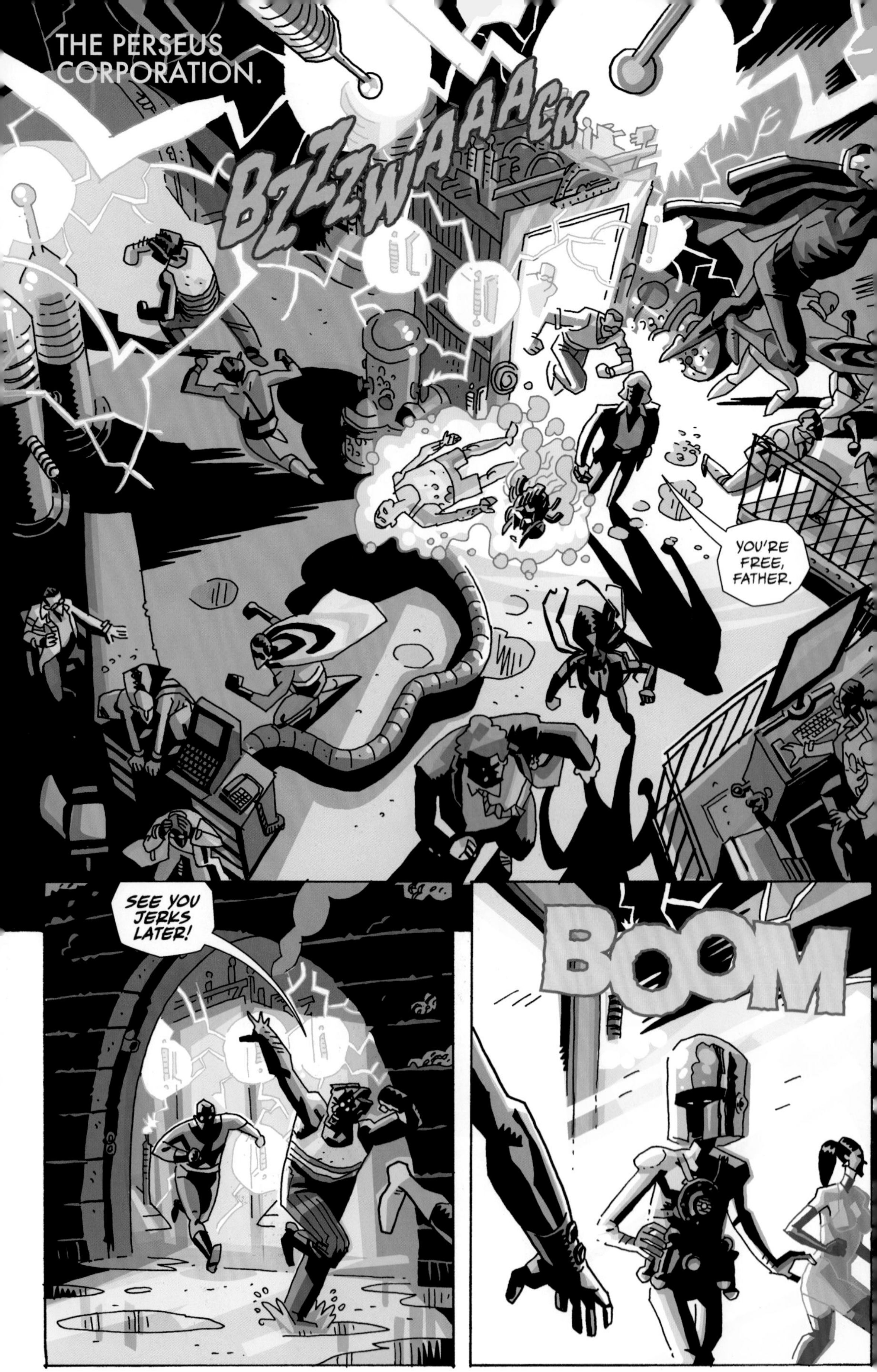
THE PERSEUS CORPORATION.
BZZZWAAAACK
YOU'RE FREE, FATHER.
SEE YOU JERKS LATER!
BOOM

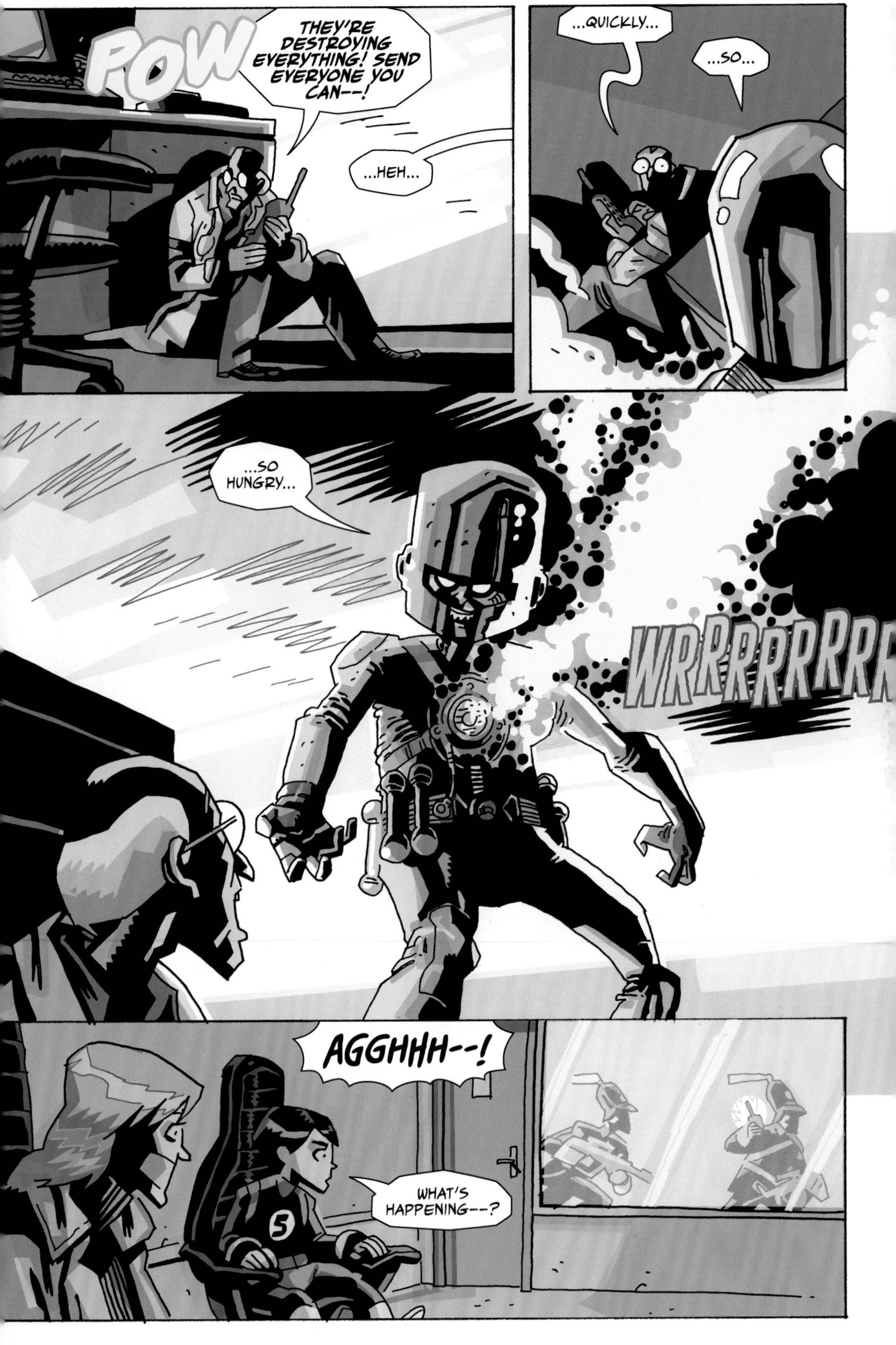
POW
THEY'RE DESTROYING EVERYTHING! SEND EVERYONE YOU CAN--!
...HEH...
...QUICKLY...
...SO...
...SO HUNGRY...
WRRRRRRRR
AGGHHH--!
WHAT'S HAPPENING--?

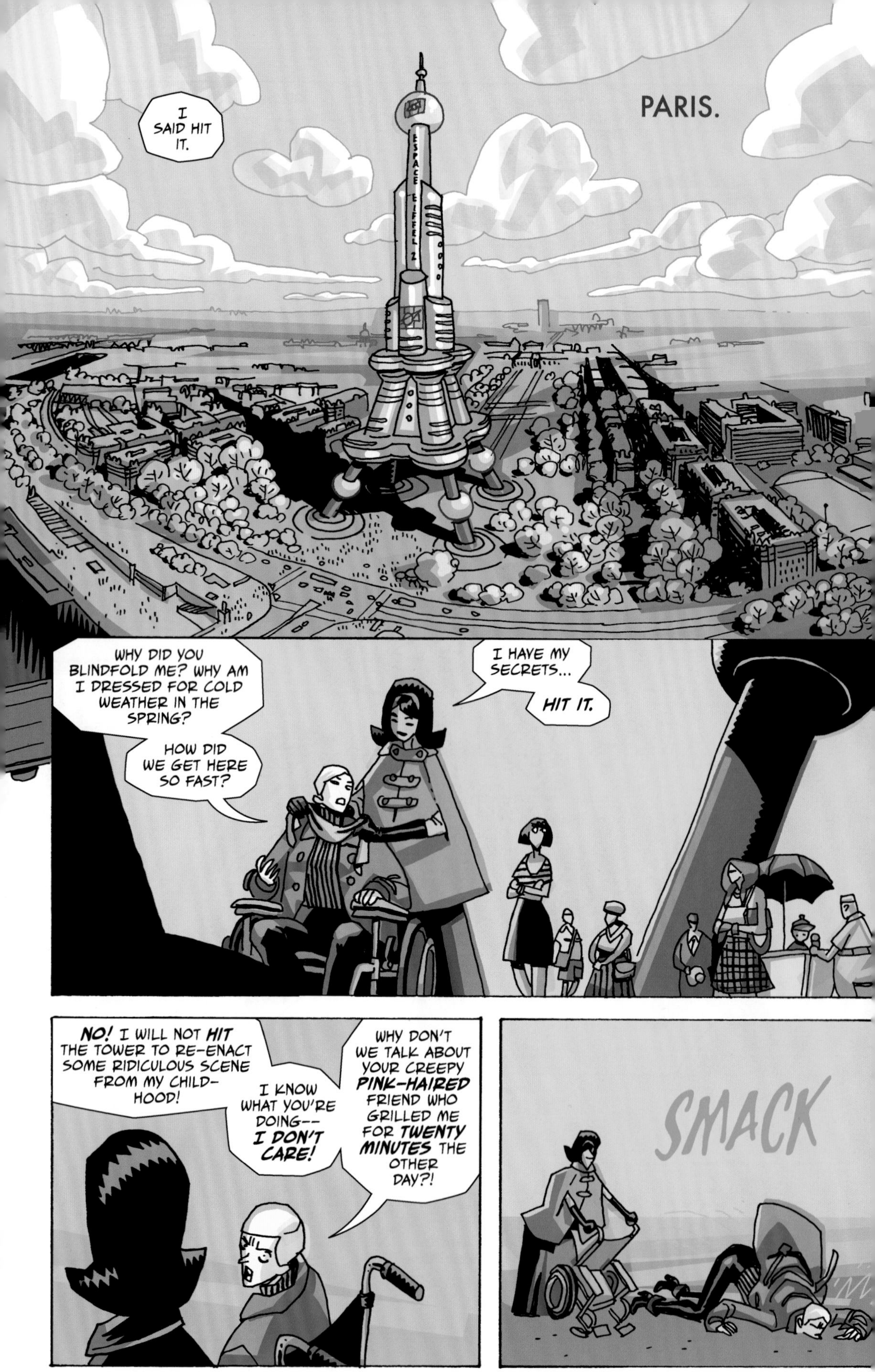
PARIS.
I SAID HIT IT.
ESPACE EIFFEL 2
WHY DID YOU BLINDFOLD ME? WHY AM I DRESSED FOR COLD WEATHER IN THE SPRING?
HOW DID WE GET HERE SO FAST?
I HAVE MY SECRETS...
HIT IT.
NO! I WILL NOT HIT THE TOWER TO RE-ENACT SOME RIDICULOUS SCENE FROM MY CHILD-HOOD!
I KNOW WHAT YOU'RE DOING-- I DON'T CARE!
WHY DON'T WE TALK ABOUT YOUR CREEPY PINK-HAIRED FRIEND WHO GRILLED ME FOR TWENTY MINUTES THE OTHER DAY?!
SMACK

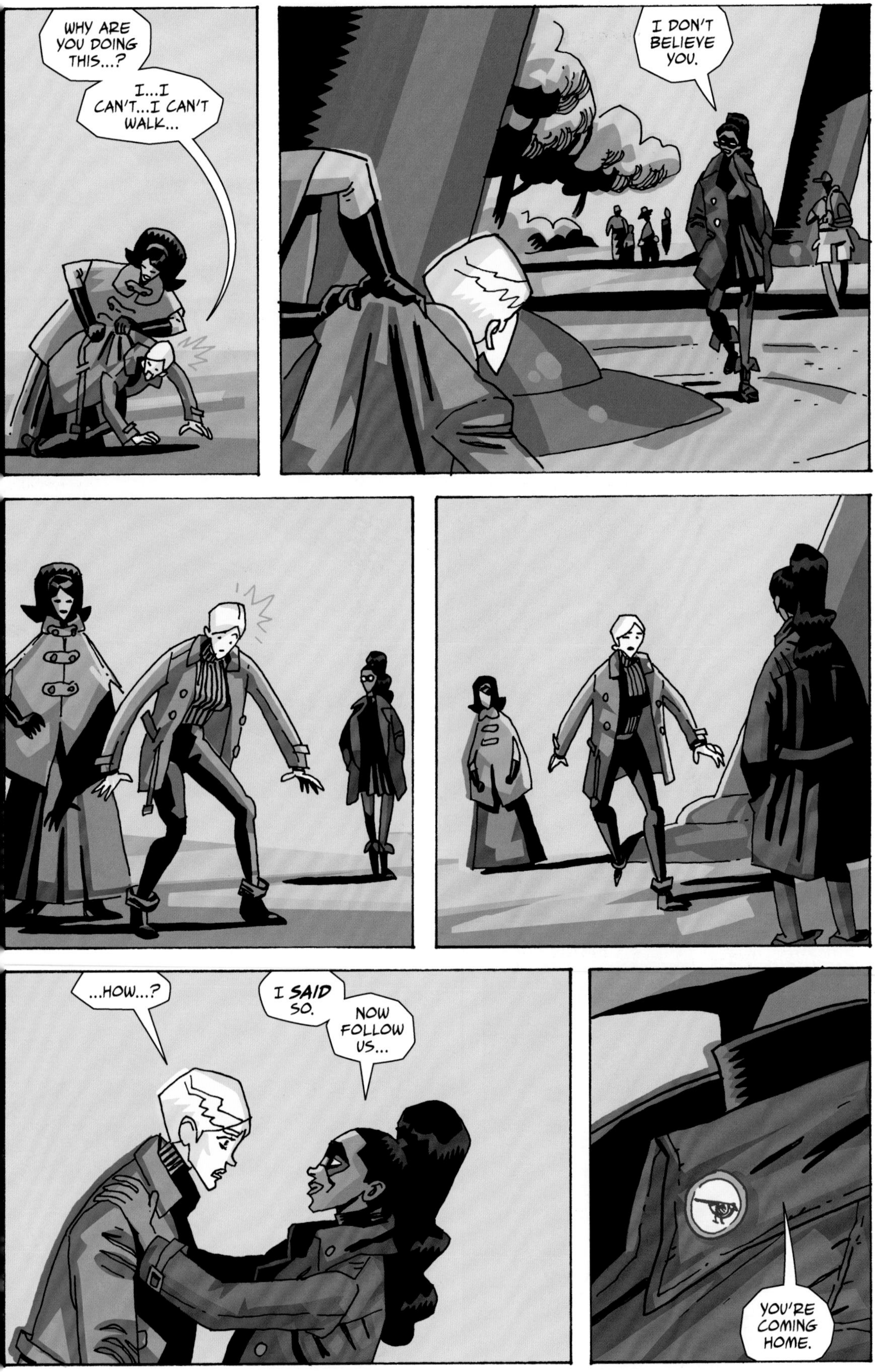
WHY ARE YOU DOING THIS...?
I...I CAN'T...I CAN'T WALK...
I DON'T BELIEVE YOU.
...HOW...?
I SAID SO.
NOW FOLLOW US...
YOU'RE COMING HOME.

THE PERSEUS CORPORATION.

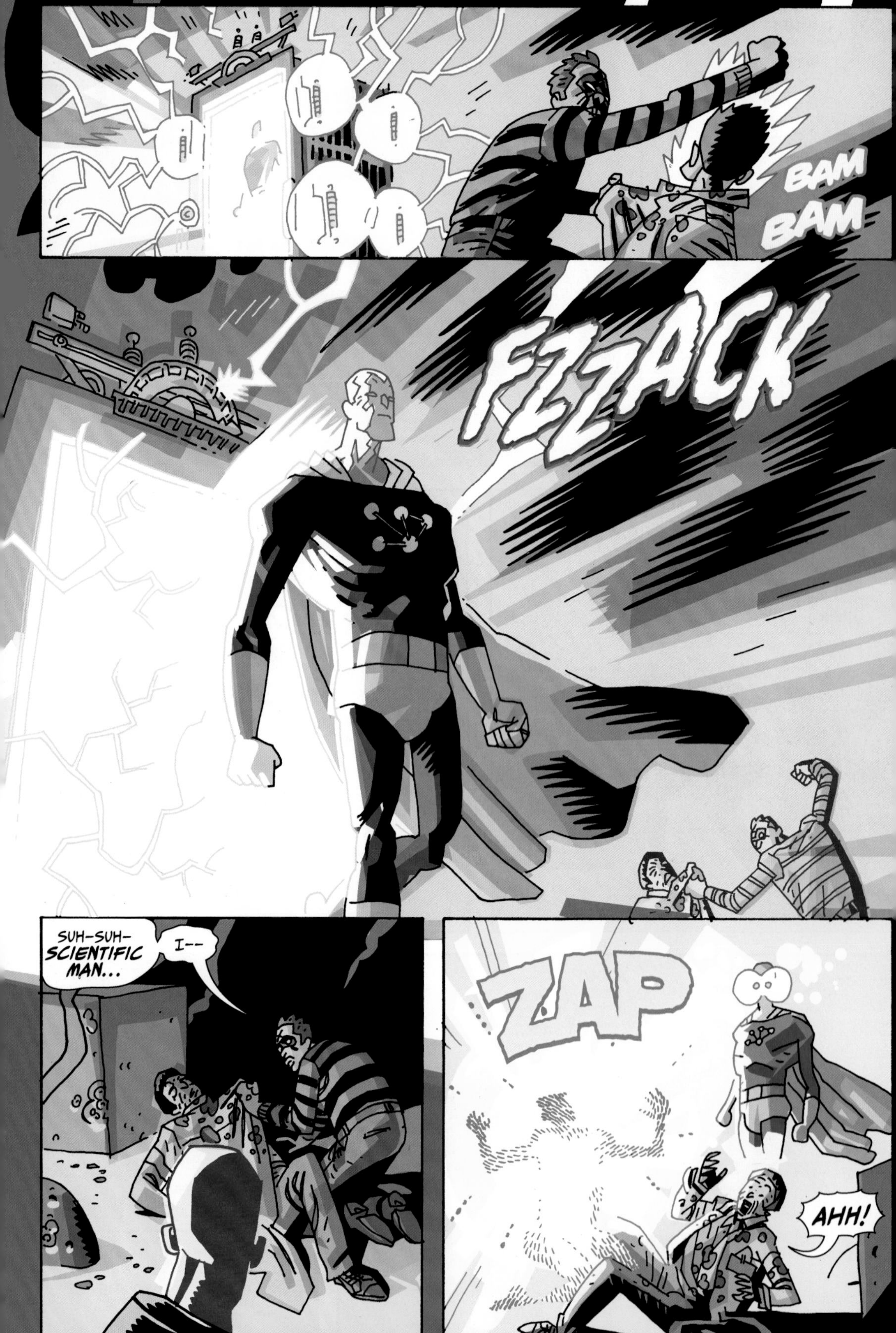
BAM
BAM
FZZACK
SUH-SUH- SCIENTIFIC MAN...
I--
ZAP
AHH!

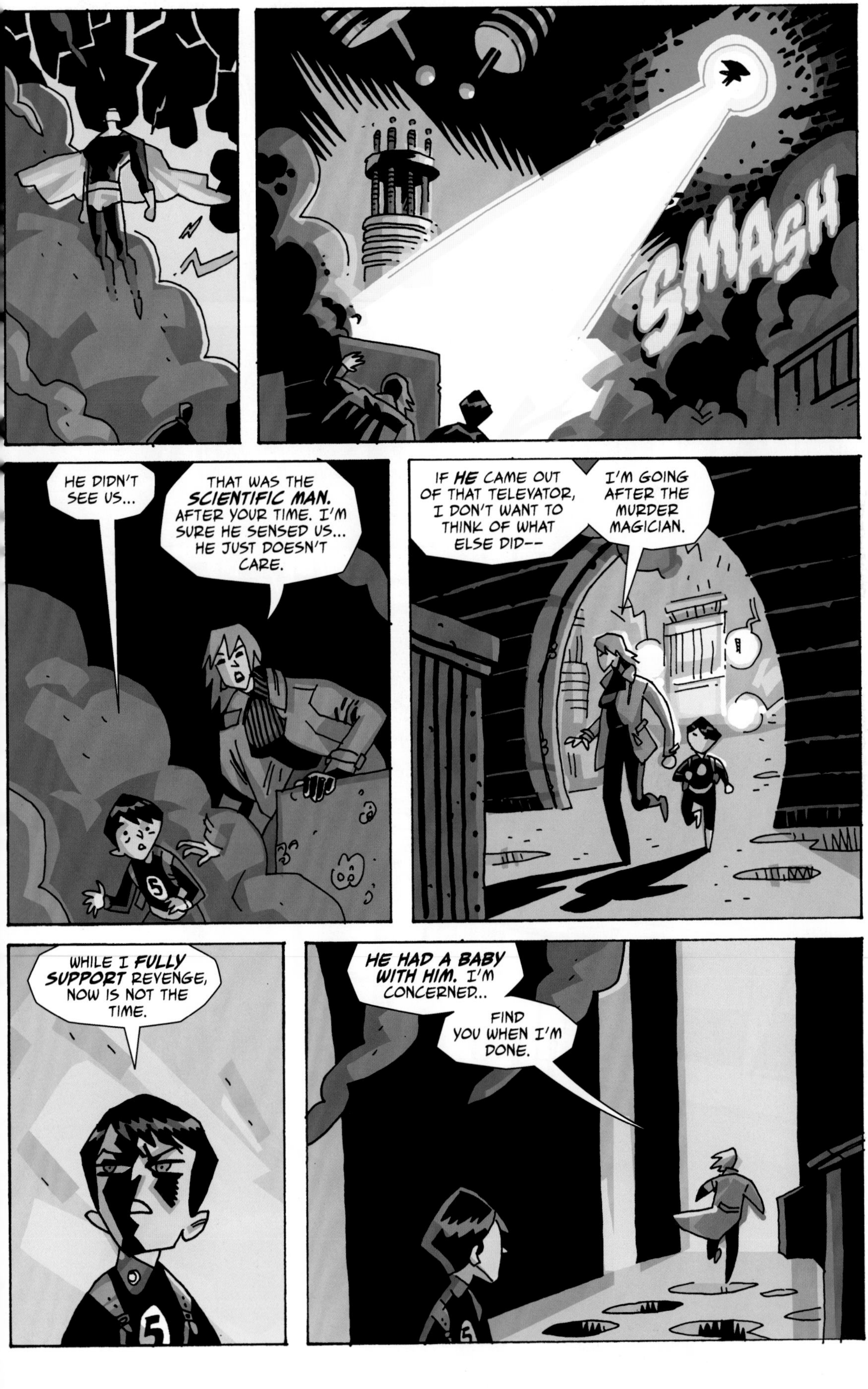
SMASH
HE DIDN'T SEE US...
THAT WAS THE **SCIENTIFIC MAN.** AFTER YOUR TIME. I'M SURE HE SENSED US... HE JUST DOESN'T CARE.
IF **HE** CAME OUT OF THAT TELEVATOR, I DON'T WANT TO THINK OF WHAT ELSE DID--
I'M GOING AFTER THE MURDER MAGICIAN.
WHILE I **FULLY SUPPORT** REVENGE, NOW IS NOT THE TIME.
HE HAD A BABY WITH HIM. I'M CONCERNED...
FIND YOU WHEN I'M DONE.

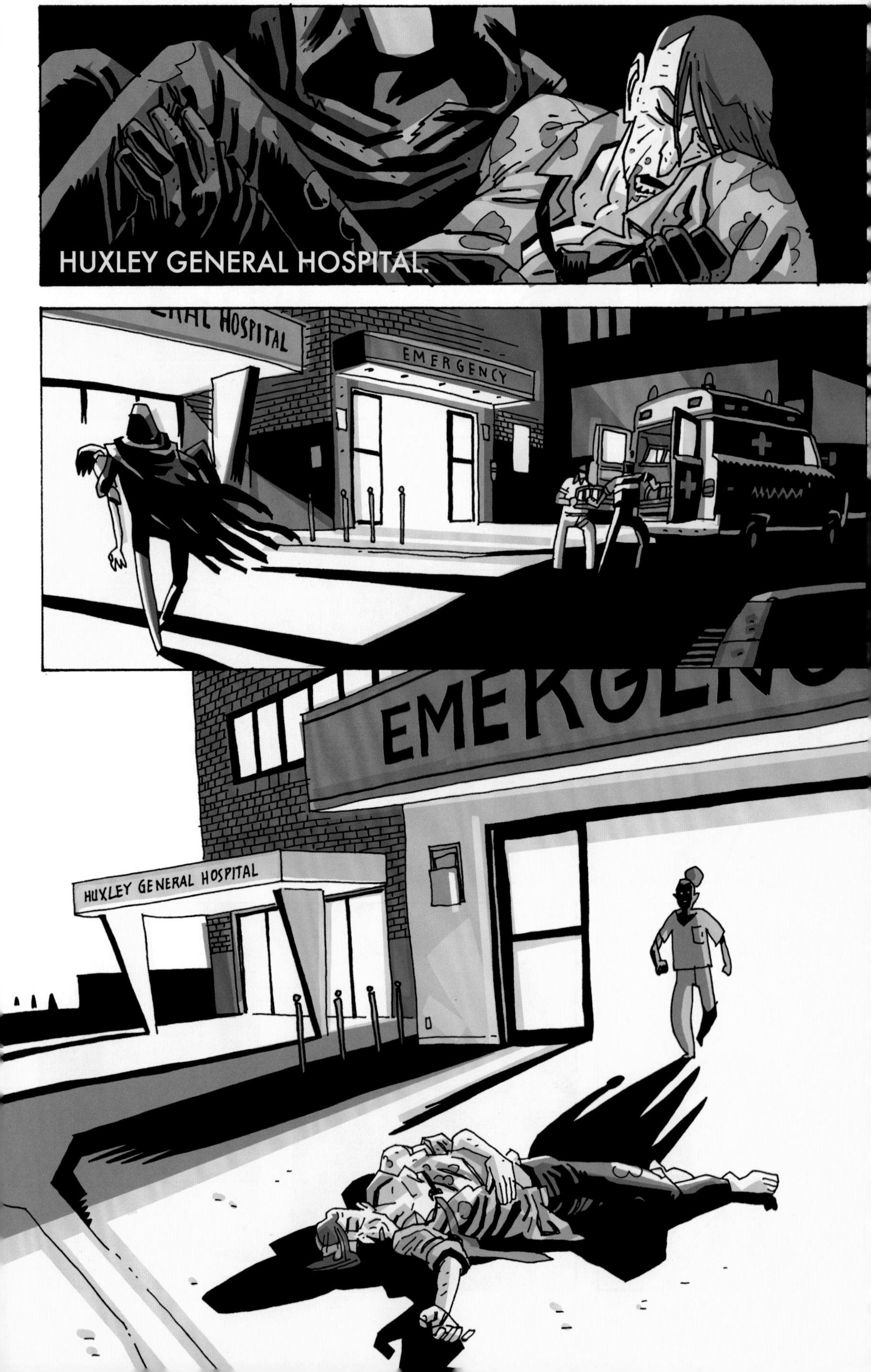
HUXLEY GENERAL HOSPITAL.
EMERGENCY
HUXLEY GENERAL HOSPITAL

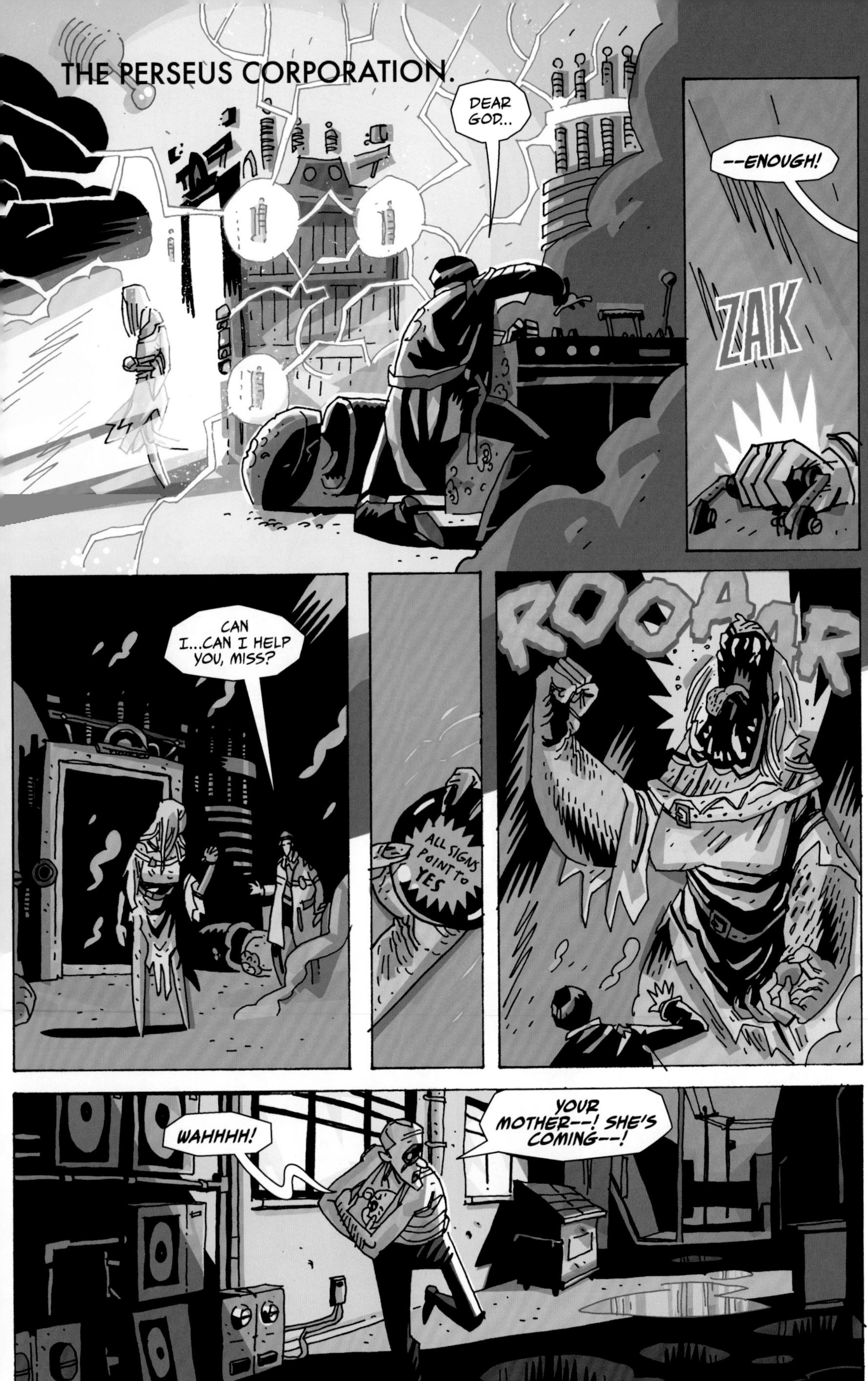
THE PERSEUS CORPORATION.
DEAR GOD...
--ENOUGH!
ZAK
CAN I...CAN I HELP YOU, MISS?
ALL SIGNS POINT TO YES
ROOAAR
WAHHHH!
YOUR MOTHER--! SHE'S COMING--!

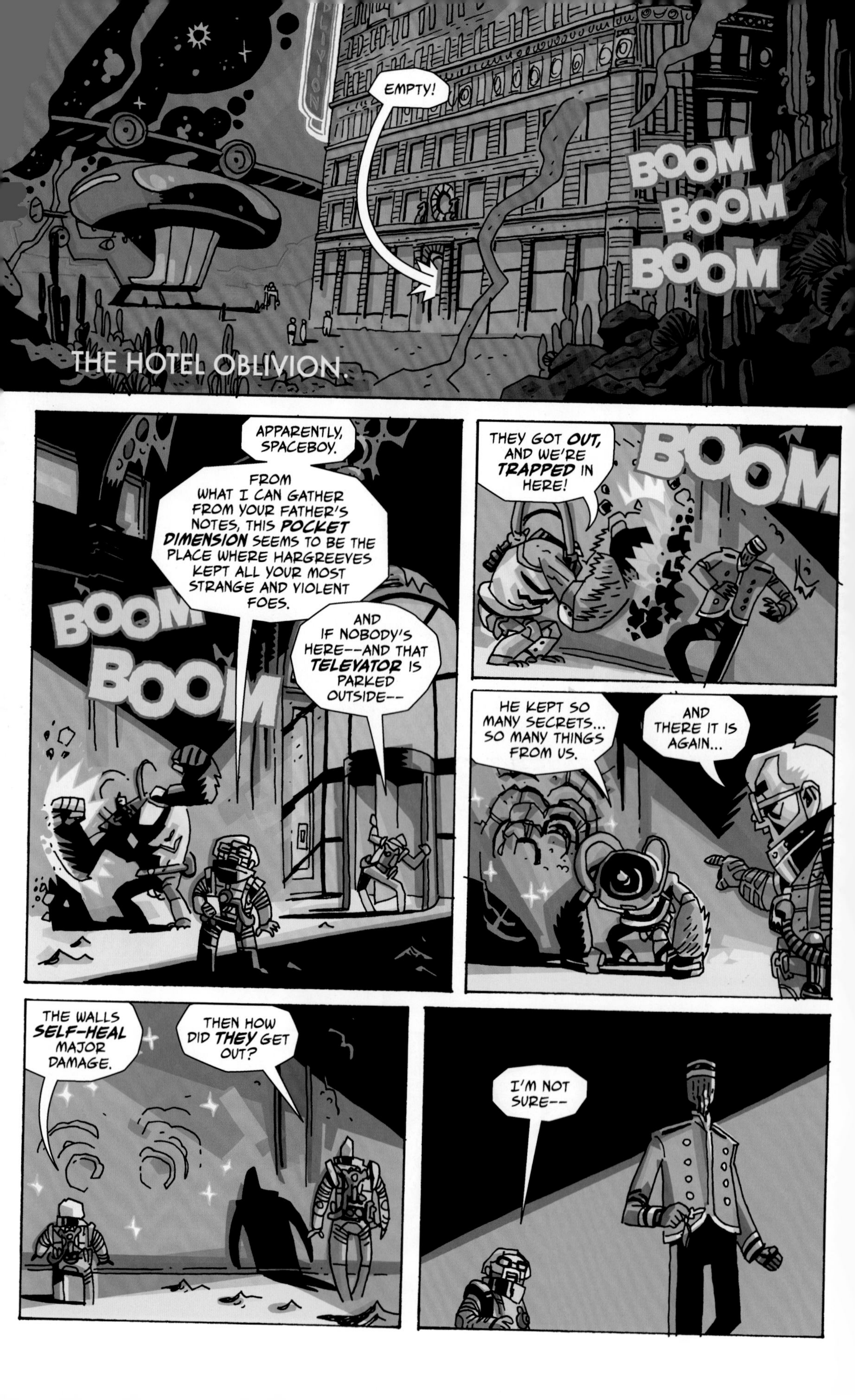
EMPTY!
BOOM
BOOM
BOOM
THE HOTEL OBLIVION.
APPARENTLY, SPACEBOY.
FROM WHAT I CAN GATHER FROM YOUR FATHER'S NOTES, THIS POCKET DIMENSION SEEMS TO BE THE PLACE WHERE HARGREEVES KEPT ALL YOUR MOST STRANGE AND VIOLENT FOES.
AND IF NOBODY'S HERE--AND THAT TELEVATOR IS PARKED OUTSIDE--
BOOM
BOOM
THEY GOT OUT, AND WE'RE TRAPPED IN HERE!
BOOM
HE KEPT SO MANY SECRETS... SO MANY THINGS FROM US.
AND THERE IT IS AGAIN...
THE WALLS SELF-HEAL MAJOR DAMAGE.
THEN HOW DID THEY GET OUT?
I'M NOT SURE--

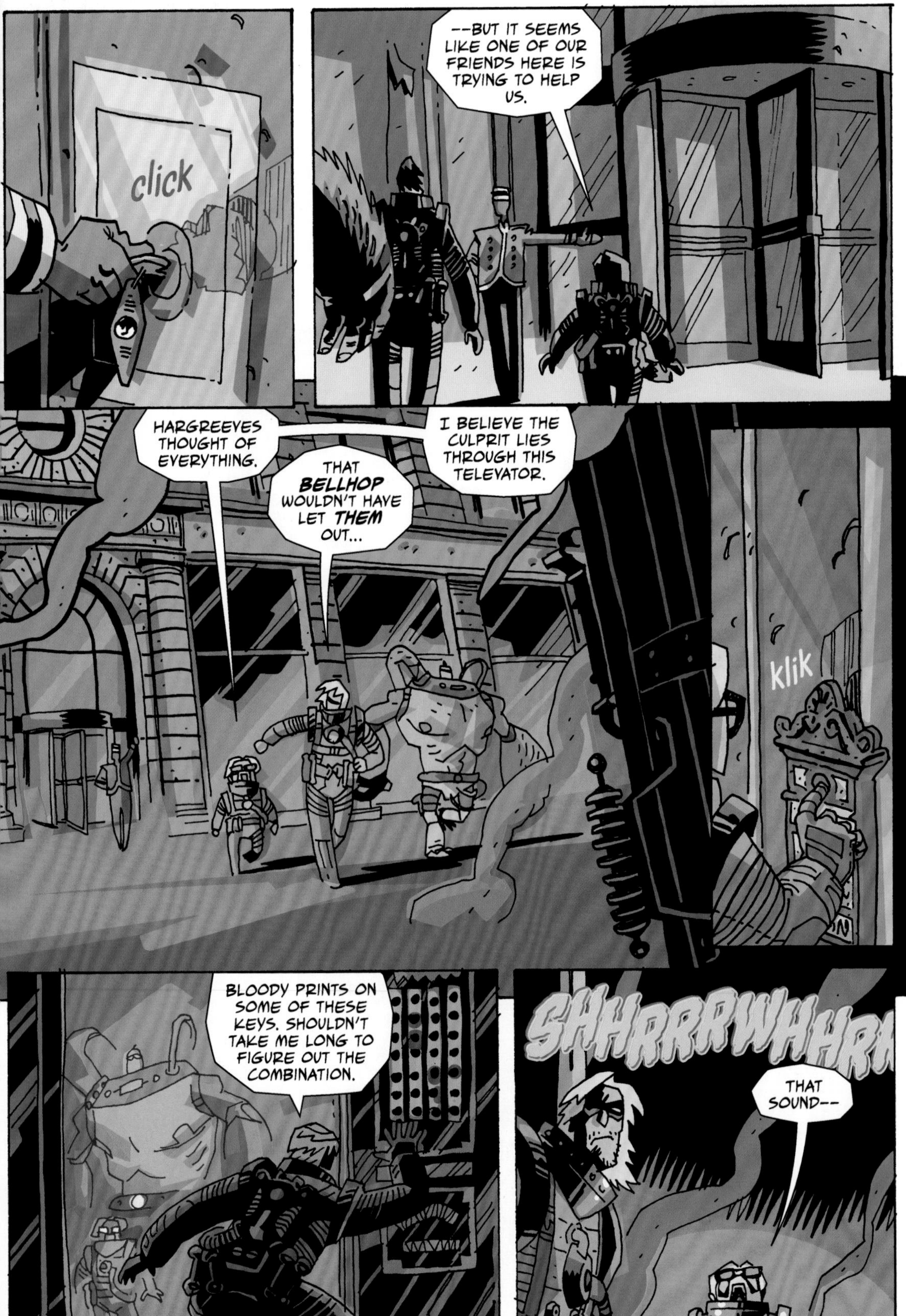
click
--BUT IT SEEMS LIKE ONE OF OUR FRIENDS HERE IS TRYING TO HELP US.
HARGREEVES THOUGHT OF EVERYTHING.
THAT **BELLHOP** WOULDN'T HAVE LET **THEM** OUT...
I BELIEVE THE CULPRIT LIES THROUGH THIS TELEVATOR.
klik
BLOODY PRINTS ON SOME OF THESE KEYS. SHOULDN'T TAKE ME LONG TO FIGURE OUT THE COMBINATION.
THAT SOUND--

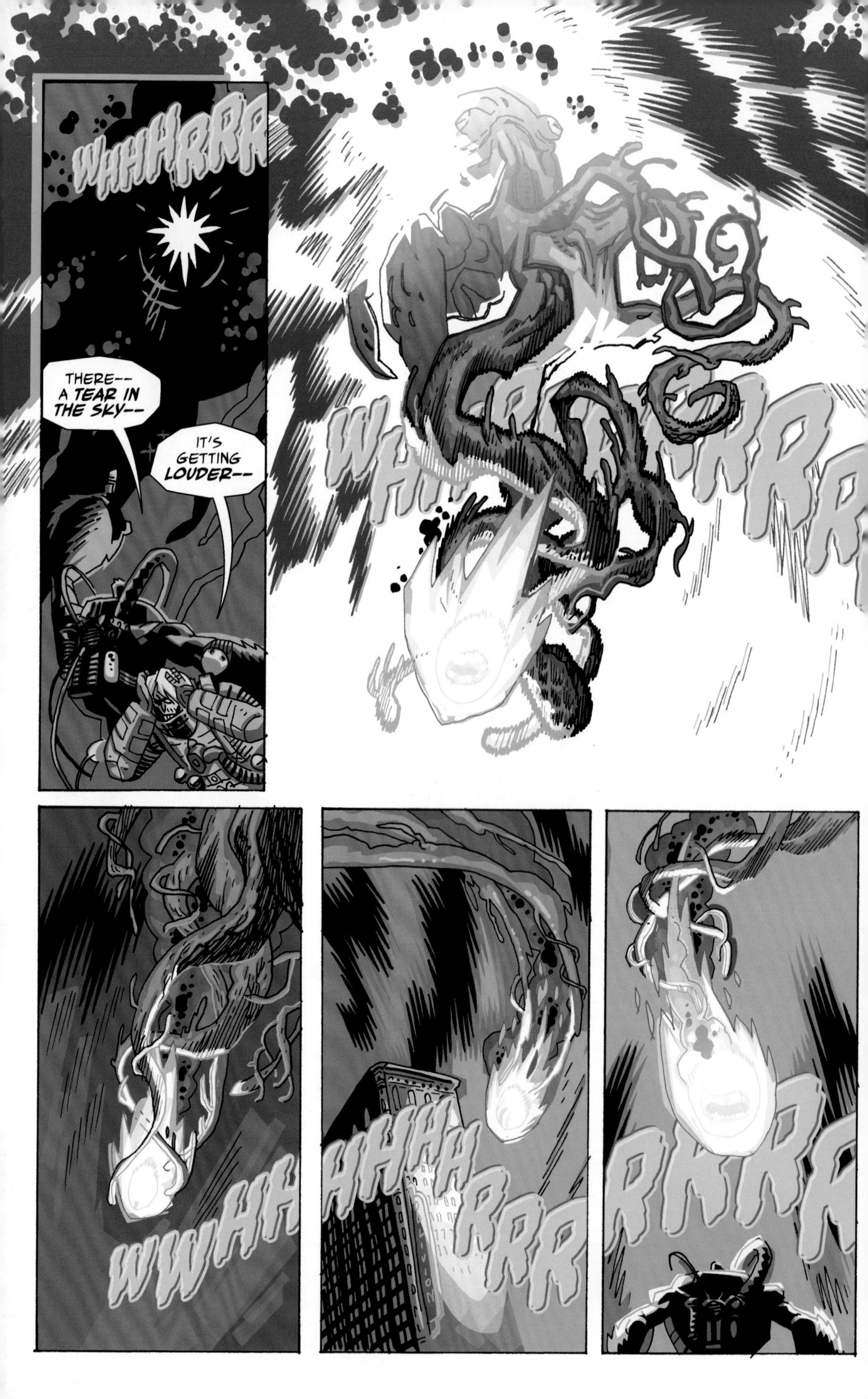
WHHRRR
THERE-- A TEAR IN THE SKY--
IT'S GETTING LOUDER--
WHHRRRRRR
WWHHHHHHRRRRRNRR

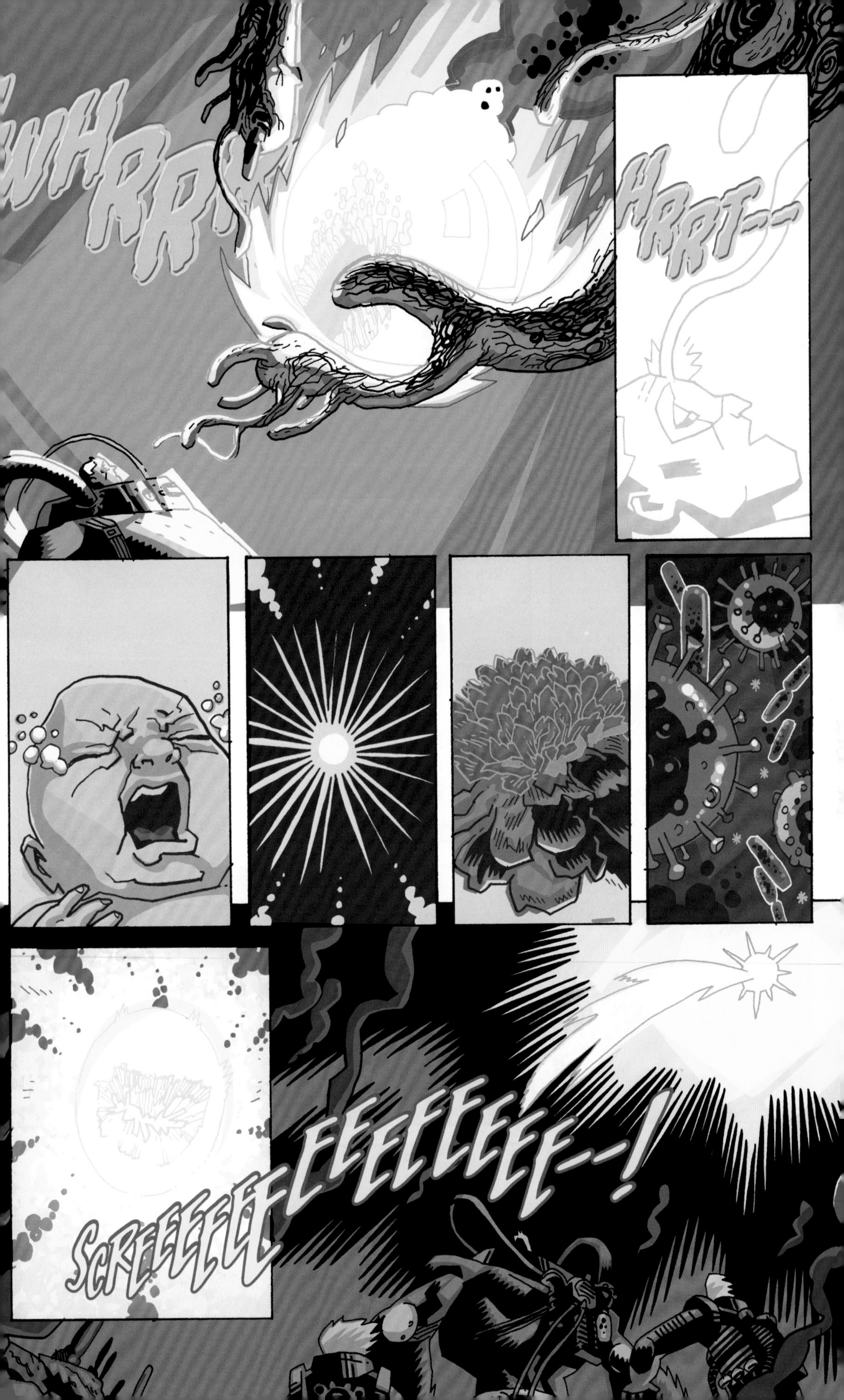
WHRRR
HRRT--
SCREEEEEEEEEEEEEEEEE--!

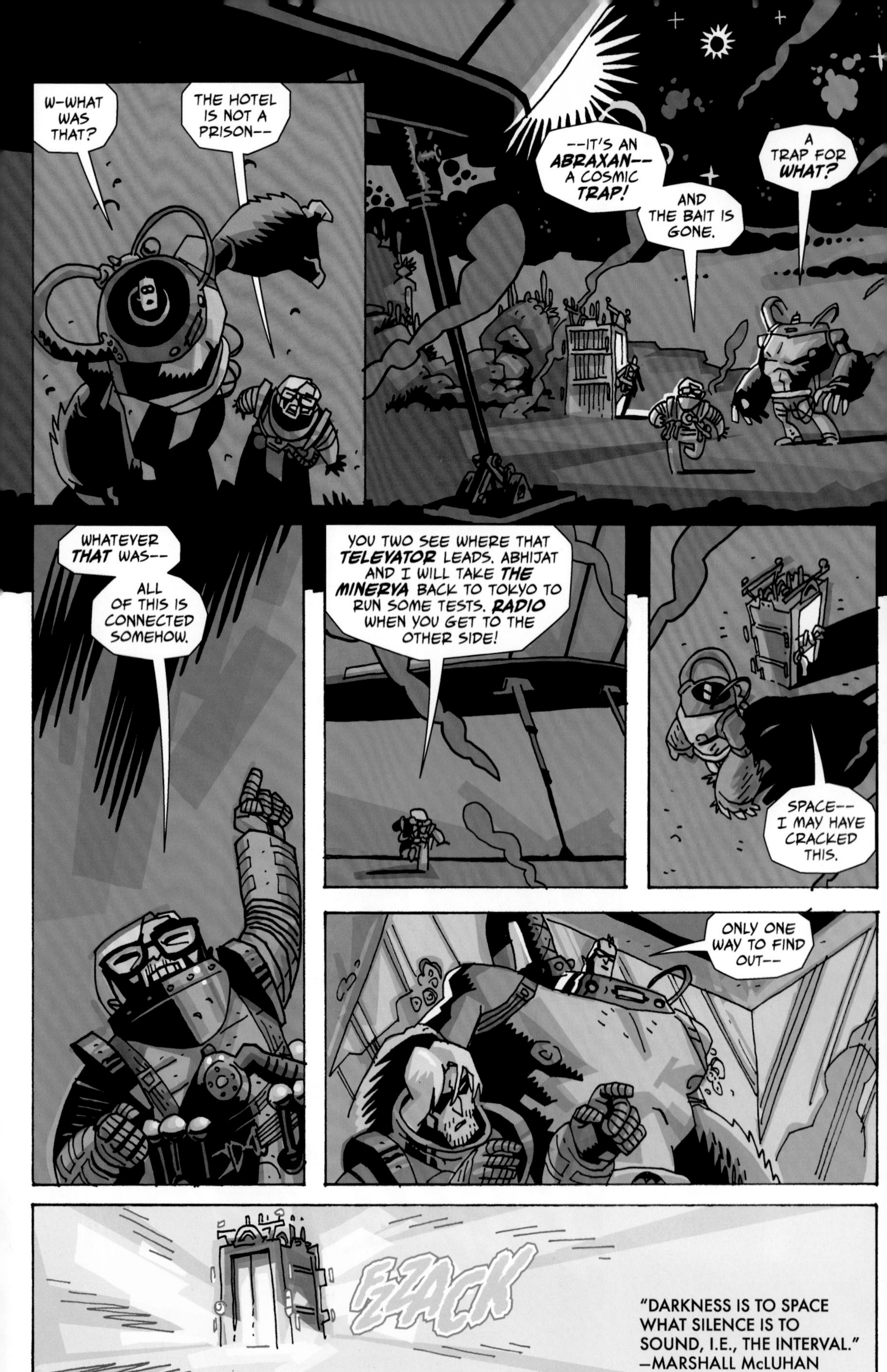
W-WHAT WAS THAT?
THE HOTEL IS NOT A PRISON--
--IT'S AN ABRAXAN-- A COSMIC TRAP!
AND THE BAIT IS GONE.
A TRAP FOR WHAT?
WHATEVER THAT WAS--
ALL OF THIS IS CONNECTED SOMEHOW.
YOU TWO SEE WHERE THAT TELEVATOR LEADS. ABHIJAT AND I WILL TAKE THE MINERVA BACK TO TOKYO TO RUN SOME TESTS. RADIO WHEN YOU GET TO THE OTHER SIDE!
SPACE-- I MAY HAVE CRACKED THIS.
ONLY ONE WAY TO FIND OUT--
FZZACK
"DARKNESS IS TO SPACE WHAT SILENCE IS TO SOUND, I.E., THE INTERVAL."
—MARSHALL McLUHAN

CHAPTER SIX

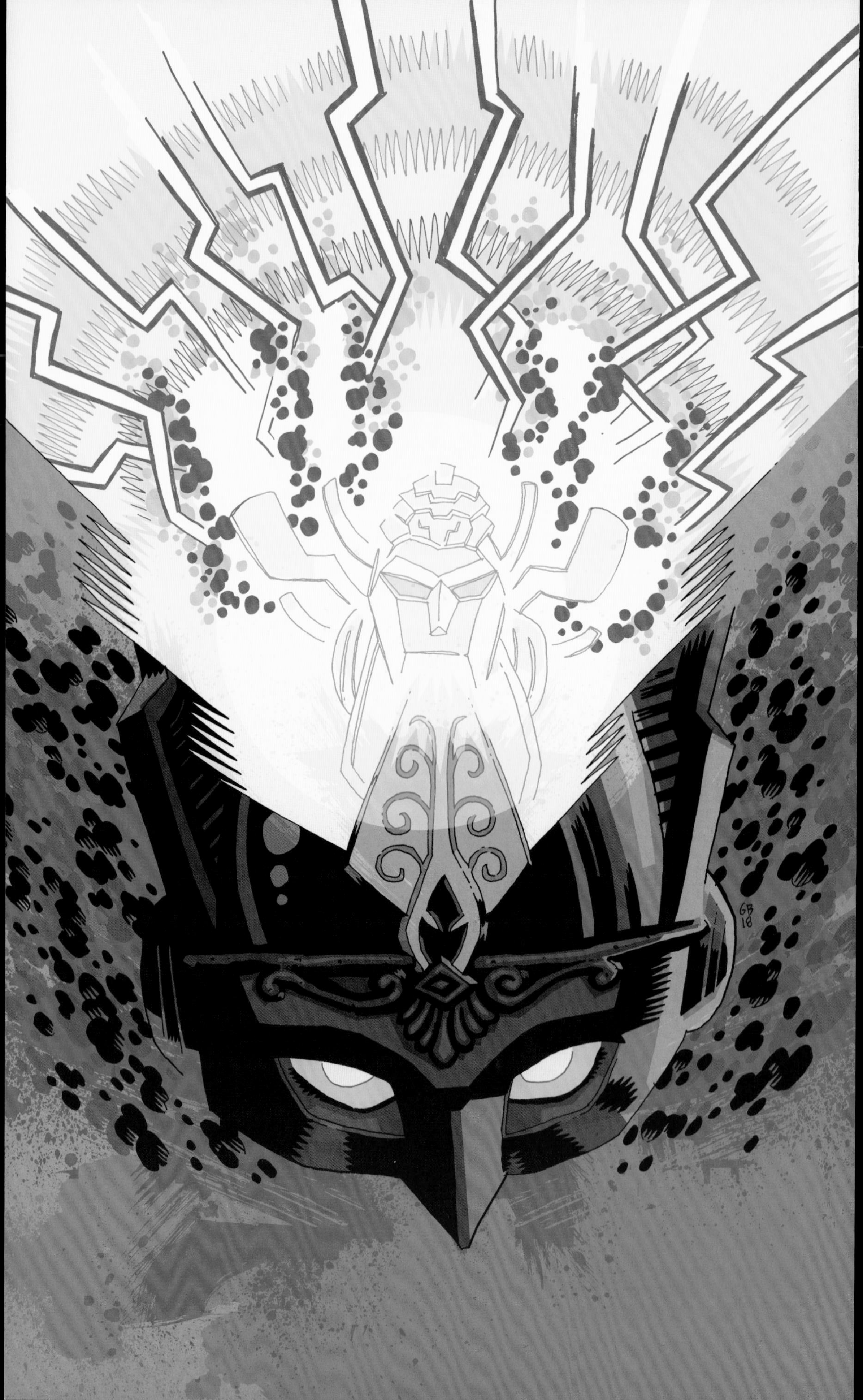
GB
18

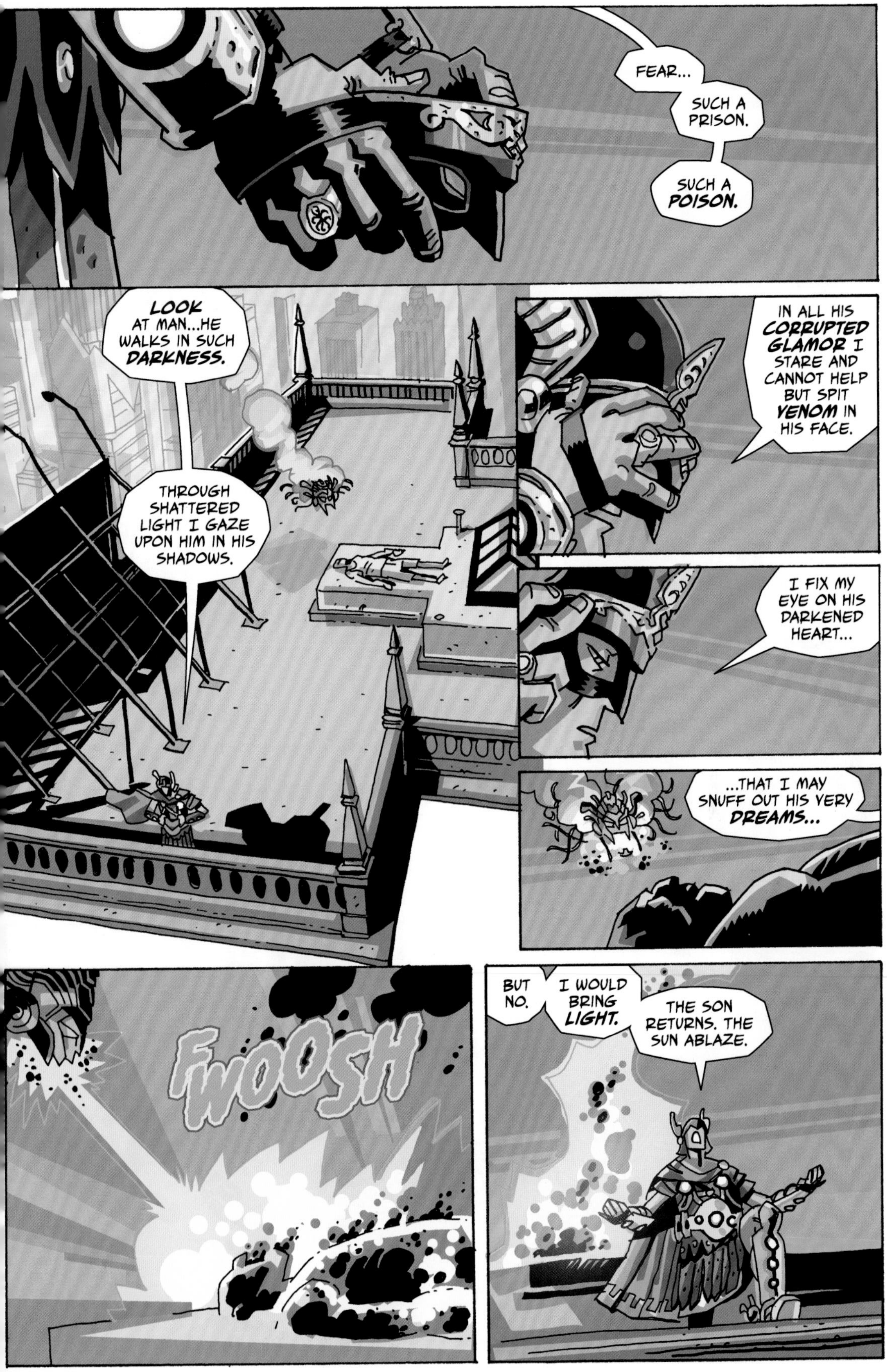
FEAR...
SUCH A PRISON.
SUCH A POISON.
LOOK AT MAN...HE WALKS IN SUCH DARKNESS.
THROUGH SHATTERED LIGHT I GAZE UPON HIM IN HIS SHADOWS.
IN ALL HIS CORRUPTED GLAMOR I STARE AND CANNOT HELP BUT SPIT VENOM IN HIS FACE.
I FIX MY EYE ON HIS DARKENED HEART...
...THAT I MAY SNUFF OUT HIS VERY DREAMS...
FWOOSH
BUT NO.
I WOULD BRING LIGHT.
THE SON RETURNS. THE SUN ABLAZE.

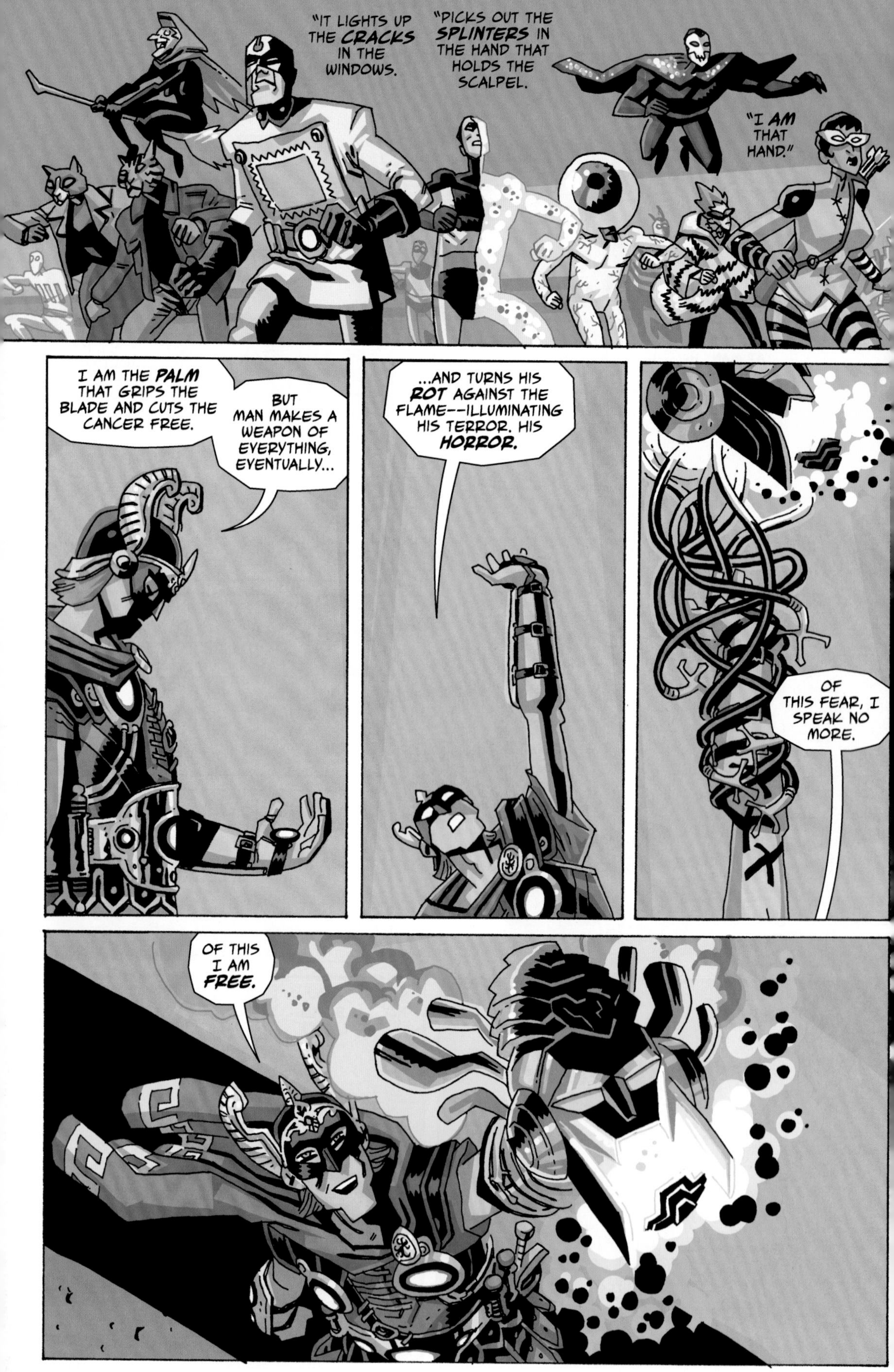
"IT LIGHTS UP THE CRACKS IN THE WINDOWS.
"PICKS OUT THE SPLINTERS IN THE HAND THAT HOLDS THE SCALPEL.
"I AM THAT HAND."
I AM THE PALM THAT GRIPS THE BLADE AND CUTS THE CANCER FREE.
BUT MAN MAKES A WEAPON OF EVERYTHING, EVENTUALLY...
...AND TURNS HIS ROT AGAINST THE FLAME--ILLUMINATING HIS TERROR. HIS HORROR.
OF THIS FEAR, I SPEAK NO MORE.
OF THIS I AM FREE.

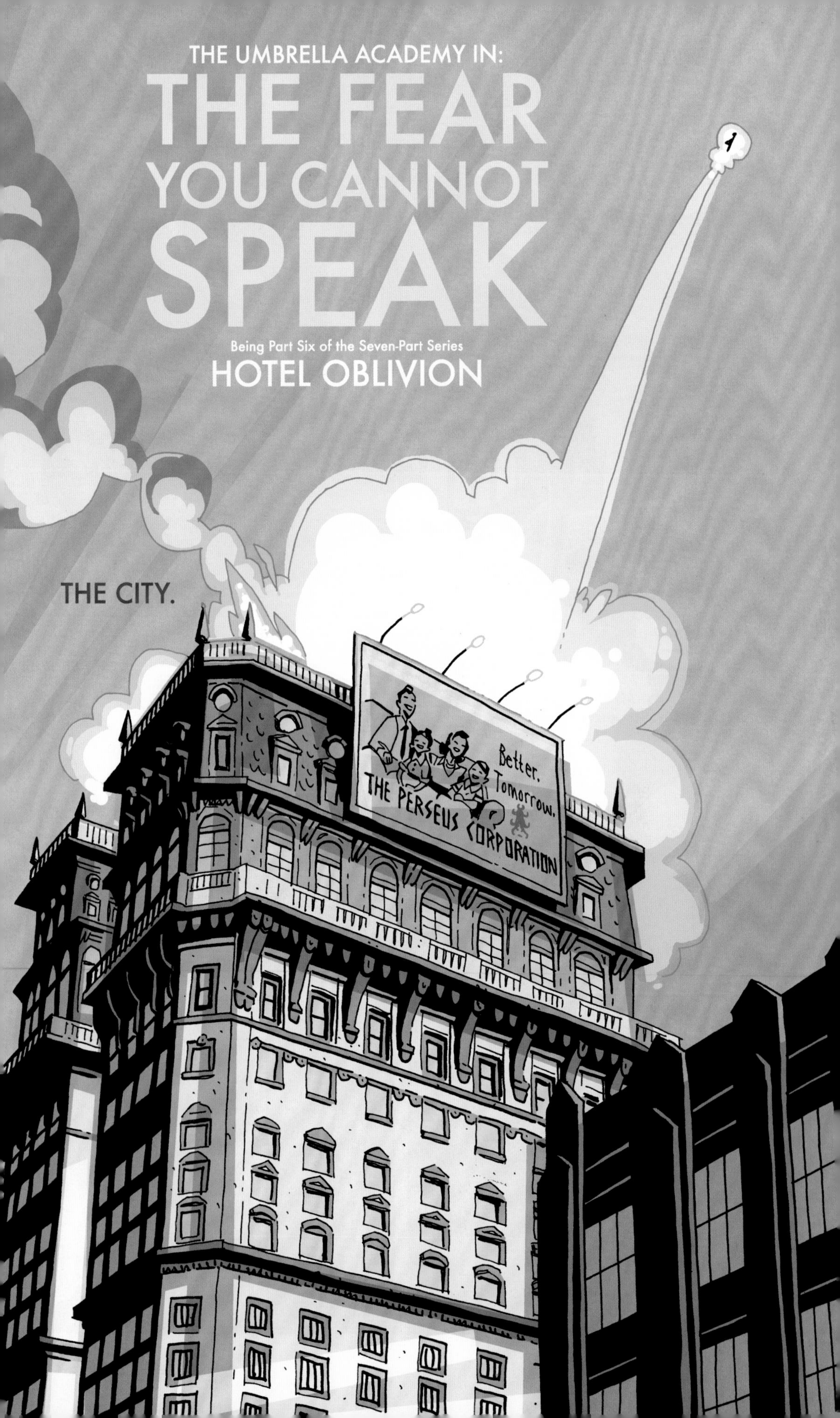
THE UMBRELLA ACADEMY IN:
THE FEAR YOU CANNOT SPEAK
Being Part Six of the Seven-Part Series
HOTEL OBLIVION
THE CITY.
Better. Tomorrow.
THE PERSEUS CORPORATION

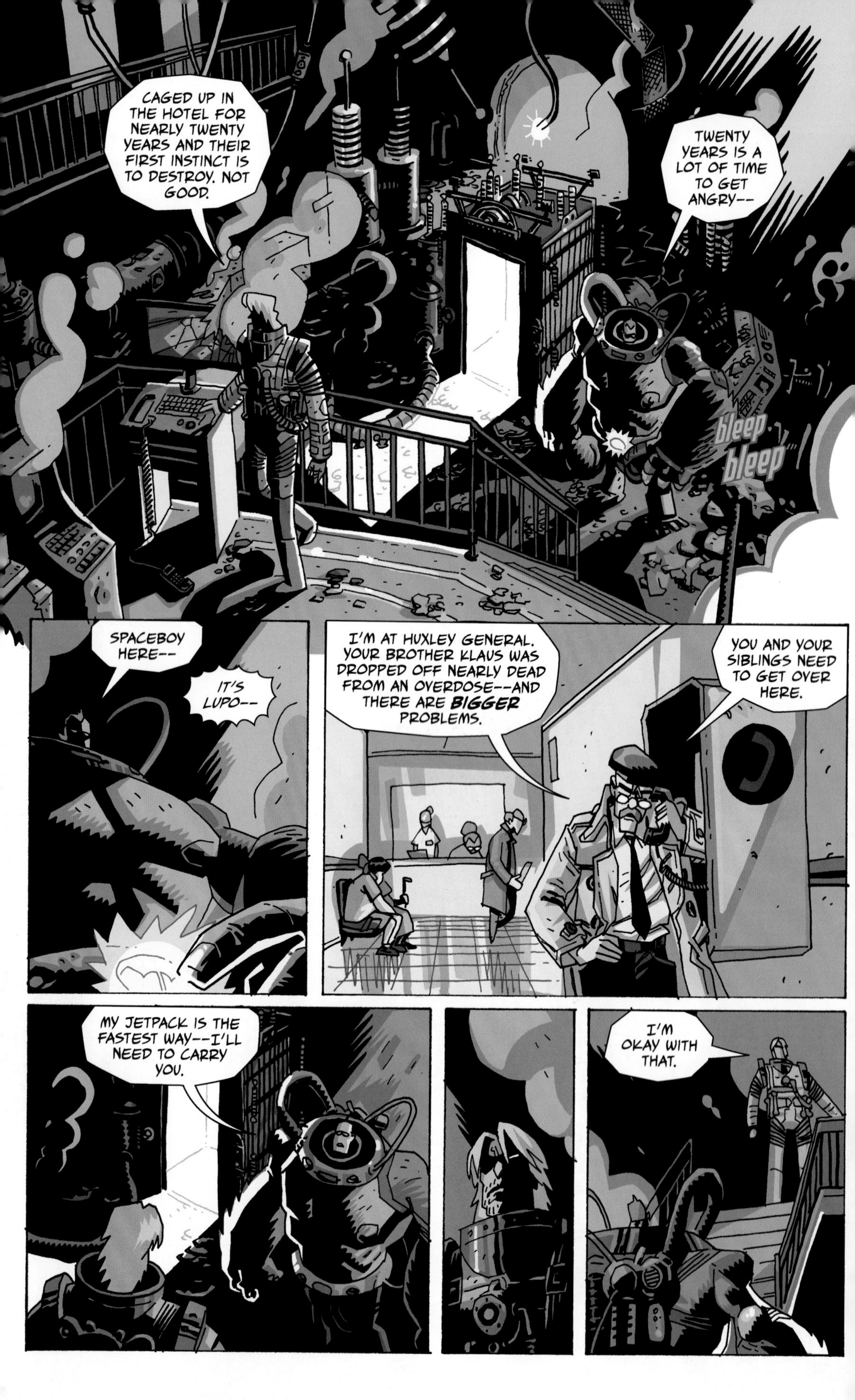
CAGED UP IN THE HOTEL FOR NEARLY TWENTY YEARS AND THEIR FIRST INSTINCT IS TO DESTROY. NOT GOOD.
TWENTY YEARS IS A LOT OF TIME TO GET ANGRY--
bleep
bleep
SPACEBOY HERE--
IT'S LUPO--
I'M AT HUXLEY GENERAL. YOUR BROTHER KLAUS WAS DROPPED OFF NEARLY DEAD FROM AN OVERDOSE--AND THERE ARE BIGGER PROBLEMS.
YOU AND YOUR SIBLINGS NEED TO GET OVER HERE.
MY JETPACK IS THE FASTEST WAY--I'LL NEED TO CARRY YOU.
I'M OKAY WITH THAT.

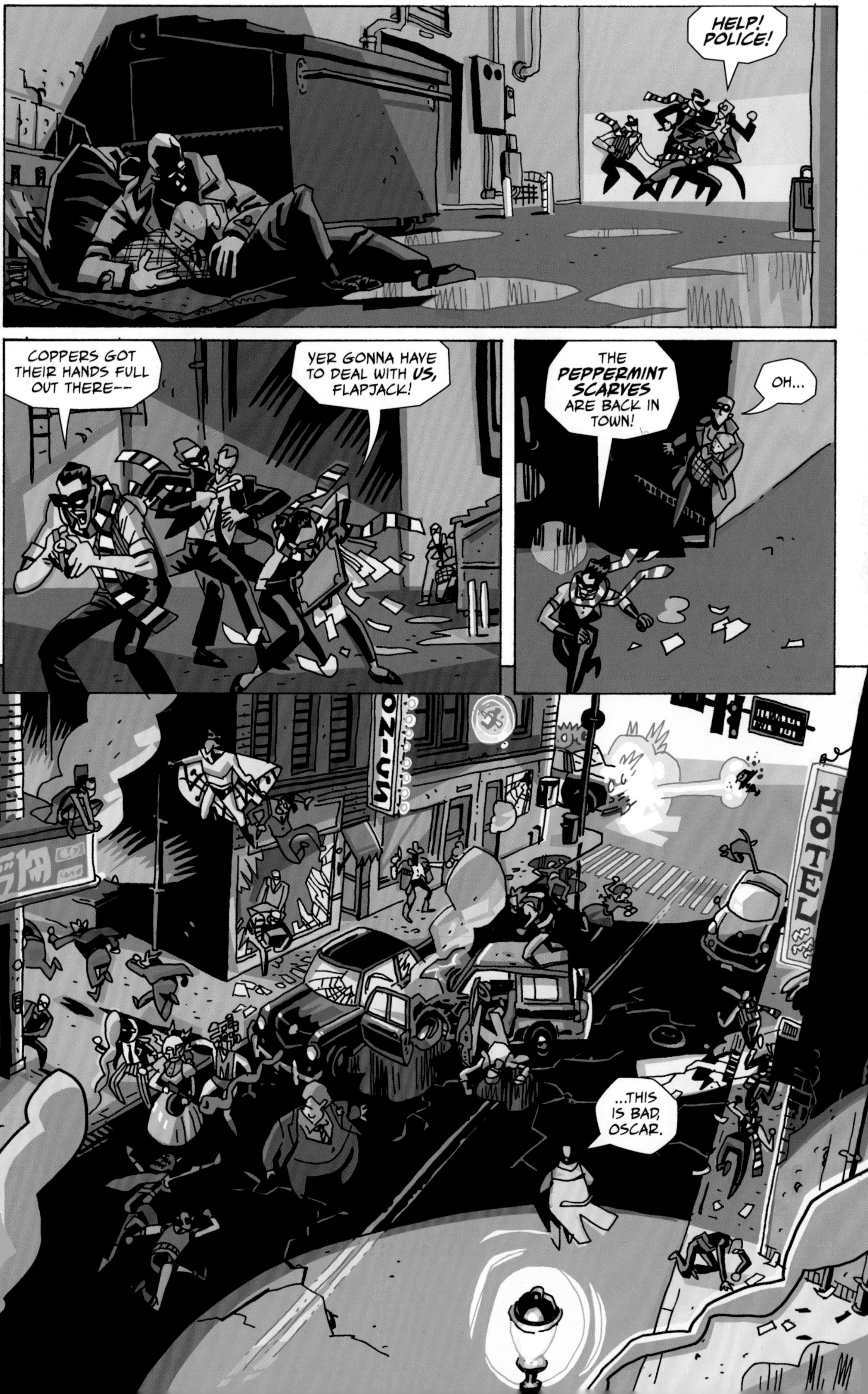
HELP! POLICE!
COPPERS GOT THEIR HANDS FULL OUT THERE--
YER GONNA HAVE TO DEAL WITH US, FLAPJACK!
THE PEPPERMINT SCARVES ARE BACK IN TOWN!
OH...
HOTEL
...THIS IS BAD, OSCAR.

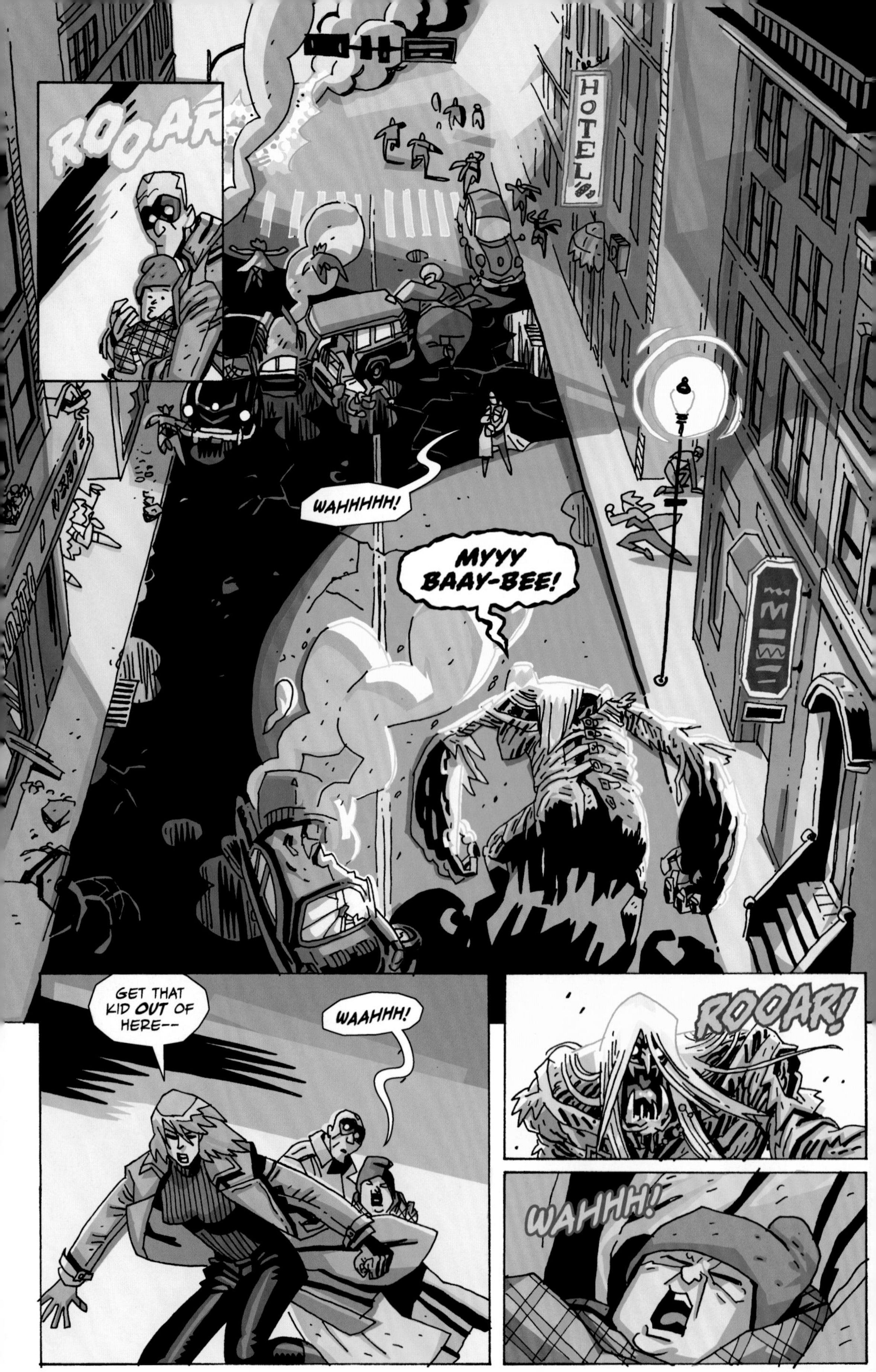
ROOAR
WAHHHHH!
MYYY BAAY-BEE!
GET THAT KID OUT OF HERE--
WAAHHH!
ROOAR!
WAHHH!

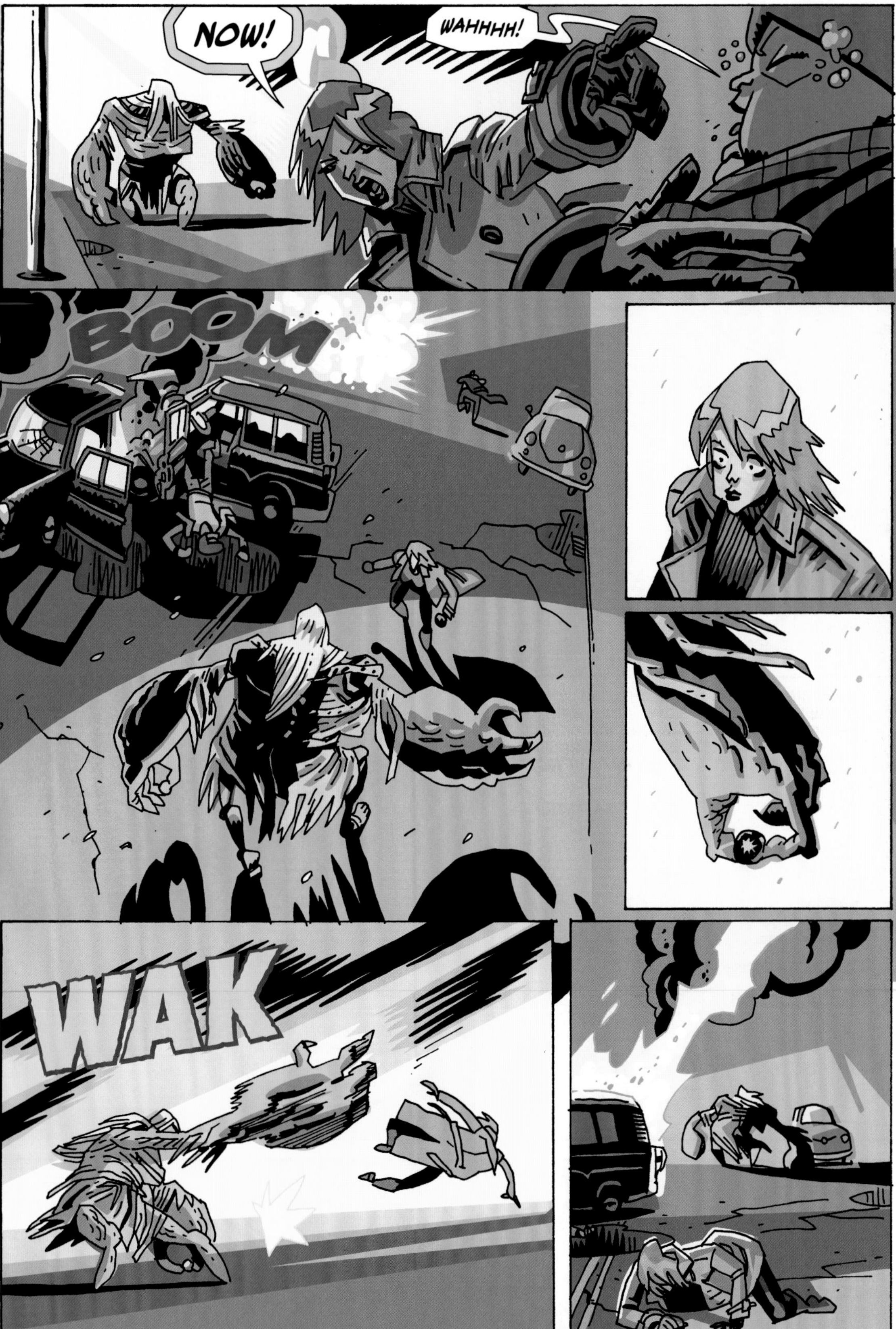
NOW!
WAHHHH!
BOOM
WAK

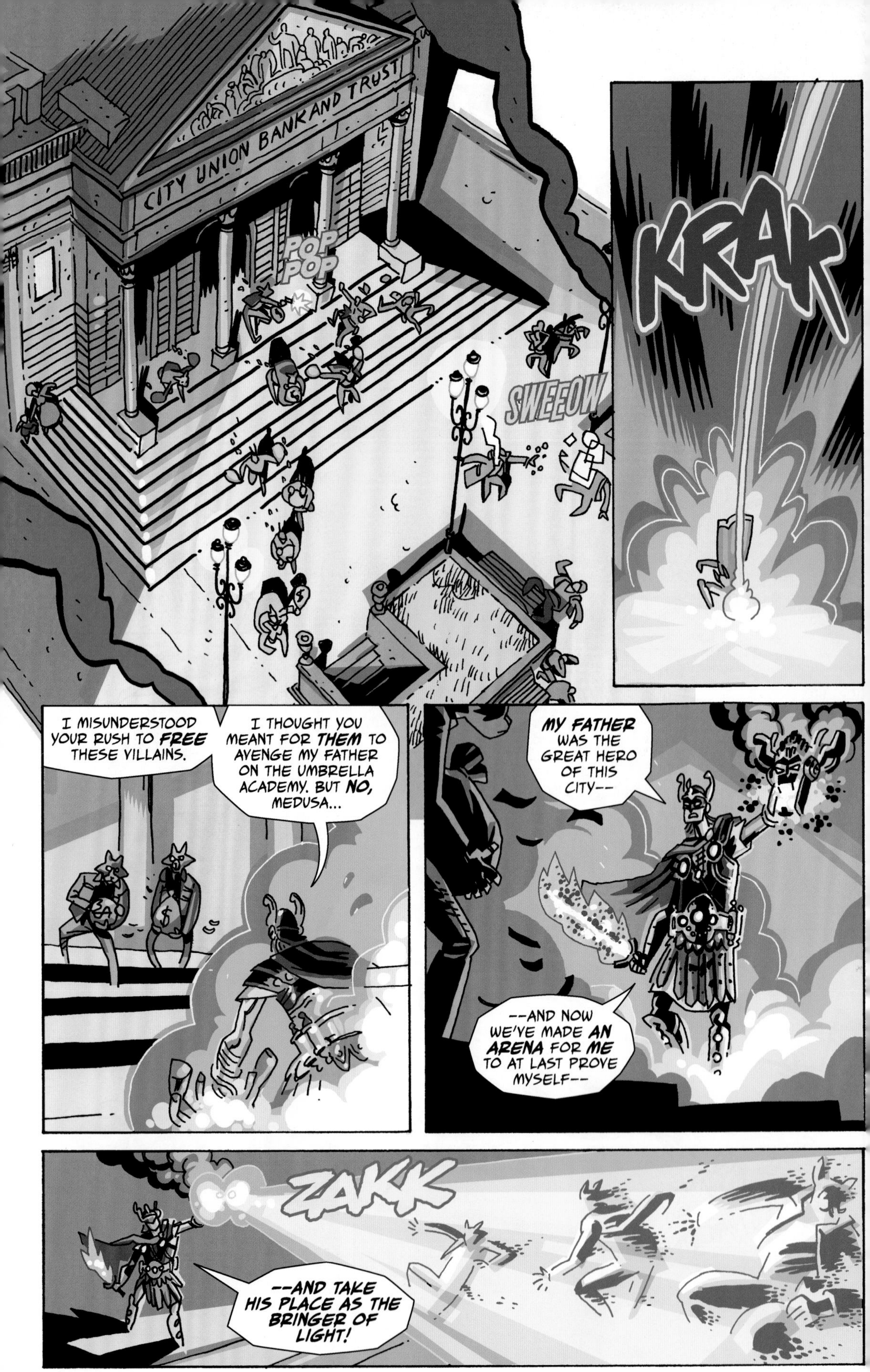
CITY UNION BANK AND TRUST
POP POP
SWEEOW
KRAK
I MISUNDERSTOOD YOUR RUSH TO FREE THESE VILLAINS.
I THOUGHT YOU MEANT FOR THEM TO AVENGE MY FATHER ON THE UMBRELLA ACADEMY. BUT NO, MEDUSA...
MY FATHER WAS THE GREAT HERO OF THIS CITY--
--AND NOW WE'VE MADE AN ARENA FOR ME TO AT LAST PROVE MYSELF--
ZAKK
--AND TAKE HIS PLACE AS THE BRINGER OF LIGHT!

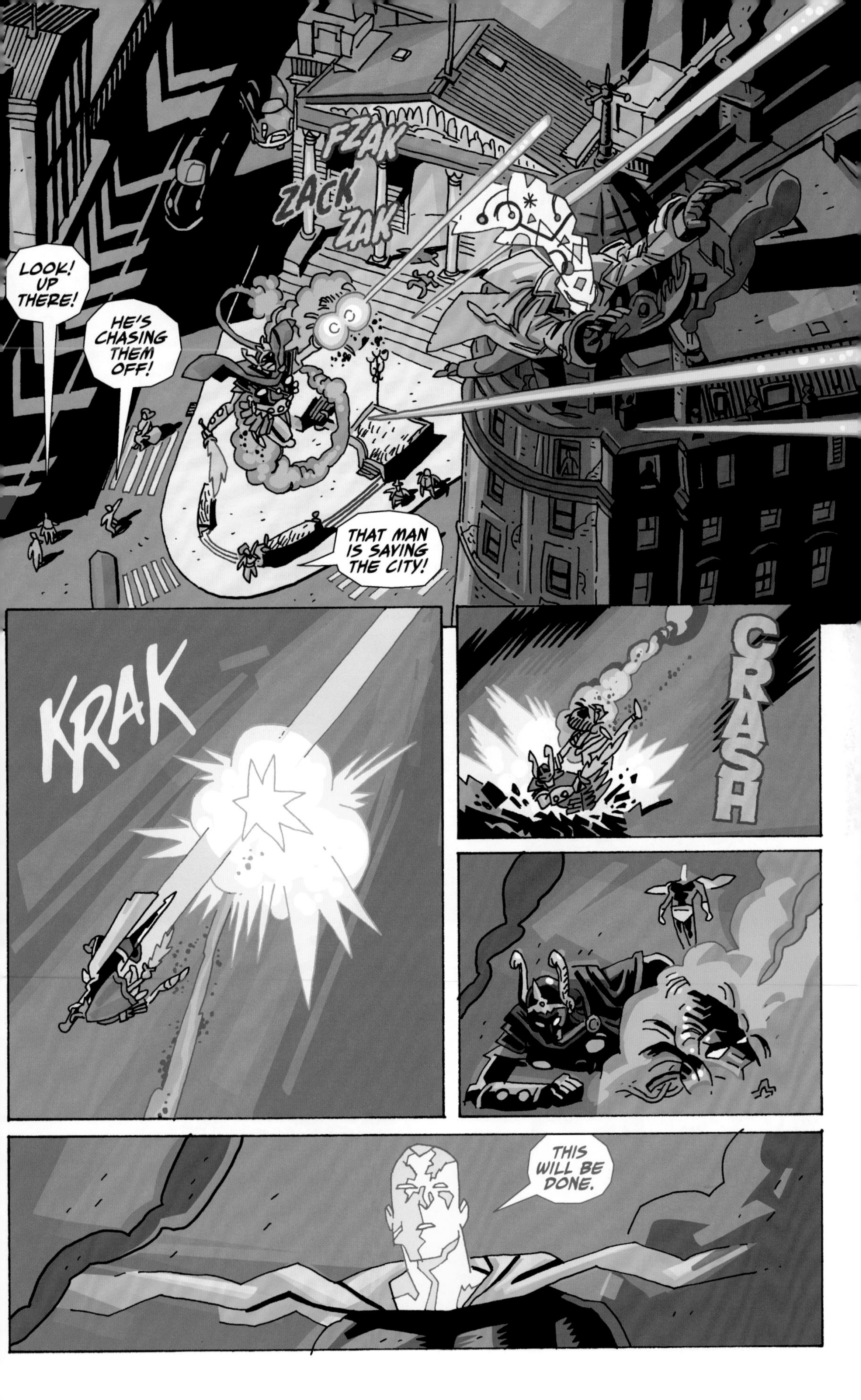
FZAK
ZACK
ZAK
LOOK! UP THERE!
HE'S CHASING THEM OFF!
THAT MAN IS SAVING THE CITY!
KRAK
CRASH
THIS WILL BE DONE.

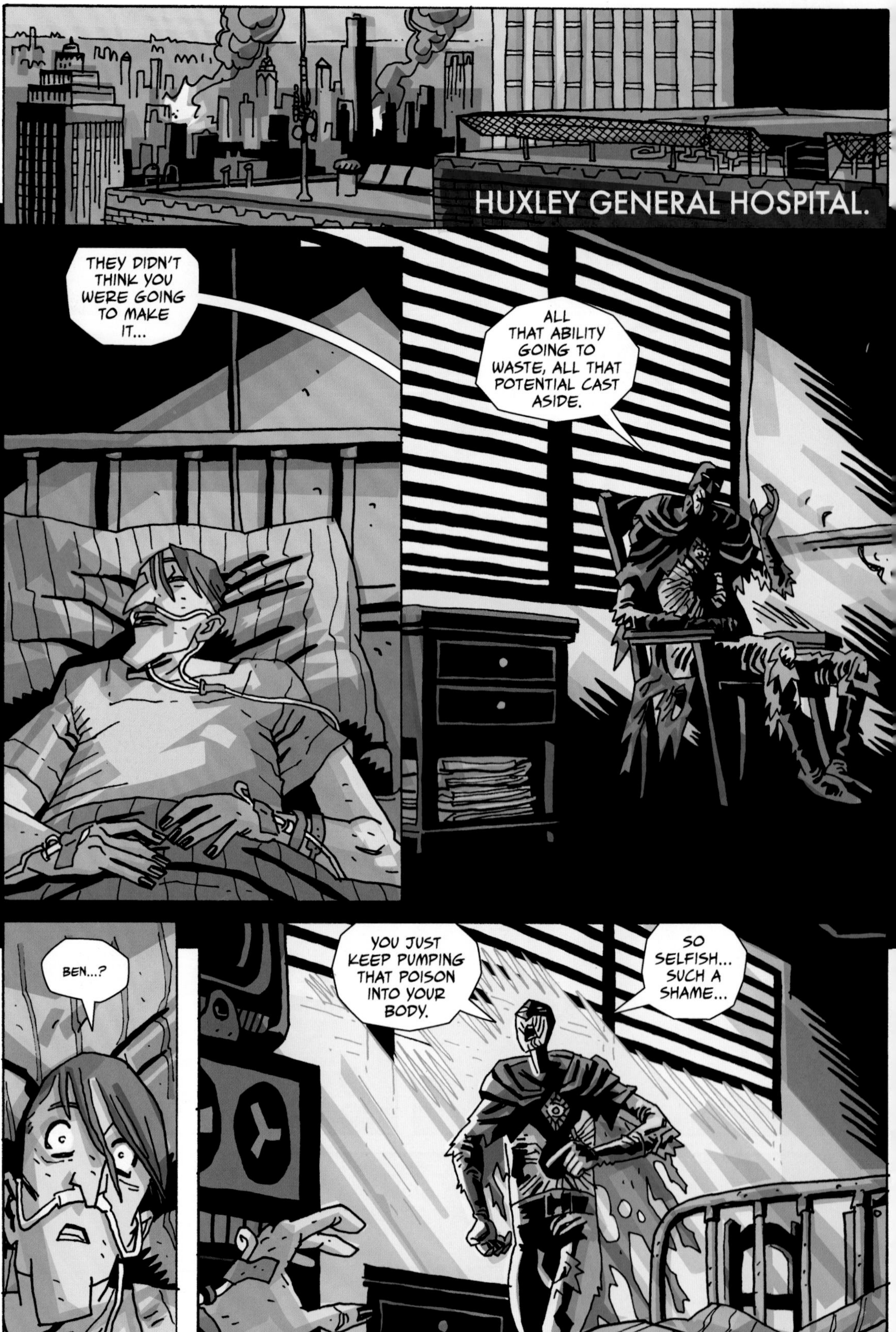
HUXLEY GENERAL HOSPITAL.
THEY DIDN'T THINK YOU WERE GOING TO MAKE IT...
ALL THAT ABILITY GOING TO WASTE, ALL THAT POTENTIAL CAST ASIDE.
BEN...?
YOU JUST KEEP PUMPING THAT POISON INTO YOUR BODY.
SO SELFISH... SUCH A SHAME...

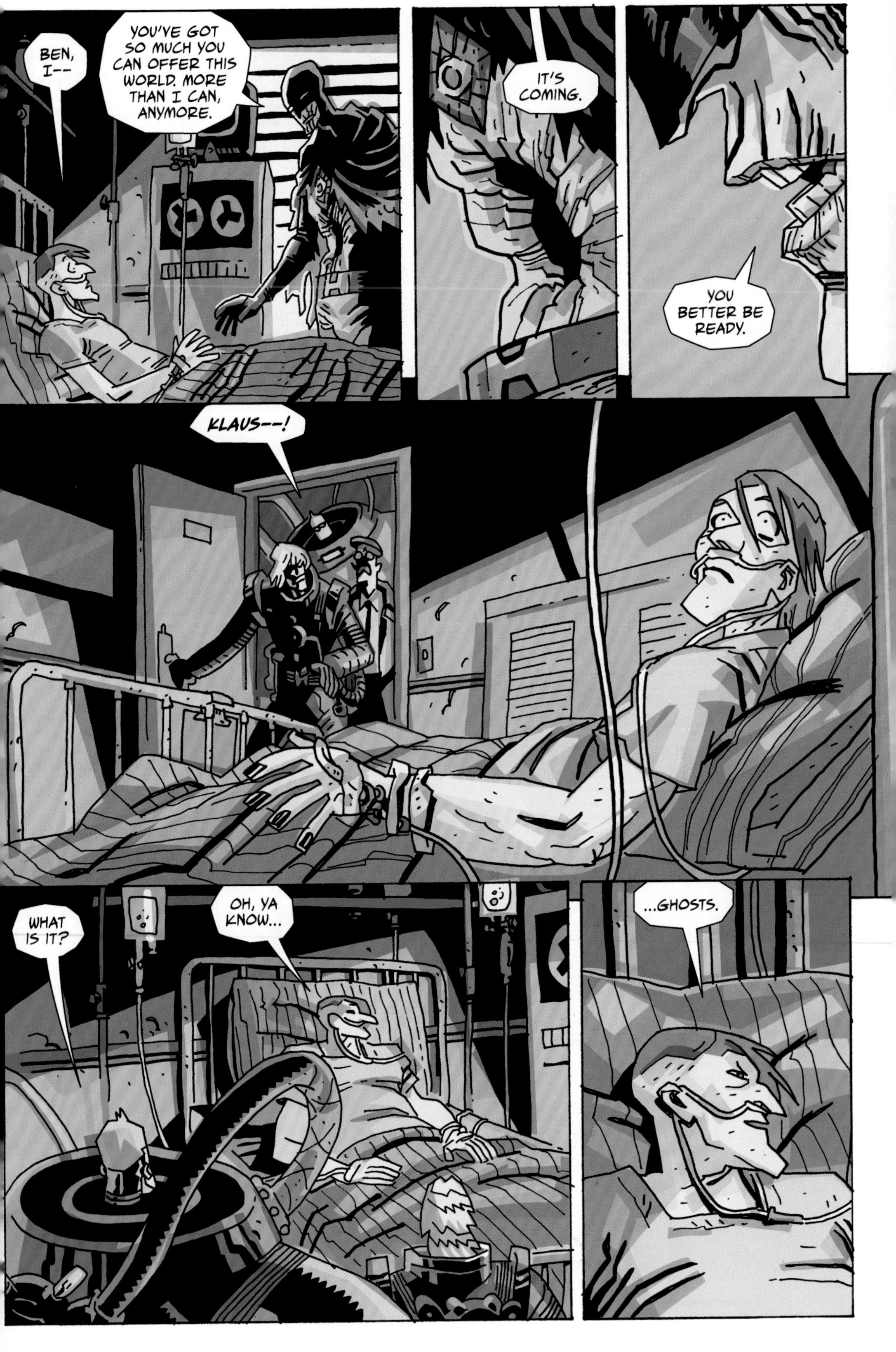
BEN, I--
YOU'VE GOT SO MUCH YOU CAN OFFER THIS WORLD. MORE THAN I CAN, ANYMORE.
IT'S COMING.
YOU BETTER BE READY.
KLAUS--!
WHAT IS IT?
OH, YA KNOW...
...GHOSTS.

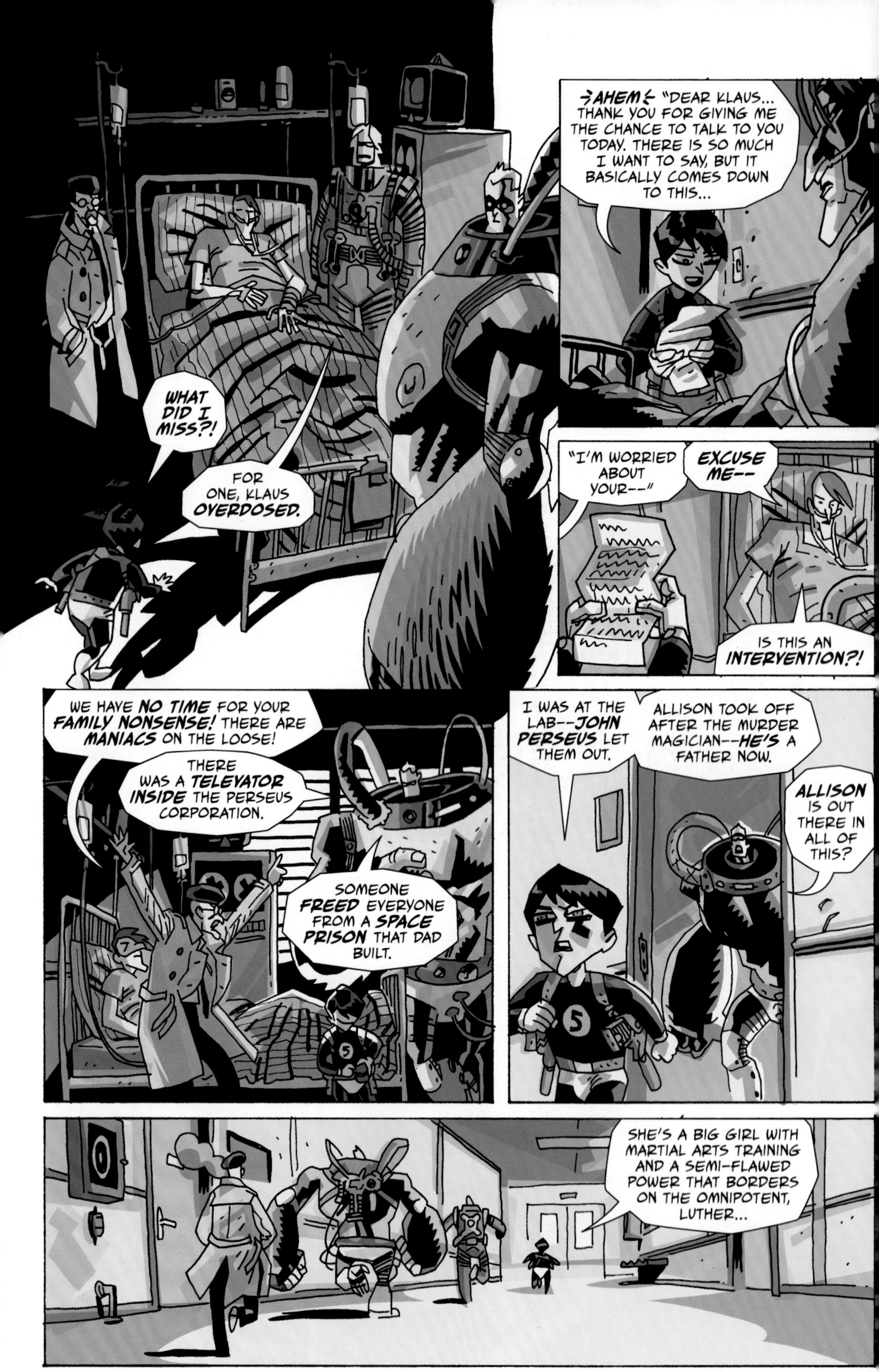
WHAT DID I MISS?!
FOR ONE, KLAUS OVERDOSED.
≥AHEM≤ "DEAR KLAUS... THANK YOU FOR GIVING ME THE CHANCE TO TALK TO YOU TODAY. THERE IS SO MUCH I WANT TO SAY, BUT IT BASICALLY COMES DOWN TO THIS...
"I'M WORRIED ABOUT YOUR--"
EXCUSE ME--
IS THIS AN INTERVENTION?!
WE HAVE NO TIME FOR YOUR FAMILY NONSENSE! THERE ARE MANIACS ON THE LOOSE!
THERE WAS A TELEVATOR INSIDE THE PERSEUS CORPORATION.
SOMEONE FREED EVERYONE FROM A SPACE PRISON THAT DAD BUILT.
I WAS AT THE LAB--JOHN PERSEUS LET THEM OUT.
ALLISON TOOK OFF AFTER THE MURDER MAGICIAN--HE'S A FATHER NOW.
ALLISON IS OUT THERE IN ALL OF THIS?
SHE'S A BIG GIRL WITH MARTIAL ARTS TRAINING AND A SEMI-FLAWED POWER THAT BORDERS ON THE OMNIPOTENT, LUTHER...

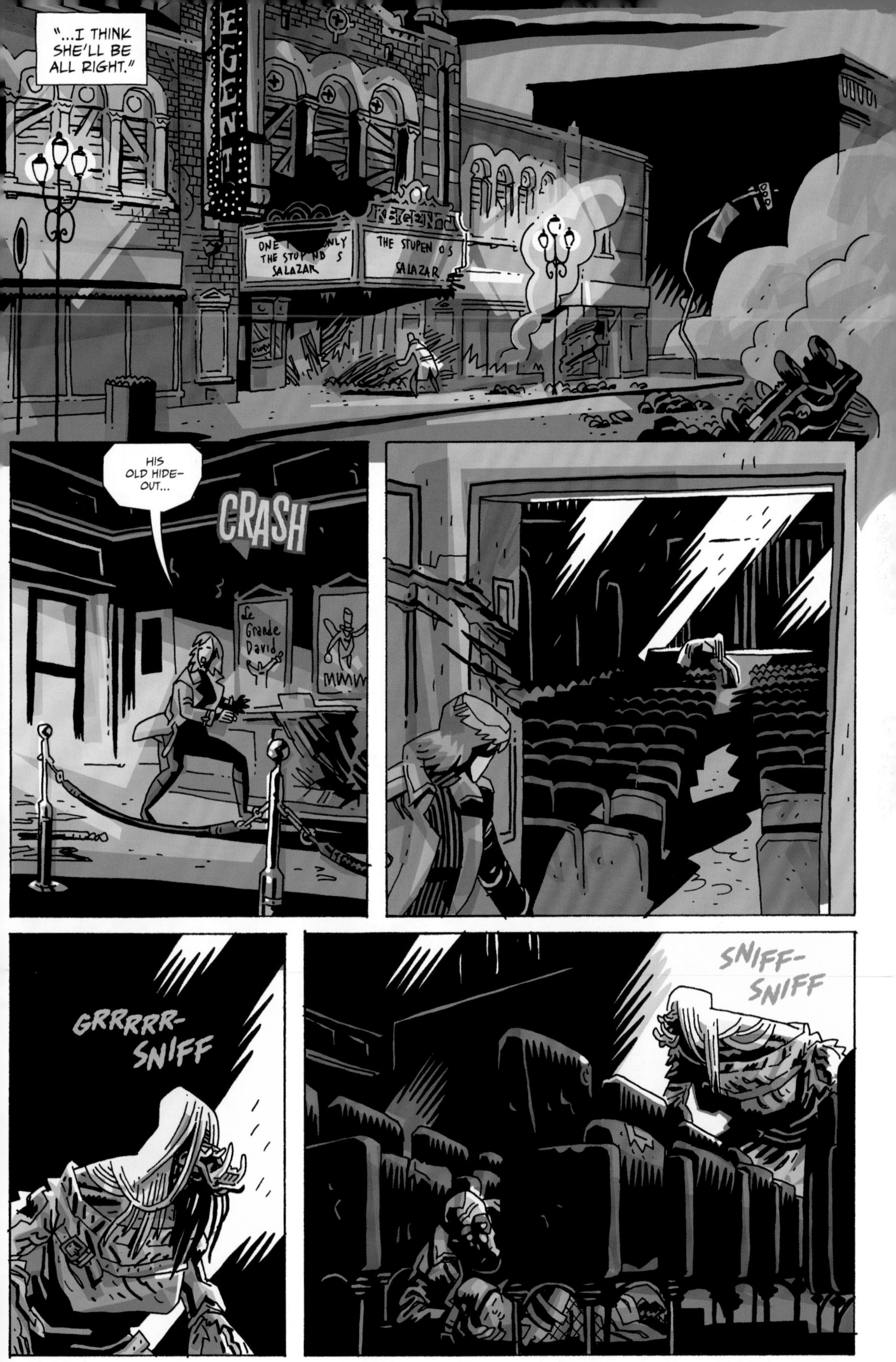
"...I THINK SHE'LL BE ALL RIGHT."
ONE NIGHT ONLY THE STUPENDOUS SALAZAR
THE STUPENDOUS SALAZAR
HIS OLD HIDE-OUT...
CRASH
Le Grande David
GRRRRR-SNIFF
SNIFF-SNIFF

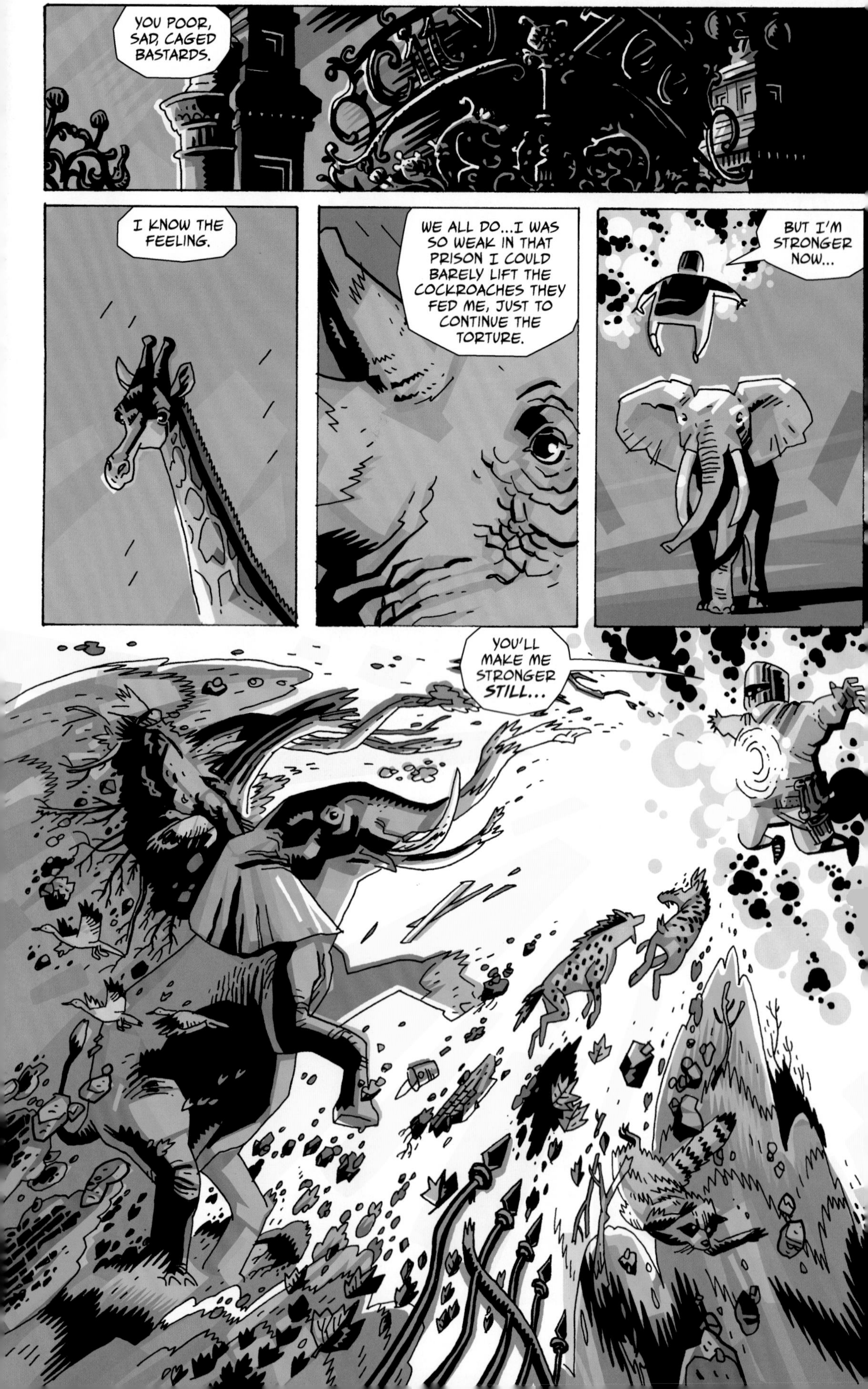
YOU POOR, SAD, CAGED BASTARDS.
I KNOW THE FEELING.
WE ALL DO...I WAS SO WEAK IN THAT PRISON I COULD BARELY LIFT THE COCKROACHES THEY FED ME, JUST TO CONTINUE THE TORTURE.
BUT I'M STRONGER NOW...
YOU'LL MAKE ME STRONGER STILL...

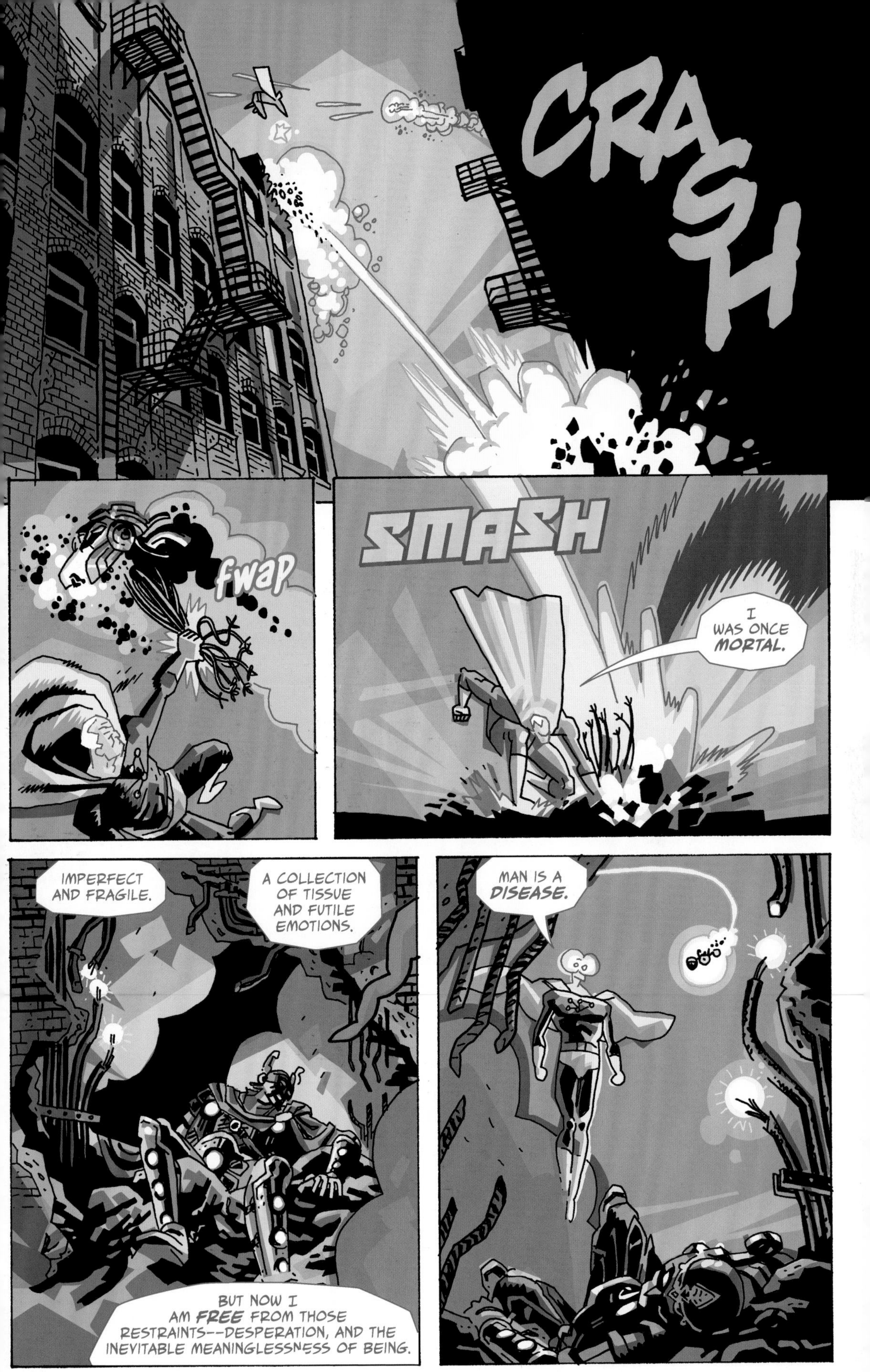

CRASH
fwap
SMASH
I WAS ONCE MORTAL.
IMPERFECT AND FRAGILE.
A COLLECTION OF TISSUE AND FUTILE EMOTIONS.
BUT NOW I AM FREE FROM THOSE RESTRAINTS--DESPERATION, AND THE INEVITABLE MEANINGLESSNESS OF BEING.
MAN IS A DISEASE.

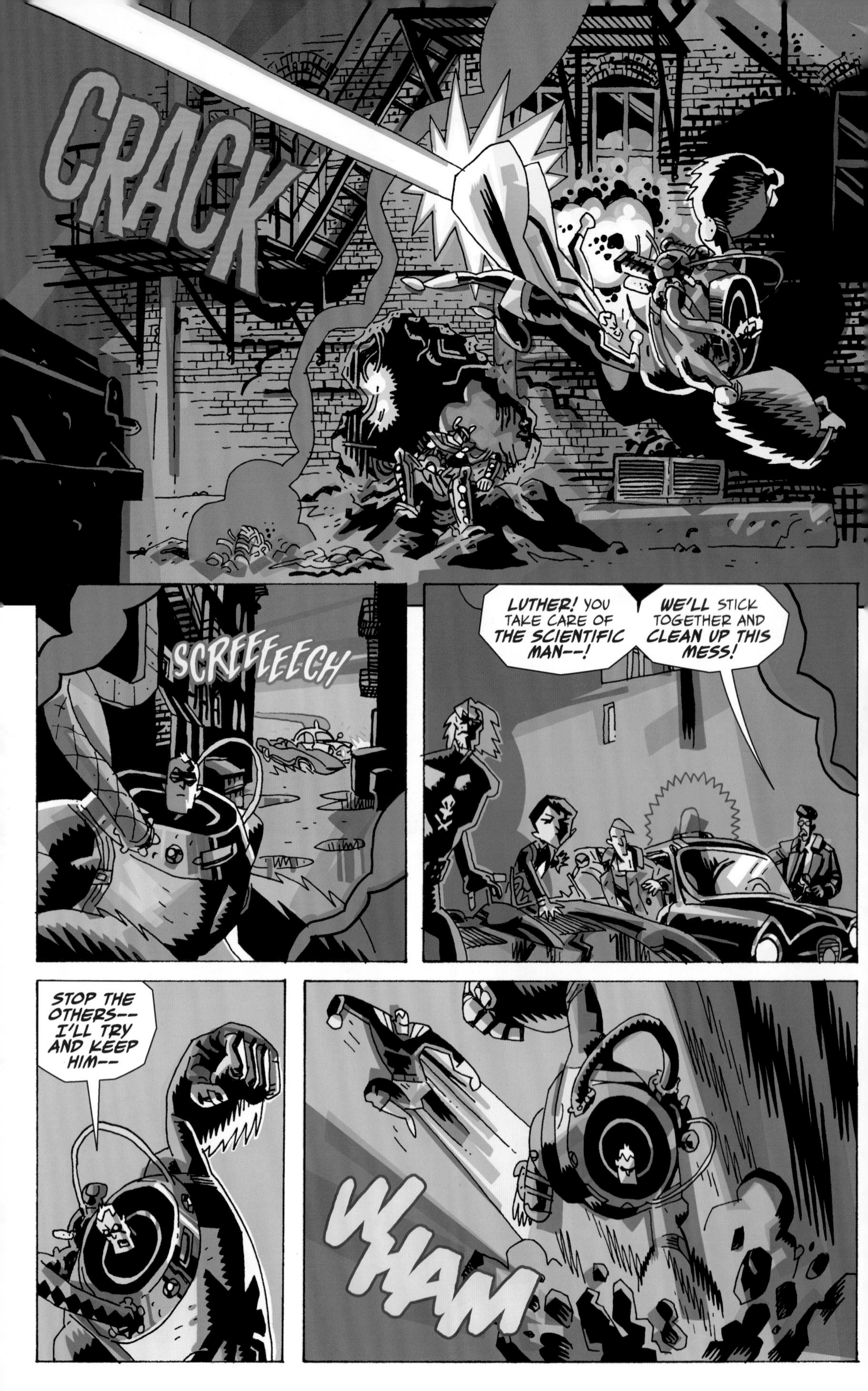
CRACK
SCREEEEECH
LUTHER! YOU TAKE CARE OF THE SCIENTIFIC MAN--!
WE'LL STICK TOGETHER AND CLEAN UP THIS MESS!
STOP THE OTHERS-- I'LL TRY AND KEEP HIM--
WHAM

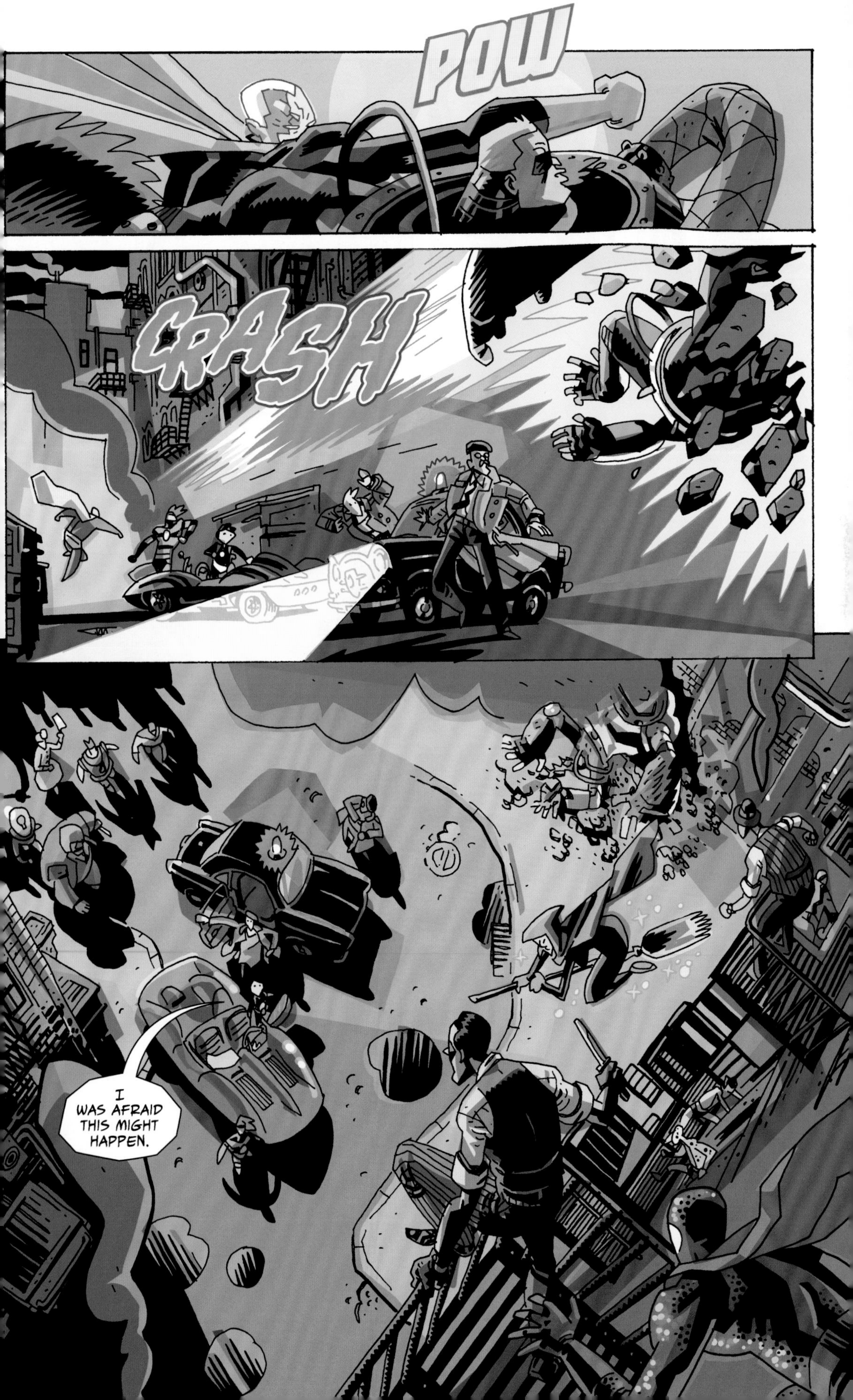
POW
CRASH
I WAS AFRAID THIS MIGHT HAPPEN.

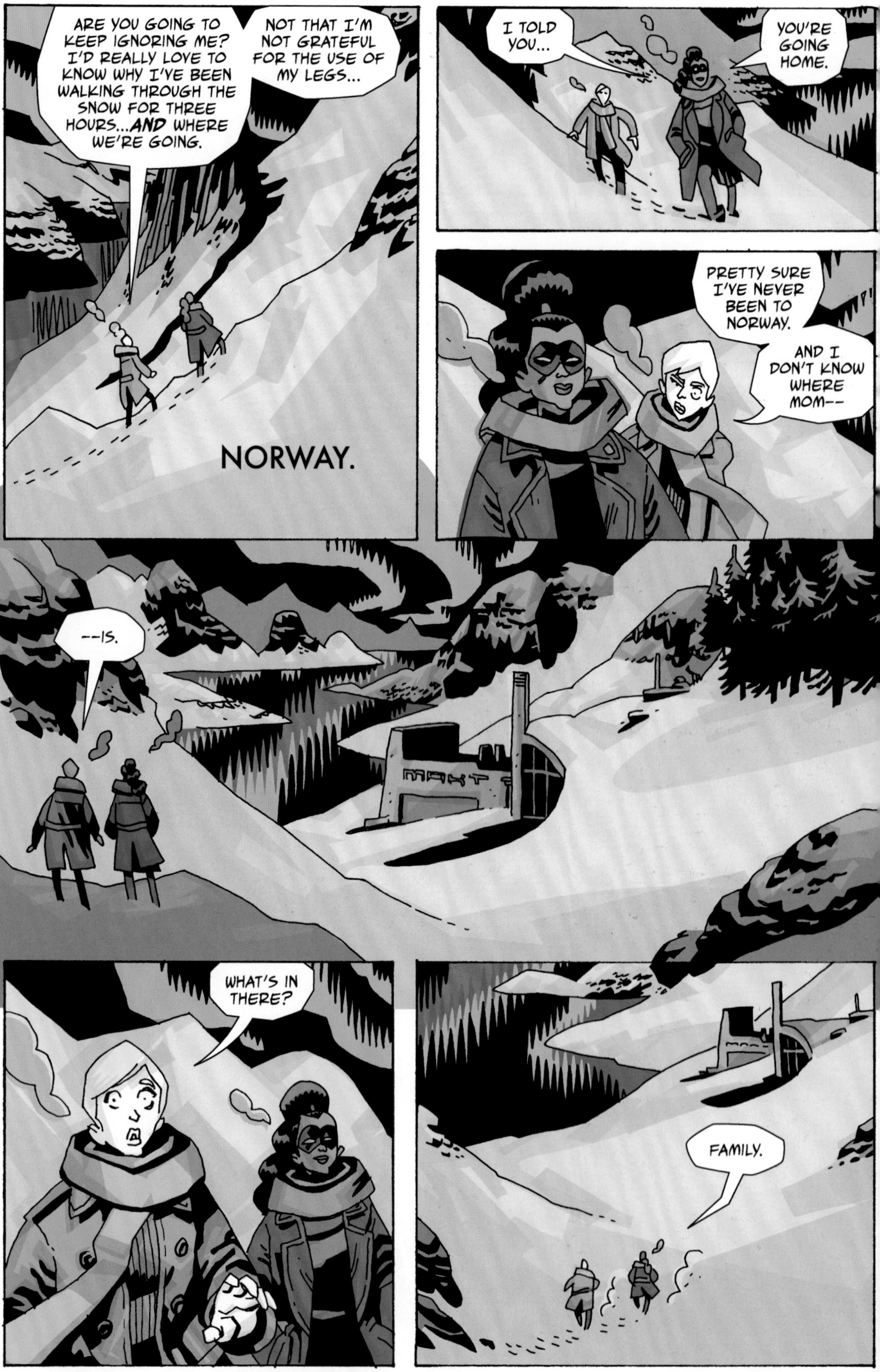

ARE YOU GOING TO KEEP IGNORING ME? I'D REALLY LOVE TO KNOW WHY I'VE BEEN WALKING THROUGH THE SNOW FOR THREE HOURS...AND WHERE WE'RE GOING.
NOT THAT I'M NOT GRATEFUL FOR THE USE OF MY LEGS...
NORWAY.
I TOLD YOU...
YOU'RE GOING HOME.
PRETTY SURE I'VE NEVER BEEN TO NORWAY.
AND I DON'T KNOW WHERE MOM--
--IS.
WHAT'S IN THERE?
FAMILY.

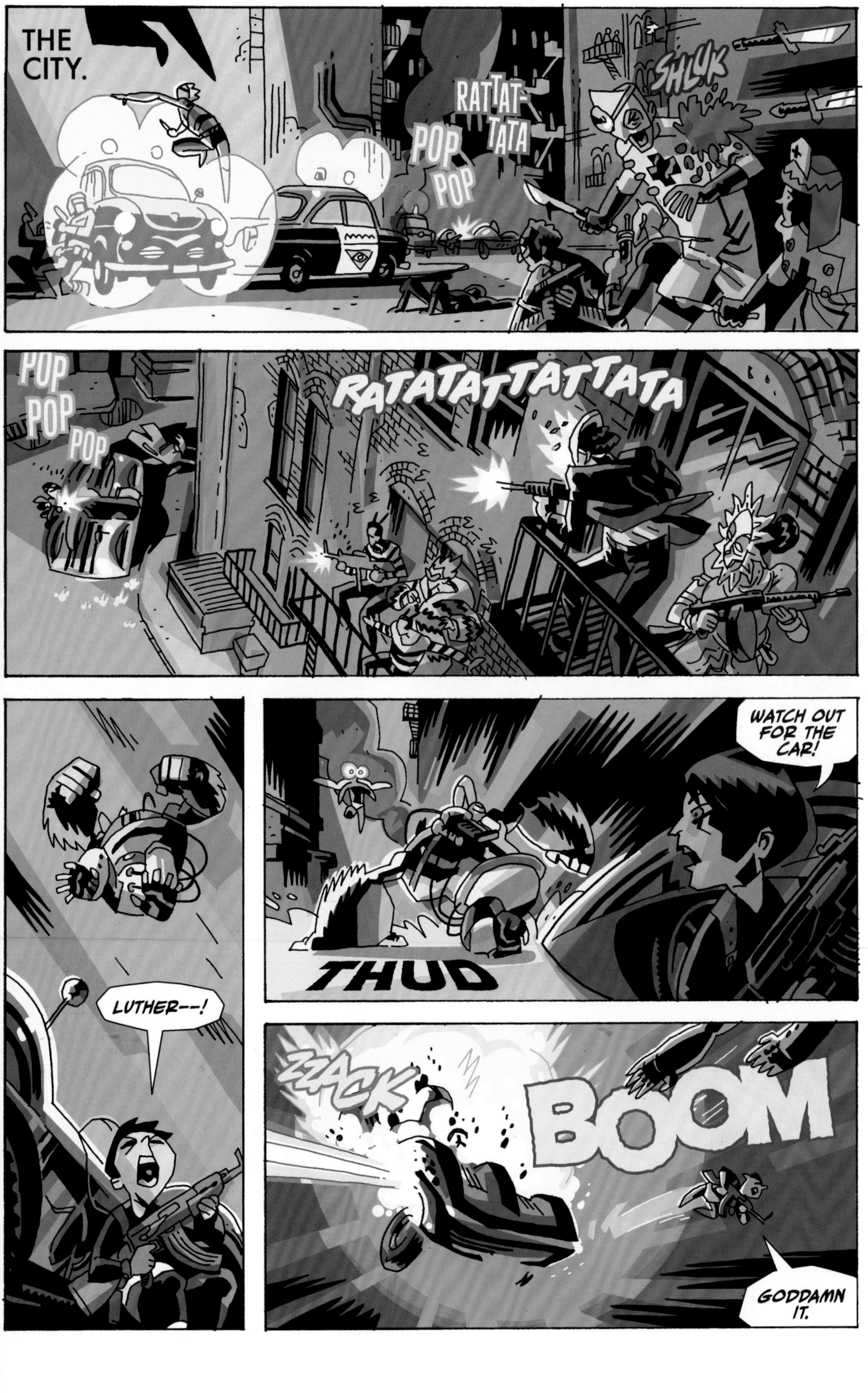
THE CITY.
POP POP
RATTAT-TATA
SHLUK
POP POP POP
RATATATTATTATA
LUTHER--!
WATCH OUT FOR THE CAR!
THUD
ZZACK
BOOM
GODDAMN IT.

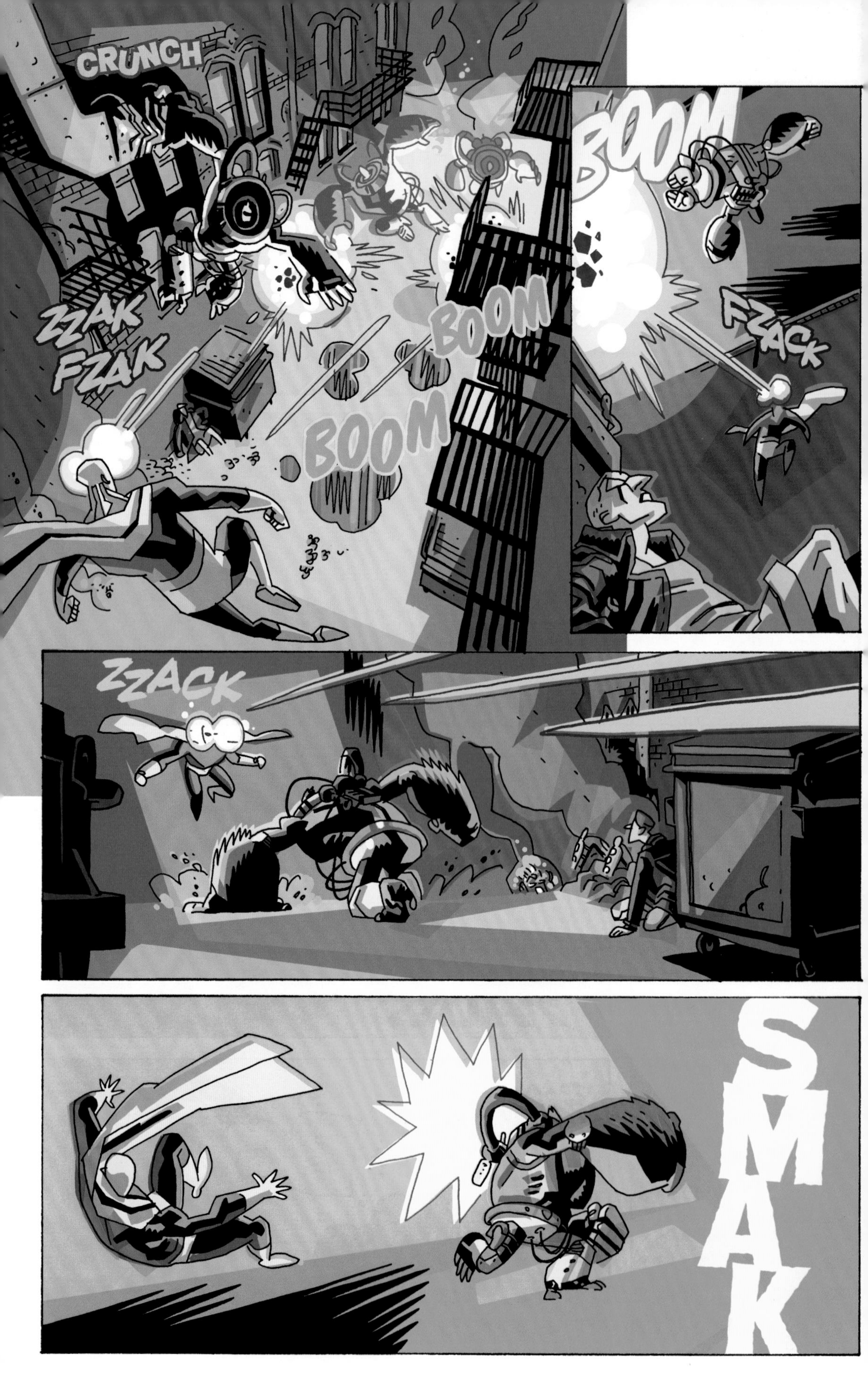
CRUNCH
ZZAK
FZAK
BOOM
BOOM
BOOM
FZACK
ZZACK
SMAK

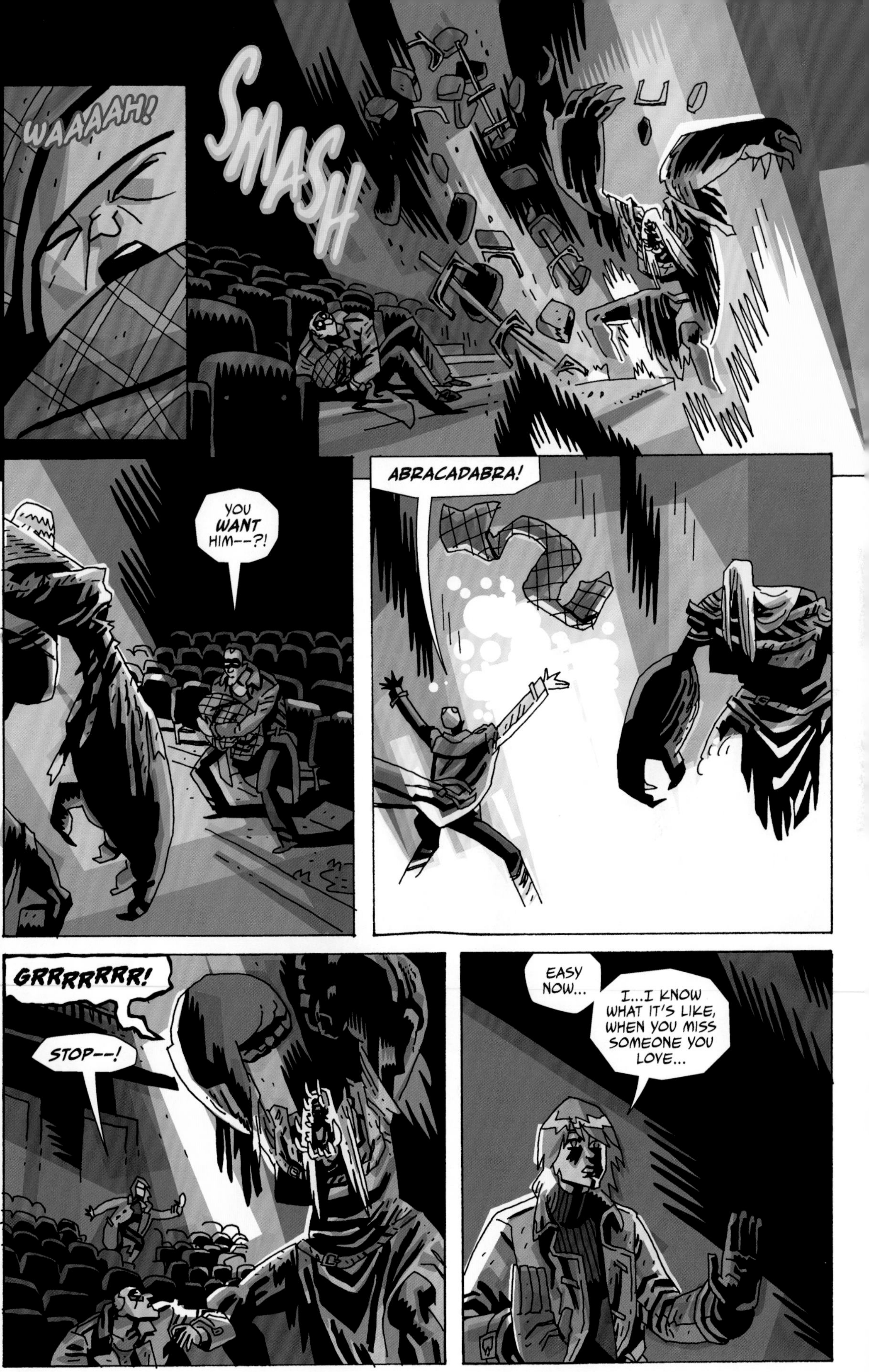
WAAAAH!
SMASH
YOU WANT HIM--?!
ABRACADABRA!
GRRRRRRR!
STOP--!
EASY NOW...
I...I KNOW WHAT IT'S LIKE, WHEN YOU MISS SOMEONE YOU LOVE...

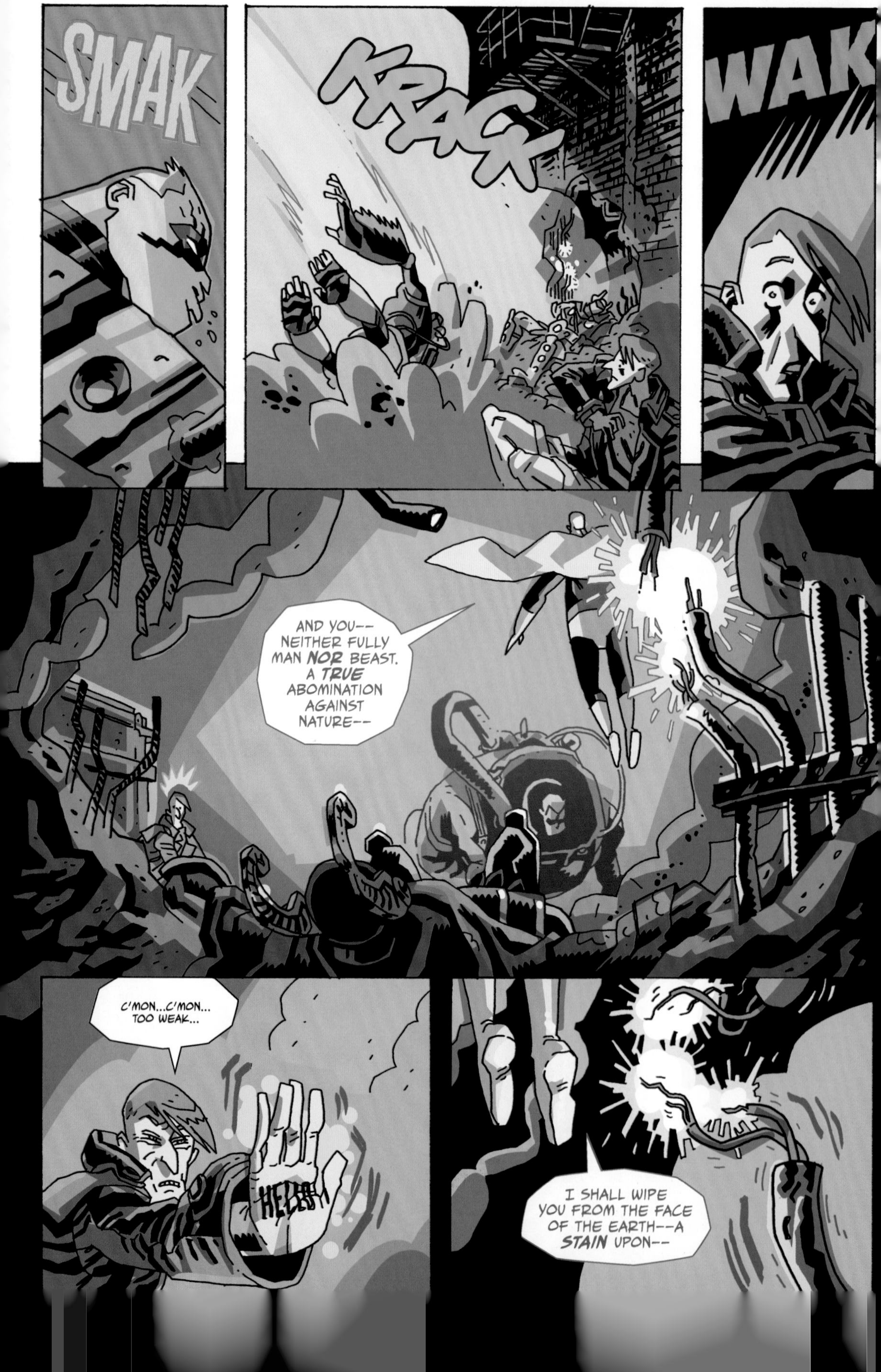
SMAK
KRACK
WAK
AND YOU-- NEITHER FULLY MAN NOR BEAST. A TRUE ABOMINATION AGAINST NATURE--
C'MON...C'MON... TOO WEAK...
I SHALL WIPE YOU FROM THE FACE OF THE EARTH--A STAIN UPON--

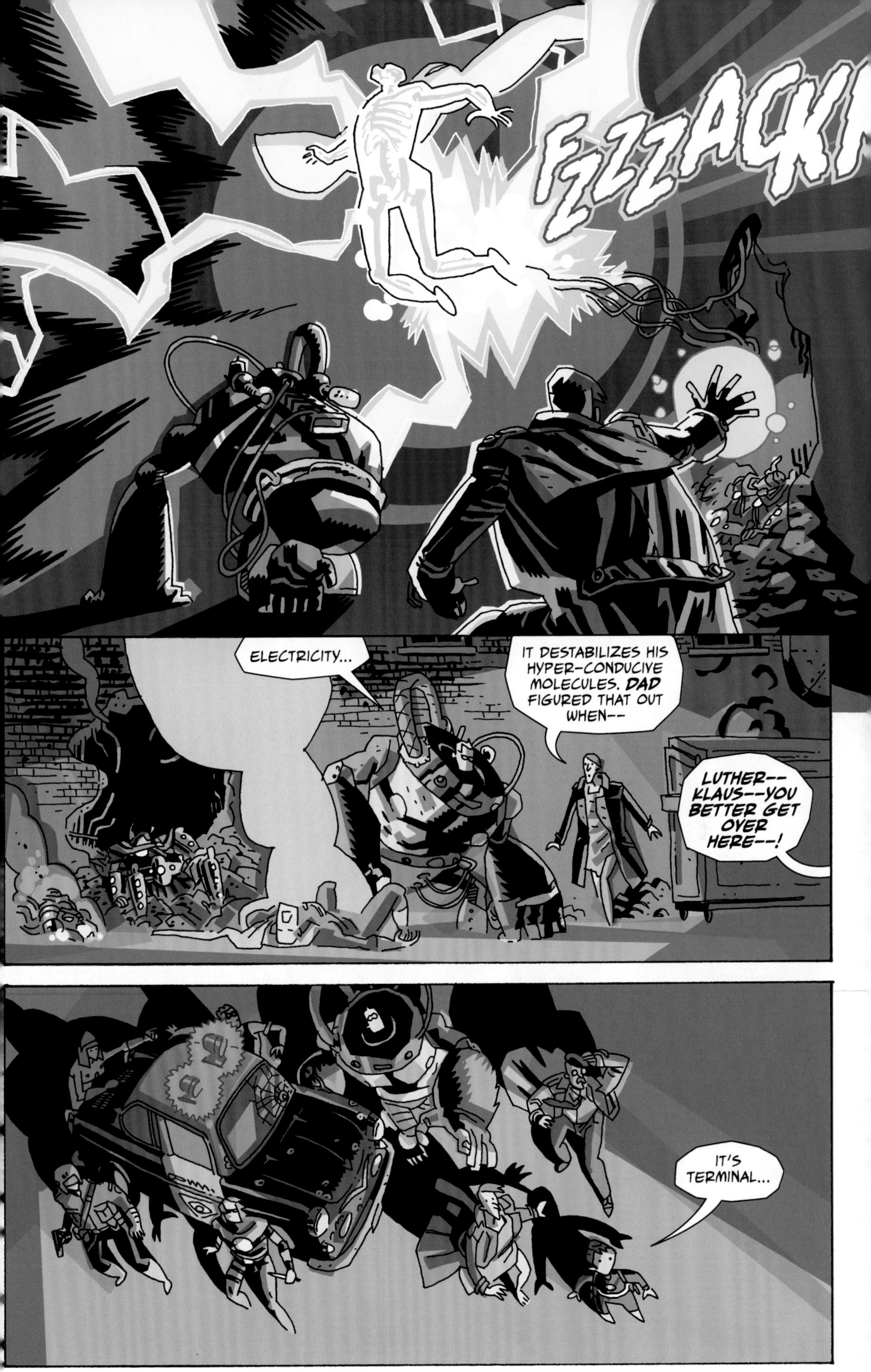
FZZZACK!
ELECTRICITY...
IT DESTABILIZES HIS HYPER-CONDUCIVE MOLECULES. DAD FIGURED THAT OUT WHEN--
LUTHER--KLAUS--YOU BETTER GET OVER HERE--!
IT'S TERMINAL...

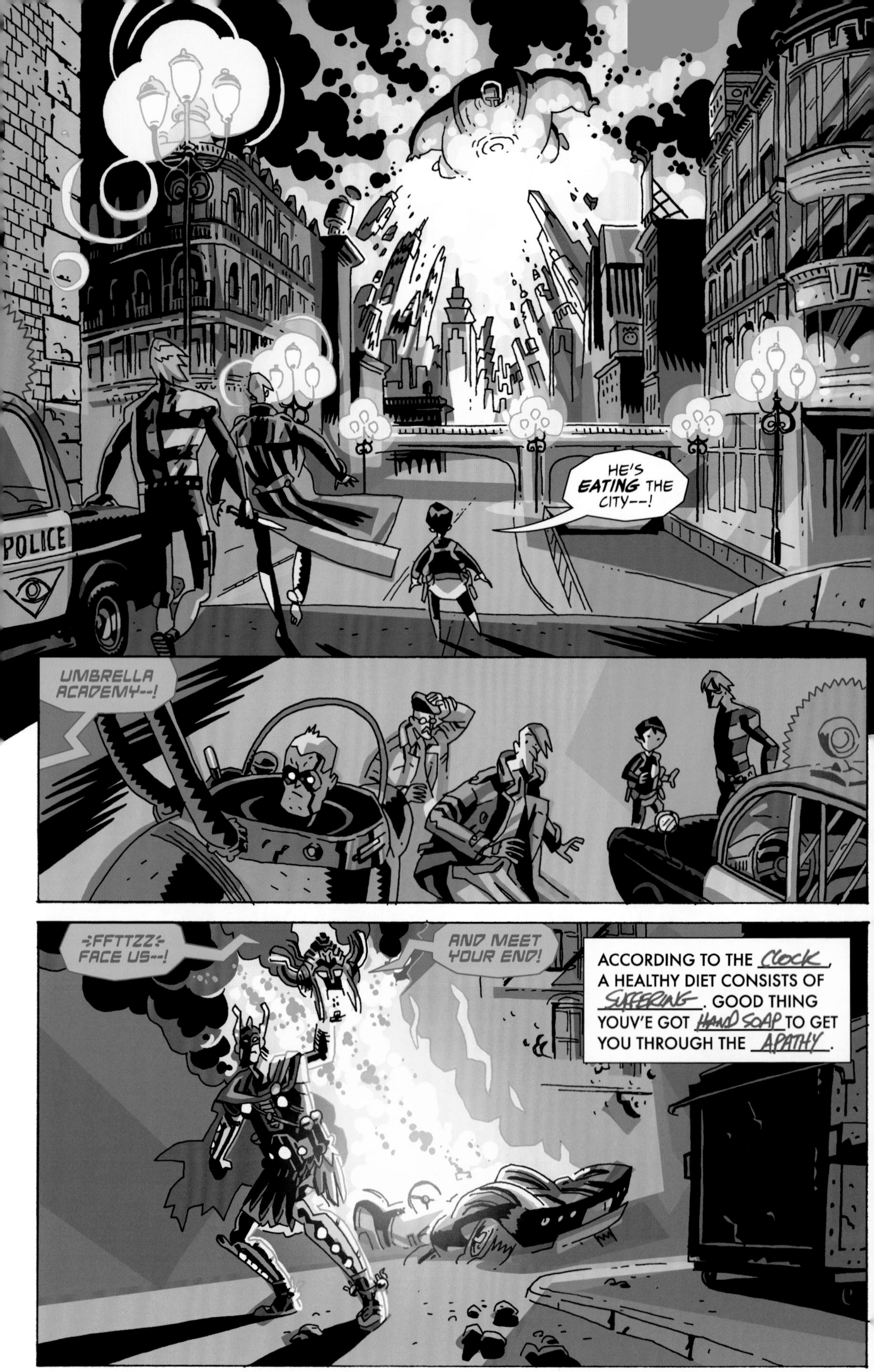
HE'S EATING THE CITY--!
POLICE
UMBRELLA ACADEMY--!
-FFTTZZ- FACE US--!
AND MEET YOUR END!
ACCORDING TO THE CLOCK, A HEALTHY DIET CONSISTS OF SUFFERING. GOOD THING YOUV'E GOT HAND SOAP TO GET YOU THROUGH THE APATHY.

CHAPTER SEVEN

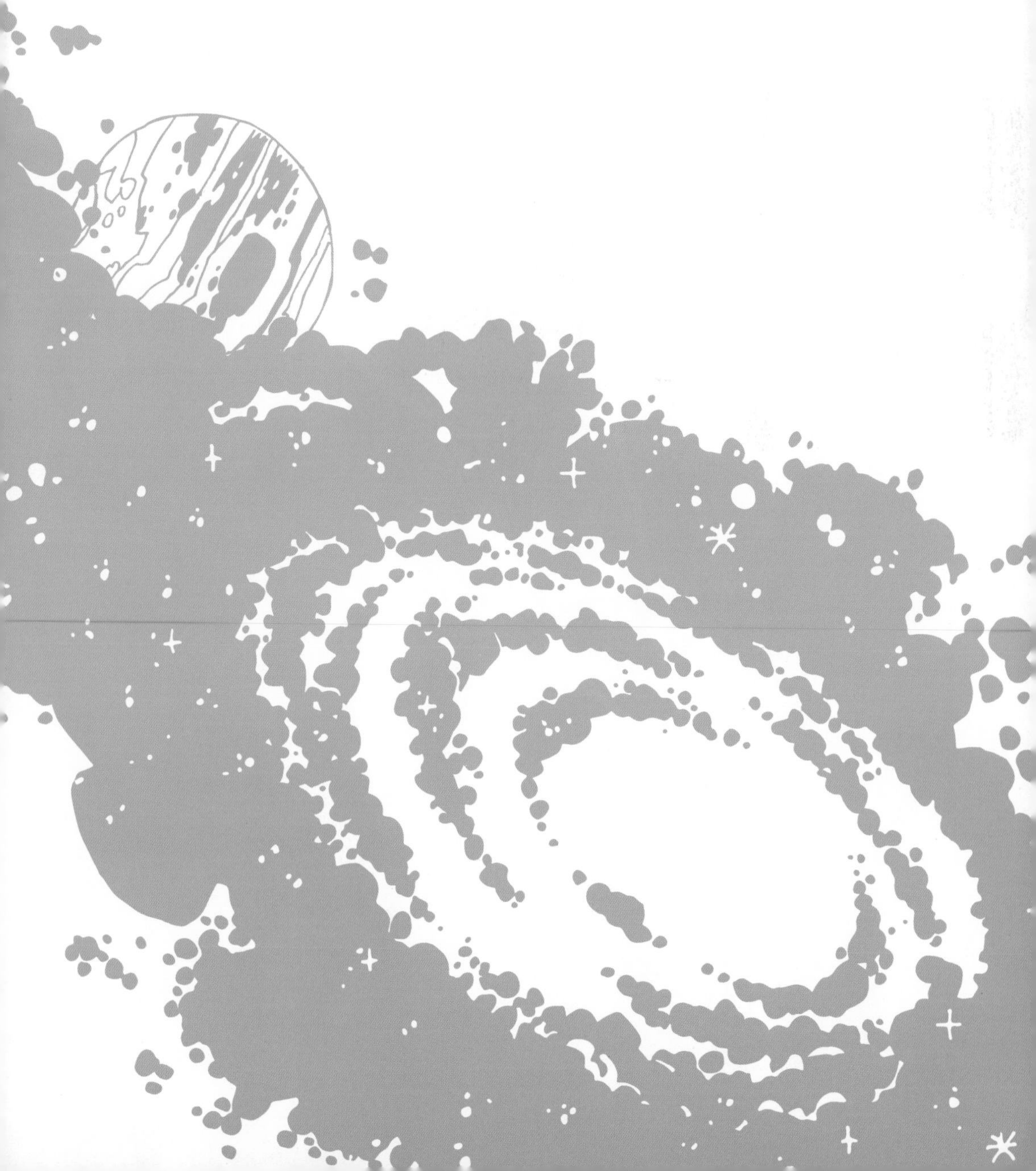

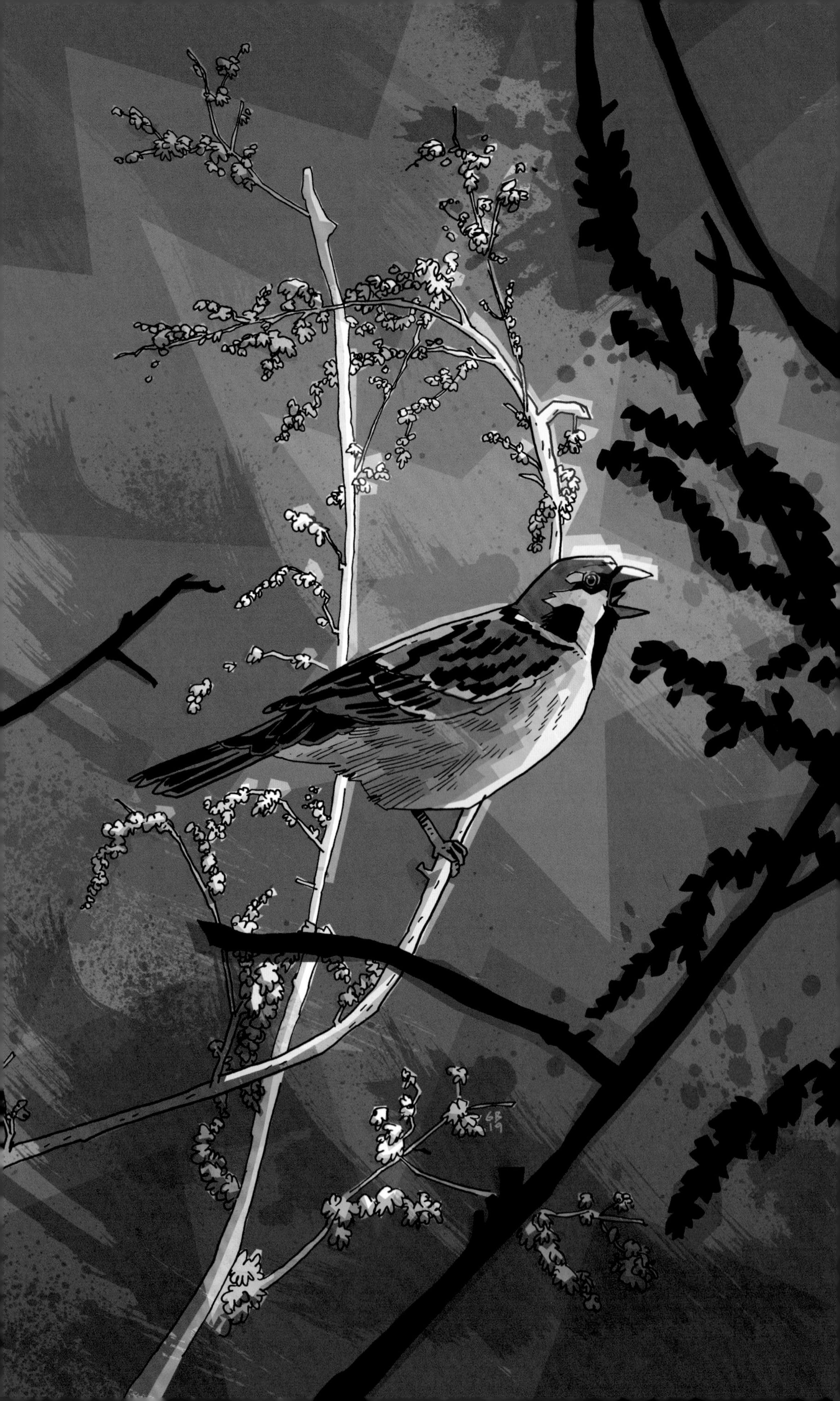
GB
'19

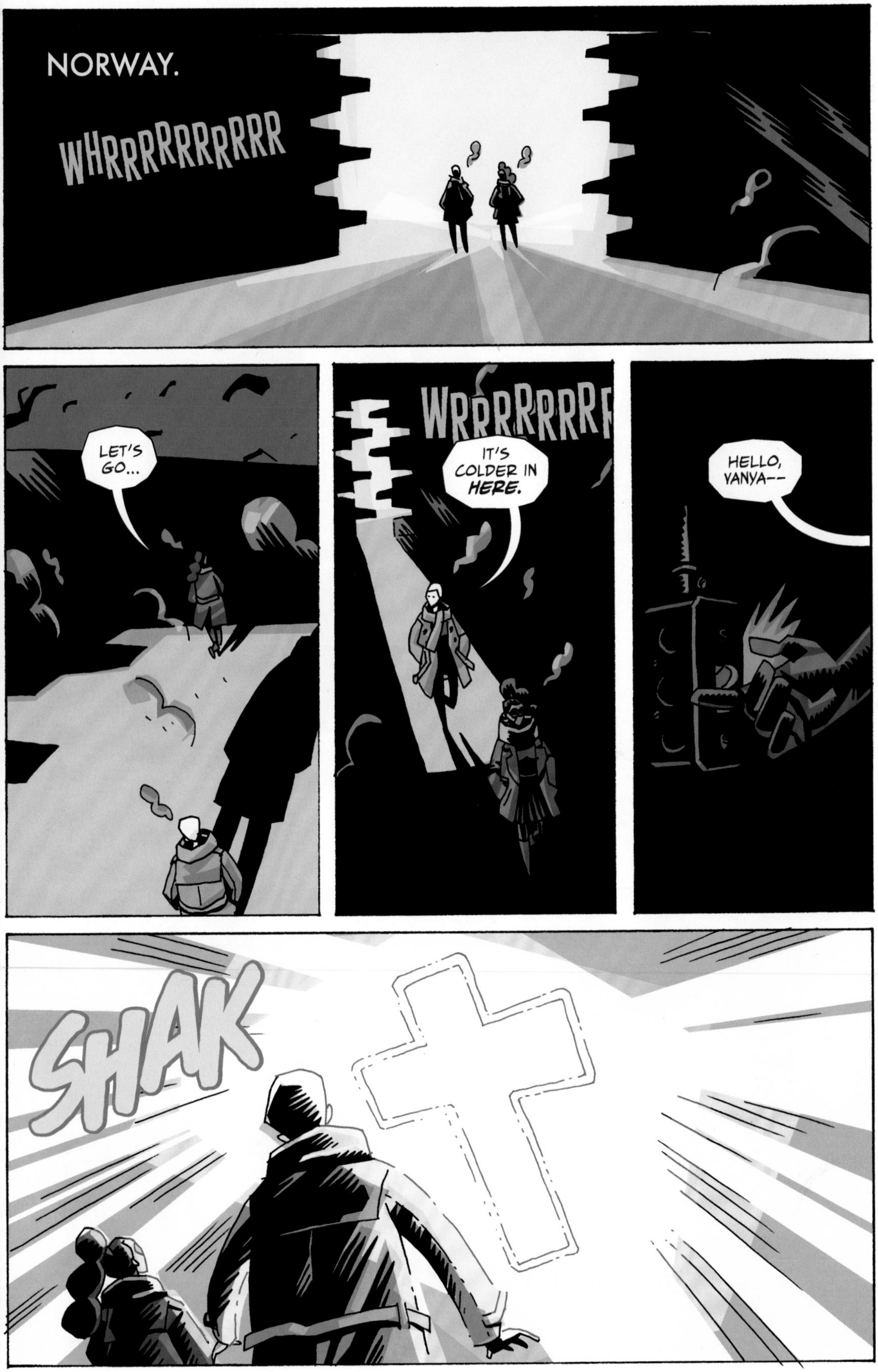
NORWAY.
WHRRRRRRRRR
LET'S GO...
WRRRRRRRR
IT'S COLDER IN HERE.
HELLO, VANYA--
SHAK

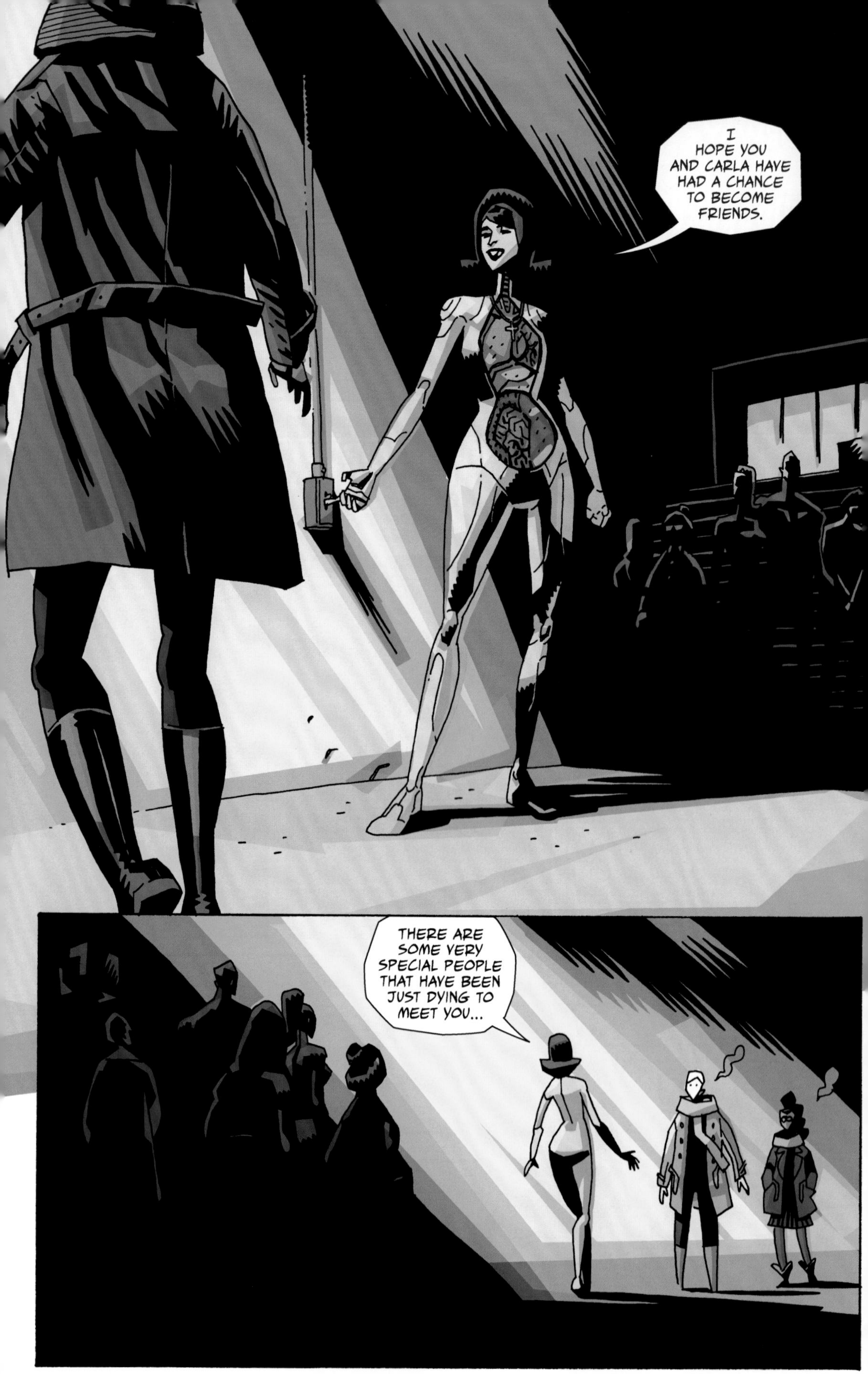
I HOPE YOU AND CARLA HAVE HAD A CHANCE TO BECOME FRIENDS.
THERE ARE SOME VERY SPECIAL PEOPLE THAT HAVE BEEN JUST DYING TO MEET YOU...

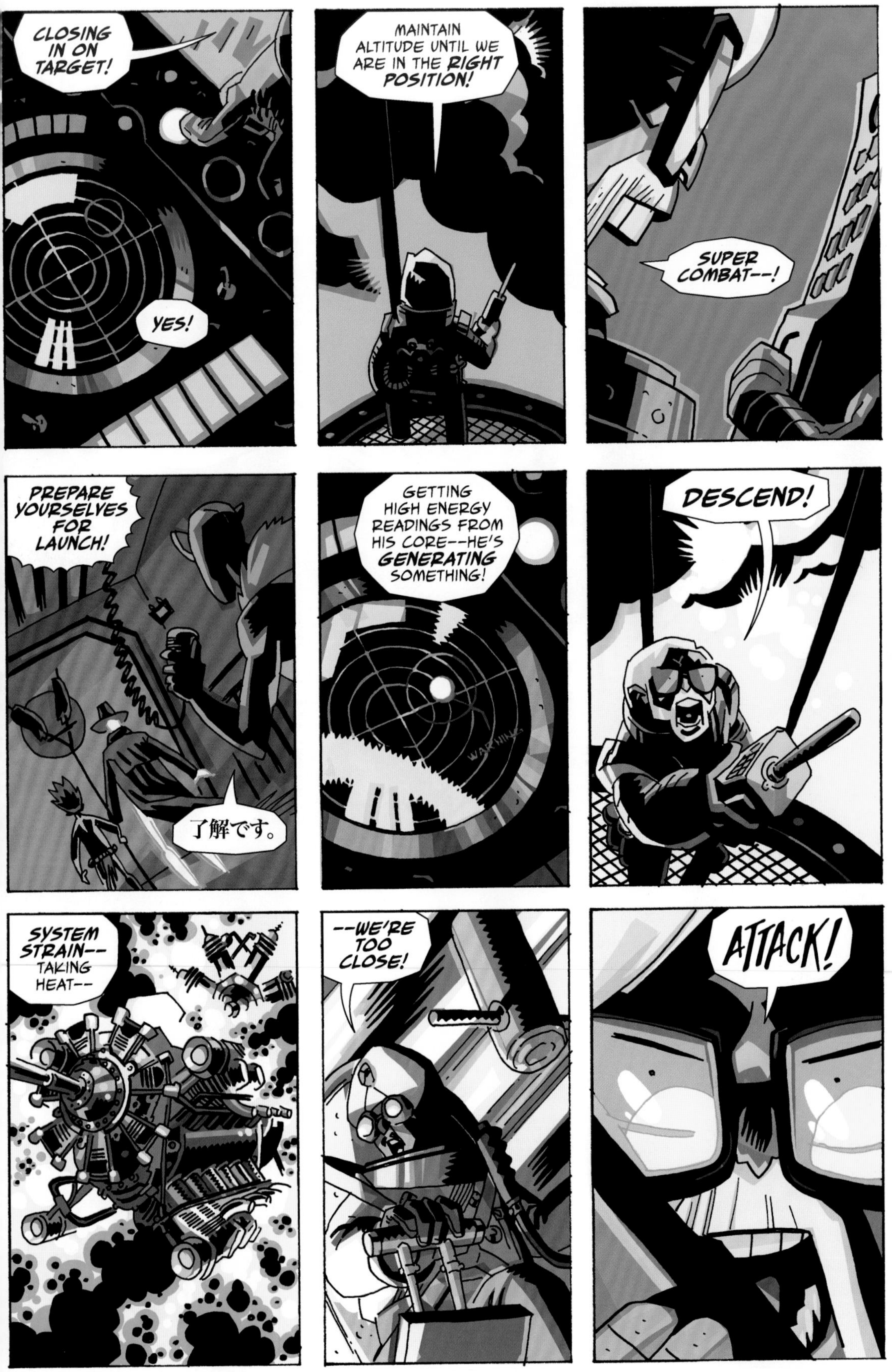
CLOSING IN ON TARGET!
YES!
MAINTAIN ALTITUDE UNTIL WE ARE IN THE RIGHT POSITION!
SUPER COMBAT--!
PREPARE YOURSELVES FOR LAUNCH!
了解です。
GETTING HIGH ENERGY READINGS FROM HIS CORE--HE'S GENERATING SOMETHING!
DESCEND!
SYSTEM STRAIN--TAKING HEAT--
--WE'RE TOO CLOSE!
ATTACK!

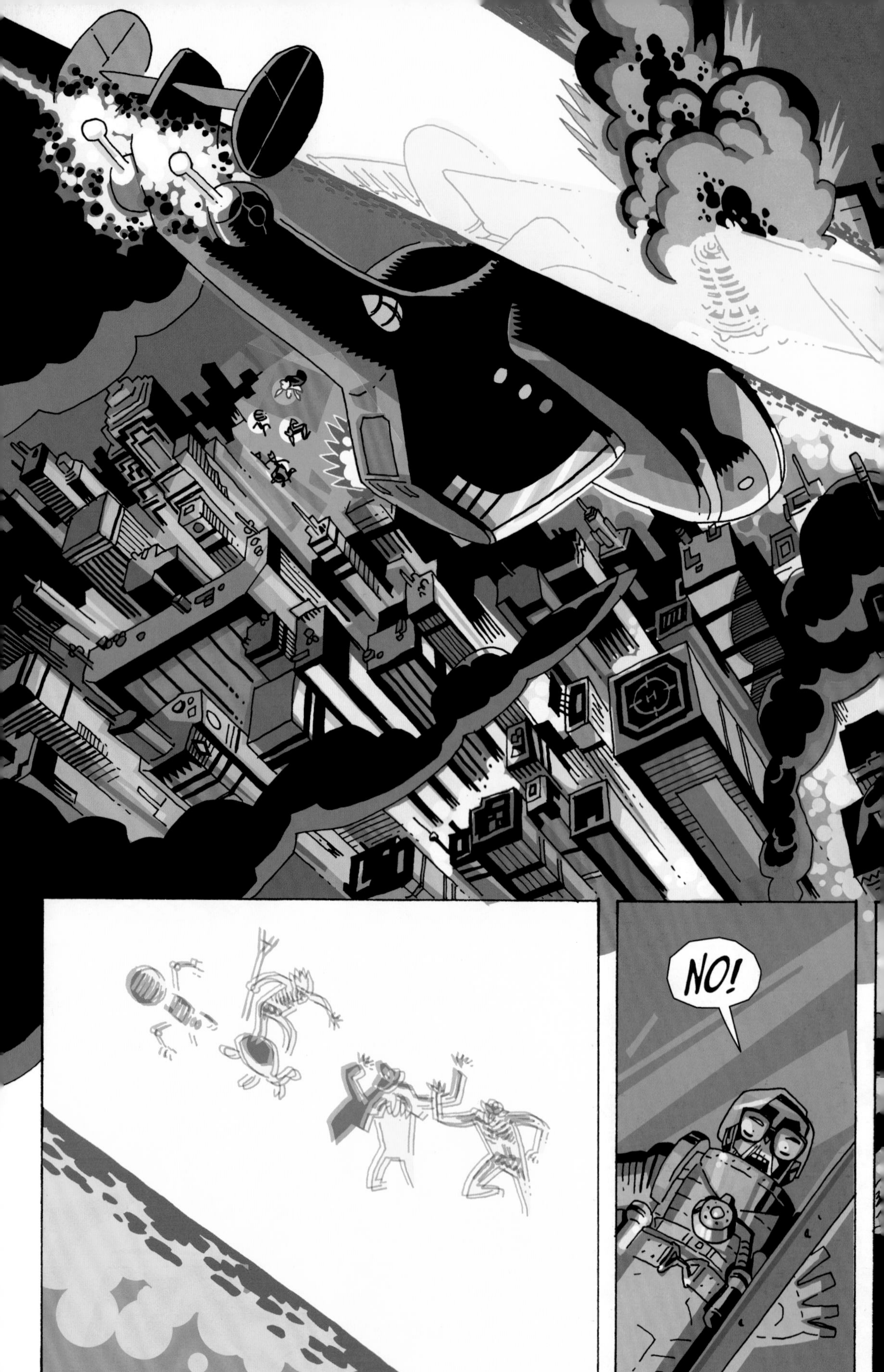
NO!

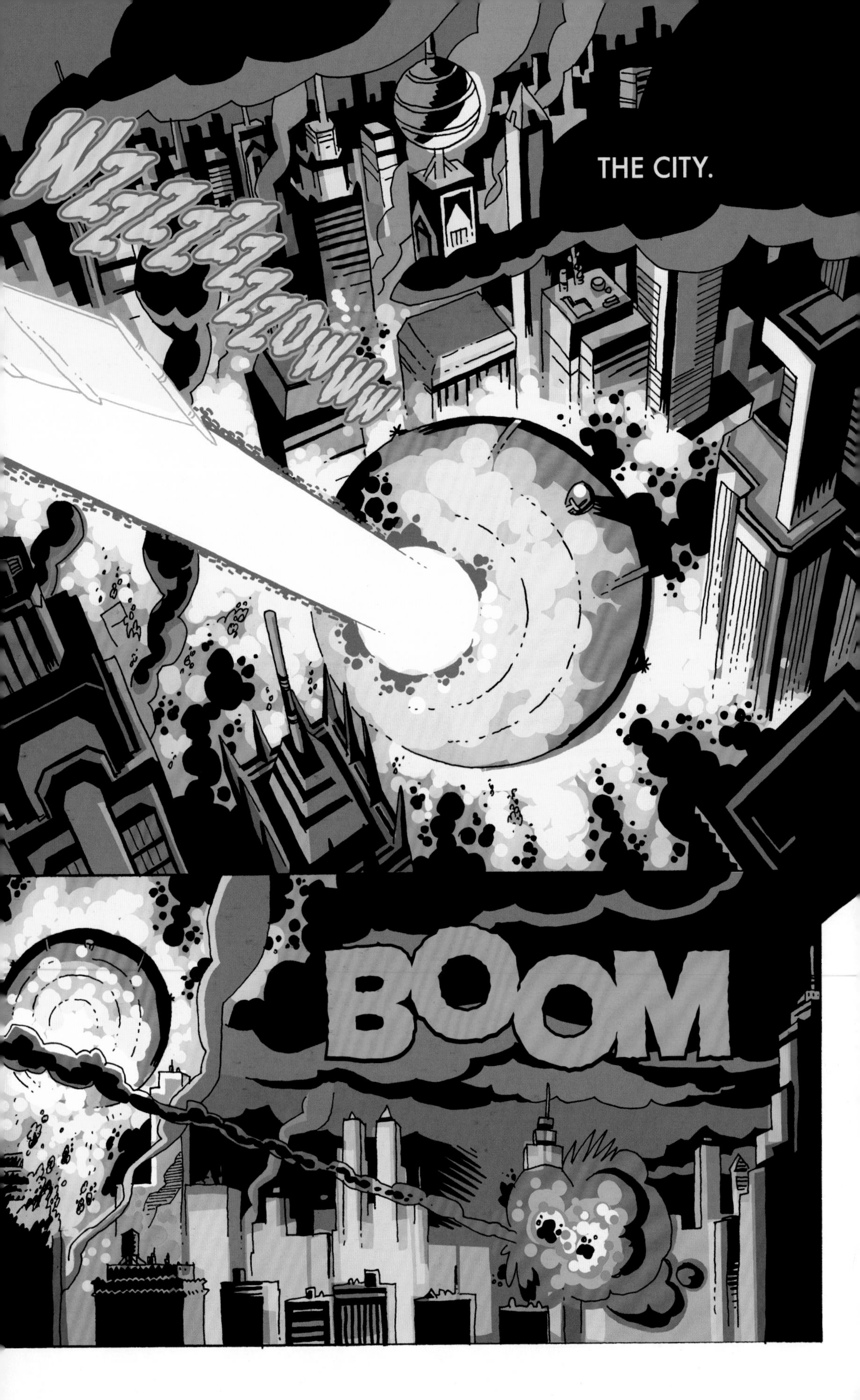
THE CITY.
WZZZZZZZZZOWWW
BOOM

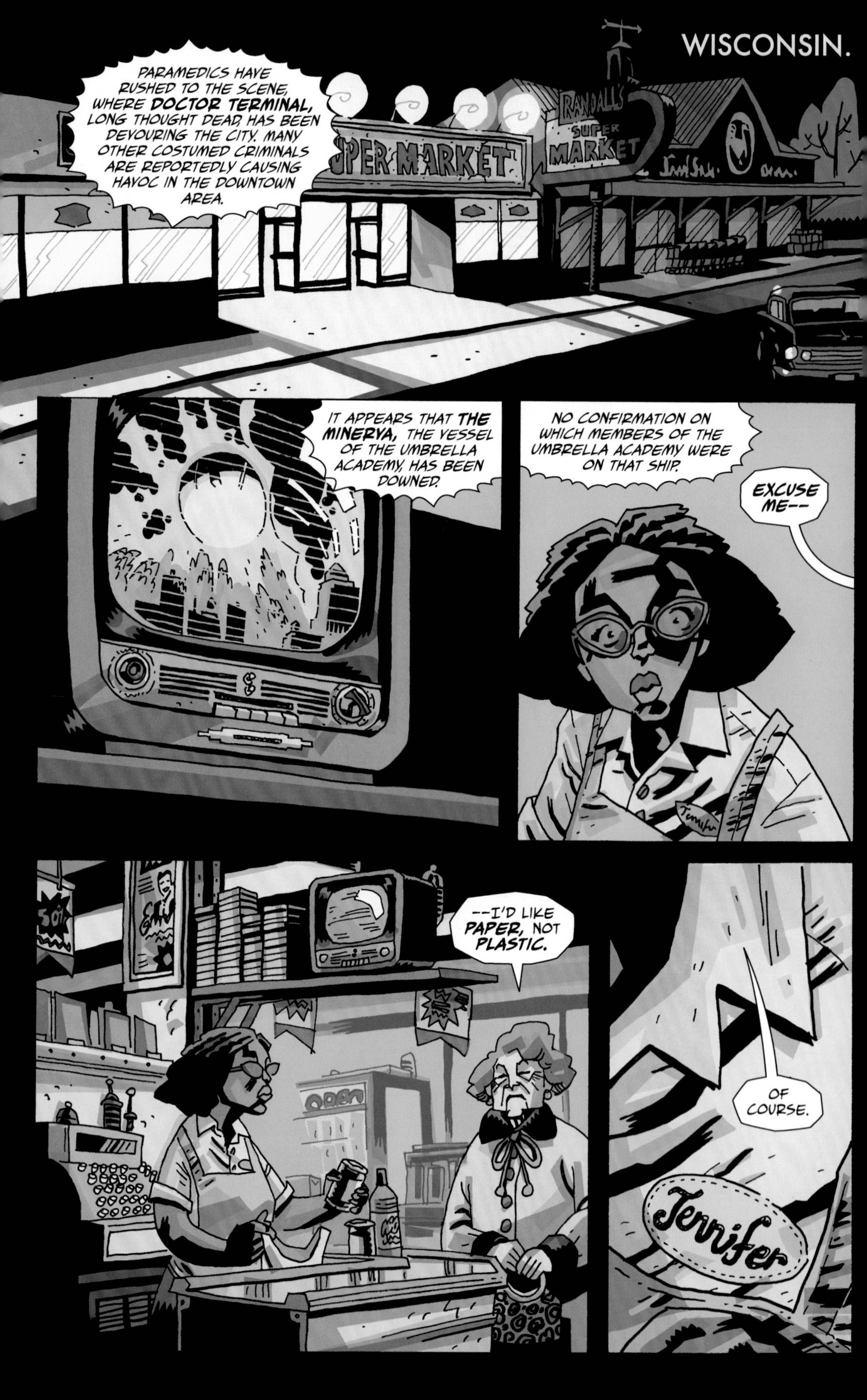
WISCONSIN.
PARAMEDICS HAVE RUSHED TO THE SCENE, WHERE DOCTOR TERMINAL, LONG THOUGHT DEAD, HAS BEEN DEVOURING THE CITY. MANY OTHER COSTUMED CRIMINALS ARE REPORTEDLY CAUSING HAVOC IN THE DOWNTOWN AREA.
SUPER MARKET
RANDALL'S SUPER MARKET
IT APPEARS THAT THE MINERVA, THE VESSEL OF THE UMBRELLA ACADEMY, HAS BEEN DOWNED.
NO CONFIRMATION ON WHICH MEMBERS OF THE UMBRELLA ACADEMY WERE ON THAT SHIP.
EXCUSE ME--
--I'D LIKE PAPER, NOT PLASTIC.
OF COURSE.
Jennifer

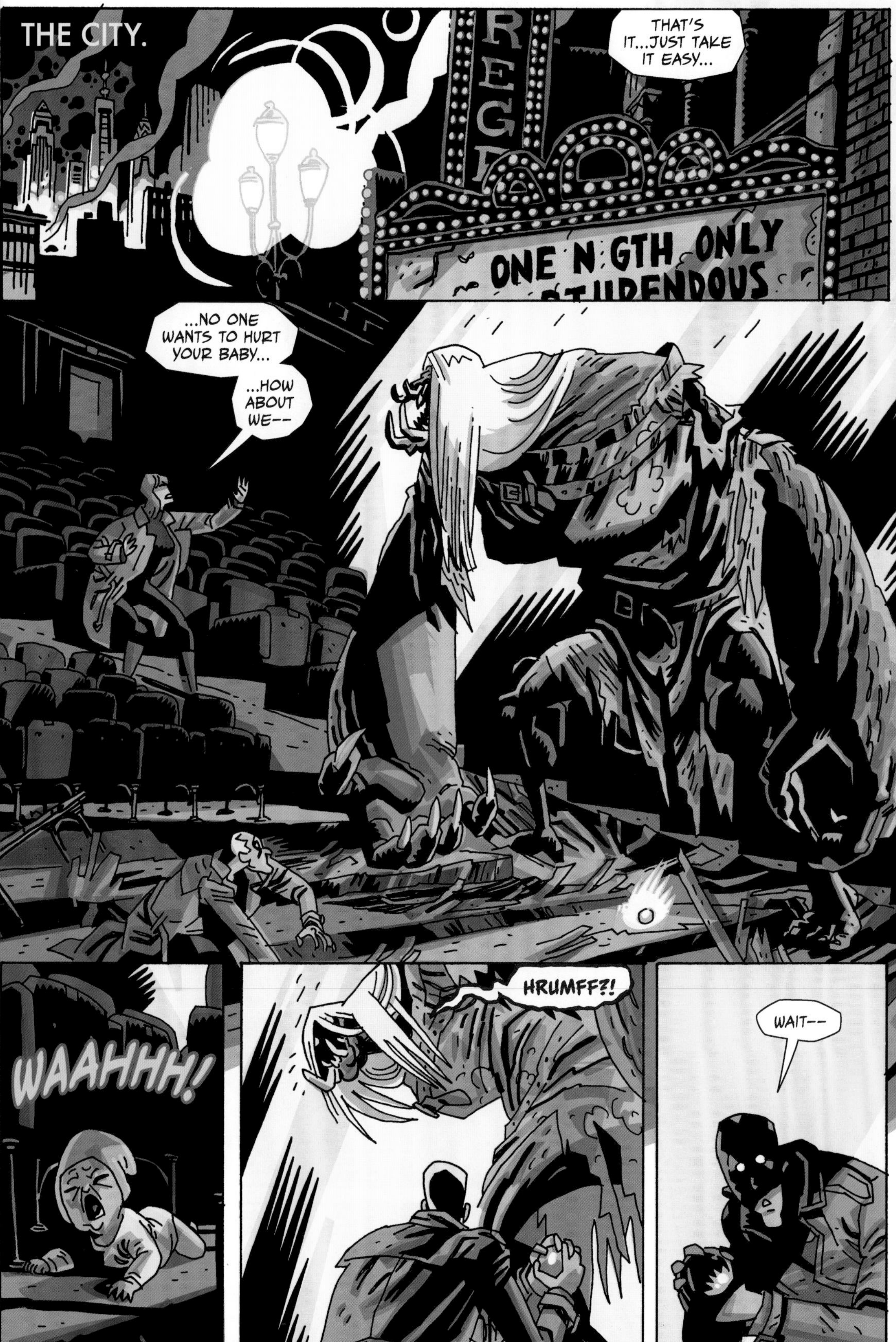
THE CITY.
THAT'S IT...JUST TAKE IT EASY...
ONE N GTH ONLY
...NO ONE WANTS TO HURT YOUR BABY...
...HOW ABOUT WE--
WAAHHH!
HRUMFF?!
WAIT--

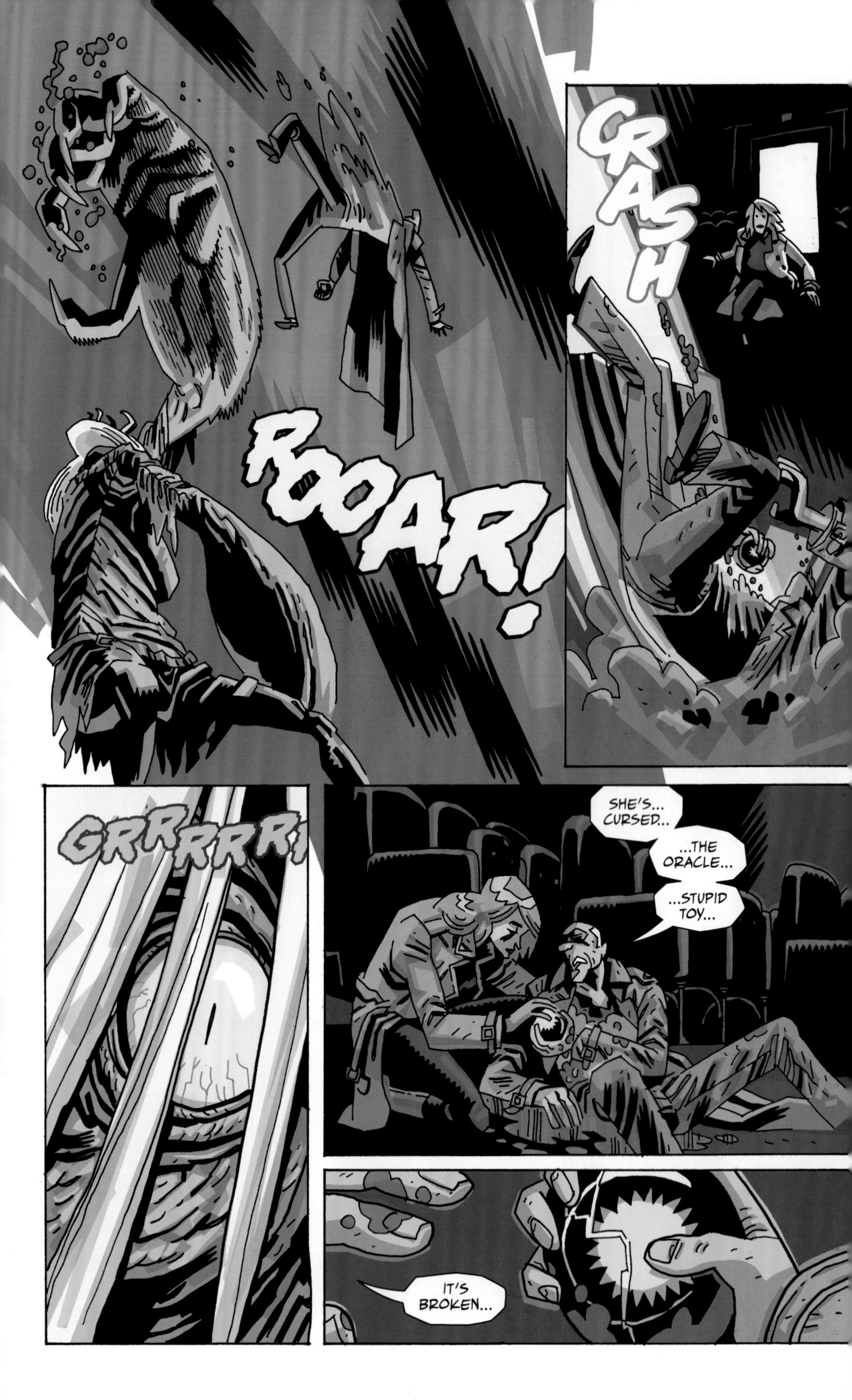
ROOOAR!!
CRASH
GRRRRRR
SHE'S... CURSED...
...THE ORACLE...
...STUPID TOY...
IT'S BROKEN...

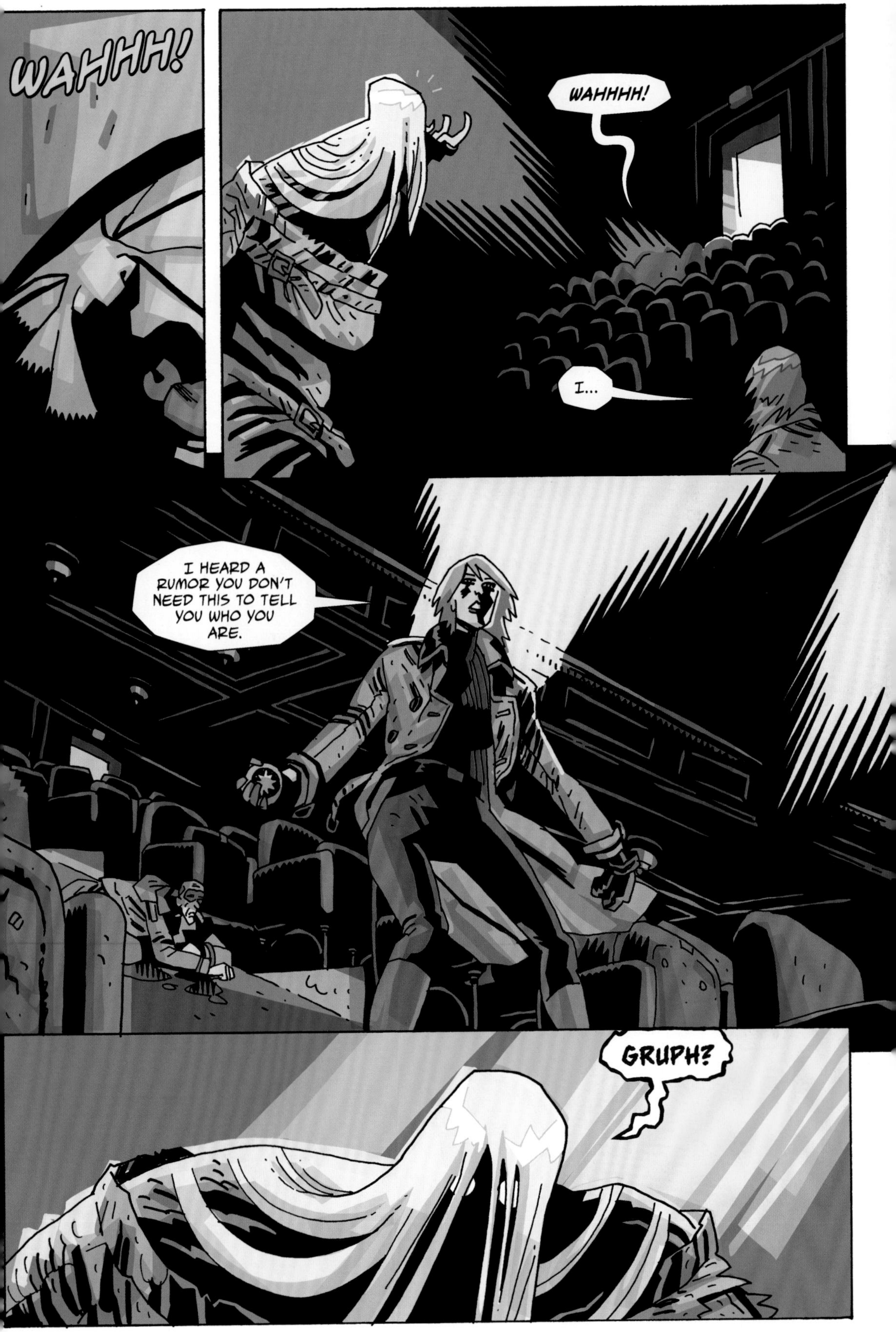
WAHHH!
WAHHHH!
I...
I HEARD A RUMOR YOU DON'T NEED THIS TO TELL YOU WHO YOU ARE.
GRUPH?

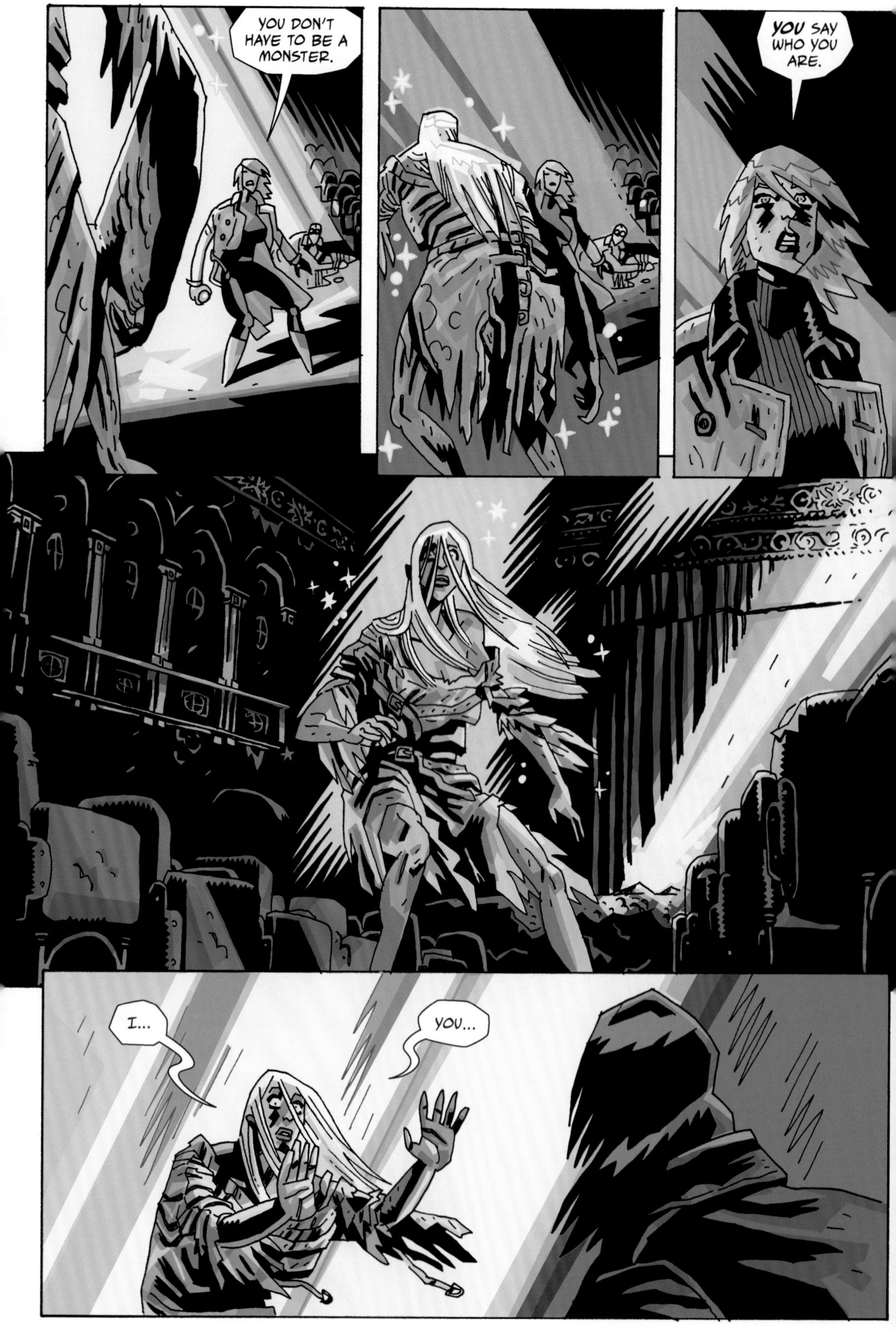
YOU DON'T HAVE TO BE A MONSTER.
YOU SAY WHO YOU ARE.
I...
YOU...

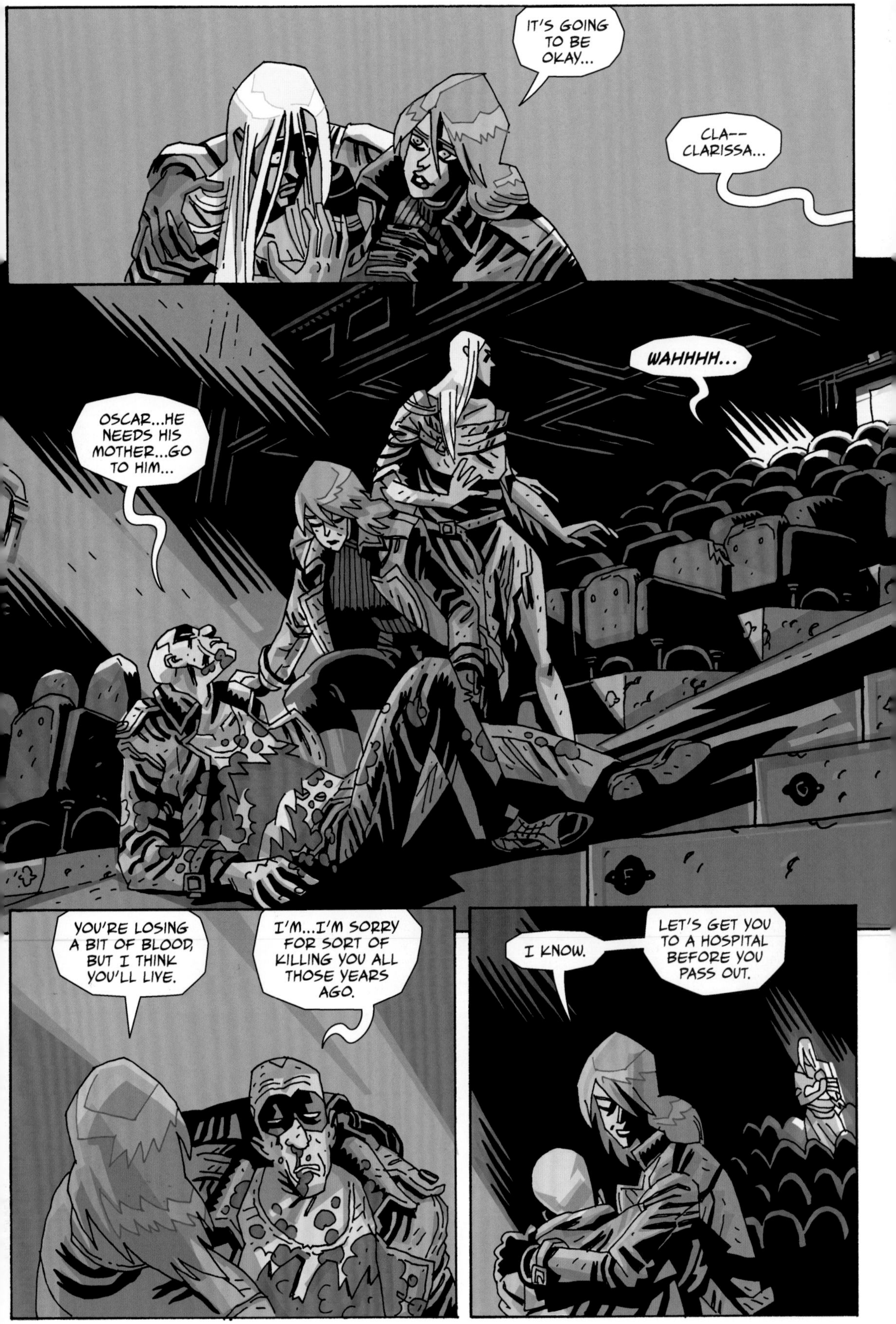
IT'S GOING TO BE OKAY...
CLA-- CLARISSA...
WAHHHH...
OSCAR...HE NEEDS HIS MOTHER...GO TO HIM...
YOU'RE LOSING A BIT OF BLOOD, BUT I THINK YOU'LL LIVE.
I'M...I'M SORRY FOR SORT OF KILLING YOU ALL THOSE YEARS AGO.
I KNOW.
LET'S GET YOU TO A HOSPITAL BEFORE YOU PASS OUT.

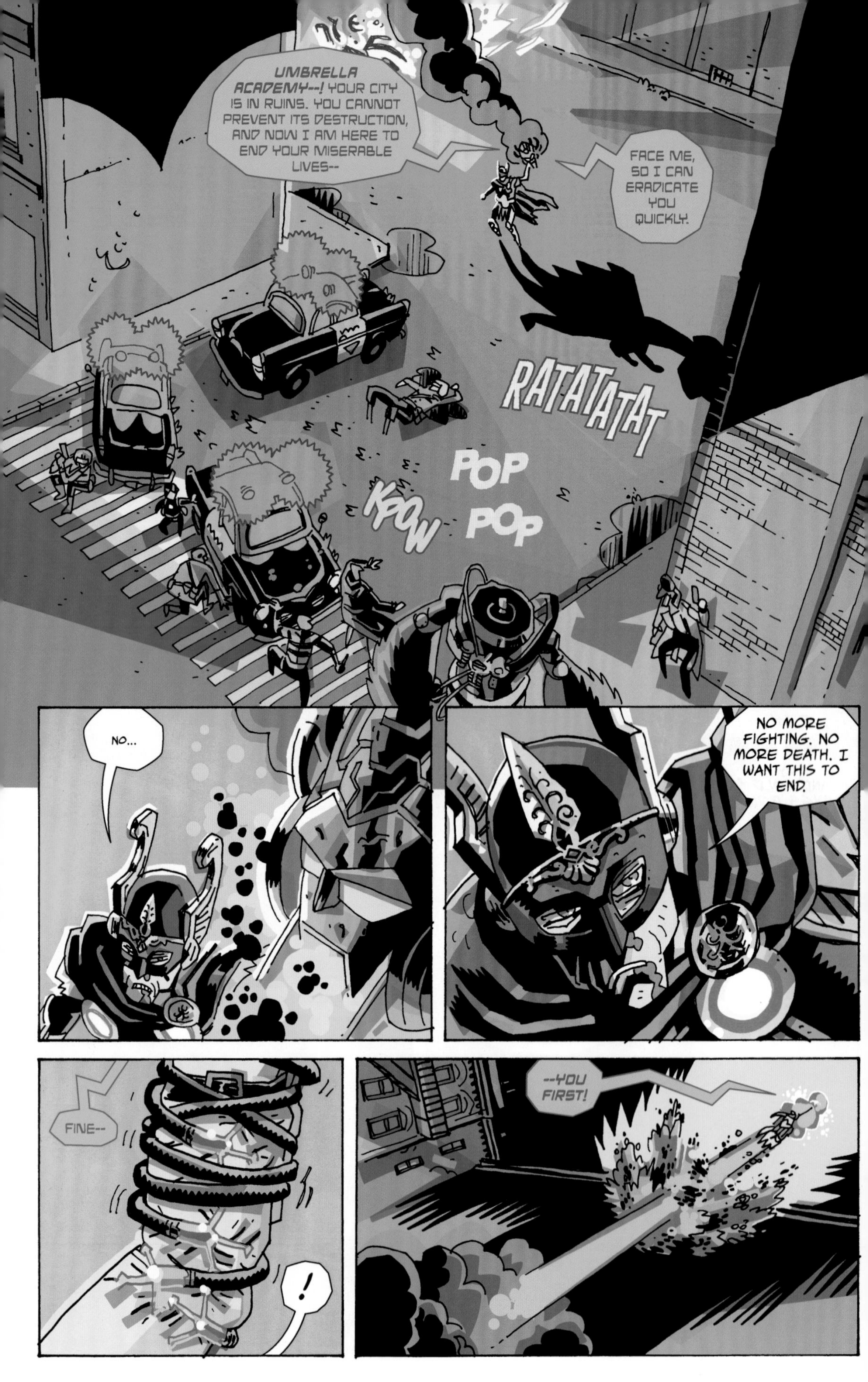
UMBRELLA ACADEMY--! YOUR CITY IS IN RUINS. YOU CANNOT PREVENT ITS DESTRUCTION, AND NOW I AM HERE TO END YOUR MISERABLE LIVES--
FACE ME, SO I CAN ERADICATE YOU QUICKLY.
RATATATAT
POP
KPOW
POP
NO...
NO MORE FIGHTING. NO MORE DEATH. I WANT THIS TO END.
FINE--
!
--YOU FIRST!

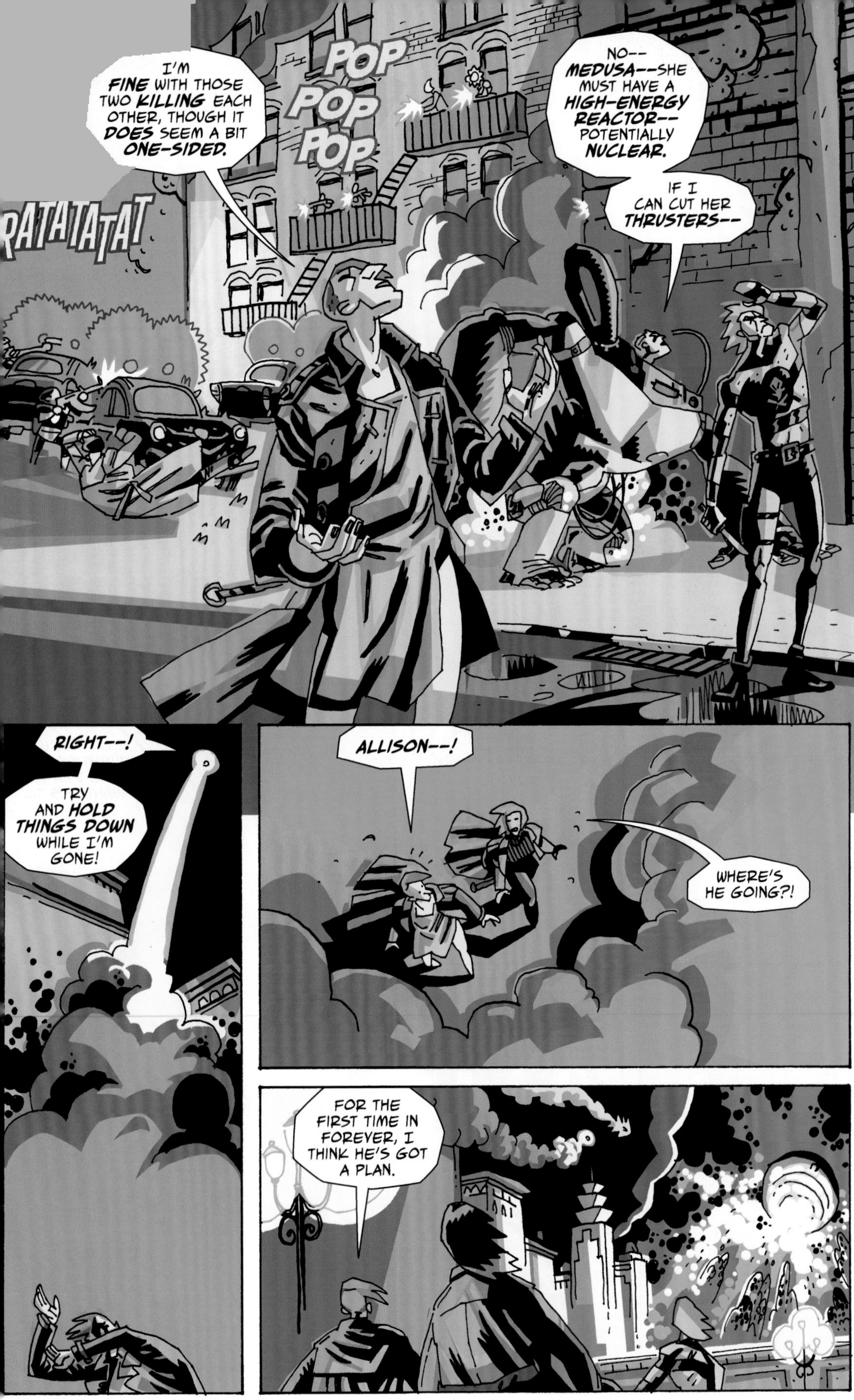
I'M FINE WITH THOSE TWO KILLING EACH OTHER, THOUGH IT DOES SEEM A BIT ONE-SIDED.
POP POP POP
RATATATAT
NO-- MEDUSA--SHE MUST HAVE A HIGH-ENERGY REACTOR-- POTENTIALLY NUCLEAR.
IF I CAN CUT HER THRUSTERS--
RIGHT--!
TRY AND HOLD THINGS DOWN WHILE I'M GONE!
ALLISON--!
WHERE'S HE GOING?!
FOR THE FIRST TIME IN FOREVER, I THINK HE'S GOT A PLAN.

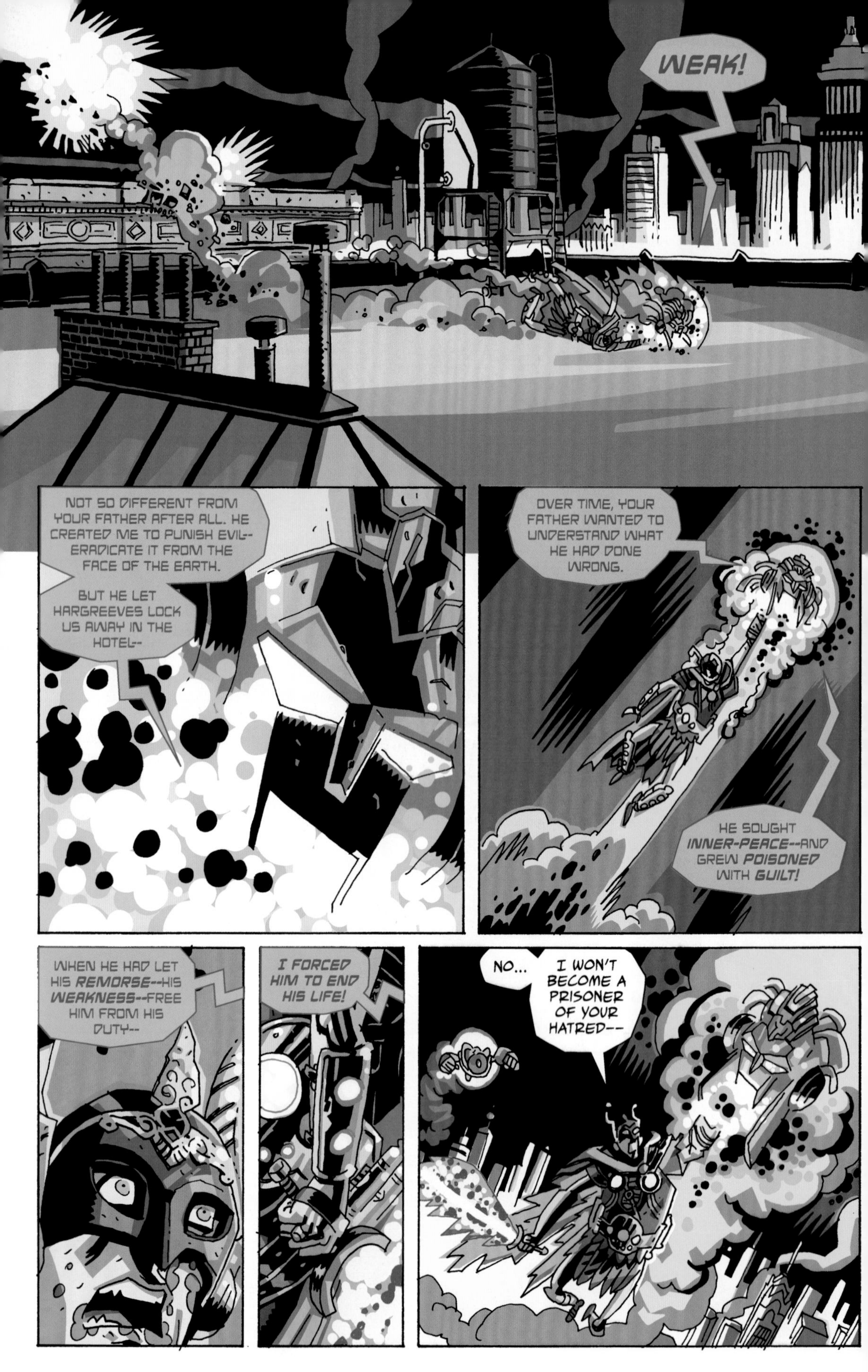
WEAK!
NOT SO DIFFERENT FROM YOUR FATHER AFTER ALL. HE CREATED ME TO PUNISH EVIL--ERADICATE IT FROM THE FACE OF THE EARTH.
BUT HE LET HARGREEVES LOCK US AWAY IN THE HOTEL--
OVER TIME, YOUR FATHER WANTED TO UNDERSTAND WHAT HE HAD DONE WRONG.
HE SOUGHT INNER-PEACE--AND GREW POISONED WITH GUILT!
WHEN HE HAD LET HIS REMORSE--HIS WEAKNESS--FREE HIM FROM HIS DUTY--
I FORCED HIM TO END HIS LIFE!
NO...
I WON'T BECOME A PRISONER OF YOUR HATRED--

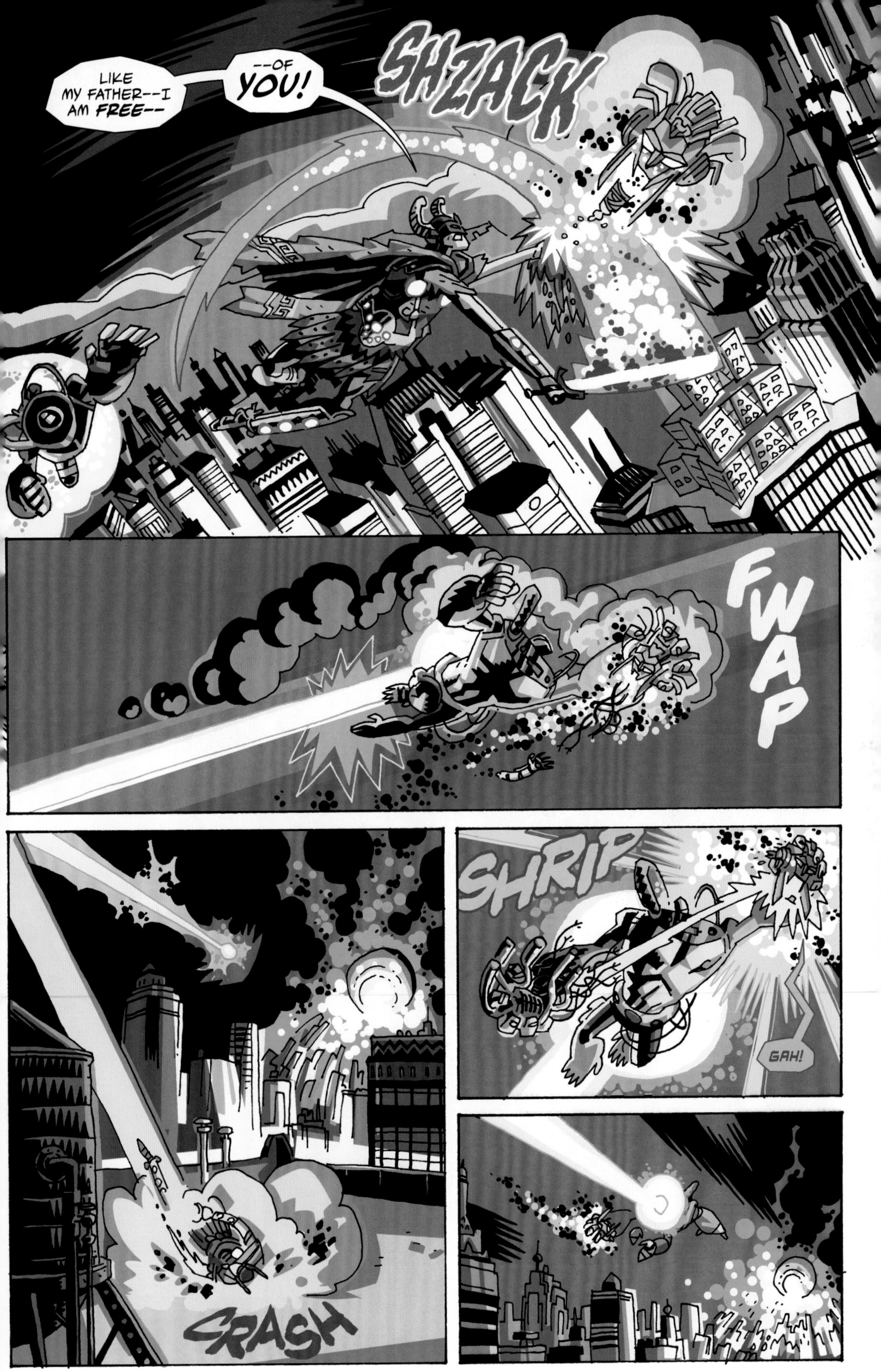
LIKE MY FATHER--I AM FREE--
--OF YOU!
SHZACK
FWAP
CRASH
SHRIP
GAH!

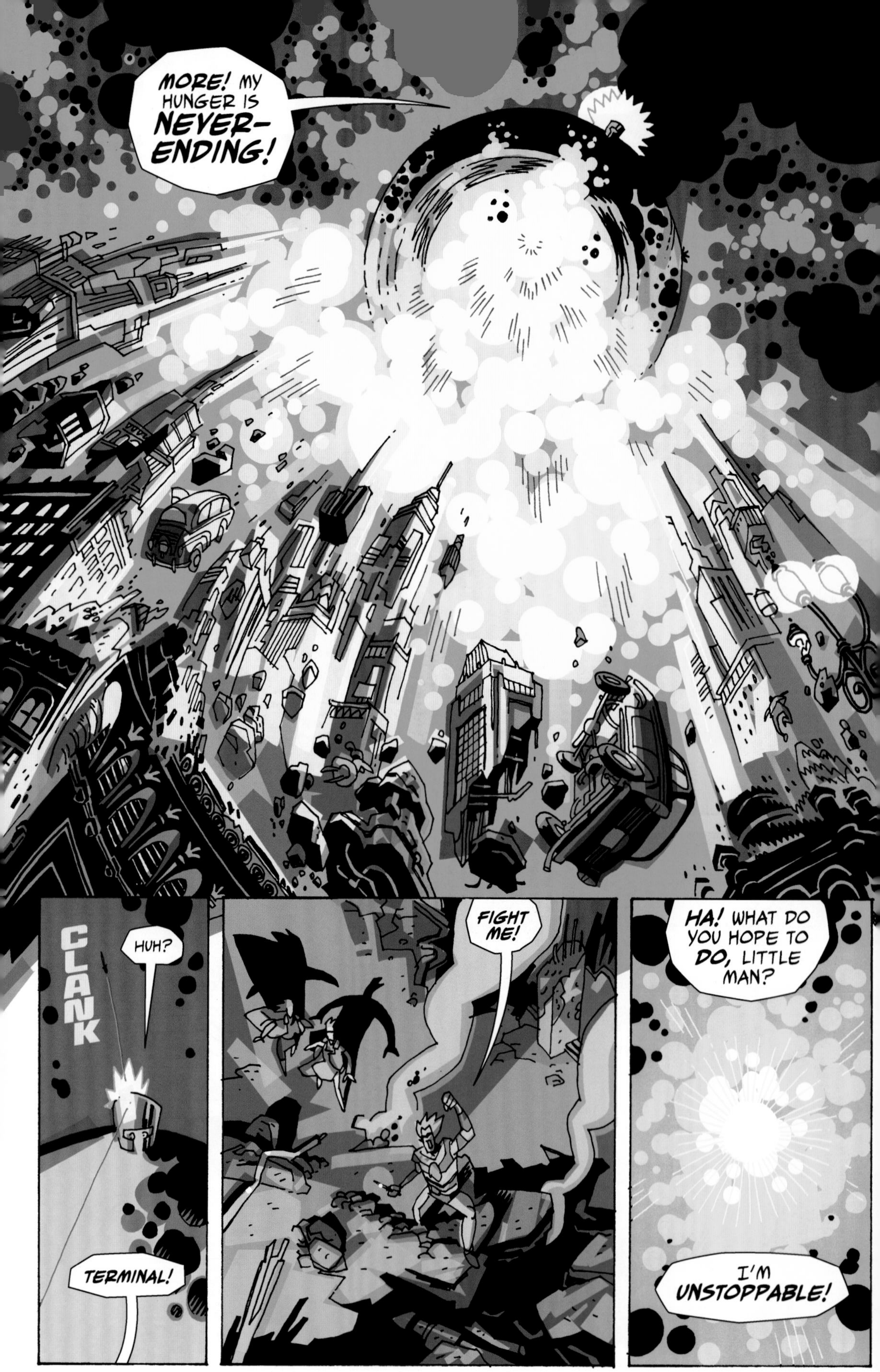
MORE! MY HUNGER IS NEVER-ENDING!
CLANK
HUH?
TERMINAL!
FIGHT ME!
HA! WHAT DO YOU HOPE TO DO, LITTLE MAN?
I'M UNSTOPPABLE!

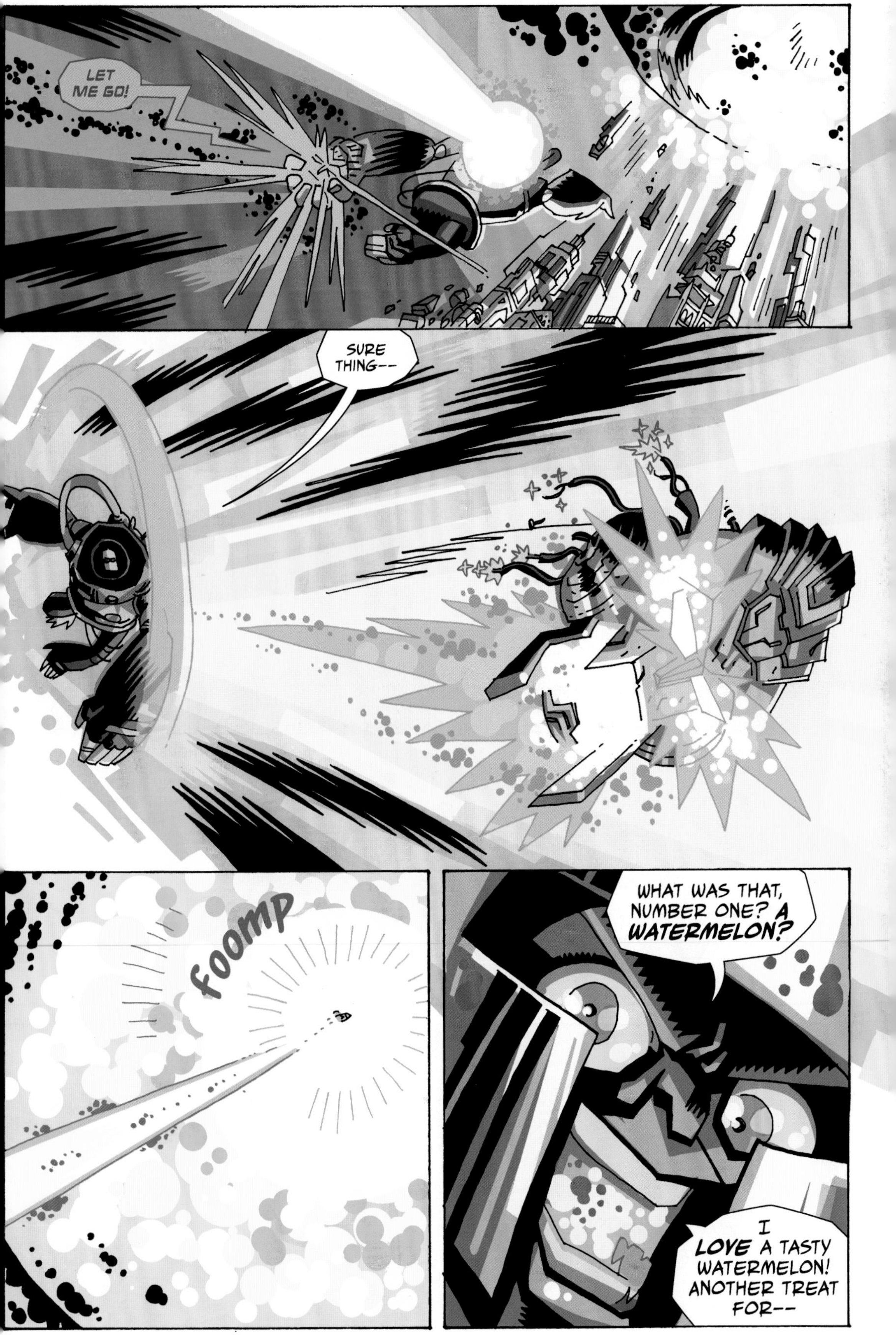
LET ME GO!
SURE THING--
foomp
WHAT WAS THAT, NUMBER ONE? A WATERMELON?
I LOVE A TASTY WATERMELON! ANOTHER TREAT FOR--

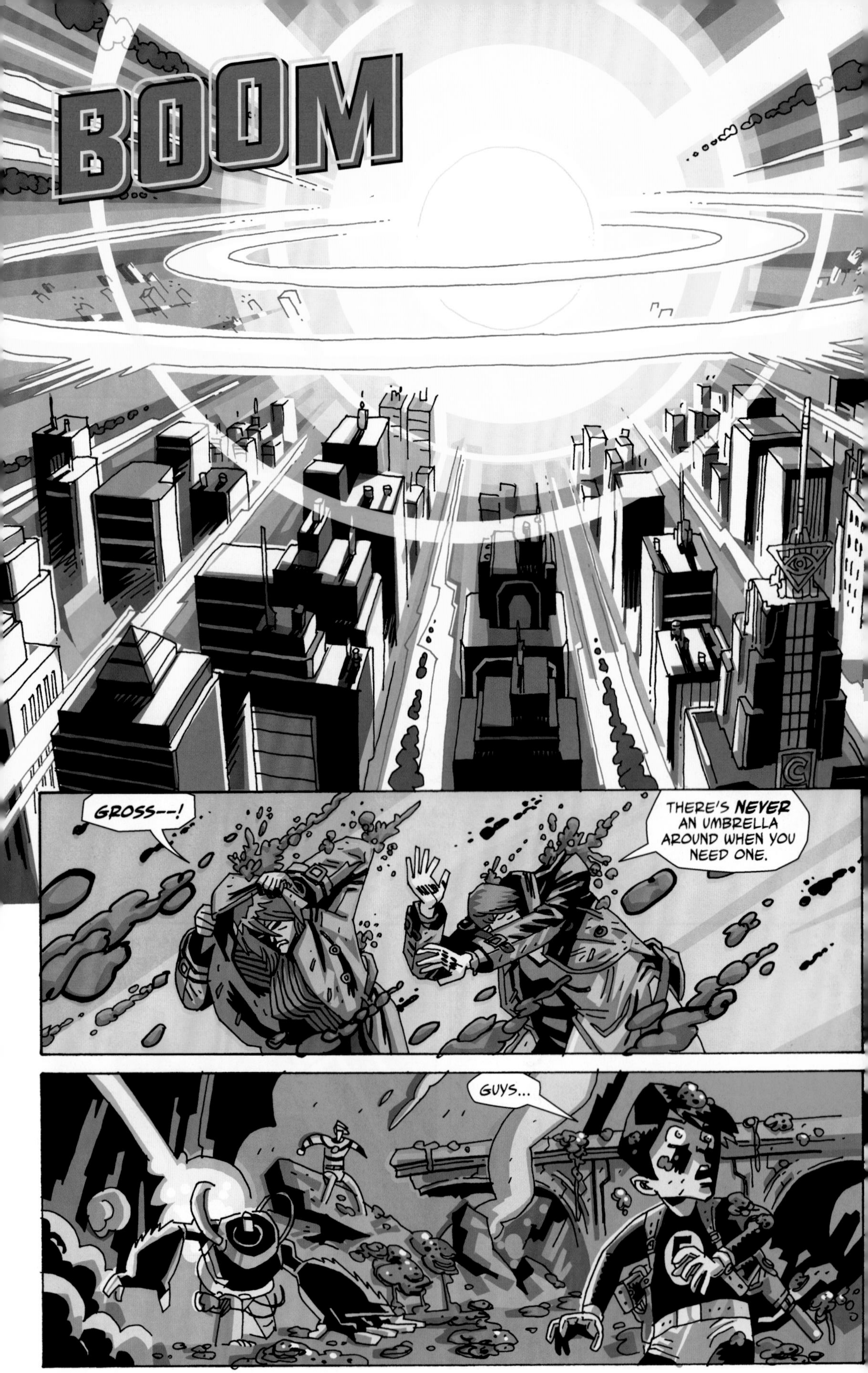
BOOM
GROSS--!
THERE'S NEVER AN UMBRELLA AROUND WHEN YOU NEED ONE.
GUYS...

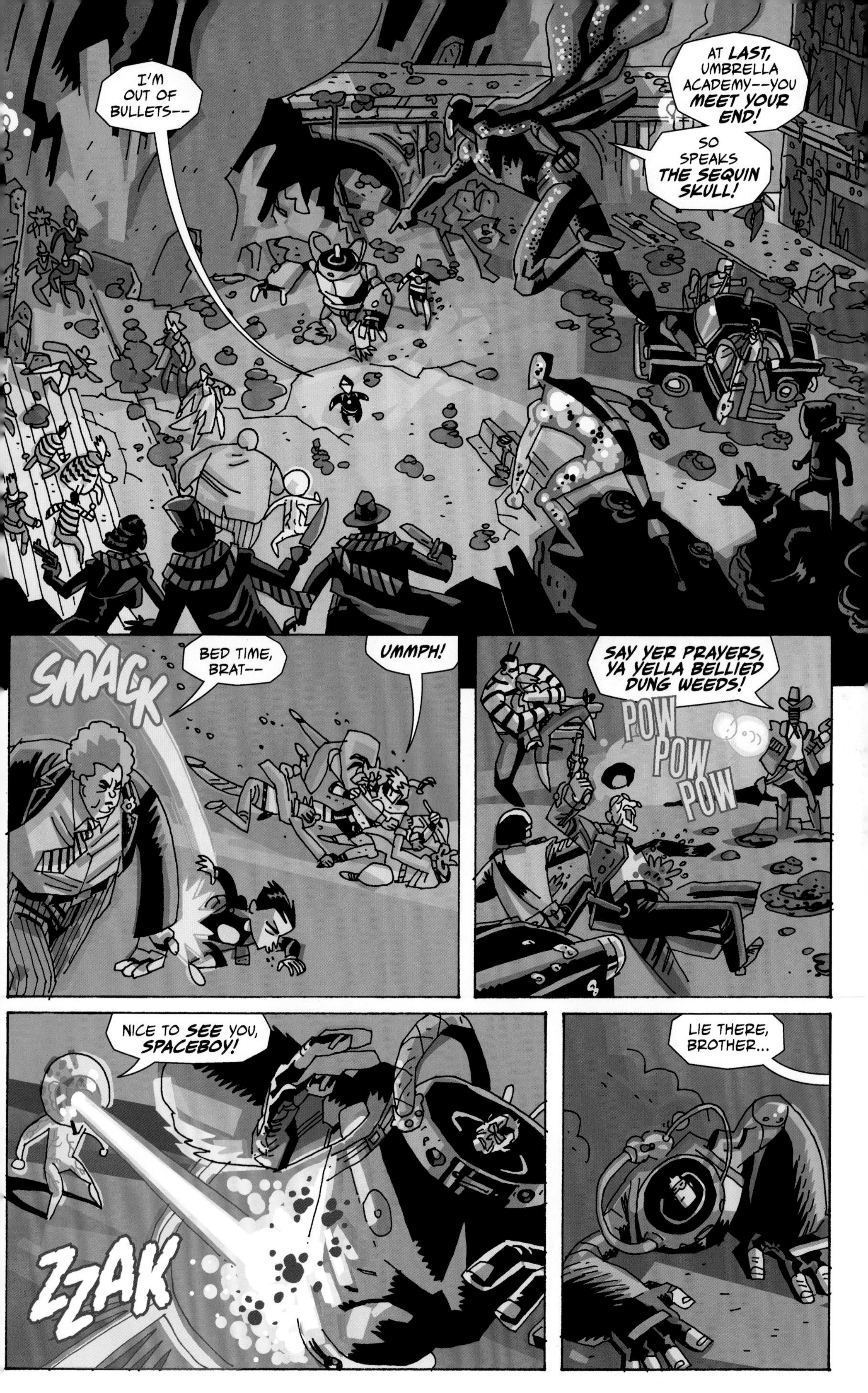
I'M OUT OF BULLETS--
AT LAST, UMBRELLA ACADEMY--YOU MEET YOUR END!
SO SPEAKS THE SEQUIN SKULL!
SMACK
BED TIME, BRAT--
UMMPH!
SAY YER PRAYERS, YA YELLA BELLIED DUNG WEEDS!
POW POW POW
NICE TO SEE YOU, SPACEBOY!
ZZAK
LIE THERE, BROTHER...

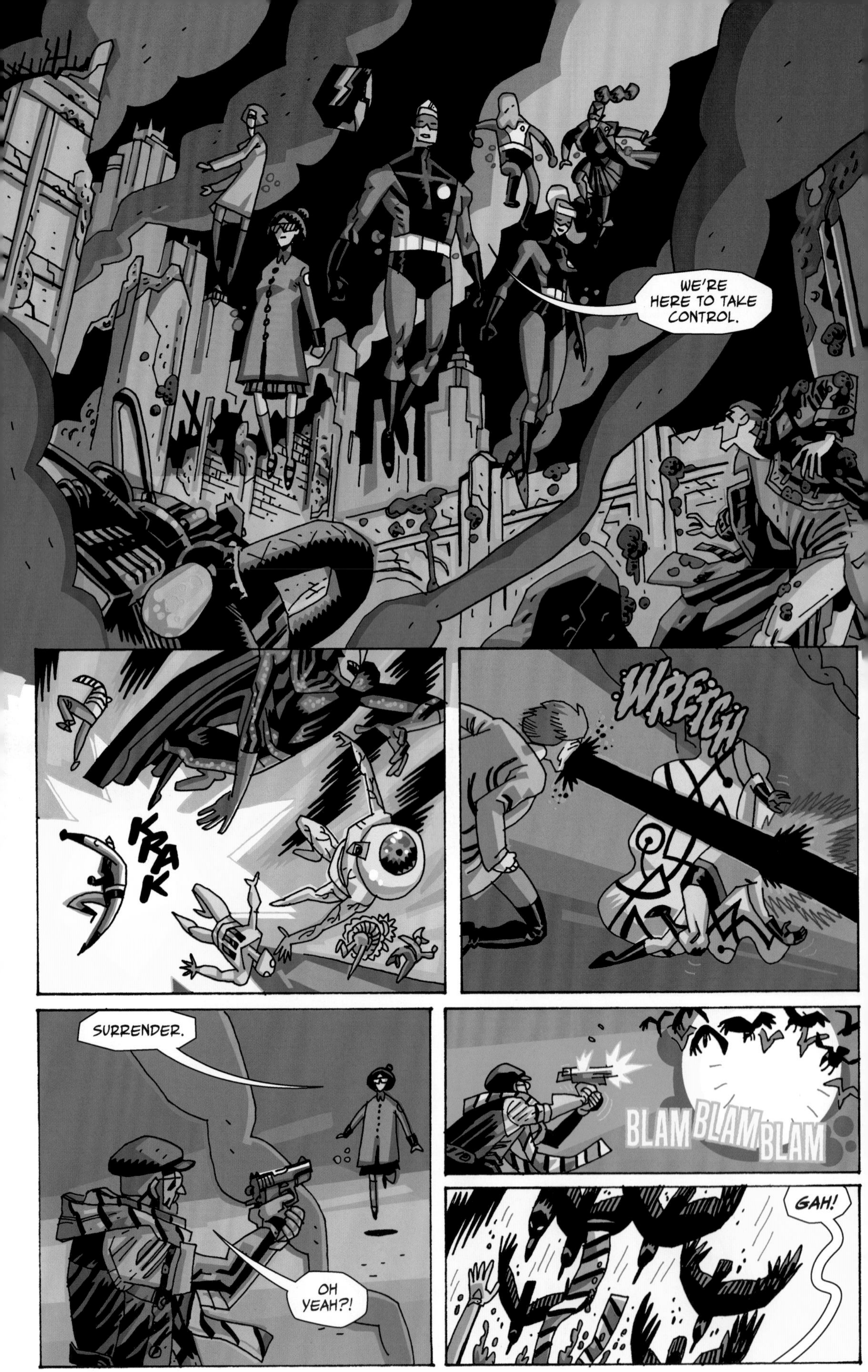
WE'RE HERE TO TAKE CONTROL.
KRAK
WRETCH
SURRENDER.
OH YEAH?!
BLAM BLAM BLAM
GAH!

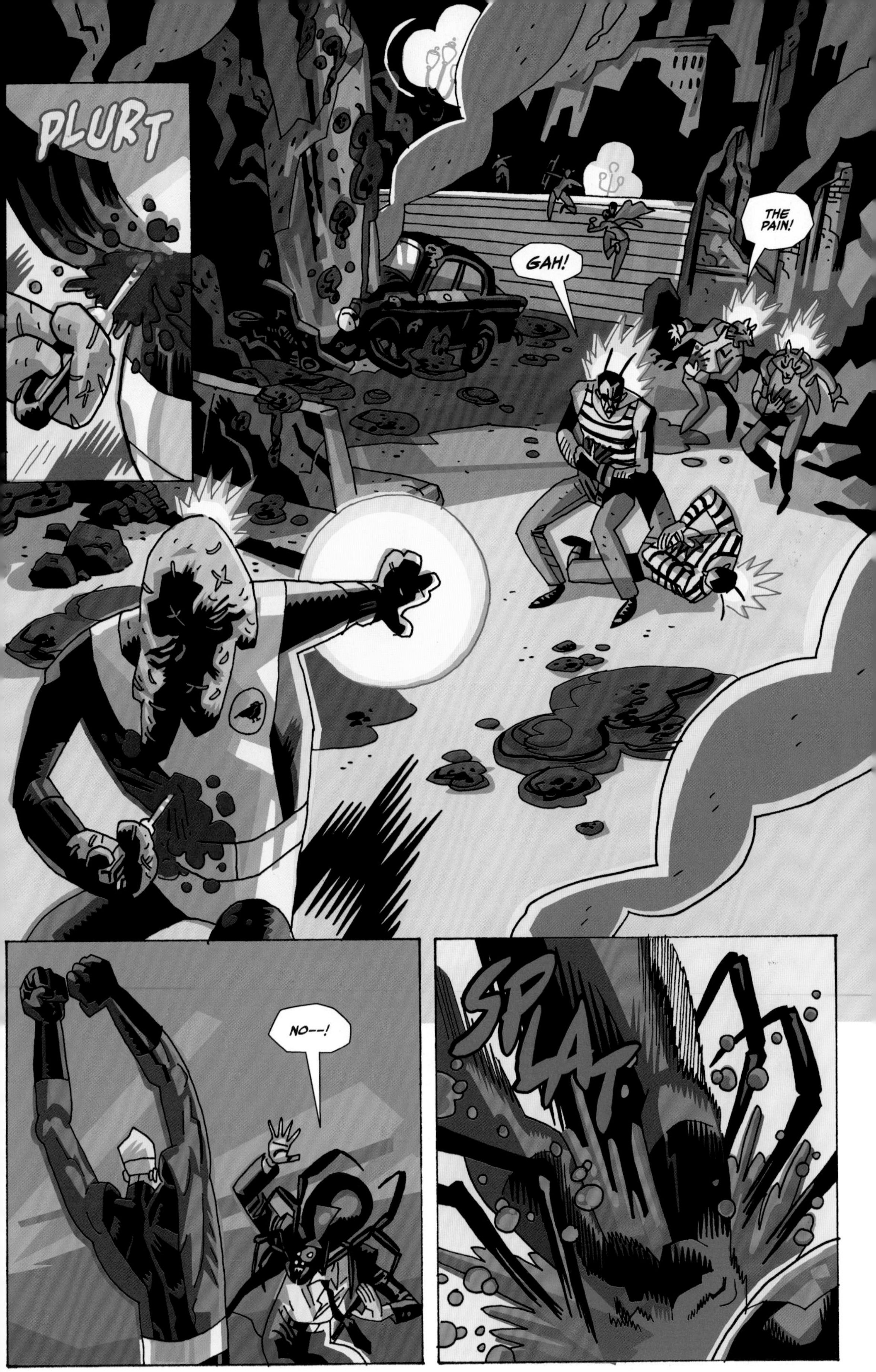
PLURT
GAH!
THE PAIN!
NO--!
SPLAT

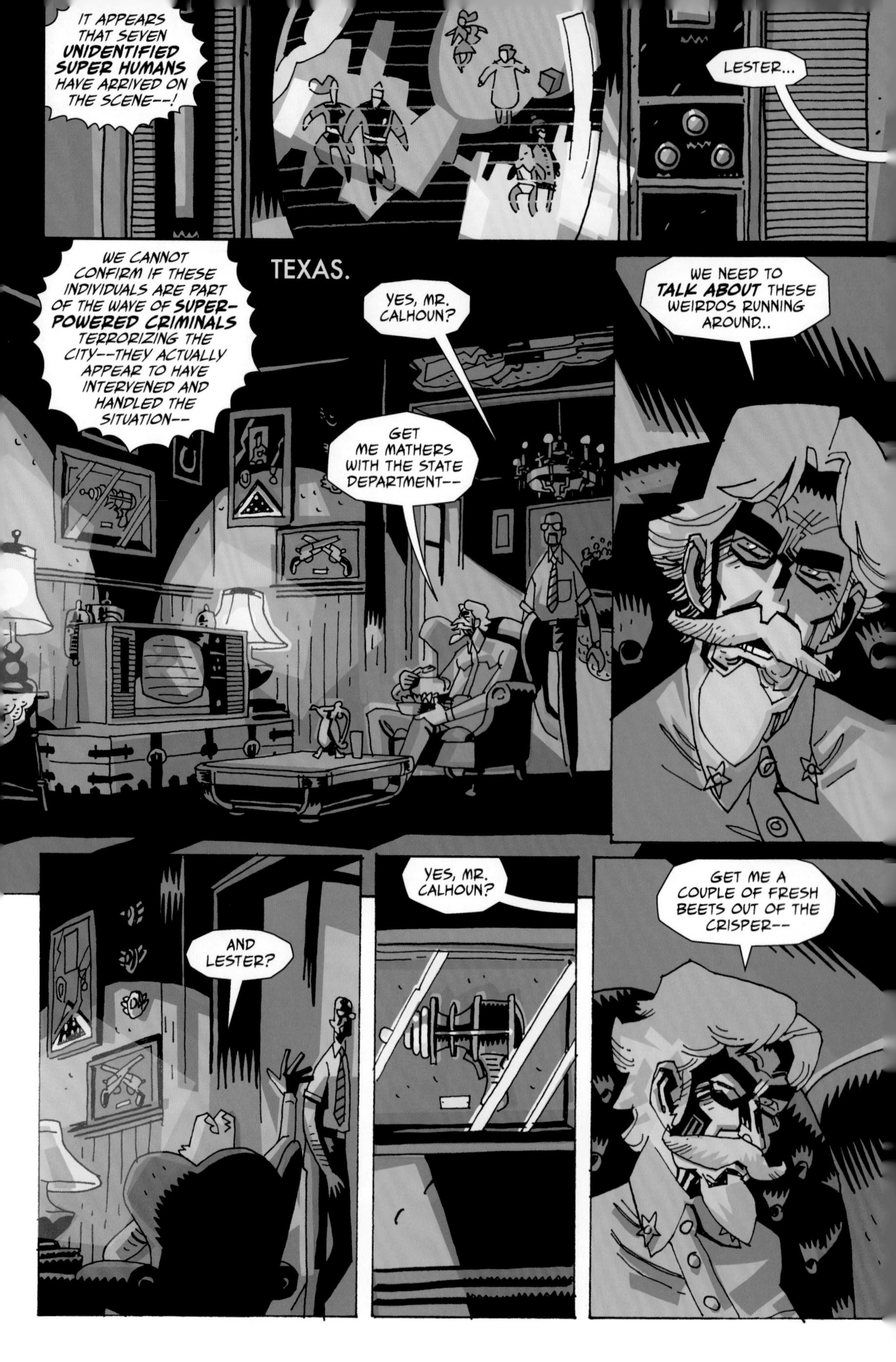
IT APPEARS THAT SEVEN UNIDENTIFIED SUPER HUMANS HAVE ARRIVED ON THE SCENE--!
LESTER...
WE CANNOT CONFIRM IF THESE INDIVIDUALS ARE PART OF THE WAVE OF SUPER-POWERED CRIMINALS TERRORIZING THE CITY--THEY ACTUALLY APPEAR TO HAVE INTERVENED AND HANDLED THE SITUATION--
TEXAS.
YES, MR. CALHOUN?
GET ME MATHERS WITH THE STATE DEPARTMENT--
WE NEED TO TALK ABOUT THESE WEIRDOS RUNNING AROUND...
AND LESTER?
YES, MR. CALHOUN?
GET ME A COUPLE OF FRESH BEETS OUT OF THE CRISPER--

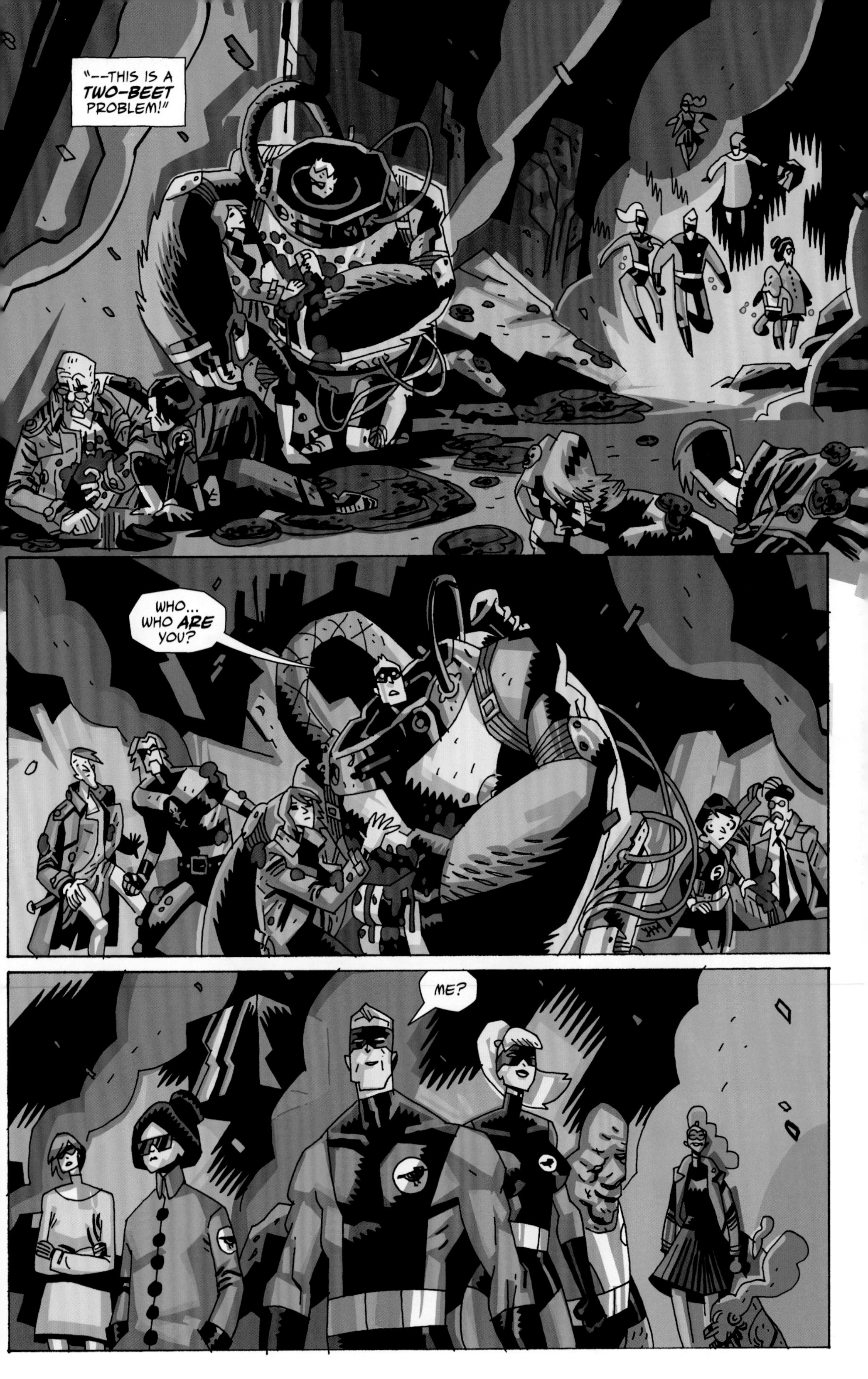
"--THIS IS A *TWO-BEET* PROBLEM!"
WHO... WHO *ARE* YOU?
ME?

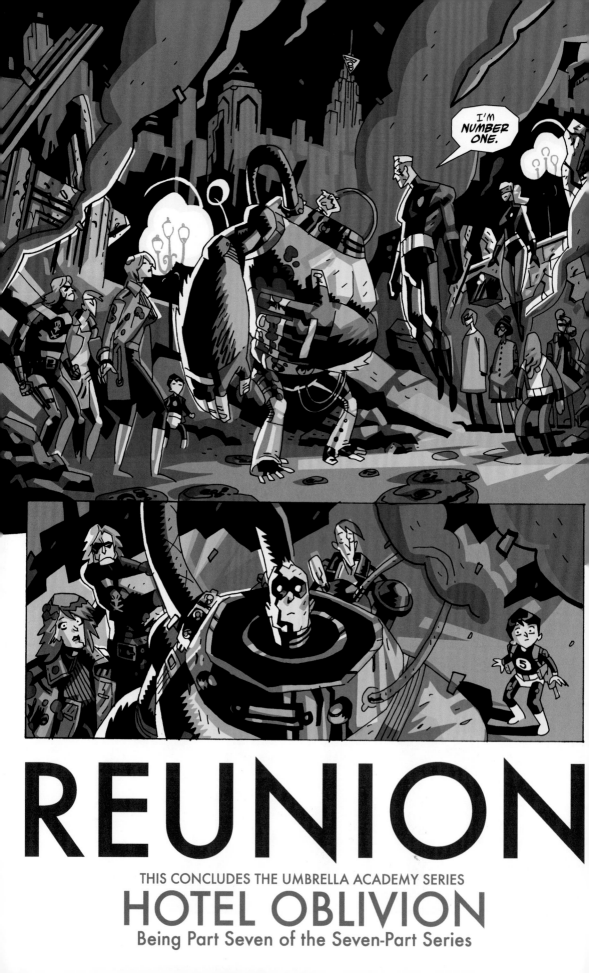

REUNION

THIS CONCLUDES THE UMBRELLA ACADEMY SERIES
HOTEL OBLIVION
Being Part Seven of the Seven-Part Series

THEY CALL ME
QUINN

MOTHER
AGONY
THE CITY
GB
18

Hotel Oblivion #2 Quinn variant cover by Gabriel

Facing: Hotel Oblivion #1 Gas Panic variant cover by Gabriel

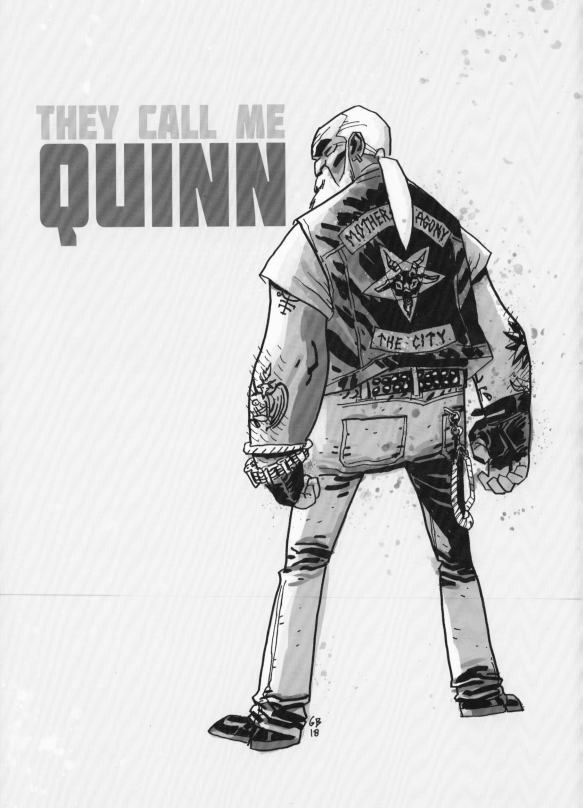

ROOMMATE WANTED

- **SEMI-PRIVATE BEDROOM**
- **SHORT DRIVE FROM CITY**
- **PRICE** ~~STEEP~~ NEGOTIABLE
- **NO NEAT FREAKS, VEGANS, ETC.**

More information:
The Umbrella Academy™ Hotel Oblivion
Story **GERARD WAY** + Art & Covers **GABRIEL BÁ** + Letters **NATE PIEKOS for Blambot™** + Colors **NICK FILARDI**
Publisher **MIKE RICHARDSON** + Editor **SCOTT ALLIE** + Designer **LIN HUANG**
+ Digital Art Technician **ALLY HALLER**
Special thanks Michael Gombos and Hieu Essin
Advertising Sales (503) 905-2315 + To find a comics shop in your area, visit comicshoplocator.com + DarkHorse.com + Facebook.com/DarkHorseComics
+ Twitter.com/DarkHorseComics

The Umbrella Academy: Hotel Oblivion #2, November 2018. Published by Dark Horse Comics, Inc., 10956 SE Main Street, Milwaukie, Oregon 97222. The Umbrella Academy™ & © Gerard Way and Gabriel Bá 2018. Dark Horse Comics® is a trademark of Dark Horse Comics, Inc., registered in various categories and countries. All rights reserved. No portion of this publication may be reproduced or transmitted, in any form or by any means, without the express written permission of Dark Horse Comics, Inc. Names, characters, places, and incidents featured in this publication either are the product of the author's imagination or are used fictitiously. Any resemblance to actual persons (living or dead), events, institutions, or locales, without satiric intent, is coincidental. Printed in Canada.

INQUIRE BY EMAIL

Ask for Quinn
DearSirReginald@darkhorse.com

Ask for Quinn
DearSirReginald@darkhorse.com

Ask for Quinn
DearSirReginald@darkhorse.com

Ask for Quinn
DearSirReginald@darkhorse.com

Ask for Quinn
DearSirReginald@darkhorse.com

Ask for Quinn
DearSirReginald@darkhorse.com

Quinn
@darkhorse.com

Ask for Quinn
DearSirReginald@darkhorse.com

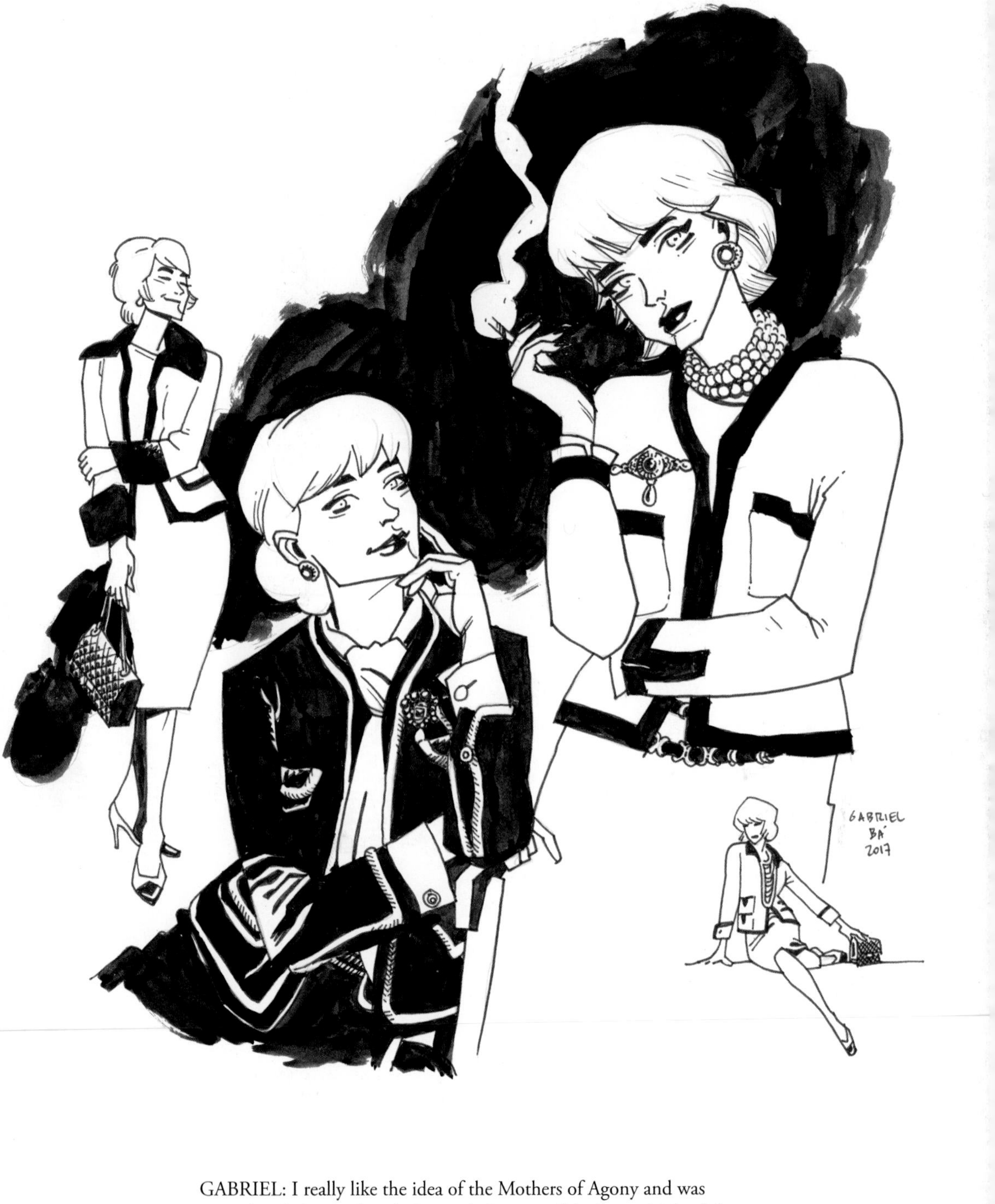
GABRIEL
BÁ
2017

GABRIEL: I really like the idea of the Mothers of Agony and was immediately inspired to design a whole gang of devil-worshiping bikers. Everything about them was visually challenging and fun: their looks, the vests with the colors on the back, their meth-lab-meets-squat house.

Contrasting that with fancy Mrs. Fairweather was something that could only happen in *The Umbrella Academy*.

Facing: Credits page from Hotel Oblivion #2—illustration by Gabriel, design by Lin Huang

MOTHERS OF AGONY
THE CITY

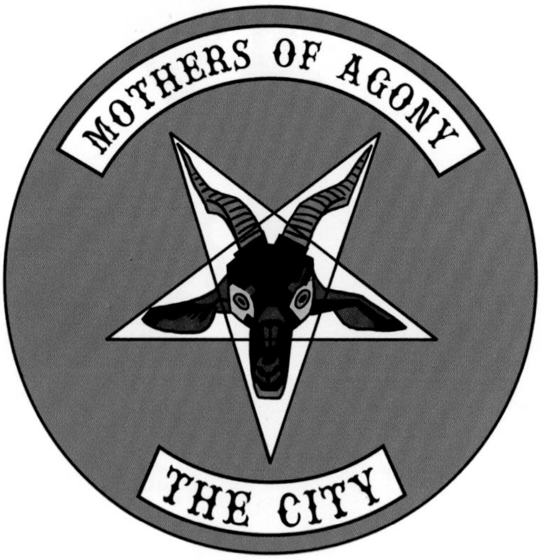
MOTHERS OF AGONY
THE CITY

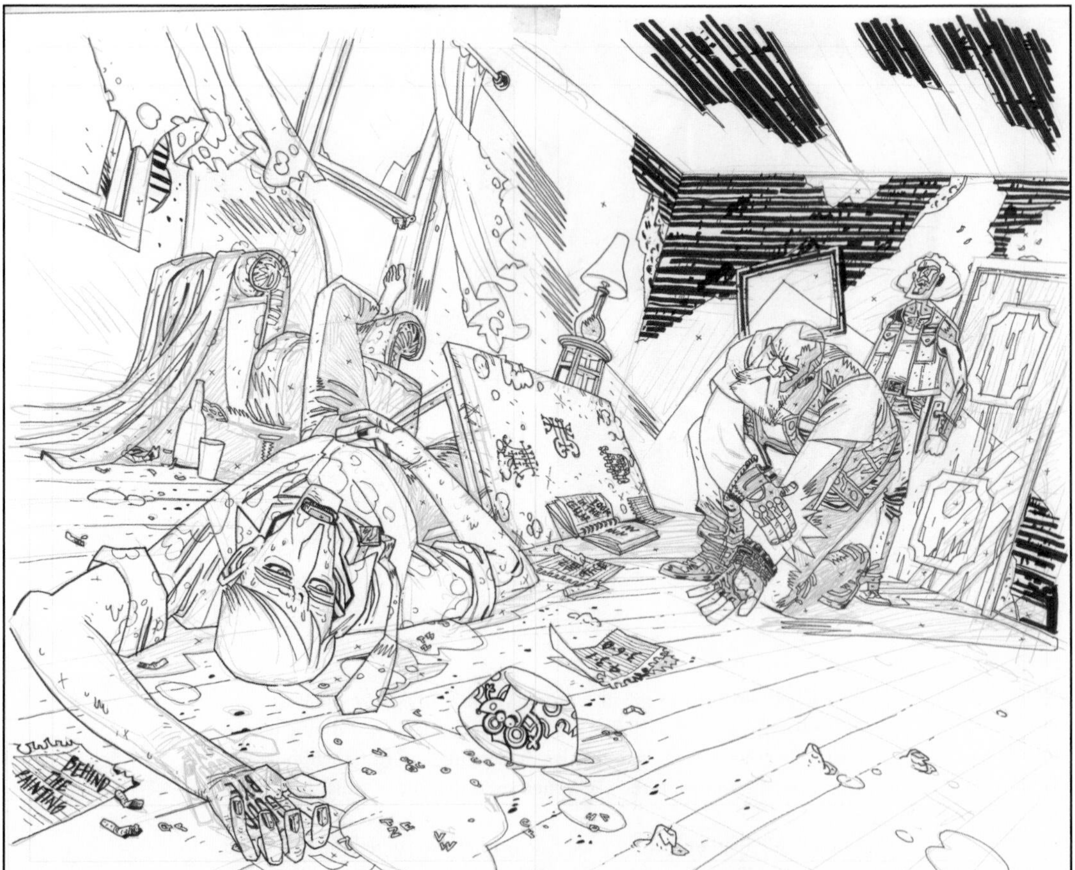
BEHIND THE PAINTING

Gabriel's design for the gang logo, and pencils for the Chapter 2 title spread

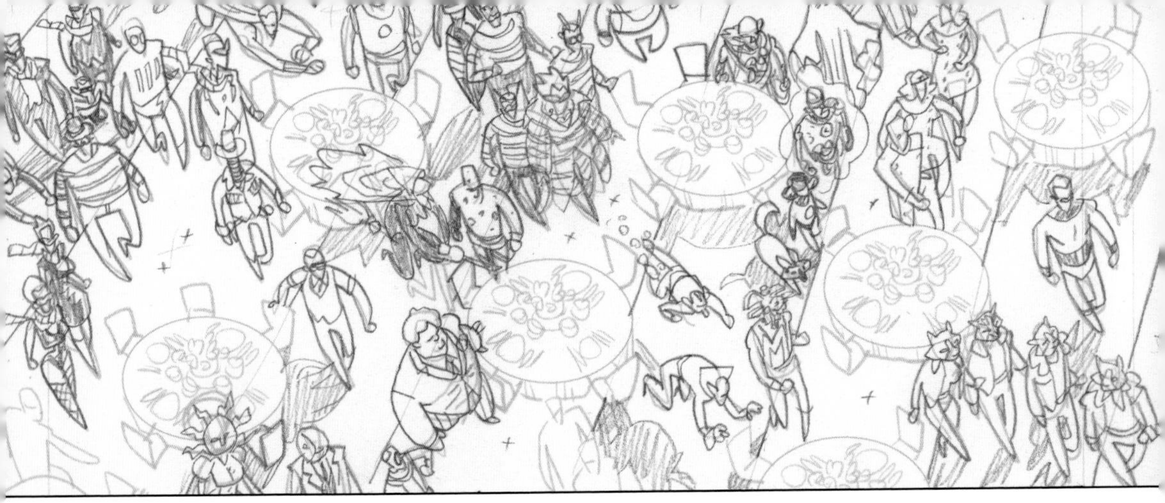

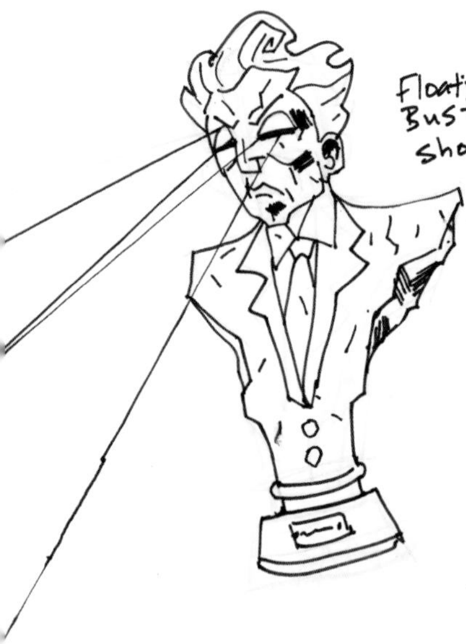
Floating Bust That shoots eye beams

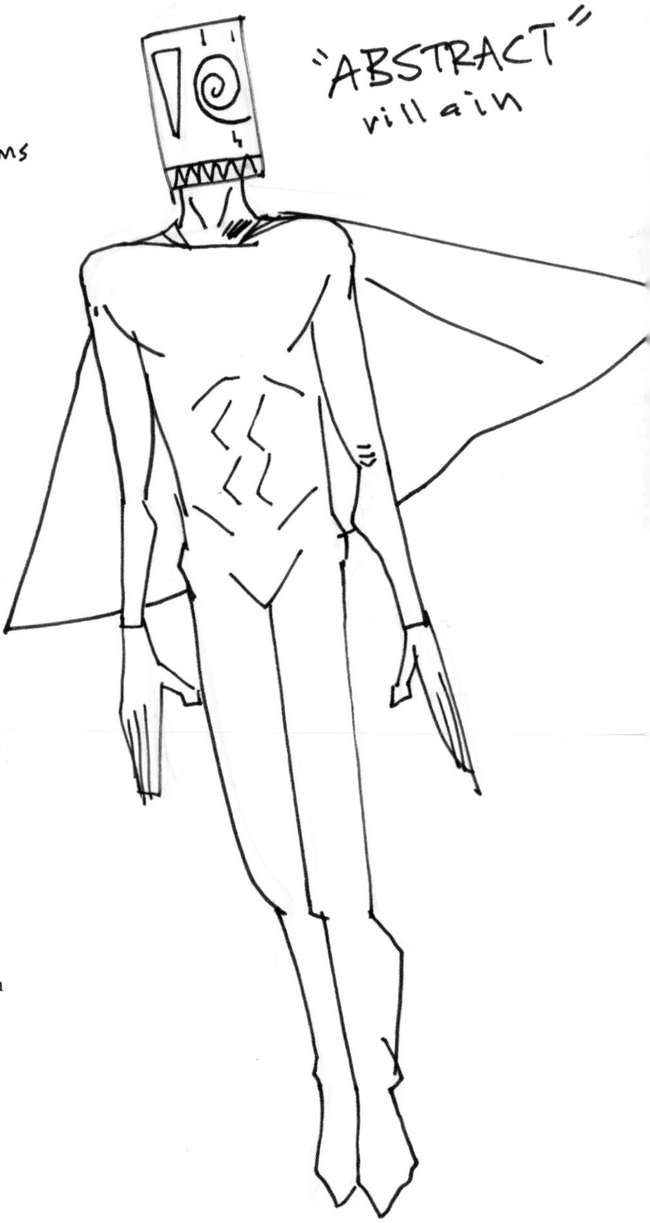
"ABSTRACT" villain

GABRIEL: Gerard created all the villains, and drew most of the designs. He has this great sense of classic hero/villain design mixed with the craziest ideas for looks and powers. It's just too much fun playing with his ideas and putting these characters on the pages, walking around, breaking things. We could literally take any one of them and tell a whole story about them, which is why I put them on the variant covers.

Gabriel's pencils from the Hotel escape in Chapter 5, and Gerard's designs for villains

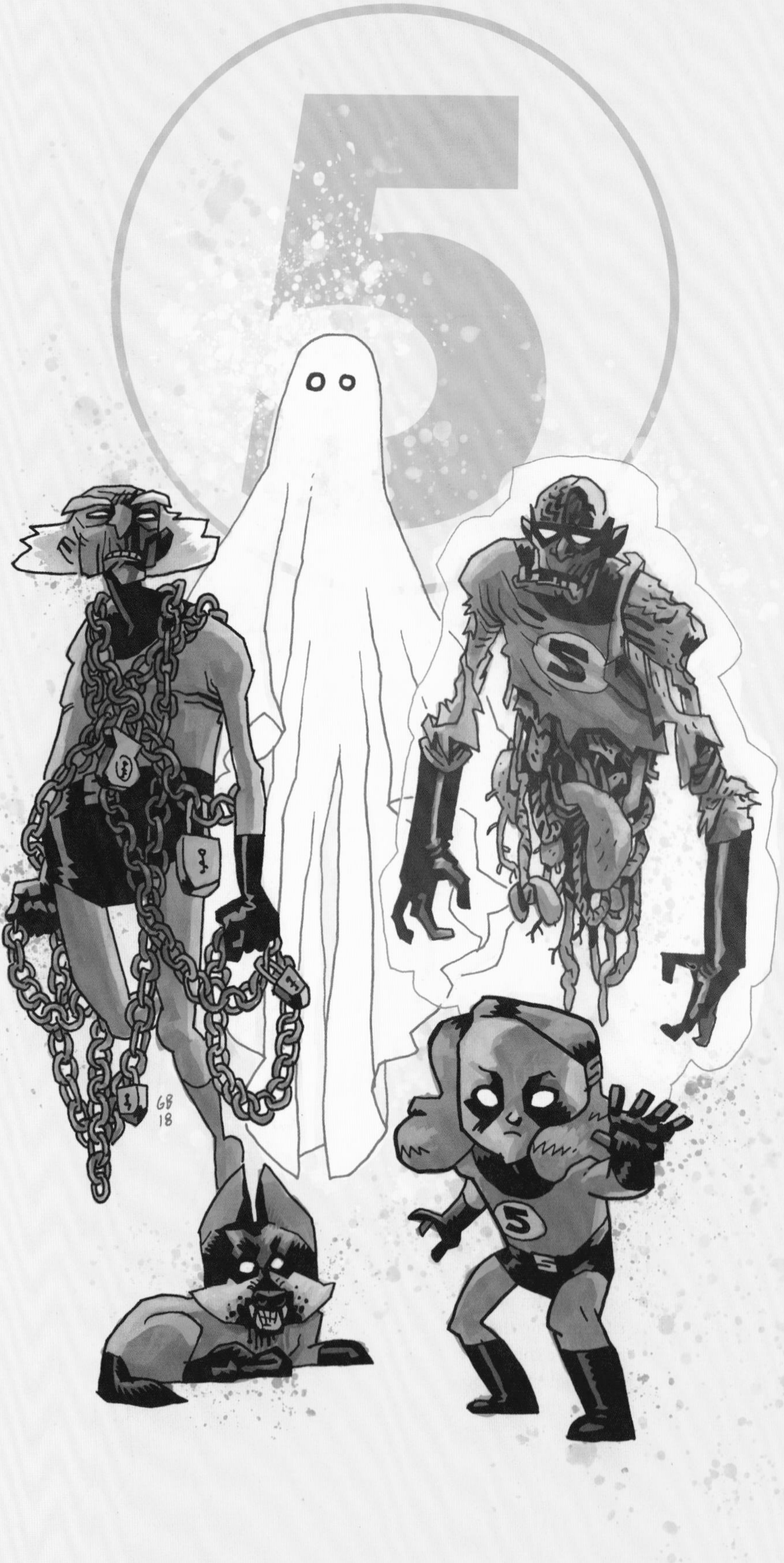
GB
18

Hotel Oblivion #5 Phantom Five variant cover by Gabriel

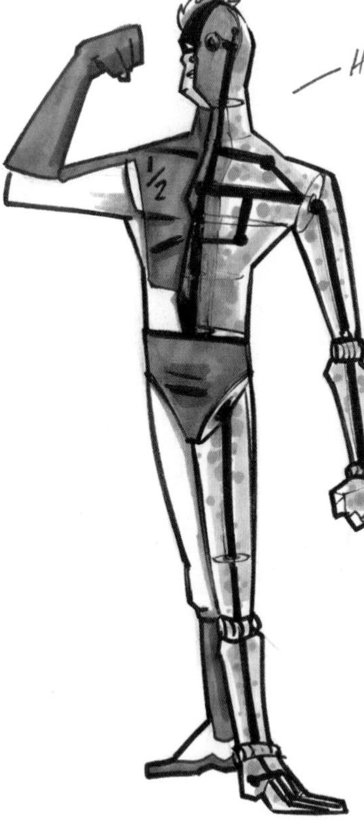
Half of Body Stuck in parallel dimension
1/2

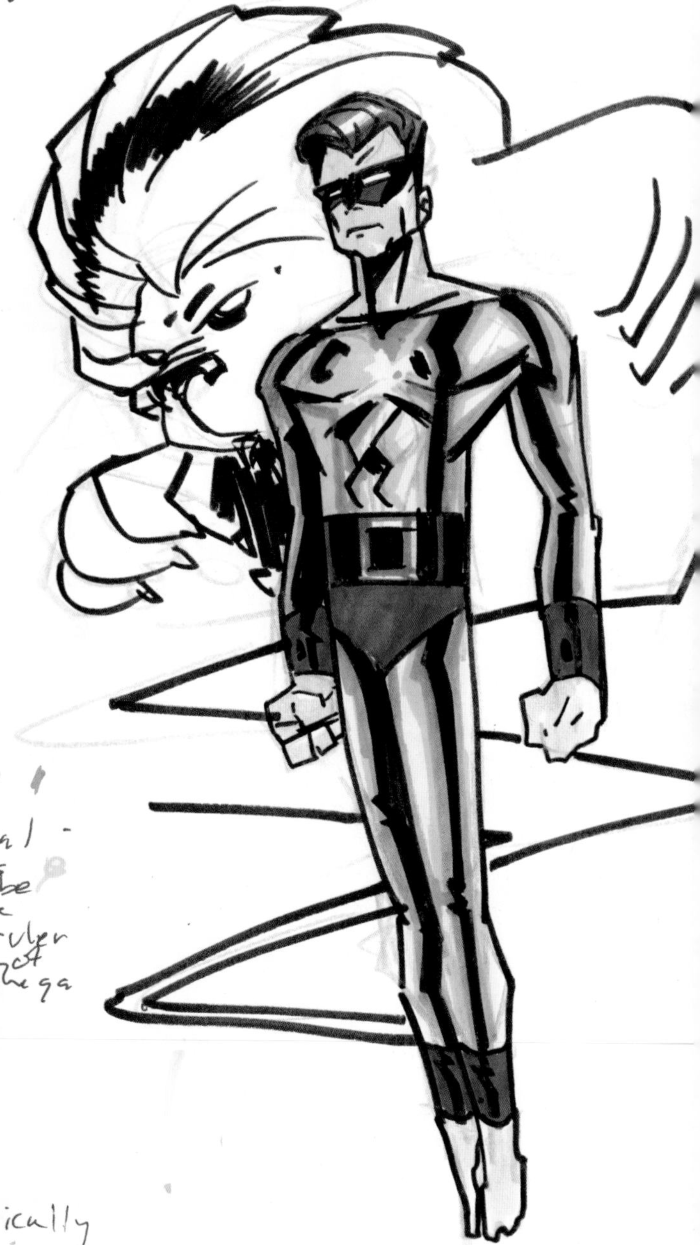

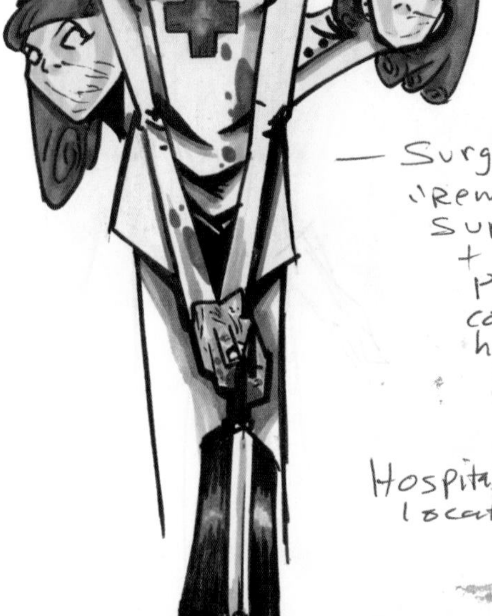
DR Bedlam — completely — delusional — wants to be the ruler of the ga
Surgically "Removes" Superpowers + turns people into compliant happy individu
Hospital changes location magically

GERARD: The inspirations for the villains in the Hotel come from many places. Some of them, such as Night Hag and the Gourmet, are old villains I introduced in an RPG I ran using Steve Jackson's GURPS system with the GURPS Supers sourcebook. The game was great fun and I remember it fondly. Maybe we will get to see other characters from the game one day.

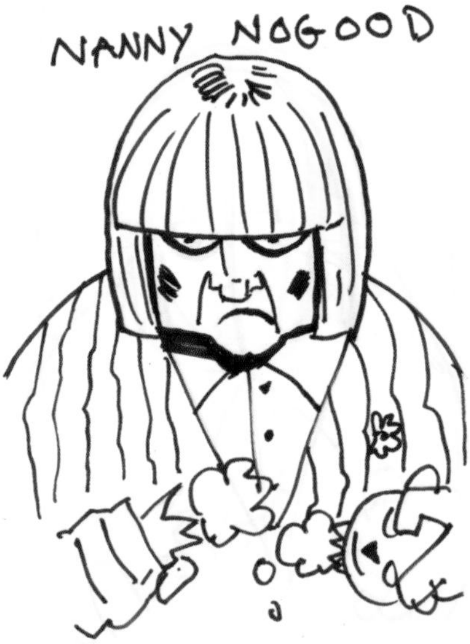
NANNY NOGOOD

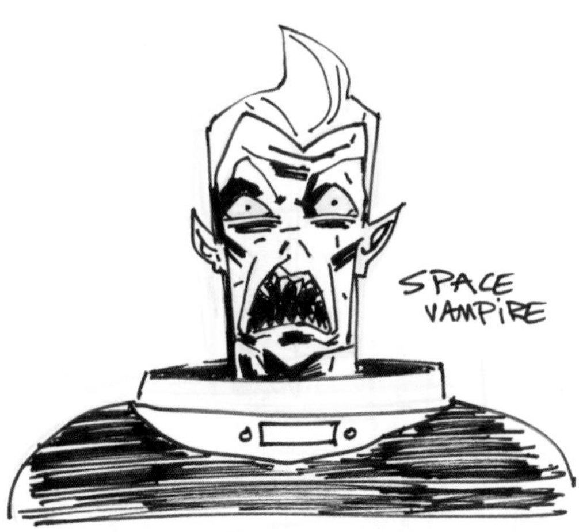
SPACE VAMPIRE

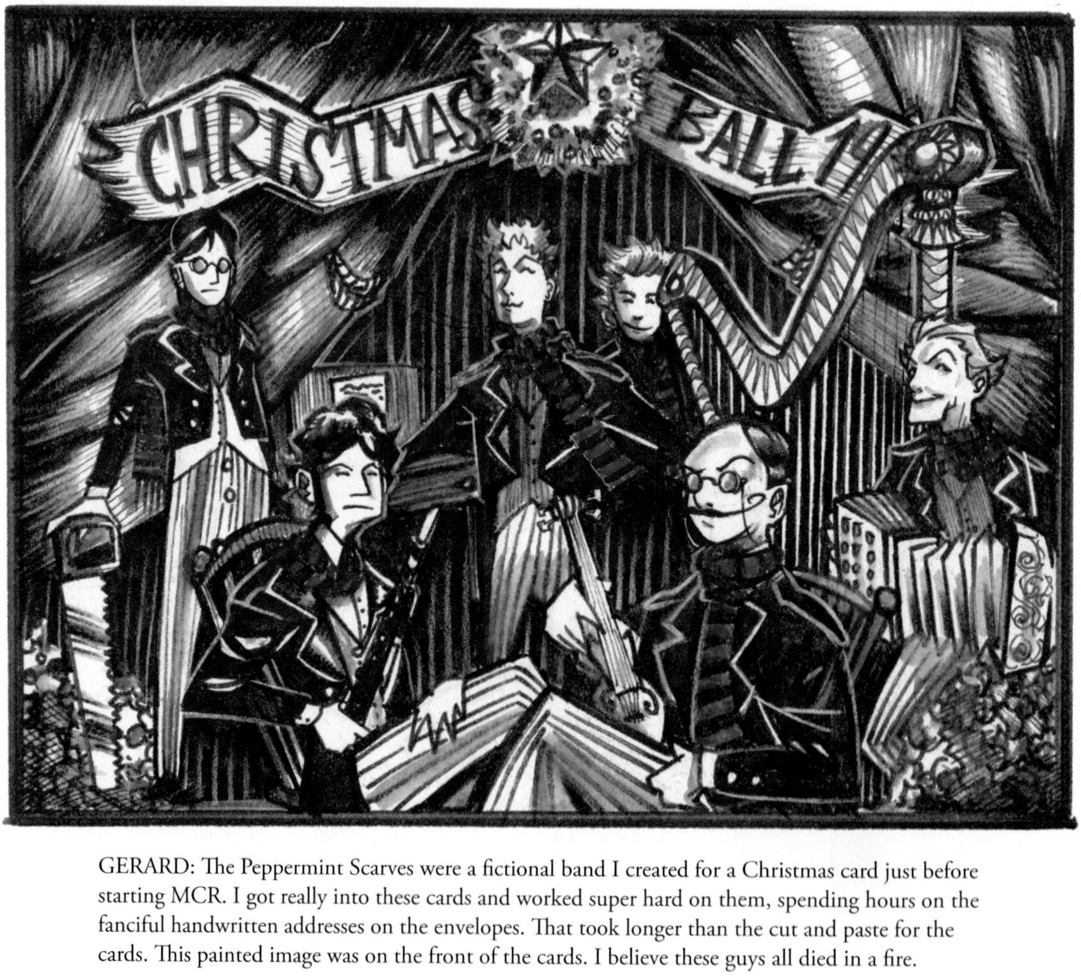
CHRISTMAS
BALL

GERARD: The Peppermint Scarves were a fictional band I created for a Christmas card just before starting MCR. I got really into these cards and worked super hard on them, spending hours on the fanciful handwritten addresses on the envelopes. That took longer than the cut and paste for the cards. This painted image was on the front of the cards. I believe these guys all died in a fire.

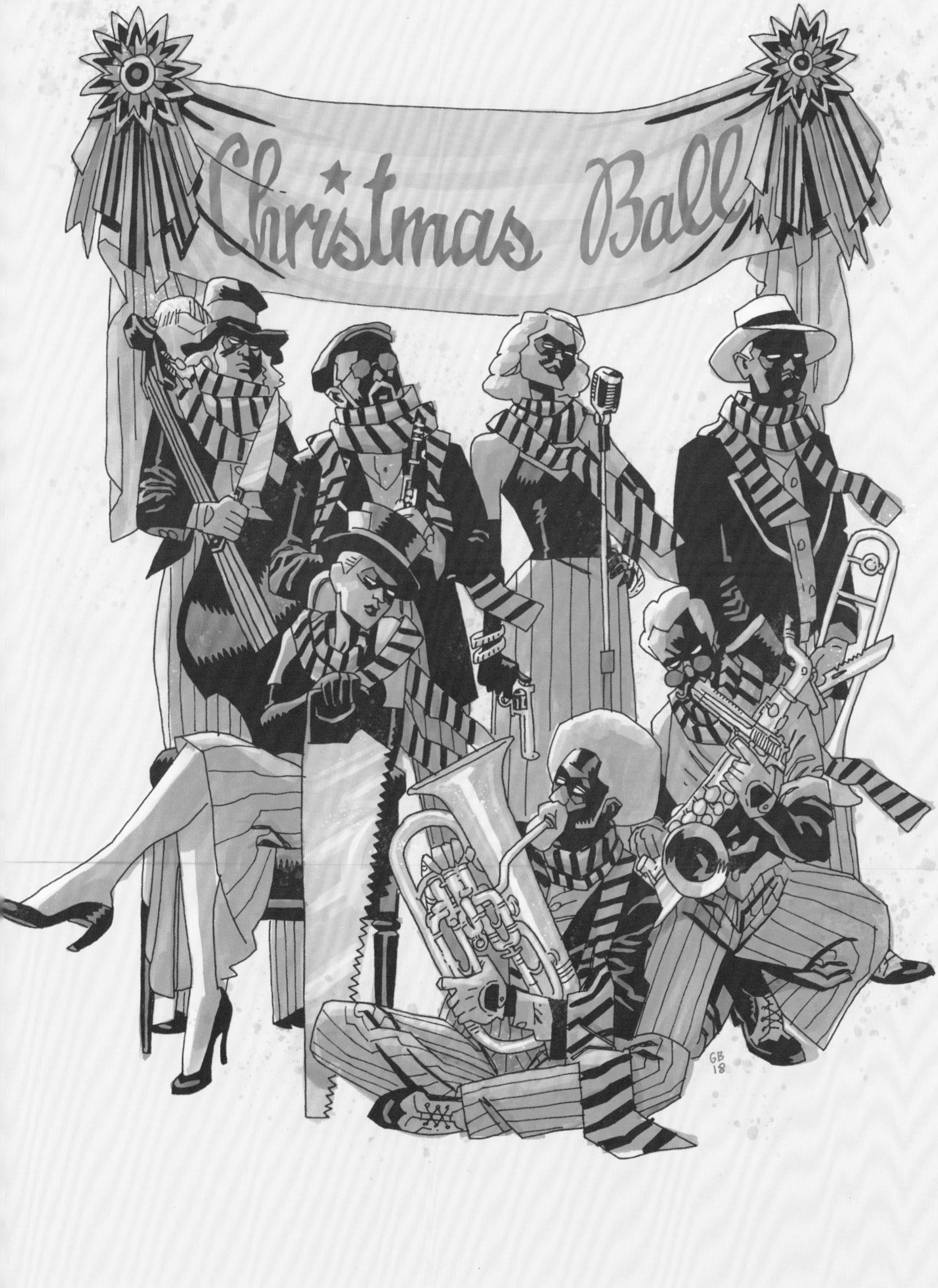
Christmas Ball
GB 18

Hotel Oblivion #6 Peppermint Scarves variant cover by Gabriel

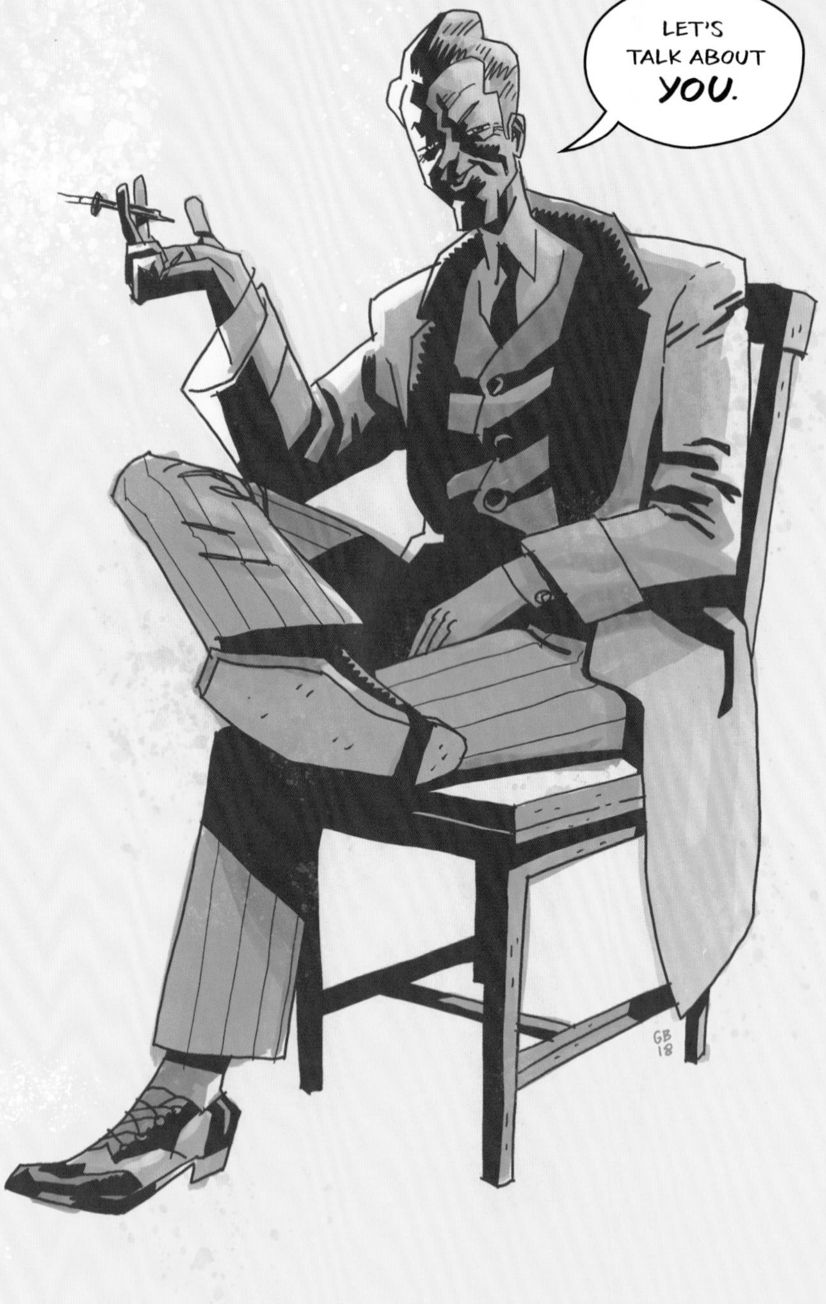
LET'S TALK ABOUT YOU.
GB 18

Hotel Oblivion #7 variant cover by Gabriel

GERARD WAY

Gerard Way began writing and drawing comics when his grandmother first put a pencil in his hand. Having developed a love of the arts, Way attended the School of Visual Arts in New York City, where he honored his skills as both writer and artist, before he made a career as a musician with My Chemical Romance. He continues to write comics to this day, including *True Lives of the Fabulous Killjoys* and *Doom Patrol*, and he enjoys it immensely. He lives in Southern California with his wife Lindsey and their daughter Bandit.

Photo by Jen Rosenstein

GABRIEL BÁ

Gabriel Bá is an Eisner and Harvey Award-winning Brazilian cartoonist, born in 1976, who has been creating comics for more than twenty years, mostly collaborating with his twin brother Fábio Moon. Together, they have published such graphic novels as the New York Times Bestseller *Daytripper* and *Two Brothers*, based on the acclaimed novel by Milton Hatoum, and *How to Talk to Girls at Parties*, based on the short story by Neil Gaiman. He also works with other writers on projects like super-spy-space-time-bending *Casanova* with Matt Fraction and *B.P.R.D.: 1947* and *B.P.R.D.: Vampire* with Mike Mignola. With *The Umbrella Academy*, he saw the opportunity to venture into the super-hero genre, and to go bold with the crazy and bizarre storytelling possibilities of the medium, while still telling personal and deep character driven stories.

Photo by J.R. Duran

ALSO AVAILABLE FROM THE CREATORS OF THE UMBRELLA ACADEMY

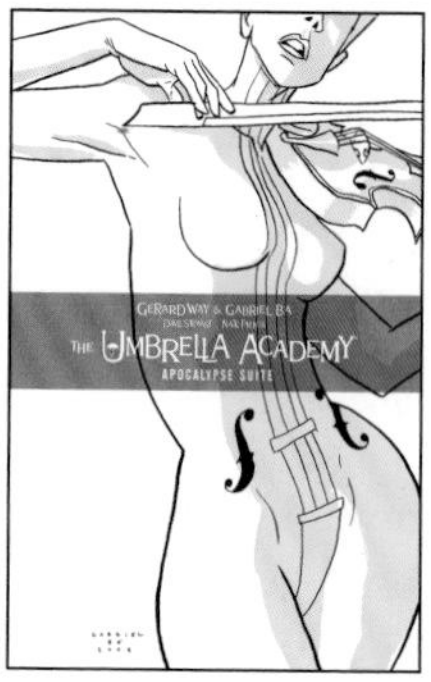
THE UMBRELLA ACADEMY
APOCALYPSE SUITE

UMBRELLA ACADEMY VOLUME 1: APOCALYPSE SUITE

By Gerard Way & Gabriel Bá

Forty-three extraordinary children were spontaneously born by women who'd previously shown no signs of pregnancy. Millionaire inventor Reginald Hargreeves adopted seven of the children; when asked why, his only explanation was, "To save the world."

TRADE PAPERBACK · $17.99 · ISBN 978-1-59307-978-9
LIBRARY EDITION · $39.99 · ISBN 978-1-50671-547-6

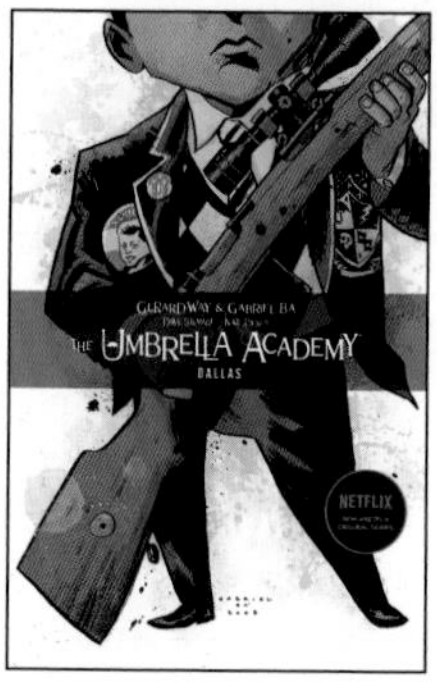
THE UMBRELLA ACADEMY
DALLAS
NETFLIX

UMBRELLA ACADEMY VOLUME 2: DALLAS

By Gerard Way & Gabriel Bá

Times are tough for this dysfunctional family of superheroes. Following the near apocalypse, the Umbrella Academy is despondent. So, it's a great time for another catastrophic event to rouse them into action.

TRADE PAPERBACK · $17.99 · ISBN 978-1-59582-345-8
LIBRARY EDITION · $39.99 · ISBN 978-1-50671-548-3

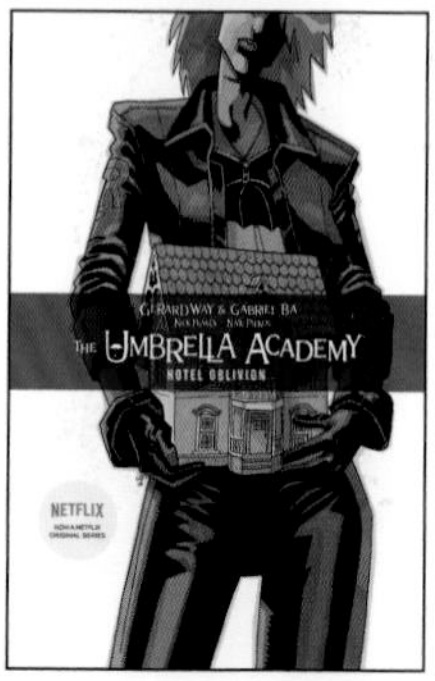
THE UMBRELLA ACADEMY
HOTEL OBLIVION
NETFLIX

UMBRELLA ACADEMY VOLUME 3: HOTEL OBLIVION

By Gerard Way & Gabriel Bá

Faced with an increasing number of lunatics with superpowers eager to fight his wunderkind brood, Sir Reginald Hargreeves developed the ultimate solution . . .

TRADE PAPERBACK · $19.99 · ISBN 978-1-50671-142-3

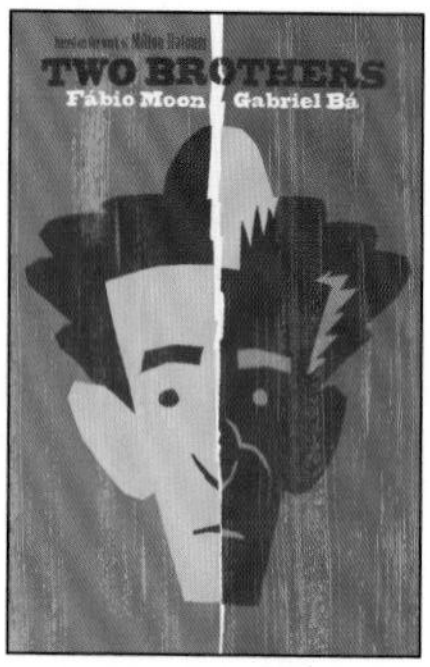
TWO BROTHERS
Fábio Moon Gabriel Bá

TWO BROTHERS

By Gabriel Bá & Fábio Moon

Family secrets engage the reader in this profoundly resonant story about identity, love, loss, deception, and the dissolution of blood ties.

HARDCOVER · $24.99 · ISBN 978-1-61655-856-7

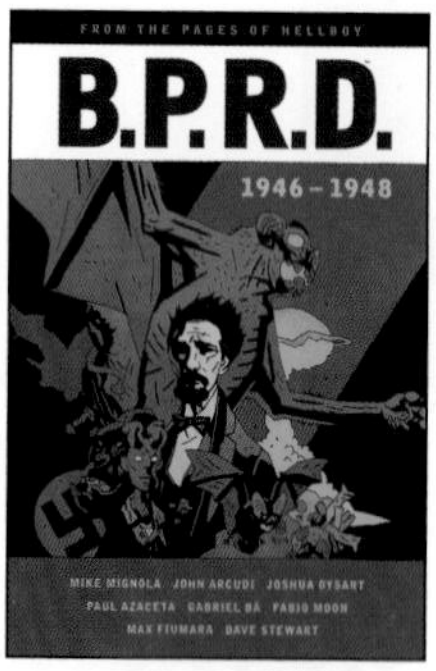
FROM THE PAGES OF HELLBOY
B.P.R.D.
1946–1948
MIKE MIGNOLA JOHN ARCUDI JOSHUA DYSART
PAUL AZACETA GABRIEL BÁ FÁBIO MOON
MAX FIUMARA DAVE STEWART

B.P.R.D. 1946-1948

By Mike Mignola, Joshua Dysart, John Arcudi, Gabriel Bá & Fábio Moon

In the wake of World War II, an occult investigator and guardian of the young Hellboy and a group of war-weary veterans investigate Hitler's top-secret Project Vampir Sturm, exposing one of the greatest villains of the Third Reich, uncovering the secret history of vampires, and leading one Bureau agent to risk his soul and his mind.

HARDCOVER · $34.99 · ISBN 978-1-61655-646-4

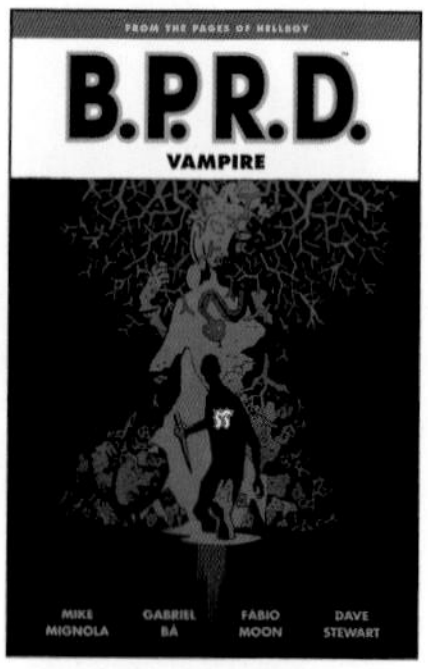
FROM THE PAGES OF HELLBOY
B.P.R.D.
VAMPIRE
MIKE MIGNOLA
GABRIEL BÁ
FÁBIO MOON
DAVE STEWART

B.P.R.D. VAMPIRE

By Mike Mignola, Gabriel Bá & Fábio Moon

A vampire-haunted occult investigator's quest for revenge turns into a rampage as he pursues a clan of undead and their gorgon-eyed queen.

TRADE PAPERBACK · $19.99 · ISBN 978-1-50671-189-8

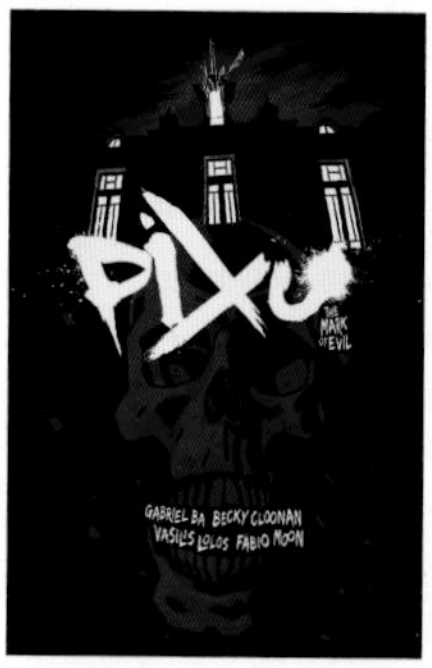
PIXU
THE MARK OF EVIL
GABRIEL BÁ BECKY CLOONAN
VASILIS LOLOS FÁBIO MOON

PIXU: THE MARK OF EVIL

By Gabriel Bá, Fábio Moon, Becky Cloonan & Vasilis Lolos

This gripping tale of urban horror follows the lives of five lonely tenants—strangers—whose lives become intertwined when they discover a dark mark scrawled on the walls of their building.

TRADE PAPERBACK · $14.99 · ISBN 978-1-61655-813-0

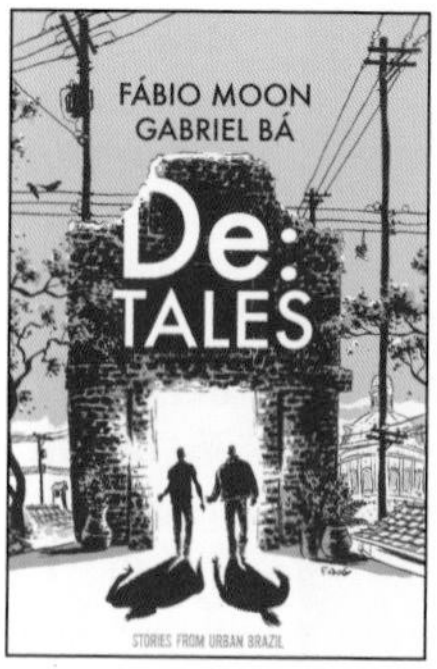
FÁBIO MOON
GABRIEL BÁ
De:
TALES
STORIES FROM URBAN BRAZIL

DE:TALES

By Gabriel Bá & Fábio Moon

Bá & Moon explore life on the streets of their native São Paulo in this collection of their early short stories.

HARDCOVER · $19.99 · ISBN 978-1-59582-557-5

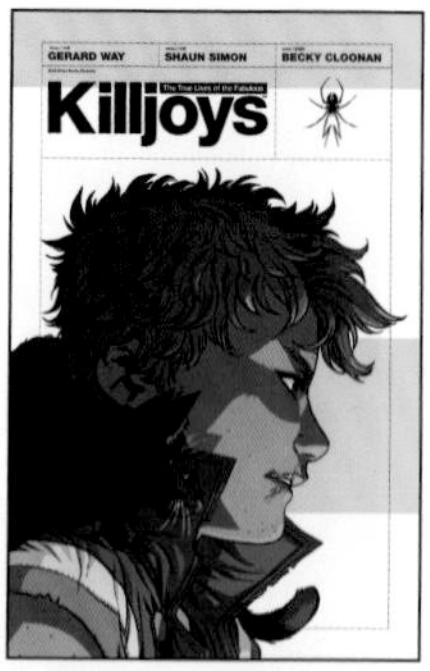
GERARD WAY
SHAUN SIMON
BECKY CLOONAN
Killjoys

TRUE LIVES OF THE FABULOUS KILLJOYS VOLUME 1

By Gerard Way, Shaun Simon & Becky Cloonan

Years ago, the Killjoys fought against the tyrannical megacorporation Better Living Industries, costing them their lives, save for one—the mysterious Girl. Today, the followers of the original Killjoys languish in the Desert while BLI systematically strips citizens of their individuality.

TRADE PAPERBACK · $19.99 · ISBN 978-1-59582-462-2

DARK HORSE BOOKS

DARKHORSE.COM

AVAILABLE AT YOUR LOCAL COMICS SHOP OR BOOKSTORE

To find a comics shop in your area, visit comicshoplocator.com

For more information or to order direct: On the web: darkhorse.com | E-mail: mailorder@darkhorse.com | Phone: 1-800-862-0052 Mon.–Fri. 9 AM to 5 PM Pacific Time.